THE NEW ZEALAND CAMPING GUIDE

Distributed by Nationwide Book Distributors Ltd
30 Stewart Street, Christchurch.
1996 Edition

Production, typesetting and layout by Gay Kerr
Published by T.O.W.Travels
82 Moana Road
Plimmerton
Wellington
04-233-8613

Written by Noni Hansen
26 Ganymede Place
Bucklands Beach
Auckland 09-534-5073

Maps and cover designed and drawn by
Dave Mc Arthur
63 Houghton Bay Road
Wellington South
04-387-2423

●

Welcome
Kia Ora
Bonjour
Wilkommen
Velkommen
Shalom

We challenge you to find a more comprehensive book on where to camp in New Zealand!
This is a no-nonsense guide with over 740 camps listed and some of them are FREE.

The chapters are in geographical sequence —from North to South–but you will also find an alphabetical listing at the back of the book. We do not attempt to grade camps. What is ideal camping for one person may be anathema to another. Some may seek just the sound of birdsong or rippling water to find their holiday paradise. Others may like meeting people and making new friends. All tastes are catered for within these pages.

We have included fun maps to help you find the location of these camps. For more detailed information you should have a general road map on hand. Our maps are a guide only and not to scale.

Preparation of this book is done by personal visits. Our opinions are expressed with the purpose of informing readers so they can make their own choice. **Every effort has been made to ensure that the information in this book is accurate at the time of publication. We cannot accept liability for any errors or omissions in the accuracy of this book. This guide was researched in 1995.**

New Zealand has a lot to offer the free independent traveller. Within our approximately 266,000 square kilometres are at least 10,000 kilometres of coast. Most of this is easily accessible and yields a huge variety of seafood from gamefish to oysters.

By contrast there are deep fiords, magnificent glaciers and volcanic mountains. Thermal activity provides an experience not to be missed–mainly in the North Island–but there are also thermal pockets in the south. The main cities are modern and evenly spaced throughout the country. Do join us as we explore the highways and byways of our Pacific nation.

Camping can be a wonderful way to meet people. We feel privileged to have made so many new friends since this book began four years ago. We welcome your comments and suggestions. Thank you for the letters we have received –we love to hear from you.

Your Pets

While most camps have a flexible policy towards pets, they reserve the right to be informed before you arrive. Some camps (particularly in conservation areas) have a definite -"No animals policy". The text of the book will provide guidelines. Where you see a 🐕 you can be confident that your dog will be accepted.

Always bear in mind that this permission is subject to your dog being well controlled and that your campsite may be in a specially allocated area. At peak holiday times **always** check with the manager before arriving with your dog.

About our entries

These "see-at-a-glance" symbols have been included to help you find inportant features more easily.The prices noted after the symbols for on-site caravans, cabins, and tourist flats are priced from that figure. We have included ALL grades of cabins under 🏠 ALL grades of tourists flats and motels are denoted by 🏠.

Legend

C   Department of Conservation Camp

🐕   Pet friendly, dogs welcome

🏠   Cabins (all grades) from

🏠   Tourist flats, and/or motels (all grades) from

🚐   On-site caravans from

⑫   This symbol on an advertisement refers to the listing number in the relevant chapter.

Each district appears in its own chapter, and where possible runs in a North to South sequence. The first eight chapters are North Island camps.

In an emergency Tel 111 for Police, Ambulance etc.

USEFUL INFORMATION

BUSINESS HOURS
Seven day shopping is now standard practice in New Zealand. Many retail shops are open Sundays and most major supermarkets. In small towns you may find more restricted hours. In some areas shops close at 5pm weekdays, instead of the customary 5.30pm.

BANKS
Most banks are open 9am to 4.30pm weekdays. ATM's are found throughout the country. Trading in overseas currency closes at 4.30 daily.

MOTORING
Motorists drive on the left-hand side of the road. It is compulsory to wear a seat belt in both the front and back seats. All children must be restrained when travelling in a car. Motorcyclists and cyclists must wear crash helmets. The open road speed limit is 100km per hour, with a top speed of 50km in built–up areas. International driver's permits are recognised, also valid licences for Australia, Canada, United Kingdom, United States, Netherlands, Switzerland, Fiji, South Africa, and West Germany.

INTERISLANDER FERRY
The interisland ferry sails several times daily between the North and South Islands. If you are taking a vehicle across the straits it is wise to book. Phone 0800 658 999 (toll free) for Interislander and rail. Operates between 7am and 9pm. New Zealand Rail Fast Ferry *The Lynx* is due to return to New Zealand waters in November 1995 and should be here all summer.

TAXIS
All city taxis run 24 hours a day, seven days a week. They operate from Taxi Stands which are clearly marked. Rates depend on both distance travelled and time elapsed. The tariff is often displayed on the outside of the car, or you can inquire from the driver.

TIPPING
Employed persons in New Zealand do not depend on tips for their income. Service charges are not usually added to Hotel or Restaurant accounts.

GOODS AND SERVICES TAX (GST)
This is charged at 12.5% on all goods and services. Duty Free shops are exempt. Visitors from overseas may be able to claim this tax back for large purchases; you will need to contact the Tax Department for details. All prices should be quoted inclusive of GST.

In an emergency Tel 111 for Police, Ambulance etc.

CREDIT CARDS
All major credit cards are acceptable in New Zealand.

TELEPHONE SERVICES
There are now a wide range of options available in New Zealand. A special booklet is available from your travel agent, or at our local Information Centres. Ask for *Telecom Guide to Travellers* or call 123.

POSTAL SERVICES
New Zealand Post shops are open Monday to Friday from 9am to 5pm. Stamps are available at many dairies and camp stores.

ELECTRICITY SUPPLY
New Zealand has (an alternating current) AC 240/volt 50/cycle system.

WATER
New Zealand has some of the cleanest water in the world. Unless otherwise notified, all tap water is safe to drink.

CLIMATE
New Zealand enjoys a temperate climate with few extremes of temperature. The summer months average 23 degrees, the winter 14 degrees Celsius. Please take care in summer; our clean clear days may mean you burn easily. We recommend the use of sunblocks. Burn times are broadcast by the media throughout summer.

TIME
Our standard time is 12 hours ahead of GMT. In summer, daylight saving comes into operation around October, and at that time clocks are advanced one hour.

ACKNOWLEDGEMENTS

We would like to thank our new teams who visited the camps and wrote the assessments for us:

Molly and Brian Ansley
Daphne Butler
Beryl and John Doran
Audrey Hudson
George Pearmain for the wonderful photos.
Marian Jefferies for all your help.
Sypko Bosch, Auckland. Your advice was invaluable.

Please accept our sincere appreciation for your assistance with our project.

What they said.....

"For anyone contemplating a camping holiday this book is a must."
New and Notable

"We're really enjoying Gay and your NZ Camping Guide."
Janet Cherrington–Auckland

"We have now used two of your Camping Guides, and I would not do
without them!"
Libby Gemmel–Napier

"I thoroughly enjoyed both the text and the cartoons."
Judith Sheehan–Christchurch

"We used the book as our bible, and recommended it to many travellers on
our way."
Joy Mildenhall–Havelock North

"Your publication *The New Zealand Camping Guide* was our constant
companion and proved invaluable. We recommend it to all our friends."
Beryl van Donk–Coromandel

"As a family with young children we truly value your tips and candid
comments. They helped us plan a 'truly special' long remembered camping
holiday."
Sue and Chris–Paraparaumu

"Your book is one of the best we have seen for a family who want to get
back to basics. Congratulations! It deserves to be a winner."
Sera and Bruce Dickenson–-Motueka

"Congratulations on an excellent publication. 'What you read is what you get
We highly recommend it to all campers."
Dudley and Barbara Vosser–Newlands.

"We used this Guide throughout New Zealand and found it well worth the
study. It provided us with several very memorable stays while travelling
around."
Pat and Janine Warnick-Bardon–Queensland

"*The New Zealand Camping Guide*–trust them, they won't lead you astray."
Judy and Russell Orsborn–Auckland

AVAILABLE OVERSEAS FROM THE FOLLOWING COMPANIES

HUNTER Publishing Inc.,
300 Raritan Center Parkway,
Edison NJ 08818
USA and Canada
Tel (703) 687 5670
Fax (703) 687 5874

REISE-KNOW-HOW -VERLAG
Darr GmbH
Im Grund 12
83104 Hohenthann.
Germany, Austria, and Switzerland.

TOWER BOOKS Wholesalers Pty Ltd
Unit 9/19 Rodborough Road
Frenchs Forest NSW 2086
Australia.
Tel (02) 975 5566
Fax (02) 975 5599

ROGER LASCELLES Cartographic and Travel Publisher
47 York Road
Brentford,
Middlesex TW8 OQP
London
United Kingdom
Tel (181) 847 0935
Fax (181) 568 3886

**SCANDINAVIAN AUSTRALIAN, NEW ZEALAND FRIENDSHIP
UNION**
Hovedkontor/Sekretariat–Danmark
Norregade 51
DK 7500 Holstebro
Denmark

CONTENTS

North Island

South Island

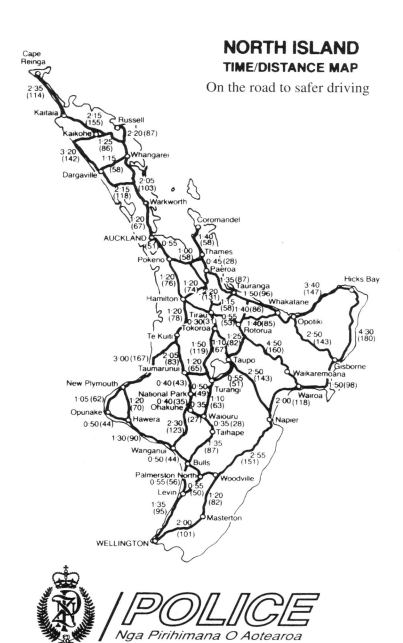

NORTH ISLAND
TIME/DISTANCE MAP

On the road to safer driving

Cape Reinga

2·35 (114)

Kaitaia

2·15 (155)

Russell

2·20 (87)

Kaikohe

1·25 (86)

Whangarei

3·20 (142)

1·15 (58)

Dargaville

2·15 (118)

2·05 (103)

Warkworth

1·20 (67)

Coromandel

AUCKLAND

0·51

0·55

1·40 (58)

1·00 (58)

Thames

Pokeno

0·45 (28)

Paeroa

1·35 (87)

1·20 (76)

1·20 (74)

Tauranga

3·40 (147)

Hicks Bay

1·20 (131)

1·50 (96)

Whakatane

Hamilton

1·15 (58)

1·40 (86)

1·20 (78)

Tirau

0·55 (53)

1·40 (85)

Opotiki

2·50 (143)

4·30 (180)

0·30 (31)

Tokoroa

Rotorua

Te Kuiti

1·50 (119)

1·10 (82)

1·25 (67)

4·50 (160)

3·00 (167)

2·05 (83)

1·20 (65)

Taupo

2·50 (143)

Waikaremoana

Gisborne

Taumarunui

0·55 (51)

1·50 (98)

New Plymouth

0·40 (43)

0·50 (49)

Turangi

Wairoa

1·05 (62)

1·20 (70)

National Park

1·10 (63)

2·00 (118)

0·40 (35)

Ohakune

0·35

Opunake

0·50 (44)

Hawera

0·35 (27)

Waiouru

0·35 (28)

Napier

2·30 (123)

Taihape

1·30 (90)

Wanganui

1·35 (87)

2·55 (151)

0·50 (44)

Bulls

Palmerston North

0·55 (56)

Woodville

0·55 (50)

Levin

1·20 (82)

1·35 (95)

Masterton

2·00 (101)

WELLINGTON

FAR NORTH DIRECTORY

Key to locations and maps in the Far North. Begins at Cape Reinga, travelling south to Waipapakauri then an easterly route south to Whananaki. Continues from Kaitaia down the west side and finishes just north of the Waipoua Kauri Forest.

Cape Reinga	1.	Tapotupotu Bay Campsite (DoC)
Spirits Bay	2.	Kapowairua Campsite (DoC)
Waitiki Landing	3.	Waitiki Landing
Te Kao	4.	Te Pua Reserve
Rarawa Beach	5.	Rarawa Beach Campsite (DoC)
Houhora	6.	Wagener Tourist Park
Pukenui	7.	Pukenui Holiday Camp
Waipapakauri Beach	8.	The Park
Waipapakauri	9.	Waipapakauri Hotel
Karikari Peninsula	10.	Karikari Bay Motor Camp
Karikari Peninsula	11.	Matai Bay Campsite (DoC)
Karikari Peninsula	12.	Whatuwhiwhi Holiday Park
Karikari Peninsula	13.	Tokerau Beach Motor Camp
Taipa	14.	Taipa Caravan Park
Mangonui	15.	Hihi Beach Motor Camp
Taupo Bay	16.	Taupo Bay Motor Camp
Whangaroa	17.	Whangaroa Harbour Motor Camp
Tauranga Bay	18.	Tauranga Bay Motor Camp
Wainui Bay	19.	Wainui Bay
Matauri Bay	20.	Matauri Bay Motor Camp
Puketi	21.	Puketi Forest Camping (DoC)
Takou Bay	22.	Takou Bay Camp
Kerikeri	23.	Aranga Holiday Park
Kerikeri	24.	The Orange Centre
Kerikeri	25.	Hideaway Lodge

Kerikeri	26.	Pagoda Lodge Holiday Park
Paihia	27.	Bay of Islands Holiday Park
Paihia (Haruru Falls)	28.	Twin Pines Tourist Park
Paihia (Haruru Falls)	29.	Falls Motor Inn and Caravan Park
Paihia (Haruru Falls)	30.	Panorama Resort
Pakaraka	31.	The Cottages Inn the Woods
Paihia	32.	Waitangi Motor Camp
Paihia	33.	The Park
Paihia	34.	Smiths Holiday Camp
Russell	35.	Orongo Bay Holiday Park
Russell	36.	Russell Holiday Park
Rawhiti	37.	Kaingahoa Camping Reserve
Bay of Islands	38.	Urupukapuka Island (DoC)
Whangaruru North	39.	Bland Bay Motor Camp
Whangaruru North	40.	Whangaruru Campsite (DoC)
Whangaruru	41.	Whangaruru Harbour Motor Camp
Oakura	42.	Oakura Motels & Caravan Park
Helena Bay	43.	Helena Bay School Camp
Whananaki North	44.	Motutara Farm Camp
Whananaki North	45.	Otamure Campsite (DoC)
Whananaki	46.	Whananaki School Camp
Whananaki	47.	Whananaki Motor Camp
Kaitaia	48.	Dyers Motel & Auto Park
Ahipara	49.	Pine Tree Lodge Motor Camp
Kohukohu	50.	The Tree House
Rawene	51.	Rawene Motor Camp
South Hokianga	52.	Okopako
Opononi	53.	Opononi Beach Motor Park
Omapere	54.	Omapere Tourist Hotel & Motel
Waimamaku	55.	Solitaire Guest House

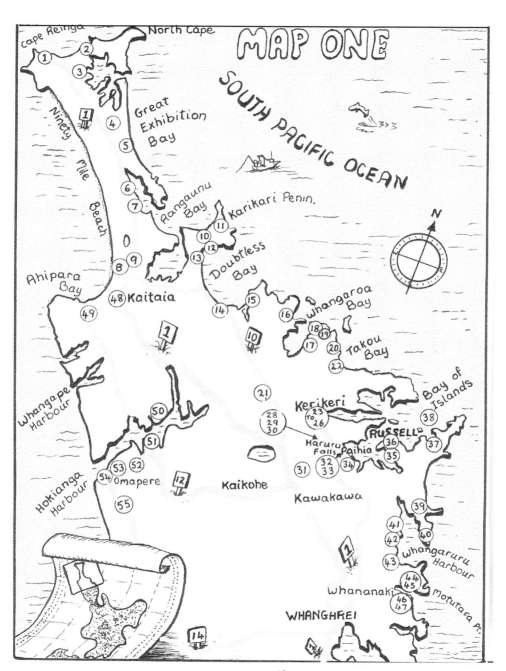

Chapter 1.

THE FAR NORTH

A treasure trove of camps awaits the traveller to Northland. Because of the abundance of coastline, the choice of beaches includes the dramatic 90 Mile Beach where the Tasman Sea rolls in. To the east a seemingly endless choice of bays, inlets, harbours and surf beaches offer something for everyone.

A drive up Aupori Peninsula ("the tail of the fish of Maui" in Maori legend) culminates in Cape Reinga. Here the waters of the Tasman Sea and the Pacific Ocean merge. It is a majestic sight, with great significance to the Maori. Most of this journey is on good roads, but for a unique experience take a bus along 90 Mile Beach.

There are many reasons why the Far North attracts the holiday maker. The warmest region in New Zealand, it is known as the winterless north. Contrasting with the delights of the open coast are the waters of Hokianga Harbour. Regular crossings are made by the Rawene car ferry. This brief journey connects you with the twin resorts of Opononi and Omapere before reaching the northern outskirts of the magnificent kauri forests.

Amongst the many holiday spots to the east, the Bay of Islands is a focal point, from the citrus orchards and artisan's workshops of Kerikeri to historic Waitangi. Fringed with sparkling beaches, Paihia bustles with pleasure craft and has a lively resort-village atmosphere. From deep-sea fishing to swimming with dolphins, all water sports can be enjoyed here. A commuters car ferry is the easy way to cross to historic Russell. The short journey begins at Opua, just south of Paihia.

The most difficult thing about holidaying in the Far North is choosing from the myriad of beaches which are strung, like clusters of pearls, beside the blue Pacific.

THE FAR NORTH (Northland)

 ## 1.   Tapotupotu Bay Campsite
Far North Road–3km South of Cape Reinga. Department of Conservation Te Kao (09) 409-7521

The northernmost camping ground! The long drive is well worth the effort. Only the last 25km are unsealed. The camping ground is nestled into a beautiful sheltered bay located at the mouth of a stream and offering excellent swimming and surfing. It is a great place from which to explore the Far North. Tapotupotu has 45 sites with an ablution block to service it. Amenities include a kitchen area (no cooking facilities) and a cold-water shower block. No pets or fires please–but you may bring insect repellent for the mosquitoes! Tapotupotu is a self-registration campground. There is a camp manager on-site during the busy summer season. Price per person is $5.

 ## 2.   Kapowairua Campsite
Spirits Bay Road. 16km from Waitiki Landing. Department of Conservation. Te Kao (09) 409-7521

A visit to Kapowairua (Spirits Bay) will guarantee you a holiday away from it all. The roads from Waitiki Landing to Spirits Bay are unsealed. This is an informal camping ground set back from the beach with 200 sites available for camping. The toilet blocks and camping sites are situated amongst clumps of manuka. Taps and cold-water showers are provided at intervals throughout the area. No pets or fires please–but bring insect repellent. Kapowairua is a self-registration campground. There is a camp manager on-site during the busy summer season. Price per person is $4.

3.   Waitiki Landing
Waitiki Landing– RD 4 Kaitaia (09) 409-7508 (phone & fax)

Just 19km south of Cape Reinga is this complex undergoing further development. At present there is a restaurant, a takeaway food service, general store and souvenir shop. You can fill dive bottles here. The grounds have 10 sites with power, around 30 tent sites and 16 cabins. Some stately palms provide both a landmark and some shade. Plans include a laundrette, kitchen and ablutions. Toilets are provided; the other amenities may be in service this summer. Your hosts the Aprea family.

4.   Te Pua Reserve
C/o Te Kao Store S Hwy 1 Northland (09) 409-7831

First collect your key from the Te Kao Store and pay a $10 deposit. Some distance north from here you will turn east down Paua Road. Environmentalist camping bounded by sheltered waters on three sides. The views are remarkable. Clear, deep water is around the perimeter, but you will have to negotiate a bank to the water or use the boat ramp, unless the tide is right. Campers must be totally independent. There is no water or any facilities. The large flat paddock lacks shade. Charges are $5 per vehicle.

5.   Rarawa Beach Campsite
Rarawa Beach Road – North of Houhora Harbour.
Department of Conservation

Rarawa camping ground is set back from the beach front and adjacent to a tidal rivermouth. The beach is long, with white sand, and is popular for its surfing and fishing. The campground itself is set among pine trees with the surrounding land farmed. Facilities are low key–cold-water showers and toilets. No pets or fires please. This is a self-registration campground run by the Department of Conservation. A caretaker visits the camp regularly over the summer season. Prices are $5 per person.

6.   Wagener Tourist Park
Houhora Heads RD 4 Kaitaia (09) 409-8564 (fax 09 409-8880)

Houhora camping ground is part of this park which has a gorgeous beachfront location at Houhora Heads. (Turn right off the Far North Road at the golf ball.) Sites are staggered and there is a special area '"Baskerville Strip" for campers with dogs. Also within the park is the Wagener Museum, souvenir shop and Cafe. The almost landlocked seaside is sheltered and picturesque. Safe swimming and shellfish are attractions, plus a boat ramp, and of course, bring your golf clubs. Only a portion of the park has power sites. Laundry facilities are excellent. There are a limited number of metered showers and flush toilets but there is no kitchen. A sewerage and dump point is available. Your hosts Lou and Val Panther. Tent sites $5. Power sites $7.50 ⏚ $25.

7.   Pukenui Holiday Camp
Lamb Road, Pukenui (09) 409-8803 (phone & fax)

This friendly Far North camp has camping above the road on several levels. Some have views and all power sites have sewerage and water connected. At the top level a well equipped bunk room has three separate sleeping areas, plus a communal lounge with sink. A key-access bathroom may be available. The main camping area is served by a central amenities building with kitchen (plenty of fridge space) TV, and coin phone. A breezeway seating area is alongside. The laundry is well equipped and ablutions are in good order.

Stroll down to the wharf; fishing is a popular pastime and the camp provides a fish-cleaning area and a freezer for your catch. You can hire kayaks at the camp. Nearby you can buy all your provisions or relax in the licensed restaurant. Diana and John Horsnell are the owner-managers here and First Aid is one of the skills they bring to the district. Yes, pets are permitted by arrangement. There are around 44 sites, most with power. Lodge accommodation and cabins. All sites $8. 🏠 $30.

8. The Park
90 Mile Beach, PO Box 71 Kaitaia (09) 406-7298 (fax 09 406-7477)

Easy to find the turnoff on the main route north, and close to the southern end of 90 Mile Beach prominent signs lead you to this complex. The focal point of the camp is a substantial building where there are quite lavish amenities, including a licensed restaurant and a bar. There is a good kitchen for campers. The ablutions are excellent, with paraplegic facilities, and hot water that provides generous showers. The laundry is equipped with automatic washing and drying machines. At the shop/office you can buy souvenirs. The grounds are not on the waterfront and are level with sheltering trees at the rear. There is a dump point provided. Special events, fishing contests, surfing, land yachts and bus tour stops draw visitors here. Your hosts the Brljevich family. No animals here please. All camping is at $9.50 per person. 🏠.

9. Waipapakauri Hotel
S Hwy 1 Waipapakauri–RD Awanui (09) 406-7408

Enjoy a free stopover here–tent sites with no extras. Use of the hotel facilities is an option. Your hosts Adrian and Pauline Clarke.

10. Karikari Bay Motor Camp
Karikari Peninsula, PO Box 163 Awanui (09) 408-7051

There are acres of farm-style sites here without power, on basically flat ground where a dramatic seascape unfolds below the camp. At the turnoff to the camp the access road is rugged, but mainly level and the distance to travel is short. Although you will need to make your own arrangements for lighting and cooking there is hot water in the ablutions. There are 12 dump points for motorhomes. Your host will use his tractor to launch your boat.. The fishing rewards are plentiful. This is a combined farm and camp, and your pets are welcome. Enjoy plenty of space, (away from the animals if you wish). At peak holiday times a small shop operates at the camp, with takeaway food. Gas bottles can be filled here too. In season there is beach horse-riding as an option. Neville and Agnes Anderson are your hosts. Tent sites $12 for family (up to 3 kids, Mum & Dad) $27 🚐 $30 (4 people) 🏠 Cottage $45 (5 people). Look for the value coupon on page 33.

11. Matai Bay Campsite

Karikari Peninsula–Doubtless Bay. Department of Conservation, Kaitaia (09) 408-2100

A very popular camping ground in a sheltered north-east facing location on the outer coast of the Karikari Peninsula. There is some unsealed road at this end of the peninsula. It is a picturesque setting on two levels where native plantings create sheltered and private sites for camping. Facilities include water supply, toilets, cold-water showers and a boat ramp. No pets or fires please. This campsite has on-site staff over the summer season; out of season it reverts to being a self-registration campsite. Price per person is $6.

12. Whatuwhiwhi Holiday Park

Whatuwhiwhi Road, Karikari Peninsula. RD 3 Kaitaia (09) 408-7202

Very well signposted off S Hwy 1, but you may encounter some unsealed road before you arrive here. The camp is nestled between some sheltering hills, but has easy, level sites. A lovely bay with placid waters and shady picnic spots is immediately opposite the camp. It is a short drive to get supplies. The central amenities block has a well kept kitchen, with microwave and hot plate cooking and fridge. There is an open patio where, for a small charge, BBQs and salads can be ordered in the Xmas/New Year period. TV and picnic tables are provided here. The ablutions were built for comfort, but have meters. There are both single-sex appointments and family-size suites. The laundry has automatic washing and dryer, with freezer space too. You can hire boats or a surf ski here. A dump point is provided. This peaceful spot has cabins on an upper level too. Your hosts, Joy and Bruce Lockart, permit pets here, by prior arrangement, off peak season only. The 16 power sites have sumps and taps and there are also 8 tent sites. Prices are from $9 per person for camping. There is a bunk room.

13. Tokerau Beach Motor Camp

Melissa Road, Karikari Peninsula. RD 3 Kaitaia (09) 408-7150

A beachside camp with fairly uncultivated grounds, although flax borders and young trees are growing. The on-site shop is only open from Boxing Day until the end of January. At the rear of the camp a large building houses the amenities. The kitchen has cooking limitations (two electric hobs) but adequate sinks and fridges. There are two auto washing machines and tubs in a semi-enclosed laundry. The ablutions provide basic showers in lockable cubicles and toilets. Your hosts Matt and Glenys Urlich. A block of tourist flats occupy one end of the grounds. These cost $30 for two people. Tent sites $5 per person. Power sites $6 per person.

14. Taipa Caravan Park
Taipa Point Road, PO Box 388 Mangonui (09) 406-0995 (phone & fax)

Just off S Hwy 10 by the bridge, this park is on the estuary and also has a beach frontage to lovely Doubtless Bay. Free parking and a boat ramp are adjacent. There are two ablution blocks and a compact kitchen provided. The laundry has automatic equipment. Very handily placed for local shopping and a licensed restaurant. The grounds are level and attractive with some shady spots. Pets are welcome by prior arrangement. This camp now welcomes guests all year round and the new owners are Rodger and Julie Dennis. All sites $9 per person or $7 per person for groups of three vans.

15. Hihi Beach Motor Camp
RD 1 Mangonui–Doubtless Bay (09) 406-0307

A sheltered beachside camp just 5km off S Hwy 10. Within Doubtless Bay this is a delightful inlet and the camping area is dotted with shady trees. Sharpen up your fishing skills or just relax on the beach. The camp has amenities in two areas, with the secondary block to the rear less well equipped. The main kitchen is a dual-purpose room set up as a games room with TV and the culinary preparation space is limited, though there are refrigerated lockers. The choice of ablutions, which include unisex showers, are of varying quality. Laundry facilities include automatic washers and a dryer. There are many "for hire" items here. A coin and card phone are available and there is a camp store. Your new hosts are Pauline and Chris. Accommodation ranges from motels to cabins. Prices are $9.50 per person for power sites and $8.50 for tents. 🔲 $30 for two.

16. Taupo Bay Motor Camp
Taupo Bay. RD 1 Mangonui (09) 406-0315 (fax 09 406-0951)

Follow the signposts off S Hwy 10, along the newly sealed road to the beachside settlement of Taupo Bay. The camp is not quite on the beach, with level grounds partially shaded by old trees. There is a well stocked community store at the camp. The communal buildings are smoke free and the kitchen is light and airy with plenty of refrigerator space. There is one full stove plus hobs for cooking. There is table tennis and pool in the games room. The ablutions are amply supplied with toilets and token-operated curtained showers, well kept, with liquid soap at the basins. The laundry has automatic washers and dryer. There is a filling station and boat-launching service. Although summer holidays are busy, this is off-the-beaten-track camping with a rural aspect. Your hosts Dorothy and George Parsons. All sites $9 per person. $30 for two. 🚐 $35 for two. 🔲

17. Whangaroa Harbour Motor Camp
Postal Service Kaeo, Northland (09) 405-0306 (phone & fax)

Across the road from the harbour and just a short hop from the intersection dividing Kaeo from Whangaroa, this is a quiet little retreat, well wooded and sheltered. The office and on-site store has basic supplies available, also a coin phone. The amenities are functional but rustic. The kitchen has meal space and TV. There is a refrigerator, but limited cooking appliances. Pets can be accepted by arrangement. ▭ backpackers accommodation is also available. Camp sites are at $8 per person plus $2 for power.

18. Tauranga Bay Motor Camp
RD 1 Kaeo–Northland (09) 405-0436

It is actually an easy drive to Tauranga Bay despite 3km of unsealed road. The sweep of pink sandy beach borders the camp and is superb for swimming. Deep-sea fishing and diving are added attractions and there is a metal boat ramp nearby. At the camp entrance is a general store; a limited choice of takeaway food may be offered here. The shop has flexible hours (7 days in peak periods) and a card phone. The 215 level sites (60 with power) are well drained but lack shade. Two sets of kitchen facilities are provided although the main kitchen has the best appointments. Showers are mainly token operated and are in the amenities building together with laundry with automatic machines. Separate blocks provide toilets. Another building has a carpeted TV lounge. In the summer holiday season there are fun activities and contests held here. Check prices before arrival. Tent sites $8 and power $9 per person.

19. Wainui Bay
Coast Road north of Matauri Bay (09) 405-0494

One of Northland's enchanting but isolated bays. Seasonal camping on the foreshore abundant with old pohutukawa trees. Both the open sea and a sheltered lagoon for swimming. Nature's abundance only, although Port-a-loos are provided. Camp fees by koha (donation).

20. Matauri Bay Holiday Park
Matauri Bay–PO Box 5, Kerikeri (09) 405-0525

The vista of Matauri Bay spreads below you as you take a leisurely pace along the gravel approach road. There is level beachfront camping, at premium prices for the water-view sites. During the busy period the web of campsites may make beach access difficult. The on-site store and office is open seven days and has a card phone. Both petrol and dive bottles are available here. The amenities block has a kitchen with plenty of sinks, communal fridge/ freezers and limited cooking equipment. Two BBQs with outdoor seating are another option. Although the ablutions have plentiful toilets, the curtained showers are less inviting, with no private dressing space. Washing machines and dryers are in separate rooms. At peak season this is a very busy camp and the casual camper would be advised to avoid the midsummer rush when the camp amenities are stretched to capacity. In charge are Garry and Leanne Morgan. Camping is at $9 per person (minimum $18 per site) summer rates with a surcharge for power. Prices vary seasonally, so check before arrival. Have for hire.

21. Puketi Forest Campsite and Hut

Waiare Road–20km northeast of Okaihau or 20km west of Kerikeri (09) 401-0109

The self-registration campsite is on the eastern edge of the Puketi Forest close to some spectacular kauri stands. The campsite is an ideal base from which to explore the forest, with its network of tracks and walks. Many kauri groves are in this vicinity. There are toilets, cold-water taps, fireplaces and wood provided at the campsite. There is also a 24-bed trampers lodge; inquire for details and prices. This can be booked by contacting the Department of Conservation at PO Box 249 Kaikohe. No pets please.

 ### 22. Takou Bay Camp

Between Matauri Bay and Kerikeri

There is a camp just behind the sand dunes for those who want a lovely isolated beach. Take your choice from shady and open sites. From S Hwy 10 the road is unsealed for about 10km. Just cold-water facilities are provided. There is no power, but abundant seafood in the bay. Your host Nora Rameka. Tent sites $5 per person.

 ### 23. Aranga Holiday Park

Kerikeri Road, Kerikeri (09) 407-9326

Country camping within a short walk of Kerikeri township. The terrain is on several levels above the Puketotara River, with the main facilities on a central terrace. The kitchen appointments are superb, with cool lockers available. A covered outdoor dining area is just outside. In the ablutions you will find good showers with a well kept look. There are also automatic machines in the laundry. For indoor entertainment an upper level TV and games room is above the amenities building. The separate new mix-and-mingle BBQ complex will cater for a crowd. It has a roll-back roof for eating under the stars, and two log-burning fireplaces, one for cooking. Meet here on Friday night, when complimentary salads are provided. Two private open-air spas and both sex ablutions are part of this facility. Although there is some long-term occupation at this camp the atmosphere is friendly and convivial. Your hosts Peter and Carol Cleghorn. Costs for two persons range from $16 for a tent site to $18 with power. 🖻 and 🏓.

24. The Orange Centre
S Hwy 10–RD 3 Kerikeri (09) 407-9397 (phone & fax)

A specialty centre where "state of the art" orange production has spawned a great visitor attraction. There is district Visitor Information here too. Ride the "Orange Mobile" to inspect the orchard. Of course there is a fruit stall and orange juice that is really fresh! A working model of a NZ village and trains is on display. Other options are Devonshire teas and the opportunity to view Northland arts and crafts. The newest innovation here is camping in the orange grove, a campervan park, where a dog kennel for your pooch will be available. Inquire from your hosts Jude and Art Hansen.

25. Hideaway Lodge
Wiroa Road, Kerikeri–PO Box 330 Kerikeri (09) 407-9773

Drive in off the southern approach road to Kerikeri near the junction with S Hwy 10. Specialising in hostel-type accommodation, but there are also plenty of lovely lawn tent sites and 10 power sites, all with taps and sumps and dotted with picnic tables and BBQs. Communal facilities are plentiful. There are two lounges, one for TV watching. The two big homely kitchens are well equipped and complete with crockery, cutlery, pots and pans. Also two modern laundries. The ablutions have both separate and unisex showers available. Outdoors there is an attractive free-form swimming pool. Horse hire is next door and you can hire bicycles as well as buy provisions at the Lodge/store/office. Occupancy is high in the dormitory accommodation, so check on availability of rooms. Your hosts Pam and David Williams. A shared room is $11 per person. Tent sites $7. Power sites $8. 🖥 and 📠

26. Pagoda Lodge Holiday Park
Pa Road, Kerikeri (09) 407-8617

In a secluded setting this camp has a water boundary to the Kerikeri Inlet. (Follow the AA signs from town, off Inlet Road.) Sites are on level lawns and it is easy to find a shady tree to drop anchor. Below the camp is a jetty, boat ramp and moorings, and campers can use the canoes and dinghies at no extra charge. A short punt on the water will bring you to the Stone Store. This is a homely little camp with adequate amenities. There is a Pagoda BBQ area. There are ample toilet facilities and metered unisex showers. A basic kitchen and a good laundry are provided and there is also a coin phone. Quiet camping on a smaller scale with 11 power sites and 6 for tents. 📠. Your hosts are Lorraine and Mike Bentley. Charges for all sites are $10 per person.

27. Bay of Islands Holiday Park
Puketona Road, PO Box 393 Paihia (09) 402-7646

Easy to find, this level park is beside the Waitangi River and a short drive to Paihia. The grounds have lovely old trees with a children's play area and BBQ in a shady spot. The office/camp store is open 7 days. There are two kitchens with contrasting equipment. At busy times campers may have to manage with good washing-up sinks but minimal cooking. Refrigerated lockers can be hired at $2 per day. The backpackers kitchen is very pleasant, light and airy with TV, dining furniture and pool table. Plenty of curtained showers, plus toilets are provided. The laundry is well equipped with automatic machines. There is a dump station. This is a large park with cabins and a lodge as well as ample camp sites. Your hosts Maurice and Linda will allow pets by prior arrangement. Prices vary seasonally. All sites $8.50 per person. ▭ $13.

28. Twin Pines Tourist Park
Puketona Road, Haruru Falls–PO Box 168 Paihia (09) 402-7322 (phone & fax)

There is a cluster of three different camping grounds at Haruru Falls and the entrances almost seem to merge. Twin Pines is nearest to the falls, with a bridge and walkway accessible from the camp, plus a jetty for boats. Picturesque, securely fenced grounds are slightly undulating and profuse with shady trees. Very well appointed amenities include two kitchens, one with gas burners. The recreation room also has a mini kitchen with fridge/freezer. In summer hangi meals can be arranged. There is a children's adventure playground . The reception building also houses a doctor's surgery. Good showers are in lockable cubicles, plus an efficient laundry with ironing equipment too. No dogs here please. Prices range from $17 for two for a tent site to $20 with power. ▭

29. Falls Motor Inn & Caravan Park
Puketona Road, Haruru Falls–PO Box 14 Paihia (09) 402-7816 (phone & fax)

Tucked away behind the Motor Inn is a level camping area with access to a private beach and boat ramp. This was once a Maori canoe landing spot and the camp has a terrific view of the falls. There are 34 power sites and just a few for tents. The facilities are not up-to-the-minute but are in clean condition. The emphasis here is on quiet family groups or older people. Campers can use the Motor Inn swimming pool on a restricted basis. Your hosts Peter and Ramona Lucie-Smith. A minimum site fee of S24 applies in December/January holiday period. Otherwise all sites are $9 per person.

30. Panorama Resort

Haruru Falls–PO Box 39 Paihia (09) 402-7525 (fax 09 402-7191)

Access to this resort is via Old Wharf Road and alongside The Falls Park. There is a boat ramp. A very elegant place to relax borders the entrance drive. There is a swimming pool in a landscaped setting. Within the level camping area, probably the tents have the prime sites. The reception office/dining room is large and merges with a bar. Licensed restaurant meals or an outdoor carvery, and smorgasbord are options. Campers have a rather gloomy little kitchen to use for their own cooking. The ablutions are good with tiled showers. The laundry is in a separate building to the rear, with automatic washers and a dryer. All guests can use the swimming pool or hire the spa pool. The office hires boats and arranges tours. At 10pm the front gate is shut. 🖥

31. The Cottages Inn the Woods

Main Road, Pakaraka–RD 2 Kaikohe (09) 405-9606

Saddle up–this is horse country. An equestrian centre offering riding or tuition if required is based at this camp. You won't see the property from the road (between Kaikohe and Kawakawa); the entrance is through the orchard, just follow the signs. The land is attractively sheltered with thickets of bamboo. There are 32 sites with power and plenty of tenting space. An amenities block contains a large utility room with access to the unisex showers, bath, toilets and hand basins. The kitchen is homely with fridge and freezer and cooking, hobs only, or a gas BBQ on the verandah. There is outdoor eating under an adjoining pergola. The laundry has an automatic washer.Beside the communal building is a fenced swimming pool and sundeck. Horse trekking etc is extra. Your hosts Douglas and Fredi Jarvis. Prices range from $6 per person for tent sites, $7.50 with power. Log 🖥

32. Waitangi Motor Camp

Tahuna Road, Paihia–PO Box 198 Paihia (09) 402-7866

Just to the north of Paihia this camp is on a flat estuary with a water boundary. The sites are well groomed with a few shady trees. The amenities offer two kitchens and the laundry has automatic washers and a dryer plus a large bath for babies. The ablutions are freshly painted with metered showers. There is a carpeted TV room available. No dogs are allowed and camp rules are strongly in evidence. Separate areas in the camp are provided where quietness is a priority. For a group booking discounts are available. All sites are $9 per person.🖥

33. The Park

Seaview Road, Paihia–PO Box 358 Paihia (09) 402-7826 (fax 09 402-8500)

The Park is an attractive complex of serviced units, camping and licensed restaurants. It is an easy stroll to the wharves and village and a stone's throw from the seashore. Fairly level lawns and shady trees are available for the camper, as is the salt-water swimming pool. Excellent ablutions, including a disabled unit are provided, but no kitchen. There is a small, but well equipped laundry. Your hosts the Brljevich family. All sites $9 (no cabins, no motels).

34. Smiths Holiday Camp
Paihia-Opua Road, PO Box 41 Paihia (09) 402-7678 (fax 09 402-6678)

This long established camp occupies a wonderful site with a private beach at its doorstep and trees and bush form the landscape. Just 2.5km south of Paihia, it is only a short drive from the main highway. The favoured location is very popular and in the holiday period is rather densely occupied. The amenities show signs of some strain when the camp is busy. There is a compact kitchen, with microwave and gas elements, also a fridge. Ablutions with showers and toilets. The laundry is well equipped with automatic machines.. There is an office and on-site store, open 7 days. Ingrid and Grant are in charge here. All sites are $10 per person.

35. Orongo Bay Holiday Park
PO Box 55, Russell (09) 403-7704

Look for this park on the Opua ferry road, 3km from Russell. It is also near the turnoff to the mainly unsealed coast road. This is a large camp and the space is well landscaped, divided by trees and toitois to give a variety of sites. There is a large range of recreational activities here and an emphasis on group bookings. The camp store is well stocked and open 7 days. There are two kitchens and two ablution blocks and automatic laundry equipment. A portion of the camp is rather distant from the kitchens. There are some outdoor taps in the grounds. A dump point is provided. Apart from the facilities provided here, most other attractions are based in Russell. Murray and Sue Campbell are in charge here. All sites are $7.50 per person..

36. Russell Holiday Park
Longbeach Road, Russell (09) 403-7826 (fax 09 403-7221)

A good vantage point above the township of Russell, this camp offers a handy location although it is back from the waterfront. There is also an on-site shop, well stocked and open daily until late. Sites are level on multi terraces, with the higher sites having good views and close proximity to the amenities block. Although the showers are metered, they offer a 6 minute soak in smart fibreglass cubicles, and the building is well maintained. Another building houses the well appointed kitchen and adjoining dining and TV annexe, which enjoys great views. There are good cobbled driveways to the various levels and a central play area for children. Campers may help themselves to the fruit growing on the property in season. Boat wash and fish-cleaning facilities are available. No dogs here please. Your hosts are Bill and Jenny, and Peter and Helen. All sites $9 (or $10 in summer). 🔲 and 🔲

Vehicle Ferry Services to Russell

The vehicle ferry offers the quickest safest route to Russell.
All roads are easy to follow and sealed. The ferry is suitable for all types of vehicles including buses and Campervans

Fullers NORTHLAND

	OPUA-OKIATO	OKIATO-OPUA
FIRST FERRY	6.50am	6. 40am
LAST FERRY	9. 00pm (Sat-Thurs)	8. 50 pm
	10. 00pm (Friday)	9. 50pm

Tel (09) 402-7421

OPUA is approximately 15 minutes from Pahia. OKIATO is approximately 10 minutes from Russell. The ferry operates as a shuttle service with crossings every 10 minutes (approximately) **TICKETS PURCHASED ON BOARD**

37. Kaingahoa Camping Reserve
Rawhiti, Cape Brett Peninsula–Northeast of Russell (09) 403-7044

On the east coast of the Bay of Islands lies Cape Brett. Rawhiti is reached by an unsealed road. When you reach this lovely bay, there is a general store for provisions. Safe swimming and good boating is across the road from the camp, which also has wonderful walking tracks. The camp sites are large and well groomed. There are hot water showers, toilets and a small kitchen for campers, while an outdoor roofed area provides meal space. The laundry has an agitator washing machine. Unlimited tent sites here plus 8 with power. There is also a homestead-style backpacker house on the property. This is a great base to explore Cape Brett or visit the whaling station at Whangamumu. Kay and Hiko Tauariki are your hosts. Tent sites $7. Power sites $9.

38. Urupukapuka Island
Bay of Islands–Department of Conservation, Russell (09) 403-7685

An ideal chance to escape on to an island for a camping holiday. Apart from Indico, Paradise and Otehei Bays, which are set aside for day visitors, campers are welcome to tent anywhere on the island. On the two main camping beaches Kupurarahurahu (Cable) Bay has fresh water and Urupukapuka Bay also has open-air cold showers. Campers need to be completely self sufficient particularly in respect of toilet arrangements and removing rubbish from the island. No pets or open fires please. Campers need to make their own arrangements for transport. Boats leave for Urupukapuka Island from Paihia and Russell daily. Camping is on a self-registration basis, with a warden on-site over summer.

39. Bland Bay Motor Camp
RD 4 Hikurangi, Whangaruru (09) 433-6759

If dusty roads don't daunt you and you want a camp that lies between two beautiful bays on the Whangaruru North peninsula, this is certainly worth a visit. Take the coastal road southeast of Russell, which is well off the usual traffic routes. The vista from the isthmus is quite delightful although the camping ground is fairly open with the occasional large pohutukawa tree for shade. Water taps are at all power sites. There are three blocks of ablutions with a BYO paper requirement. The showers are metered. Cooking facilities are adequate but there is no refrigeration or other appliances. Automatic laundry equipment is provided. The Bland Bay camp store supplies provisions for the district and the campers. You will also find a coin phone and dive bottle filling station. Pets may be permitted under leash control. Your host Don Read. Extra charges apply for waterfront sites. These are the minimum charges. Tent sites $6. Power sites $7.50.

40. Whangaruru Campsite
30km southeast of Russell. Department of Conservation, Russell (09) 403-7685

Whangaruru camping ground is at Puriri Bay within the Whangaruru North Head Scenic Reserve. Access to here is on partly sealed roads from Russell or from north of Whangarei. The area is very attractive with sheltered waters providing excellent opportunities for walking, swimming, boating and other water sports. The campground faces west, overlooking the Whangaruru Harbour and accommodates 60 to 80 sites. The ground is flat to gently sloping with scattered native plantings. Three toilet blocks are provided throughout the site and an open air cold shower is situated centrally. Use of the rubbish recycling system is requested. Please report to the camp manager on arrival. Whangaruru campsite is closed over winter from 1 July to 30 September. No pets or fires please. Prices per person are $5.

41. Whangaruru Harbour Motor Camp
Oakura–RD 4 Hikurangi (09) 433-6806

One of those delightful destinations with no passing traffic. The camp overlooks a picturesque beach. There are food vendors on the site in the holiday period. Camping is mostly flat, on varying levels climbing slightly to the rear, where there is a communal building with card phone and campers amenities. The kitchen has an island bench with hot plates. There is a fridge, but no other appliances. Washing-up sinks are plentiful. There is automatic washing and drying equipment in the laundry. Ablutions include a babies bath. The metered showers are well lined, with lockable cubicles. Above the facilities is a backpackers lodge with spectacular views of the beach. A large communal room opens to a homely kitchen and 14 bunks are provided. The whole building has a full verandah for wave watchers. No dogs here in peak season please. Your hosts Joe and Lesley Pickens. Charges are $18.50 for two persons with power. Backpacker beds are $12 each.

42. Oakura Motels & Caravan Park
Oakura Bay–PDC Whangarei (09) 433-6803

Amongst a coastline of delightful beaches Oakura Bay is a popular spot. This camp is about a block back from the beach and is a well manicured park with little white fences defining the camp sites, which also have their own drainage and water and are shaded by plenty of trees. All your shopping requirements (with Eftpos) are handy including a wine shop and petrol. There is also a dive filling station. The camp store has a book exchange. Enjoy the heated or cool indoor swimming pool, which has viewing from both the recreation and TV rooms alongside. A private spa can be hired. This camp focuses on the needs of family groups with a pleasant quiet environment. The ablutions are almost like home, no meters and also a separate babies bathroom. There is hot -plate cooking in the kitchen. Refrigerated lockers are provided. There are two laundries with automatic washers and a dryer. Your hosts Joy and Grant Robertson will help with boat hire and dive-bottle refills. Pets will be accepted by prior arrangement. All sites $17 for two.

43. Helena Bay School Camp
Helena Bay–Hikurangi District (09) 433-6716

A little backwater camp where you would be unlikely to find crowds. This tiny settlement has camping available within the Helena Bay school grounds, which have plenty of play equipment for the youngsters. Large trees offer shelter and the grounds are relatively level and reasonably close to the beach. If you are fussy about facilities this will not appeal. However showers and toilets are provided, as well as a kitchen and a primitive laundry. The independent camper may enjoy being away from the mainstream camps. All sites $6 with a surcharge for power.

44. Motutara Farm Camp
Whananaki North, RD1 Hikurangi (09) 433-8252

A sprawling camp in a spectacular position with beaches galore and views towards Poor Knights Islands. In fact this is a seaside farm just up the hill from Whananaki settlement. There is no power here, but fridge and freezer space is available. A tractor service will carry your gear to your site. These vary from sloping, roughly terraced, to flat but untamed and there are big pohutukawas for shade. Despite the lack of facilities (only some cold-water showers and long-drop toilets) this camp is well booked for summer. No bonfires are to be lit here, and cooking fires are by permission only. Mountain-bikes are for hire, but leave your dog at home. Your hosts, the Barron family, live at the camp entrance. Charges for adults (over 12 years) are $5 each.

 ### 45. Otamure Campsite
Rockell Road, Whananaki North. Department of Conservation, Whangarei (09) 438-0299

A beautiful coastal conservation campground 2km past Whananaki village . It has a beachfront setting fringed with large pohutukawas. Water supply and toilets are provided. No pets or fires please. Price per person $4.

46. Whananaki School Camp
PDC Whananaki via Hikurangi–Northland (09) 433-8231 (phone & fax)

Only in use for campers in the school holidays and weekends, there are level sites and some shady trees here. There is excellent play equipment for children and use of the tennis courts. The harbour estuary is easily accessible. There are no sites with power and no hot water. Facilities are limited to toilets and hand basins. Tent sites $5.

47. Whananaki North Motor Camp
22km east of S Hwy 1, Private Bag, Whananaki–Northland(09) 433-8896

This fully serviced camping ground is directly behind the local general store with takeaway food plus everything from fishing tackle to ice creams. There are also dive-tank fills, kayak hire, petrol and oil. The level grounds extend to a safe harbour estuary at the back. As yet there are no shady spots but trees are growing. A modern communal building houses a roomy kitchen with hot plate or microwave cooking and a freezer, but no dining area. The ablutions are clean and fresh with hot water limitations in the late evening. The laundry has automatic washer only. A modest-sized camp, it has 20 power sites all with taps and plenty of room for tents. This is a small resort area with easy sealed road access. No pets here please. Your hosts Ray and Jayne Kensington. Tent sites $7.50. Power sites $8.50 ⌂ $30 for two.

48. Dyers Motel & Auto Park
67 South Road, Kaitaia. (09) 408-0333

Close to the Kaitaia township, this park has convenience shopping right next door and a card phone at the gate. Camping is to the rear of the motels on level sites unrelieved by any landscaping, but many sites have their own sump. The camp has good laundry facilities and a car wash and plenty of taps. The kitchen is rather short on cooking equipment and finding your way round the ablutions is a bit of a challenge. There is a good-size games room with TV room adjoining. A rather ordinary swimming pool is open in summer. Your friendly hosts here are Keith and Pam Brott. Camping (with or without power) will cost you from $8 per person. 🚐 $12.50 per person. 🏚

49. Pine Tree Lodge Motor Camp
Ahipara Bay, Ahipara, Northland (09) 409-4864

This camp is a short drive from Kaitaia and 3km from Rawene Road. Ahipara is at the southern end of Ninety Mile Beach, but this is not a seafront camp. It has a somewhat rural aspect with pine trees and random sites. The oval swimming pool with sun deck blends well with its environment. An exceptional indoor dining and recreation room has a big stone fireplace and is the focal point of the camp. Alongside is a camp kitchen in need of some upgrading, and a roofed BBQ area is an alternative. Meals are offered by arrangement. Catering for groups is popular here. The ablutions have curtained cubicles, but the laundry equipment is minimal. Jim and Merlene Tatnell are your hosts. There is chalet accommodation and power sites at $10 per person. Tent sites are $8.50. 🏚

50. The Tree House
C/o PDC Kohukohu, Hokianga (09) 405-5855

On the northwest` side of the ferry landing it is just a few minutes to the well-named Tree House. The smoke-free communal building is delightful, surrounded by a verandah with a card phone, and almost enclosed by trees and a grape arbour. Excellent dual kitchen facilities are alongside the peaceful recreation room (no TV). Other facilities are up-to-the-minute shower suites and automatic laundry equipment. The focus here is on backpacker accommodation in cabins or in the lodge. For campers there is a choice of tent sites, either in the orchard or in the (foot traffic only) main camping area. Campers with cars must leave them in the carpark provided. There is no provision for caravans, but motor homes can be accommodated although only one power point is available. This is a short-stay resort; bookings are for a maximum of 3 days. Ideal for environmental do-it-yourselfers. Your friendly hosts Phil and Pauline Evans. Tent sites $8.50. Independent vans $6.per person.

51. Rawene Motor Camp
Marmon Street, Rawene (09) 405-7720

Access by the regular crossings of the Hokianga Harbour by the Rawene car ferry brings you to this little local township. The camp is sheltered by bush and is above the town, but not visible from the road. The general impression is of a secluded environment with amenities of a rare vintage. The kitchen is barely family-size, but has crockery as well as one of everything except a fridge. Ablutions are similarly limited, but cleanly kept. The laundry has an agitator washer and here you will find fridge and freezer space. A gently shabby TV room is carpeted and has soft chairs, bookshelves and a pool table. There may be a spa room available. Tent sites $7. Power sites $8. 🚐 $12. 🏠 $16.

 ## 52. Okopako
Mountain Road, South Hokianga C/o PDC Opononi (09) 405-8815

The Wilderness Farm. Look for the signpost between Rawene and Opononi. The approach road looks unlikely, climbing slightly through farmland to reach the farm gate. This is primarily a lodge with comfortable facilities and great views from the verandah. There is a congenial kitchen with gas cooking and refrigerator. Unisex ablutions are provided; campers share with lodge guests. Other facilities will be added. Camp sites are reasonably level but do not have power. This is a farming experience holiday with a huge surrounding territory to explore. Horse treks are an option. Shearing demonstrations and feeding the lambs can be arranged. Your hosts Nils, Lois and Anna King. Tariff from $6 (no cooking) to $8.50 full use of lodge. $14 a bed in lodge. All animals are permitted provided they are under control.

53. Opononi Holiday Park
S Hwy 12–Opononi, PO Box 16 (09) 405-8791

On a pleasant, slightly elevated site and an upgrading program, this camp is across the road from the beach. There is a vista of sand dunes and sparkling waters from most parts of the camp. The kitchen offers gas hot plate cooking and fridge. Table and chairs are provided. Ablutions are tidy but shower space is limited and beachy. The laundry has automatic washers. Very well placed for the traveller, with shopping and petrol nearby. You can hire "Banana Boats" from the camp. Your new hosts Jenny and Harry Barlow. Tent sites $8. Power sites $10. 🏠 $15.

54. Omapere Tourist Hotel & Motel
S Hwy 12–Omapere, PO Box 19 (09) 405-8737 fax (09) 405-8801

This magnificent waterfront location is also a site of historical interest. From the hotel the water views are superb, and an inviting free-form solar-heated swimming pool is available for guests and campers, as are hotel meals if required. Camping is in the hotel grounds on level sites with some hard stands for vans. A useful amenities block is provided for the 39 power sites, with further sites for tents. Pets are permitted by arrangement. Charter launch trips can be booked here and there is an adjacent jetty and boat ramp. For a comfortable multi-purpose resort close to Opononi this is very attractive. Harry and Erica will welcome you. All camp sites are $9 per person.

($4.50 for children).

55. Solitaire Guest House
S Hwy 12–Waimamaku (09) 405-4891

Not strictly a camp site, but a good stopover place some 6km north of the Waipoua forest. There is a small village nearby. The guest house has an attractive aspect and 2 power points for vans could be available. There is also room for a few tents. Campers would share the house facilities. Lloyd and Betty White are your hosts.

NEAR NORTH DIRECTORY

Key to locations and map of the Near North. Starts at Ngunguru (just north of Whangarei) and continues down the east coast to Orewa and Whangaparaoa Peninsula. Across to Helensville (Parakai), taking in the South Head before skirting the Kaipara Harbour and going north to finish at the southern end of the Waipoua Kauri Forest.

Ngunguru	1.	Ngunguru Bay Holiday Park
Whangarei	2.	Whangarei Falls Caravan Park
Kamo	3.	Kamo Springs Caravan Park
Whangarei	4.	William Jones Motor Camp
Whangarei Heads	5.	Tropicana Holiday Park
Whangarei Heads	6.	Blue Heron Holiday Park
Whangarei Heads	7.	Treasure Island Trailer Park
Whangarei	8.	Alpha Mini Motel & Caravan Park
Otaika	9.	Otaika Motel & Caravan Park
Whangarei	10.	Blue Goose Caravan Park
Ruakaka	11.	Harbour Lights Motel & Caravan Park
Ruakaka	12.	Paradise Point Motor Camp
Ruakaka	13.	Ruakaka Reserve Motor Camp
Bream Bay	14.	Uretiti Campsite (DoC)
Waipu Cove	15.	Waipu Cove Reserve Motor Camp

NORTHLAND–NEAR NORTH

Mangawhai	16.	Mangawhai Heads Motor Camp
Mangawhai	17.	Mangawhai Beach Hideaway
Mangawhai	18.	Mangawhai Village Family Camp
Mangawhai	19.	Riverside Caravan Park
Pakiri Beach	20.	Pakiri Beach Motor Camp
Wellsford	21.	Castlecourt Motels & Caravan Park
Leigh	22.	Goat Island Camping
Whangateau	23.	Whangateau Camp Ground
Takatu Point	24.	Tawharanui Regional Park
Warkworth	25.	Sheepworld Caravan Park
Warkworth	26.	Sandspit Motor Camp
Martins Bay	27.	Martins Bay Holiday Camp
Mahurangi West	28.	Mahurangi Regional Park
Hauraki Gulf	29.	Motuora Island Camping Ground
Orewa	30.	Puriri Park Holiday Complex
Orewa	31.	Orewa Beach Holiday Park
Red Beach	32.	Pinewoods Motor Park
Whangaparaoa	33.	Shakespear Regional Park
Parakai	34.	Aquatic Park Holiday Camp
Shelly Beach	35.	Shelly Beach Reserve
Paparoa	36.	Paparoa Motor Camp

Pahi (Northern Kaipara)	37.	Pahi Motor Camp
Tinopai (Northern Kaipara)	38.	Tinopai Camp
Ruawai	39.	Travellers Hostel
Dargaville	40.	Selwyn Park Motor Camp
Te Kopuru	41.	Glinks Gully
Nth Head, Kaipara Harbour	42.	Kellys Bay
Baylys Beach	43.	Baylys Beach Motor Camp
Kaihu	44.	Kai Iwi Lakes (2 camps)
Kaihu	45.	Kauri Coast Holiday Park
Donnellys Crossing	46.	Trounson Kauri Park Campsite
Kaihu north	47.	Waipoua Forest Campsite (DoC)

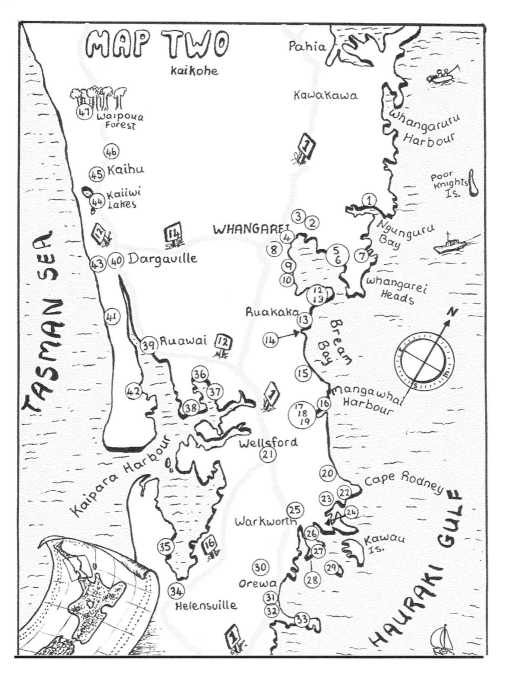

Chapter 2

NEAR NORTH

This is a favoured holiday spot for the nearby Auckland residents, as well as having almost universal appeal for its choice of rural or beach locations.

Big city bustle is left behind. Whangarei is the only truly urban area. However each community is well served by shops and eating places.

The eastern coast offers such a selection of beaches, from the sweep of surfing coast to intimate bays, that you are spoiled for choice. The water is never far away, whether it is a gentle estuary, a river or the open sea. Unique in this area is Goat Island, a marine sanctuary just off the coast north of Leigh. It is just as appealing for its scenery as it is for the abundance of marine life that will share the water with you when you swim or dive.

 The Hibiscus Coast combines the appeal of a holiday resort with home base to those who prefer a quiet suburb within an easy drive from Auckland. It has a lively beach atmosphere in summer.

If you choose to go west you can enjoy the thermal waters of Parakai at the southernmost end of the Kaipara Harbour.

The route through to Dargaville offers smaller-scale camps, often notable for their fishing opportunities. The charm of Kai Iwi Lakes attracts many holidaymakers with their placid waters and unspoiled scenery.

A journey up to the Waipoua Kauri Forest should not be missed. The giant kauri trees date back over 1000 years and are easily accessible. On the fringes are camps with an away-from-it-all charm.

This picturesque gateway to Northland has so many holiday options that you should be prepared to stay a while. Don't be tempted to rush by and miss all that this area has to offer.

NEAR NORTH (Northland)

 1. Ngunguru Motor Camp
Water's Edge–Papaka Place, Ngunguru RD3 Whangarei
(09) 434-3851 (phone & fax)

A visually attractive spot to drop anchor. The water's-edge location is delightful, being a calm little bay with good shelter. Camp sites are level and most have shady trees and picnic tables. The amenities, though slightly dated, provide adequate ablutions, auto washers and dryer and a kitchen with plenty of refrigeration. A breezeway gives the youngsters a pool table and TV venue. There is an on-site dairy and grocery shop which also has a video library. Boat hire or fishing trips can be arranged. This offers superb fishing opportunities and it is only a 5-minute drive to the deep-sea fishing port of Tutukaka. This is dog-friendly territory, except for the December-January holiday period. Your hosts are Stuart and Sheryl Goldstone. All sites $10 per person. and $35 for two. Look for the value coupon on page 55.

2. Whangarei Falls Caravan Park
Kiripaka Road, PO Box 7013, Tikipunga, Whangarei (09) 437-0609

This camp is on the main Whangarei to Tutukaka Road and just a stone's throw from Whangarei Falls. It is a small well-tree'd spot with some reasonably private sites. The ablutions are quite smart with plentiful hot water. There is a basic laundry with iron and ironing board. The kitchen is serviceable. The private spa pool and fenced outdoor swimming pool are alongside the central amenities block. The recreation and TV room is comfortable and homely, with a card phone provided. The BBQ area becomes a focal point in summer; inquire about the possible outdoor meals at a small extra charge. Taps are at all power sites. No animals here please. Your hosts Barbara and Jim Mowat. All camp sites are $7.50 per person. Bunk room $13. $24.

3. Kamo Springs Caravan Park
55 Great North Road–PO Box 4237, Kamo, Whangarei (09) 435-1208

The Kamo shopping centre is 2km south of this park, but it has a dairy and tearooms right alongside. This is a S Hwy 1 location, so it is very easy to stop here. Appointments are excellent. The showers have a seat and dressing cubicle and hand towels are provided at the basins. A spacious kitchen is equipped with all the necessary appliances and the laundry has automatic machines. There is a very comfortable TV room. The grounds are level with some big shady trees and there are privacy hedges between some sites. A children's playground is provided. The mineral springs provide a tepid pool, or you can use the fresh cold-water swimming pool. Private spa pools are available by prior arrangement. Bryce and Daphne Taylor are the managers here and the gates are shut around 11pm. Tent sites are $7 and power sites are $8 each person. There is a waste dump point here.

4. William Jones Motor Camp
24 Mair Street, Whangarei (09) 437-6856

Very close to the heart of Whangarei and merging with the adjacent Mair Park, these grounds are manicured and divided into separate areas, dotted with walnut and citrus trees and dense hedges. There are also kowhai trees and stands of kauri nearby. The amenities block divides the camp, with holidaymakers separated from those who have set up for long-term stays. A coin phone is provided, but no camp store. The kitchen is well equipped, including cooking appliances to almost catering standard. The ablutions are excellent, with metered showers in lockable cubicles. The laundry, with metered appliances, has both automatic and agitator machines and dryers, plus ironing table. It also contains 2 fridges. A new TV room offers cosy relaxation. In the grounds are plenty of taps and a car wash. Great camping in an urban location, it will cost you $7 per person with power, or $6.50 for tents.

5. Tropicana Holiday Park
Whangarei Heads Road, RD 4 Whangarei (09) 436-0687 (phone & fax)

This seafront park is level with plenty of lovely shady trees. There is a selection of accommodation as well as 50 power sites (mostly with taps) and 25 for tents. A swimming and toddlers pool are protected by a fence and there is a safe tidal beach. Small boats are for hire, as is the private spa pool. A play area is provided for children. There is a modern kitchen with microwaves, but the full stove is metered. A flagstone-paved terrace just outside is a mealtime option. At the waterfront a breezeway-style, well lit BBQ/dining area with sink, zip and fridge offers an alternative. The ablutions are smart with metered showers, and have liquid soap and paper towels. The laundry is supplied with good automatic equipment. There is a comfortable games and TV room. Breakfasts, a morning paper and a courtesy car can be arranged for guests. The office contains a mini camp store, while a card phone is on hand. The owner/operators here are Diane and Steve Russo. Power sites cost $9 per person or $8.50 for tents. Inquire for other options.

6. Blue Heron Holiday Park
Scott Road, Whangarei Heads–RD 4 Whangarei (09) 436-2293

On a promontory almost surrounded by the waters of the Whangarei Harbour, this camp has a lot of potential. The better sites are out on the point where they have unobstructed water views. There is a boat ramp and easy access to the water. A 7-day office/shop offers basic supplies and snacks, with a coin phone available. The amenities are sparse and past their prime, but automatic machines are provided in the laundry. Your friendly host is Maureen Ross, who will accept dogs here by prior arrangement. Prices are from $15 for two persons for tents to $16 with power.

7. Treasure Island Trailer Park
Pataua South–RD 1 Onerahi (09) 436-2390

This Whangarei Heads camp has chosen not to supply details for our book. Please call them for information.

8. Alpha Mini Motel & Caravan Park
34 Tarewa Road, Whangarei (09) 438-9867

On a main access road to Whangarei city and very handy to shops and services. There is a pedestrian bridge at the rear for easy access to a good shopping centre. Night tennis is available right next door for a small charge. Racquets and balls will be provided on request. The park itself is not large, but you can enjoy the shade of a large willow tree with a BBQ and seating beneath its branches. There are level sites, 30 with power and plenty for tents. The facilities provided are excellent, with a "focal point" kitchen, well equipped and with room for the helpers! A comfortable lounge has a smoke-free environment, with easy chairs, TV and books. There is a tidy pool/table tennis table as well. The ablutions are excellent with well maintained shower cubicles, all bright and clean. There is good automatic equipment in the laundry. Close to the bus station. Your friendly hosts Dawn and Ken Carter. All camp sites are $14 for two persons. Look for further information on page 56.

9. Otaika Motel & Caravan Park
136 Otaika Road, Whangarei (09) 438-1459 (phone & fax)

To the visitor this is also S Hwy 1. The park mainly appears to be motels but a surprisingly extensive level camping area is tucked away to the rear and bordered by trees. A proportion of the sites are occupied long term. The amenities are centrally located with tiled floors and vanity mirrors in the ablutions. There are automatic machines in the laundry. The kitchen is smallish, without tea-making facilities, but has fridge/freezer (locked) with a deposit payable for a key. Hot plates or rangette cooking, with table and chairs and TV here. It lacks, perhaps, the comfort of a communal lounge, although a games room is provided. Within the pleasantly sheltered grounds is a basic play area, swimming pool and spa pool. A card phone is available and there is a range of shopping just across the road. Your hosts Allan and Mary Gibb will allow pets by arrangement.   For tenters it is $16 for two persons or $15 with power. ⊕ $30 for two ⊟ $45

10. Blue Goose Caravan Park
S Hwy 1,Whangarei (09) 438-3801

South of the city, this camp is to the rear of a 7-day store. This is a very utilitarian camp with about 20 power sites and plenty of tent sites available. Mostly this is a long-term residential camp with little provision for holidaymakers. Unappealing if you want a holiday atmosphere. Occasionally there is a flat available. No animals please. Power sites cost $10 for two persons or a tent site will cost $5 for two.

11. Harbour Lights Motel & Caravan Park
128 One Tree Point Road, RD1 Ruakaka (09) 432-7651

At S Hwy 1 take the Marsden Point turnoff to Ruakaka. Harbour Lights has an attractive aspect from the road, and you won't be disappointed when you drive in. The camping sites are well groomed and varied, some with shade and divided by hedges. There are 30 power sites with taps and about 12 for tents. The amenities are very comfortable, the shower cubicles have seats, and the basins are supplied with soap and a towel. The laundry has automatic equipment and a dish-washing area, as there is no kitchen. There is a lovely carpeted social room with pool and table tennis tables and a TV annexe. This can double as a mini-conference facility. A bonus is the private sandy beach to the rear, with direct access from the camp. There are also tandem bikes for hire. Children have a priority here, with early evening videos provided, plus the occasional treasure hunt. You can order breakfast too.   Inquire for other accommodation. Your new hosts are Shirley and Roger Neal. All camping is at $8 per person ⊟

12. Paradise Point Motor Camp
One Tree Point, RD 1 Ruakaka (09) 432-7228 (phone & fax)

Laid-back camping right on the beach with a boat ramp. Fishing folk are regular patrons of this camp. This sometimes leaves less room for the casual camper. However there are both power and tent sites available. There is plenty of free space to park your boat or trailer. During the summer season vendors call with fruit and vegetables. The amenities include metered showers, well kept toilets and a laundry with automatic machines, plus outdoor tubs. There is a mini kitchen. You will find your hosts Kay and Bert Aart have the camp office in their house on the right of the camping paddock. All sites are $7.50 per person.

13. Ruakaka Reserve Motor Camp
Beach Road, Ruakaka (09) 432-7590

On the Bream Bay coast, this extensive camp is divided into six interesting areas. There are 178 power sites and more than 100 for tents. Big stands of pine trees separate different areas of the camp. Choose from a wide variety of sites. Some overlook the wetlands and sand dunes. This camp has bird conservation areas and resident ducks. There are excellent ablutions with 10 cent metered showers in 7 different blocks, plus facilities for the disabled. The automatic laundry equipment is first class. The kitchens are tidy, with limited appliances. For the active camper there is volleyball, tennis plus fishing and other seaside options. You can walk through the camp to a 7-day grocery shop. Lots of space here and there are on-site caravans and cabins for rent. A sewerage and dump point and car wash facilities are provided. Please no pets here. Your hosts, Brian and Eileen Sloper, lock the camp at 11pm. Tent sites $12 for two. Power sites $14 for two. Under-15-year-olds with two adults are free.⬚ and ⬚. Look for further information on page 56.

14. Uretiti Campsite
S Hwy 1–34km south of Whangarei. Department of Conservation, Whangarei (09) 438-0299

Uretiti is located on the beachfront. Turn off S Hwy 1 between Waipu and Whangarei (look for the signpost). The camp area is relatively undeveloped but is in a spectacular setting overlooking the Hen and Chicken Islands and the sweeping coastline of Bream Bay. There is a range of naturist seaside activities on this attractive stretch of beach which has large shady trees and grassy sites. The camp itself has a remote aspect with low-key facilities (toilets, taps and cold-water showers). There are close to 100 sites available on flat to gently undulating land, generally sheltered and private. This is a self-registration campsite, although a camp caretaker is on site over the summer. No pets or fires please. Prices per person is $5.

15. Waipu Cove Reserve Motor Camp
Cove Road–RD 2 Waipu Cove (09) 432-0410

Surfing anyone? This camp is right on the foreshore of a lovely stretch of curving beach which is well known for its good surfing conditions. Within the camp are 225 sites, most with power. Despite the space, high density camping predominates. Although there are two blocks of ablutions they are stretched to capacity, as are the kitchens when the camp is busy. The laundry has automatic equipment. There are improvements in progress. Within the camp is a boat ramp and a medical facility which is manned in summer. No animals here please. Beside the camp further reserve land offers picnic spots and playgrounds for children. Your new hosts are Neal and Ailsa Pope. Power sites are $20 for two persons, or $17.50 without power.

16. Mangawhai Heads Motor Camp
Mangawhai Heads Road, Mangawhai (09) 431-4675

Right on the estuary seafront, this camp is divided by the entrance road. On one side is the open flat area with up to 80 power sites and beach-style ablutions that use 50 cent tokens. There is a basic kitchen with new hot plates and plenty of bench space. A good automatic laundry is alongside. The other side of the road has more of a garden setting with a children's play area and some pretty sheltered spots for tenting. The camp office is here, also some cold-water showers. This is a lovely coast if you don't mind the camping limitations. The new hosts here are Andrea and Peter Newing. Power sites are $5.50 per person.

17. Mangawhai Beach Hideaway Motor Camp
Moir Point Road, PO Box 96, Mangawhai (09) 431-4251

Well-named, this camp merges comfortably into the sheltering trees. There are a variety of sites; some are grouped in little platforms amongst the bush. Sites are level, but the terrain is varied. At the top of the camp is the shop/office for basic supplies with a verandah for relaxing. Nearby is a new ablution block, with an integral laundry. At the lower end of the camp there are water's-edge lawn sites served by a multi-purpose amenities block. There is a spacious kitchen-social room which is light and airy with picnic tables and a coin phone. The ablutions have curtained shower cubicles. There is extra fridge/freezer space in the laundry, which also has auto washer and dryer. A dump point is provided. The beach frontage also has shady trees and a boat ramp. There are close to 90 sites here. Your hosts Harold, Hazel and Neal Foote. Sites are $8 per person.
🔲 tucked into the bush.

18. Mangawhai Village Family Camp
Moir Road, PO Box 12, Mangawhai (09) 431-4542

Camping in a garden style, close to the local shops and central to the many resorts in this area. There are 64 sites which are roomy and level with some shady trees. The amenities are well sited in the centre with a small kitchen, ample appliances in a fairly spartan setting. The ablutions have overhead showers and there are automatic machines in the laundry. There is a games room and outdoors there is mini golf, children's playground and a trampoline. A fenced swimming pool and spa pool are provided also. The office/camp store and outbuildings have a pleasant cottage-style appeal. The hosts here are Acker, Vera and Adam Gavin. Tent sites are $5 per person, power sites are $7.50 per person, and dogs, by arrangement, an extra $2. 🖼 .Look for the value coupon on page 55.

19. Riverside Caravan Park
Black Swamp Road, PO Box 2, Mangawhai (09) 431-4825

There is a warm welcome waiting here, just over the bridge and right on the estuary. The drive-in entrance is neatly divided from the exit by a little grove of citrus trees. There are over 100 power sites (with taps) and some for tents on well groomed lawns dotted with young trees. Large trees and a private beach, with boat ramp, are on the borders. A central complex houses the communal kitchen, which has eye-level oven and plenty of equipment. Adjoining there is a TV and dining area, including camp library. A large recreation room with pool table completes this very useful building. Other amenities are in two ablution blocks with metered showers. There are automatic laundry machines. All amenities are well kept and clean. Dinghy or kayak hire is available. The friendly new hosts are Loraine and Dave Hartley, who welcome casual holidaymakers, with or without their dogs. All sites $9.50 per person. 🖼 $40 for two.

20. Pakiri Beach Motor Camp
Pakiri River Road, RD 2 Wellsford (09) 422-6199

Just to the north of Leigh, this camp is right on a pleasant east coast beach. There is some unsealed road to travel. At the camp there is a store at the entrance and a card phone. Among the 50 power sites are 17 with TV plugs. There are ample tent sites, all on level ground. A children's playground is set up in a tree-shaded corner, while infant trees are getting well established around the grounds. The ablutions are in two blocks, with well lined and roomy metered showers. The laundry has good commercial wash and drying machines and an ironing board. A large kitchen has plenty of benches and a table, hot plate cooking and fridge/freezer. A sturdy recreation room houses TV. This is country camping with horse-hire stables across the river. Definitely no dogs at the camp. Your new hosts Noela and Tony Adams are planning many more services at this camp. All camping sites are $9 per person. 🖼 $30 for two. 🖼 $50 for two.🖼 $65.

21. Castlecourt Motels & Caravan Park
S Hwy 1, Wellsford (09) 423-7705

Easy to spot this prominent complex on the main north route. A gravel driveway is offered for campervan parks, which are adjacent to the main highway. Many of these are now available as on-site vans for hire. In the main building a communal room with Sky TV, a pool table and sink and fridge is for the use of campers. Also motel-style ablutions and a laundry with automatic machines. There is a private spa pool for hire. There are now also tent sites on the rear paddock. Your host Darla Archer. Tent sites $11.95 for two persons, or $20 for two for a van park. 🚐 $20 for two.

22. Goat Island Camping
Goat Island Road, Leigh–RD 5 Warkworth (09) 422-6185

The experience of Goat Island is one that draws many families in the summer months. In the sheltered bay you can swim amongst the colourful fish; diving and snorkelling is very rewarding. Absolutely NO fishing as this is a marine reserve. Just up from the beach in a rural setting there is a camping spot which enjoys sea views. It is a modest little camp with only 15 sites (8 with power) and it is also a working farm. (Check availability during the winter.) The amenities building is modern and clean with a well equipped homely kitchen. A fridge/freezer and a phone are available. There is limited laundry equipment, and there are nice single showers and toilets for each sex. The grounds are fairly level with some play equipment for children and a nice paved communal eating area with two gas BBQs. A simple camp in a favoured location where you may be able to bring your pet. Your hosts Jackie and Jock Baker. Power sites are S17 for two and tent sites are $14 for two. Group concessions may be available.

23. Whangateau Domain & Camp
Whangateau Beach–Leigh (09) 422-6305

There are prominent signposts at each end of this camp, where many sites are right on the water's edge. It is beside a football field with camping around the perimeter. All sites are level and some have shady pohutukawa trees. Although the amenities buildings are past their prime, they have a good standard of upkeep. The kitchen is dominated by a refrigerated drinks machine; there is also a fridge but a minimum of cooking options. The laundry has good automatic washing and drying machines. Blocks of toilets are at either end of the grounds, and there are metered showers in the main building. 26 power sites plus tent sites here. You will find the managers, Sue and Stu, in residence on the grounds. No animals here please. Tent sites $13 for two. Power sites $15 for two.

24. Tawharanui Regional Park
Takatu Point–via Warkworth or Leigh (09) 422-7711 or (09) 366-2166

This is an Auckland Regional Park where camping permits must be obtained from the city office. If you are looking for the tranquillity of a remote camp bounded by a variety of beaches and endless open spaces in harmony with pockets of native bush, you will enjoy the freedom of this park. Be prepared to negotiate 6km of unsealed road; the final 3km are marginal for towing a caravan. Otherwise this is a lovely drive and the roading within the park is good. There are delightful picnic spots, with the camping ground in a designated area, through the farm gates. There is no power available. This area will cope with 180 campers. You will find good clean toilets and taps at intervals. The grounds are level to undulating, well groomed with rubbish recycle bins. There is access to the nearest beaches and sand dunes over the stiles. The camp ground is sited within a Marine Reserve, but there are other parts of the park where you can fish to your heart's content. No dogs or fires are permitted here. Check on the park closing times before arrival. The gates are closed at night. Look for further information on page 96.

25. Sheepworld Caravan Park & Camping Ground
S Hwy 1–PO Box 536, Warkworth (09) 425-9962 (phone & fax)

Leave the city behind you and make this first stopover with ease. Continue on the main route north just past Warkworth (about an hour's drive north of Auckland). The Sheepworld sign is easy to spot, and you will find refreshments at the neighbouring cafe. Check out the luxury sites for motorhomes—they include most with private en-suite units. In addition to these, there are a myriad of rural tenting sites. This is a peaceful location, well back from passing traffic. $25 for an en-suite site. Your hosts are Ian and Gail.

26. Sandspit Motor Camp
PO Box 40, Warkworth (09) 425-8610

It is just 7km from Warkworth township to this coastal camp. The ferry to Kawau Island leaves practically from the doorstep. Enter this long established camp between the tall trees and under the hanging sign. There are 10 cabins, 30 power sites and 40 tent sites. A boat and trailer park is available. This is an idyllic location in a peaceful corner, with a sheltered little beach and a jetty. There are a variety of level sites with mature shady trees. An on-site store is open 7 days between Labour weekend and Easter and dinghies can be hired. Although the amenities belong to an older era there are good hot metered showers in the freshly painted ablution area. The kitchen has basic equipment, with a microwave as well. In the laundry are automatic machines and there is also an outdoor tub and wringer. The TV room is "picture theatre" style. No animals here please. Your new hosts are Brian and Vanessa Morrison. Tent sites $9 per person. Power sites $10 per person 🏠 $34 per person..

27. Martins Bay Holiday Camp
Martins Bay (09) 425-5655 (cellphone 025 762-357)

Martins Bay is at the foot of a newly sealed, no-exit road via Snells Beach. The holiday camp and picnic area virtually occupies the whole of Martins Bay. There are about 200 power sites and 30 for tents, very fully occupied in the summer season. Level sites are fairly open, though large pohutukawa trees are prominent. An area is set aside for boat and trailer parking and there is a boat ramp. Many sites are occupied on a long-term basis. The central amenities block has a card phone alongside. The building has a very basic kitchen with hot plate cooking and possible use of a freezer. There are automatic machines in the laundry. The ablutions are well-lined and nicely kept with metered showers and clean toilets. There is a secondary small block of ablutions at the far end of the grounds. A dump station is provided. Good new play equipment is for the use of the under 10 year olds. The only provisions available come in by vendors in the Xmas holidays. Also in summer a St Johns medical centre is open and a marquee is erected for communal entertainment. If you want to be part of "Caravan City" come here in the holiday season, but be sure to book. Your hosts Ray and Ruby Close. All sites.. $9 per person. .

28. Mahurangi Regional Park
Mahurangi West Road, Warkworth district. (09) 366-2166

This is an Auckland Regional Park where camping permits must be obtained from the city office. Turn off S Hwy 1 towards the coast 12km south of Warkworth. There is another 7km to travel, the last 3km unsealed. There are various remote camping sites within the park (no power) but for vehicle access there is level lawn camping adjacent to a delightful beach with grassy banks and pohutukawa trees for shade. Facilities are toilets and cold water. Permission must be obtained to use the sheltered camp fire site, tucked away in its own area. The park also has wheelchair-access toilets and a phone, both close to the entrance. No dogs here please.

29. Motuora Island Camping Ground
Motuora Island, Kawau Bay, Department of Conservation (09) 422-8882

The main access to Motuora Island is by private or charter boat from Sandspit. A minimum facility camping ground in a delightful rural setting on a small island near Warkworth. There are toilets, cold showers and an open fire BBQ. It is a great destination for sea kayaking trips. On and around the island there are opportunities for walking, swimming, diving, sailing, boating, and fishing. Intending campers need to book through the Department of Conservation C/o Mansion House, Kawau Island, Private Bag 910,

Warkworth. Also available for rent is a four-bed cottage. Motuora is rodent free so please check through all personal luggage before visiting the island. The island operates a "pack in-pack out" rubbish policy, so please be prepared to take all rubbish off when you leave. Prices are $4 per adult.

30. Puriri Park Holiday Complex
Puriri Ave, Orewa (09) 426-4648

Favoured with a beautiful setting on level grounds with magnificent specimen trees and sheltering hedges, this park is at the northern end of Orewa. The beach is within a short stroll along the avenue and across S Hwy 1. There is virtually no passing traffic and on one border is Eaves Bush, with a licensed restaurant adjacent. The office and shop complex are prominent here and a good selection of grocery items, icecreams etc are stocked. Video games are right alongside. There is a fenced 30-metre swimming pool with a 50 cent gate charge for campers, a pleasant play area for children, even a skating rink. There are new ablutions here to add to the facilities, which are well placed throughout the grounds. There is a well equipped laundry and an adequate kitchen, with another communal hall and limited kitchen facilities available for groups, also TV, or table tennis is an option. The camp has plenty of BBQs and good lighting. Bird life is encouraged, so pets are not permitted. Your hosts are Joan and John Shadbolt. All casual camping is $9 per adult, 🔲 $35 for two. 🔲 $54.

31. Orewa Beach Holiday Park
S Hwy 1 –Orewa (09) 426-5832

Beachfront camping at the southern end of lovely Orewa Beach where you drive in beside the traffic lights. The land is flat, with big pohutukawa trees, and there are 321 power and tent sites plus 10 cabins. This large camp is efficiently managed, with excellent amenities, splendidly maintained, including paraplegic toilets. There are sunny kitchen/dining areas plus electric BBQ. Both laundries have automatic equipment. Two alternative recreation rooms give separate options for relaxing. The park has plenty of taps too and a new children's playground. There is a boat ramp. Orewa has many holiday attractions and an excellent selection of shops. This is a very popular camp.No dogs here please. John and Shirley Tailby can usually find you a site, even in summer and they will accept all discount vouchers. All sites are from $9 per person. 🔲.

32.   Pinewoods Motor Park
23 Marie Ave, Red Beach (09) 426-4526

More like a mini village than a camping ground, this park rambles along the hills above the northern end of Red Beach. There are narrow winding streets, individually named, and clusters of own-your-own cottages with permanently leased sites. There is an attractive communal area at the base of the park, sheltered by mature trees and featuring an excellent playground for children. Alongside is a recreational hall with connecting ablutions and kitchen. Although the land is steeply contoured there are level sites for vans and tents. Around 20 have power, and there are close to 150 in all. There are six small amenities blocks of varying quality. Xmas and New Year entertainment is a feature here. Dogs are not permitted. A Jacob's Ladder gives direct access to the beach. Your hosts Irene and Graham Lee. All sites are $16 for two adults.

33. Shakespear Regional Park
Army Bay, Whangaparaoa (09) 366-2166

This is an Auckland Regional Park where camping permits must be obtained from the city office. Right at the tip of the Whangaparaoa Peninsula, it is well signposted all the way. This is a recreational area with camping occupying a site at Te Haruhi Bay. Through the gate to the Countryside Camp Site which is level, with picnic tables and plenty of cabbage trees, but minimal shade. There are a couple of outdoor sinks and flush toilets with basins and paper towels. No power here. You may not see the lovely beach from your camp site, but it is only a few steps away. No animals here please. The whole park is alive with bird life, and resident peacocks will share their park with you. *Look for further information on p 96.*

34. Aquatic Park Holiday Camp
Cnr Parkhurst and Springs Road, Parakai (09) 420-8998 (phone & fax)

This is the thermal heart of the Helensville district, northwest of Auckland. Look for the tall palm trees of Parakai, well known for its many swimming pools, water slide and warm mineral waters. The camping ground is adjacent, but quite separate from the pools. A nice level park having plenty of big trees, picnic tables and some hard stands for vans. The park holds 98 power sites and 40 for tents. A good well equipped kitchen has no dining space, but plenty of preparation benches and fridge. The laundry facilities are excellent. The ablutions have free lockable shower cubicles in a functional style. Toilet facilities are here, with another block provided near the camp entrance. The pools complex can provide casual dining, video games and is a popular entertainment centre. The camping ground is locked at 10pm. Under new management; inquire from Gary. All sites are from $12 per person and this includes free entry to the pools.

35. Shelly Beach Reserve
Kaipara Harbour, RD 1, Helensville (09) 420-2893

This is a pretty harbourside spot with some provision for camping. Northwest from Helensville, it is rather a long drive, but the roading is good. The power sites are all level and on gravel, with a view of the water. Pohutukawas give partial shade and there is possibly room for some tents. The camping area runs parallel with the road and has a play area for children alongside. Boaties will enjoy the access to the Kaipara Harbour from the 120-metre wharf or the boat ramp. The on-site shop with tea-rooms is also the camp office. Minimal amenities are cold-water showers and toilets. It is a $12 per site to park here.

36. Paparoa Motor Camp
Cnr S Hwy 12 and Pahi Road (09) 431-7300

Weary travellers will easily find this nearly new camp not far from the renowned Matakohe Kauri Museum. Paparoa is a small community with shopping and services. The camp will mainly suit motorhome drivers as there are 20 power sites on gravel. A small grassed area offers some tent sites. The amenities include a good paraplegic suite with quality fittings, and ablutions on a small scale. A multi-purpose room has a basic kitchen with full stove and fridge. Laundry equipment occupies the far end of the room and there is no charge for the automatic washer; a dryer is not supplied. There is a "no animals" policy here. Your host Lavaunne Balchin. Power sites are $15 for two and $4 per person for tents.

37. Pahi Motor Camp
RD 1 Paparoa–North Kaipara Harbour (09) 431-7322

The little spit of land on which the Pahi Motor Camp is sited is ideal for the boating and fishing enthusiast. An excellent wharf, boat ramps, and the sheltered inner harbour is great for swimming too. The camp sites are all level, some with sheltering trees, but the most impressive of these is an historic Moreton Bay fig tree, one of the largest in the world. The communal building is attractive, with a high standard of cleanliness. The kitchen and dining are complete with TV. The equipment includes 2 full stoves (some pots and pans) plus good refrigerator and vertical deep freeze with individual drawers for hire. A selection of books and a chair on the verandah looks inviting. The ablutions have spacious showers and hand towels provided. There is a toilet for the disabled. Some public toilets at the water's edge will help out when the camp is busy. The laundry is tidy, with agitator washing machines and tubs only. There is a dump point here and 36 power sites. No dogs permitted. Your hosts are Neil and Mary. All sites are $7.50 per person.

38. Tinopai Camp
North Kaipara Harbour (09) 431-7263

If fishing matters more than facilities, a waterfront camping site here will suit. A boat ramp is available and the sites are level and on grass. There are public toilets and cold-water showers for the campers, also a basic laundry facility. However a well stocked general store is across the road with Eftpos available and a card phone. There is no resident caretaker, but Alec Ross is nearby for information, or contact the Kaipara District Council. The power sites are $10 for two people, or $9 for tents.

39. Travellers Hostel
Off S Hwy 12. Ruawai (09) 439-2283

A home-like accommodation lodge, this has a garden where there is provision for camping. A lawn is available for tents with gas BBQ and attractive surroundings. A nice spot to rest up and perhaps enjoy the comfortable lounge with wood-burning stove. Ruawai has local shopping, country pub and swimming pool. It is reasonably close to the Matakohe Kauri Museum, which should be on your itinerary. Your hosts Stuart and Sue Butcher. $16 for two people for a power site here.

40. Selwyn Park Motor Camp
10 Onslow Street, Dargaville (09) 439-8296

An orderly, all-purpose camp in the heart of Dargaville. The grounds are dotted with flowering trees and sites are level. A fenced, above-ground swimming pool is a new facility. There are playing fields and a children's playground alongside. The indoor recreation room is a pleasant spot, with TV corner, plenty of dining tables and chairs, books to borrow or play pool. A coin phone is available. Optional cooking in the kitchen with 2 microwaves, full stove, rangette and hot plates. The ablutions have paper towels provided, and the laundry has automatic equipment. At the office some basic items can be bought. Please make arrangements first if you want to bring your dog. Your hosts Rob and Mary Clark also have standard and tourist cabins here. Tent sites $14 for two. Power sites $18 for two. ▦ $28 for two.

41. Glinks Gully
Te Kopuru. C/o Kaipara District Council (09) 439-7059

Offering rather a rugged aspect above a magnificent stretch of the Tasman coast, this camp is south of Dargaville where a cluster of mainly holiday homes have braved the isolation. An ablution block with cold-water showers and flush toilets are the only amenities. It is an open secret that this a great place to fish. You will also enjoy the purified drinking water, free of chemicals. Your host Donald Drummond. Economical camping at $8 for two with an extra $1 per site for power.

42. Kellys Bay
North Head. C/o Kaipara District Council (09) 439-7059

Situated 54km south of Dargaville on North Head, this is an inner Kaipara location, with good fishing. The waters are tidal here, and there is a boat ramp. Minimal amenities are long-drop toilets and cold running water. There are 10 power sites. The previous costs for Glinks Gully also apply here.

43. Baylys Beach Motor Camp
Seaview Road, RD 7 Dargaville (09) 439-6349

This seaside suburb of Dargaville has camping in a residential location, although the camp is not beachside. There are 8 holiday chalets, room for plenty of tents and 16 power sites in an environmentally pleasant setting. The kitchen is large, with plenty of eating areas, both inside and out, but not overly supplied with cooking facilities. There is a wood-fired BBQ available. Showers are token operated, in clean, but not plentiful numbers. The laundry has automatic wash and dry. There is a card phone at the gate and 7 day shopping with light meals available nearby. Sites are level and there is a dump station. Low-key camping in a quiet spot. Your hosts are Ian and Jean Chase. Tent sites $7.50 and power sites $8.50 per person 🛏 $26 for two.

44. Kai Iwi Lakes
Taharoa Domain, Kaihu. Private Bag, Dargaville (09) 439-7059

Lake Taharoa is the largest lake of the three commonly known as Kai Iwi Lakes. The area contains two camping grounds. Around 32km north of Dargaville turn off S Hwy 12 into Omamari Road.
Pine Beach Camping Ground has provision for 500 campers on the grassy eastern shores of the main lake with a picturesque backdrop of pine forest. Water laps the white sand beaches and there is an adventure playground for children. A coin-operated BBQ is available.
Promenade Point Camping Ground accommodates up to 100 campers on the opposite side of Lake Taharoa, a tree dotted corner at the narrow end of the lake where there are less vigorous sports and you can hunt for shellfish.

Despite the lack of electric power to this Domain it is very popular in summer, when food stalls service the area. Otherwise it is a long way to shopping. There are toilets and water taps available at both camps, while Pine Beach also has cold-water showers. The Kai Iwi Lakes Water Ski Club and Dargaville Yacht Club are based at the lakes, which are the major water skiing venue for the north. Other sports popular are canoeing, windsurfing, trout fishing and swimming. Caretakers are on-site in the main holiday season, when booking is advisable. All sites are $5 per person, for school children $3. Absolutely no dogs permitted on Taharoa Domain.

45. Kauri Coast Holiday Park
Trounson Park Road , Kaihu (09) 439-0621 (phone & fax)

Bush-clad hills are a backdrop to this delightfully secluded camp. Easy to find, it is just a short distance from the highway and about 33km north of Dargaville. Cyclists can go to and from the camp on a separate cycle track. There are level sites (two brick paved) and all enjoy proximity to a bubbling river. Canoes can be hired and horse treks arranged. A play area for children includes a large sandpit. View glow worms and kiwis at night; there are guided walks arranged. The amenities sparkle with cleanliness, with lockable shower cubicles plus a paraplegic suite. The immaculate kitchen has hot plate and microwave cooking, fridge/freezer and a high chair is provided. A generous laundry has auto washing and dryer. Pets can be accommodated here, but arrangements must be made beforehand. Your friendly hosts Keith and Isobel Lowrie have a little on-site shop for basic supplies. Camping will cost you $9 per person, with or without power. There is a small selection of other accommodation. ▭. Look for the value coupon on page 55.

46. Trounson Kauri Park Campsite
40km north of Dargaville, on Donnellys Crossing Loop Rd. Department of Conservation

The campground is adjacent to a beautiful pocket of mature kauri forest. Trounson Kauri Park has full facilities including hot and cold water and showers, kitchen with stove and fridge and 4 power points for vans. Guided night walks are available to hear kiwi and see glow worms. No pets or fires please. Price per person is $6.

47. Waipoua Forest Campsite and Cabins
23km north of Kaihu, S Hwy 12, down Visitors Centre Road. Department of Conservation

A great base from which to explore the great kauri forest of Northland. There are plenty of walking and tramping tracks in the forest. The campsite is at the forest's Visitor Centre, near the Waipoua River, where you can make your booking. The camping ground operates on a self-registration system and there is a resident caretaker. Facilities include hot and cold-water showers, toilets and communal cookhouse with refrigerator if required. There are also cabins and a cottage available. Advance bookings can be made through Waipoua Forest Visitor's Centre, Private Bag, Dargaville. No pets or fires please. Price per adult is $6. ▭.

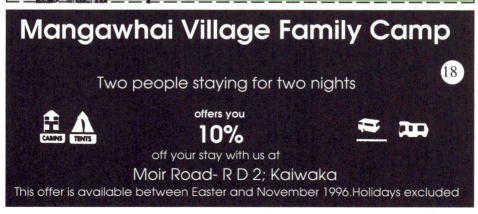

AUCKLAND AND THE COROMANDEL DIRECTORY

Key to locations and map of Auckland, and the Coromandel. Begins on the East Coast Bays north of Auckland travelling south then across to the northwestern suburbs including the coastal resorts west of the Waitakeres. After including the city and islands, continues south skirting the Manukau Harbour to the west. Across to the Firth of Thames and the coast roads– Great Barrier Island is to the north. The Pacific coast (on the east of the peninsula) finishes at Whangamata.

Stillwater	1.	Stillwater Motor Camp
North Shore	2.	Takapuna Beach Motor Camp
North Shore	3.	North Shore Caravan Park
North Shore	4.	Kontiki Caravan Park
North Shore	5.	Birkenhead Caravan Park
Henderson	6.	Western Caravan Park
Henderson	7.	Tui Glen Motor Camp
Muriwai Beach	8.	Waterfront Camp
Piha	9.	Piha Domain Motor Camp
Whatipu	10.	Whatipu Lodge
Huia	11.	Karamatura
Huia	12.	Huia Dell Motor Camp
Auckland	13.	Avondale Motor Park
Auckland	14	Remuera Motor Lodge & Camping
Hauraki Gulf	15.	Home Bay Campground (DoC)
Hauraki Gulf	16.	Motuihe Island Campground (DoC)
Waiheke Island	17.	Waiheke Backpackers
Waiheke Island	18.	Palm Beach
Waiheke Island	19.	Whakanewa Regional Park

AUCKLAND-COROMANDEL

Auckland	20.	Otahuhu Caravan Park
Auckland south	21.	Green Acres Caravan & Cabin Park
Auckland south	22.	Meadowcourt Caravan Park
Auckland south	23.	Manukau Central Caravan Park
South Maraetai	24.	Omana Regional Park
Takanini	25.	NZ Holiday Parks
inner Manukau	26.	Clarks Beach Holiday Park
Waiuku	27.	Sandspit Motor Camp
Waiuku north	28.	Awhitu Regional Park
Manukau Heads	29.	Big Bay Motor Camp & Store
Manukau Heads	30.	Orua Bay Motor Camp
Ramarama	31.	South Auckland Caravan Park
Orere Point	32.	Orere Point Holiday Park
Waimangu Point	33.	Tapapakanga Regional Park
Waharau	34.	Waharau Regional Park
Kaiaua	35.	Kaiaua Motor Camp
Miranda	36.	Miranda (Hot Springs) Park
Thames District	37.	Kaueranga Valley (DoC)
Thames	38.	Dickson Holiday Park
Thames	39.	Boomerang Motor Park
Thames	40.	Waioumu Bay Holiday Park
Tapu	41.	Tapu Motor Camp
Tapu	42.	Tapu Creek Farm
Coromandel	43.	Long Bay Motor Camp
Coromandel	44.	Coromandel Holiday Park
Coromandel	45.	Shelly Beach Motor Camp
Coromandel	46.	Oamaru Bay Tourist Flats

Coromandel	47.	Papa Aroha Holiday Park
Coromandel	48.	Anglers Lodge Motor Park
Cape Colville	49.	Otautu Bay Motor Camp
Cape Colville	50.	Coromandel Farm Parks (DoC)
Great Barrier Island	51.	Akapoua Bay (DoC)
Great Barrier Island	52.	Awana (DoC)
Great Barrier Island	53.	Mickeys Place Campground
Great Barrier Island	54.	Haratonga (DoC)
Great Barrier Island	55.	Whangaparapara (DoC)
Great Barrier Island	56.	Medlands (DoC)
Great Barrier Island	57.	Whangapoua Campground (DoC)
Coromandel east	58.	Whangapoua Camping Ground
Kuaotunu	59.	Kuaotunu Motor Camp
Kuaotunu	60.	Kuaotunu Beach Tourist Park
Coromandel east	61.	Otama Beach Remote Area
Whitianga	62.	Whitianga Holiday Park
Whitianga	63.	Aladdin Motor Camp
Whitianga	64.	Buffalo Beach Resort
Whitianga	65.	Waters Edge Motor Lodge
Whitianga	66.	Mercury Bay Motor Camp
Whitianga	67.	Harbourside Holiday Park
Whitianga	68.	Flaxmill Bay Hideaway Camp
Whitianga	69.	Cooks Beach Motor Camp
Hahei	70.	Hahei Holiday Resort
Hot Water Beach	71.	Hot Water Beach Holiday Park
Tairua	72.	Paku Lodge & Caravan Park
Tairua	73.	Tairua Holiday Park

AUCKLAND-COROMANDEL

Tairua	74.	Pine Lea Motor Camp
Pauanui	75.	Pauanui Airtel & Auto Park
Pauanui	76.	The Glade Holiday Resort
Coromandel ranges	77.	Broken Hills (DoC)
Opoutere	78.	Opoutere Park Beach Resort
Whangamata	79.	Settlers Motor Camp
Whangamata	80.	Whangamata Motor Camp
Whangamata	81.	Pinefield Holiday Park

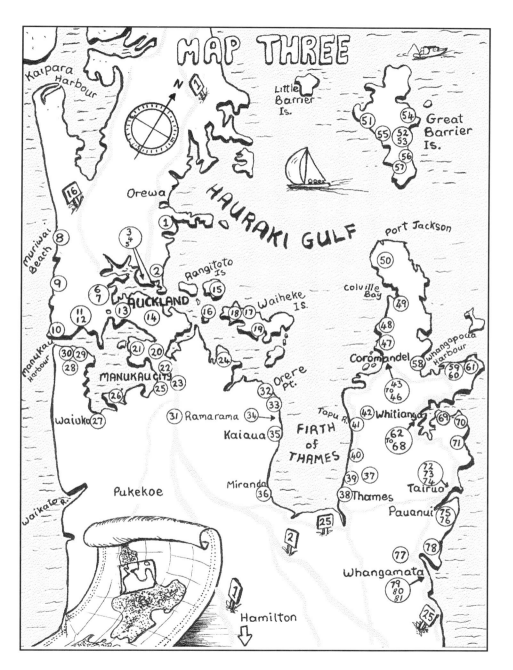

Chapter 3.

AUCKLAND–THE COROMANDEL

Welcome to Auckland and the contrasting region of the Coromandel.

Auckland is a delight for the city dweller. The sea permeates the mood of the city. It is accessible to all, while boating is a favourite pastime. The Harbour Bridge is a busy traffic corridor leading to greater Auckland and northern New Zealand. Auckland's landmark volcanic cone, Rangitoto, is only a short journey by boat from the heart of the city. Dramatically placed, its almost perfect shape is visible from many vantage points. A visit and a walk to the crater should not be missed. The views are breathtaking.

Yet another harbour is to the south of the city. The Manukau Harbour has a more industrious image but there are also many delightful settlements on its far-flung perimeters. Fishing is a rewarding pastime, especially along its southern shores.

Between these water boundaries is a city that offers the visitor a cosmopolitan atmosphere, with a particularly Polynesian flavour. As the busiest entry point, by air and sea, overseas tourists will find plenty of options here. If you haven't explored Auckland yet, a call at any Visitor Information Centre may leave you wishing you had planned to stay longer. Apart from the glorious beaches, there are even thermal pools to be enjoyed on its outskirts.

The waterfront of Auckland is alive with things to do. A brand new casino dominates the inner city. There are a cluster of satellite cities in the surrounding area, also offering quiet bushy suburbs and intimate beaches. It is no wonder that Auckland has the largest population base in New Zealand and is still growing vigorously.

From Auckland to the Coromandel is not a long journey. This peninsula represents "laid-back" living and idle holidays. There are innumerable beaches to enjoy, but the roads are not for the traveller in a hurry. The peninsula is bisected by a rugged dividing range with beach settlements on either side. Coromandel township is an interesting medley of history, recreation and quaint shops. When you tire of the urban attractions of Auckland, the Coromandel offers beach resorts, wilderness camping and a back-to-nature experience. Set aside some time to explore its unique environment.

AUCKLAND–THE COROMANDEL

1. Stillwater Motor Camp
Duck Creek Road –RD 3 Silverdale   (09) 424-7518

Stillwater is a picturesque community which borders the rural countryside lying between the Hibiscus Coast and the East Coast Bays of Auckland. Look for the signposts off the East Coast Bays Road. From this holiday spot tranquil views of the Wade River would surely inspire any artist. For the fisherman there is a boat ramp and jetty with easy access to the open sea. Ample shady trees and an abundance of water boundary enhance the nice level sites. Amenities are fitted with a high standard of ablutions, while there are also excellent auto laundry machines. The kitchen is well provided with fridges, and has a wall oven and hot plates. There is a dual-purpose recreation room, which has a homely TV lounge opening to a large hall for more active pursuits. There is a dump station provided. At the gate to the camp is a general store with all basic supplies and takeaway meals, open 7 days. Stillwater is otherwise not well serviced with shops. A restful retreat which also has other accommodation. No pets please Your hosts Brian and Lesley Turner. Camp sites are $10 per person. Bunk house $10 per person 🖶 $40 minimum. Look for the value coupon on page 95.

2. Takapuna Beach Motor Camp
22 The Promenade, Takapuna–Auckland   (09) 489-7909

A prime site at one of Auckland's most desirable beaches, yet the busy Takapuna commercial area is within a few minute's walk. It is an unpretentious camp with a practical rather then aesthetic aspect. There is minimal privacy; however some sites and the communal building have great sea views. A outdoor deck alongside the kitchen has a gas BBQ, the kitchen has hot-plate cooking only, plus good refrigeration. A large laundry offers automatic equipment and ironing board. The ablutions are in efficient condition with lockable shower cubicles, and a key system operates for "guests only" use. At the camp entrance is a general store and card phone. A car wash is available. There is a nominal amount of play equipment for the children. Kevin and Chris Harvey are the owners here and advise that around 25 casual sites are provided, plus 10 on-site vans. No animals here please. Premium waterfront sites may incur an extra charge and there is a deposit (refunded) for the ablutions key. Tent sites $18 for two. Power sites $23 for two. 🚐 $40 for two. 🚐 $31.50 for two. A 🖶 $50 for two.

3.   North Shore Caravan Park
52 Northcote Road, Takapuna–Auckland. PO Box 36-139 Auck 9,

(09) 418-2578 (fax 09 480-0435)

Drive in beside the Pizza Hut to this very elegant camp, situated on Auckland's North Shore. The grounds are well back from passing traffic and are immaculately presented with groomed lawns and planter boxes a feature. Every site has a picnic table and some also have canopies. There are some hard stands for vans. Facilities are maintained to a very high standard. There is a light and airy kitchen with hot-plates set in a tiled island bench, plus a cluster of refrigerated lockers and a boiling-water service. The ablutions are squeaky clean, tiled, with instant hot-water and moulded shower linings in individual cubicles. There is a lavish amount of mirrors and plenty of toilets plus a nicely set up babies bath and paraplegic facilities. The laundry is superb with banks of automatic equipment, clean and spacious with sorting table. A practical TV room is available, as is a "cafe style" dining room. By this summer a new swimming pool and communal BBQ should be installed. No pets please. Your hosts Wally and Shirley Browning. All sites are $23 for two people. Bunkroom $37 for two. 🔲 $45 for two. 🍴 $68 for two. Leisure Lodge $68 for two.   Look for further information on page 96.

4.   Kontiki Caravan Park
Council Tce, Northcote–Auckland   (09) 480-5684

A roadside camp opposite Little Shoal Bay, a popular boating anchorage. Sites are only available for up to a week as space is limited. The ground is level with some sheltering trees and to the rear is the Northcote Bowling Club and reserve land alongside. There appears to be a camp community of long-term residents. The kitchen is homely with plenty of refrigeration, but limited cooking. The laundry has a good automatic washer and dryer. Although the ablutions are in the "past their prime" category, they appear clean and serviceable. (There are additional public toilets nearby)   Casual camping is at $15 for a power site and $10 for tents. No dogs are permitted here. Your host Graeme Sim.

5. Birkenhead Caravan Park
2 Rangitira Road (Verrans Corner) Birkenhead   (09) 482-0666

Just a small camp on Auckland's North Shore, this is a short drive from the Harbour Bridge and past the Highbury shopping centre at Birkenhead. Although it is immediately off a fairly busy road (with shops and a bus depot opposite) the entrance is bush-lined and opens out to a level area with surrounding bush views. There are 14 power sites, and some tent sites. While there is a large amount of hard-sealed space in the centre, lawn camping is provided around the perimeter. The communal building is large and pleasant with plenty of room to socialise, watch TV or play table tennis. A home-style compact kitchen, all very clean and tidy, serves this area. The laundry is semi-enclosed, with an automatic washer and dryer. The ablutions are not numerous, but include a full paraplegic suite. No dogs here please. The focus here is on long-term residents. Costs are from $90 per week. Casual camping is $20 for two.

6. Western Caravan Park
524 Swanson Road, Ranui   (09) 832-2995

This camp specialises in long-term occupancy. It is an urban camp on the fringe of Henderson and not really geared for casual holidaymakers. The usual camping amenities are here, TV lounge, ablutions with roomy showers. Excellent automatic equipment in the laundry, and kitchen with hot plates and grillers, a table and chairs. No dogs permitted here. Malcolm Spencer and Priscilla Fairbrother are the managers. There is a weekly charge from $65 for one person on a power site. 🖼. Tent sites $10 for two. Power sites $15.

7. Tui Glen Motor Camp
Edmonton Road, Henderson   (09) 838-8978

A traditional camping ground, claimed to be the first motor camp in New Zealand. It has a relatively secluded location despite being very close to Henderson shopping centre and major traffic routes. Amongst the trees are clusters of cabins and tourist flats with good accessibility by individually named streets. Camp sites are level and well groomed. The central amenities block contains a kitchen where, perhaps, cooking takes second place to the coin-operated drinks and snacks machine and TV. There is good automatic laundry equipment. Ablutions are well kept, although more showers would be an advantage. There is plenty of lawn and a play area supplied for the youngsters. Located adjacent to the Olympic Pool, there is also bowling and croquet next door. No dogs here please. Your hosts Joyce and David Gilbert. Tent sites $8 per person. Power sites $10 per person 🖼 $38 🖼 $48.

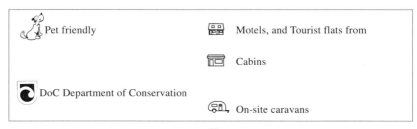

Pet friendly	Motels, and Tourist flats from
	Cabins
DoC Department of Conservation	On-site caravans

8.   Waterfront Camp
General Store & Cafe–Regional Park, Muriwai Beach   (09) 411-7763   (fax 09 411-7426)

Muriwai Beach is one of the more spectacular beaches in the greater Auckland area. The focal point here is a well stocked store and cafe (with public phones) and a generous rural park for camping. All the grounds are separated from the beach by a road and some grassy banks. There are at least 66 power sites and over 100 for tents with plenty of taps throughout. Sheltering trees are dotted throughout the park. There is an adjacent golf course (not a camp facility) , but this location is more notable for its surfing, and rock and beach fishing. There is a patrolled swimming area. Amenities are sturdy and clean with a large kitchen, plenty of sinks and benches and adequate cooking, but no fridge. There are metered showers, and shaving points, flush toilets are provided in the main block, with other toilets and basins separately located in the grounds. Dump points are provided for vans. The laundry is housed in a large room with automatic washers and campers have keys. Muriwai is notable for its gannet colony and several environmental and geological features. Your hosts Kath and Bill Moore. All camping here is from $8 per person.

9.   Piha Domain Motor Camp
Seaview Road, PO Box 52 Piha. (09) 812-8815

Piha is on the coastal fringe of the Waitakere Ranges but the Scenic Drive on a good sealed road makes it within easy reach of the city. Above the camp the hills provide a backdrop and dramatic seascape views. The camp occupies the only large flat site in the district. Lion Rock is prominent on the seaward side of the camp. The other boundaries are playing fields, a tennis court and a lagoon for the children, who also have an adventure playground. The amenities building is rather elderly and basic, but it does provide hot showers, automatic laundry equipment and a kitchen with reasonable equipment, plus a microwave and fridge. At the entrance to the camp is an attractive building for public use. A rather curious internal layout provides open-style cold-water showers, for both sexes, toilets plus a paraplegic toilet. There is a store and phone opposite the camp. Attractions here are the surfing and fishing. The surrounding hills have a scenic bush reserve laced with walking tracks. Your friendly hosts are Jo and John Harris. Tent sites $7 per person. Power site $7.50 per person 🔲 $12 per person. Look for the value coupon on page 95.

10. Whatipu Lodge
Whatipu–West Auckland   (09) 811-8860 (phone & fax)

An outpost resort accessible via Titirangi and Huia where the west coast beaches finish and on the fringe of the Manukau Harbour entrance, this is a remote area serviced by an unsealed road and having lodge accommodation as the priority. However there is a fairly smooth camping area, with lots of space and no trees and no power for the intrepid camper. The beach has miles of black sand and is recommended for surfcasting. You will have to be independent as there are no kitchen or laundry facilities for the camp. A minimal amount of cold-water showers and toilets are provided. There is no national grid power here, so only the Lodge has power from its own generator. Pets are allowed, if kept under control. You can really "get away from it all" here. A well stocked shop and a public phone is on the property, but for petrol you will have a 20km drive to fill up. The hosts here are Mary and Neil Roberts and camping will cost you $8 for up to four people.

11. Karamatura, Huia
Huia Road, Southern Waitakeres   (09) 811-8897 or 09) 817-7134

Barn Paddock is an Auckland Regional Council campsite on the western side of Huia Bay. Camping is by permit only. It combines camping with an operating farm, drive in through the farm gates. Discover Auckland's last frontier at Huia. This is remote camping on undulating grassy sites surrounded by high, thickly wooded hills. There are many walking tracks. Facilities are cold-water, long-drop toilets and an all-purpose building with sinks, storage capacity or shelter from the elements. A power supply is pending. Make enquires from the Ranger. Tent sites $2 per adult without vehicle. Tent sites $5 with vehicle.

Kiwianis Huia Camp is a well set-up bunk accommodation unit for groups only. A very pleasant setting with catering facilities and outdoor activities, ideal for school groups. Inquire from the Ranger.

Huia Lodge another bunk accommodation option, overlooking the sea, but not as well sited as Kiwianis. Also groups only are permitted here. Inquire from the Ranger. These Auckland Regional Parks have a No Animals – No Fires restriction. Look for further information on page 96.

12. Huia Dell Motor Camp
1196 Huia Road, Huia–Titirangi (09) 811-8627

The quiet charm of Huia, with its backdrop of bushclad hills and tranquil sea views seems worlds away from the bustle of Auckland. However it is a pleasant drive out, on good sealed roads through the bushy Waitakere suburbs. The camp rambles through cleared patches of bush with rustic facilities for pioneer camping. There is controlled hot water and antique laundry facilities, ablutions, toilets and a bushman's kitchen. At the gate is a general store and tearooms, with a card phone. Apart from a children's play area and the lovely sheltered beach you will have to create your own entertainment. One area of the camp is dominated by a group of cabins, but there is ample privacy for tents, also 10 power sites in a bushland atmosphere. Pets are accepted here by prior arrangement. It will be necessary to book your site over Xmas. Your host Janice Campbell. Tent sites $6 per person. Power sites $8 per person. 🏠 (with kitchen) $30 for two.

13. Avondale Motor Park
46 Bollard Ave, Avondale   (09) 828-7228

Quiet camping in a western suburb, where the neighbours are not in evidence. Plenty of trees surround the grounds, which also have a boundary stream. Two public phones are installed here. The site is flat with a variety of permanent accommodation. The kitchen is airy, with a metered wall oven and microwave or gas ring cooking. There is an outdoor pergola alongside with picnic table and chairs on a flagstone base. The ablution block is in reasonable condition and there is a separate babies bathroom provided. The recreation room is a bit cramped, but has a pool table and TV. There is an excellent laundry with plenty of automatic equipment. There is a car wash and a dump station here. Children have a play area. Very central camping in older Auckland. No animals at this camp please. Your hosts Sally and Eric Redit. Power sites are from $9 per person, or $8 for tents On-site caravans and other accommodation is available.

14. Remuera Motor Lodge & Camping Ground
16 Minto Road, Remuera–Auckland   (09) 524-5126   (fax 09 524-5639)

Unexpectedly, Remuera has a camping ground, in an "old garden" setting and just off Remuera Road. This secluded site is within a short stroll of the village shops and is in close proximity to the racecourse, hospital and city generally. The grounds have level lawn sites on three terraces, 45 with power, and around 11 for tents. At the entrance the office and generous swimming pool are on the upper level. There is other accommodation, and the backpackers lodge is well equipped and handy to the road. The central communal building houses the kitchen with refrigeration and has a "campers pantry" plus basic utensils (pots and pans, and all things you may have forgotten!) . The laundry has auto washing and drying, ironing and hair driers as well. There are homely touches in the tiled ablutions, which have metered showers. There is a dump station here. Your hosts Ron and Barbara Parker. All sites are $15 per person or $24 for two. There is a backpacker lodge at $20 per person. (1br) 🏠 $69 for two. Weekly rates are by negotiation.

15. Home Bay Campground
Motutapu Island Recreation Reserve–Hauraki Gulf Department of Conservation   (09) 372-7348

There is a daily summer ferry-boat service to this campground but the most common transport mode is by private boat. Access is also available from Islington Bay on Rangitoto Island, by a one-hour walk across the walkway to Home Bay. This is a minimum-facility camping area with toilets, a water supply and fireplaces, but no kitchen, showers or power points. From the campground visitors have access to the farm park on Motutapu Island, historic buildings and coastal recreation. It is a great stop-off for sea kayakers. Large groups need to book through the Department of Conservation, Motutapu Island, Private Bag 68908, Newton, Auckland.

16. Motuihe Island Campground
Motuihe Island Recreation Reserve, Hauraki Gulf, Department of Conservation (09) 534-8095 (phone & fax) or (09) 534-5419

With its beautiful sheltered beaches, fascinating island walks, either around the foreshore or through the farm-park, Motuihe offers a holiday destination with a difference. This 180-hectare island in the Hauraki Gulf is just a short harbour cruise away from Auckland City. The western headland is the site of the minimum-facility campground, with water and toilets. There are solar showers and BBQs for hire, and a conveniently located shop which also provides meals and takeaways. The campground is run by a concessionaire. Also available is accommodation in a bunkhouse (formerly used by naval personnel) with basic facilities. Bring your own sleeping bags and gas cooker. A second accommodation unit is the Homestead with full facilities (but bring your own towel and sleeping bag) . All sites $4 per adult.

17. Waiheke Island Backpackers
Hekerua House, 11 Hekerua Road, Waiheke Island (09) 372-8371

Privacy in the trees. This is a bushland setting, mainly offering hostel accommodation. However a small level lawn can be used for tents. All facilities are shared by campers and guests alike. There is a domestic style kitchen with all utensils provided.
There is a laundry with automatic washers and dryers. A roomy shower suite for each sex is available. The house has a very comfortable lounge opening to a wooden deck with gas BBQs and an outdoor sink.
Your host is Maggie, who will charge you $10 for a tent site.

18. Palm Beach Backpackers
54 Palm Road, Waiheke Island (09) 372-8662

Across the road from Palm Beach, one of the many glorious Waiheke beaches, this resort has a friendly welcome and a cosmopolitan atmosphere. The main building has extensive verandahs. Just outside the kitchen you can use the 5-burner gas BBQ, or two alternative washing-up sinks. The kitchen itself is well equipped for self-catering, with all the equipment and utensils. Plenty of fridge and freezer space is provided. The servery opens to the dining room, with a setting of family-group tables and chairs. There are plenty of alternative relaxing options. Two comfortable lounges as well as one activities room with air hockey, table tennis, pool and darts. Adjacent to the main house are well maintained ablutions with lockable shower cubicles and vanity basins. A set of tubs and a clothes line are provided in a breezeway for your laundry. Campers will find around 35 tent sites on lawns; choose your favourite spot. There are also 3 chalets to rent. The bus from the ferry stops at the door and you can hire kayaks and mountain bikes here. A convenience store/dairy and takeaway food outlet is close by. Your helpful hosts Carol Handin and John Ball. Tent sites $10 per person or $15 per bed in the lodge.

19. Whakanewha Regional Park
Off Gordons Road, Half Moon Bay–Waiheke Island (09) 372-5647 or (09) 366-2166

The nearest settlement is Rocky Bay, look for O'Briens Road then Gordons Road. This park is being developed for camping and picnicking. Collect your camping permit at the ARC or DoC Information Office at the ferry buildings before you catch the ferry to Waiheke. There are shuttle buses from the ferry landing to within easy reach of the park. If you are driving there is a short stretch of unsealed road leading into the camping area. A lovely curving beach is on one border with clear water that is very shallow for some distance. Ideal for the children. There are two camping areas, both reasonably level. One has young nikau palms and the shade of an old pohutukawa for picnics. This is environmentalist camping–expect no mod cons. Go back to nature for a week or two and create your own activities. Horse hire is nearby and there are many bridle paths to explore. A car club has dirt-track racing and an aerodrome has scenic flights just on the outskirts for more excitement. This park is in the care of your friendly Ranger Andy Spence. *Look for further information on p 96.*

20. Otahuhu Caravan Park
26 Majorie Jayne Cresc, Otahuhu   (09) 276-6815

This camp caters for long-term residents in a industrial area in Otahuhu. It is unlikely that provision is made for casual overnight stopovers. Amenities and grounds are reasonably tidy. Your hosts Graham and Robyn Grace. A van site will cost $70 per week for one person plus $15 per extra adult. On-site caravans are from $105 per week minimum charge.

21. Green Acres Caravan & Cabin Park
124 Favona Road, Mangere (09) 275-5553

A level camping ground surrounding a substantial accommodation block which is not available for casual guests. The campers have ablutions and laundry, all adequately equipped. The kitchen offers plenty of sinks and benches, but don't expect any properly functioning appliances. Home base to a number of residents, this offers useful sites for stopping over, especially if you are travelling by plane. Sites are well serviced with power, TV and sumps, but the grounds are devoid of trees and appear haphazardly kept. There is an adventure tower and swings in fairly utilitarian surroundings. Power sites are $10 per person and there are on-site caravans. Your hosts Keith and Angie.

22. Meadowcourt Caravan Park
630 Great South Road, Papatoetoe   (09) 278-5612

A large level camping ground bordered by trees. Located on a busy road, it has quite a relaxed and spacious "feel" and commuting to most Auckland destinations is easy. Shops, particularly Manukau City Centre, are within a short distance. There is a good stock of groceries at the camp store and a card phone. Long-term residents occupy a portion of the camp but there are unlimited tent sites and plenty of power sites, plus on-site caravans. Plenty of outdoor taps and a dump point are provided. The amenities are usefully signposted. Two blocks of ablutions include a paraplegics toilet. There is excellent equipment in the three laundries. The kitchen is clean with minimal cooking equipment and a tiny fridge. There is a spartan but tidy TV room. An airport courtesy car is available. No dogs at this camp please. The managers here are Bob and Iris Devonshire. Power sites are $12 per person or $14 for two. Tent sites are $8 per person or $12 for two. 🚐 $30 for two.

23. Manukau Central Caravan Park
902 Great South Road, Manukau City   (09) 266-8016 (phone & fax)

Highly recommended for the traveller who appreciates the good housekeeping of a well kept camp. Included in the 53 power sites are two with individual en-suite services. For the others the communal buildings are well appointed and spotlessly clean and include a paraplegic suite with wheelchair available. The kitchen has refrigeration and TV and a pleasant dining area. Excellent laundry equipment is provided. The grounds are attractive and edged with trees. They are well back from passing traffic with good sized sites, some with concrete pads for vans. There is a dump point here. A restaurant is next door and other shopping is nearby. Bring your pets by agreement with your hosts John and Cathy Isbister and family. Personal en-suite sites are $24. Tent sites are $8 per person. Power sites are $20 for two. Look for further information on page 94.

24. Omana Regional Park
Omana Beach Road, Maraetai   (09) 536-6007 or (09) 366-2166

An extensive area for camping that is reached through an appealing picnic park just above the beach. It is dotted with large trees and the rolling lawns have picnic tables and BBQs. There is a purpose-built campfire site. For campers there are taps, toilets (which include paraplegic access) and outdoor cold showers. The park is well groomed and spacious. Adjacent to the entrance is an adventure playground for children. There is an information office at the park with a public phone. The gates are closed at night. Maraetai has local shops and services reasonably handy. Look for further information on page 96.

25. New Zealand Holiday Parks
7 Rountree Place, Takanini   (09) 298-0499   (09) 298-0599   (fax 09 537-0782)

You can see this camp from the southern motorway approaches to Auckland. Look for the camping symbols on the fence and take the Takanini turnoff. Follow the blue signs on the bus shelters when you reach the Great South Road. At the entrance is a shop and card phone and a security system operates 24 hours. Most of this park is designated for long-term residents, but the aspect is tidy, with casual campers located in a separate area. There are also cabins available. The communal buildings are generous, with a large well kept kitchen that has gas-ring cooking. The ablutions have push-button showers and a paraplegic toilet. The laundry has plenty of fully automatic machines. There is a large all-purpose social hall, while outside there are BBQs and an adventure playground for children. There is a dump station here. Your host is Mike Smillie. Tent sites $10 per tent. Power sites $20 for two. ⊕ $25 for two. ⊟ $45 for two.

26. Clarks Beach Holiday Park
Torkar Road Ext., Clarks Beach–RD 4 Pukekohe   (09) 232-1685

This is a popular spot for weekenders, being only a pleasant hour's drive from Auckland. The landscaped grounds are next to the golf course and over 100 level sites enjoy many facilities. Beside the camp office is a new games room with some serious gym equipment. There is a large covered solar-heated swimming pool with picnic and BBQ facilities. The recreation room is upstairs with pool table, piano and TV, plus a kitchenette and a camp library. It opens to a balcony with sea views. Most sites have power, water and sewerage. The kitchen offers one full stove, a microwave and electric hobs. It supplies a fridge and preparation area, but not dining space. There are neat well-lined shower cubicles (10 cent meters) in the ablutions which also have a babies bath and paraplegics toilet. Excellent laundry equipment provides automatic washers and dryers, iron and board, even a wringer. There is a dump point here. Try the mini golf within the camp. Boaties will enjoy the boat ramp, boat park, fish-cleaning sink and fish smoker. The waters of the Manukau Harbour are at your doorstep. Bring your own food, or shop at the nearby community shops. No dogs here please. Your hosts Alan and Janet Deed will discuss discounts. All sites are $10 per person. $37 for two. Chalets $48 for two.

27. Sandspit Motor Camp

Rangiwhea Road, Waiuku   (09) 235-9913 (phone & fax)

The nearest motor camp to the township of Waiuku and alongside a public reserve and a sandy beach. In a pleasant quiet street this small camp is not geared for entertainment, but has a well stocked on-site store and coin phone. Sites are mostly elevated but cabin-style accommodation predominates. The amenities have not been updated in recent times. Basic ablutions have single or unisex facilities. There is a modestly equipped kitchen and laundry provided. Play equipment is on the foreshore, Swimming or hire dinghies is an option. Net fishing in season. Pets by arrangement with your host John Crighton.
Tent sites here are $7.50 per person and power sites $15 for two.

28. Awhitu Regional Park
*Off Brook Road, between Waiuku and Manukau Heads   (09) 235-1106
or   (09) 366-2166*

Lifestyle camping in an easy-to-access ARC park some 30km north of Waiuku. There is a vast choice of sites within two defined areas, **The Brooks** camping ground or **The Peninsula** camping ground. It is all basically level with grassy sites and clusters of trees. Although it is a coastal camp the two beaches are reached by walking tracks. There are clean toilets, but the only other facility is an outdoor cold-water shower. Campers must be independent of power and no animals are permitted. There is an attractive 9 hole golf course alongside the park.   Look for further information on page 96.

29. Big Bay Motor Camp & Store
South Head, Manukau Harbour–RD4 Waiuku   (09) 235-1132

The tip of the Awhitu Peninsula is a pleasant drive through rural countryside from Waiuku to the Manukau Heads. At Big Bay there is a safe sandy beach and a sheltering bluff. There is a small settlement here amongst the surrounding hills, but the motor camp is on mostly level ground across the road from the beach. It supplies most items from its general store, open 7 days, or you can partake of a tasty snack at the adjoining tearooms. This is the commercial centre of Big Bay with a postal agency and coin phone as well. The camp sites are sheltered, some with shady trees. An attractive BBQ and social gathering spot is roofed and has hot water and lighting. There is an indoor social room; the structure may be old, but the comforts are provided. The amenities are rather humble, with a clean homely kitchen that has meal space and a high chair. The ablutions belong to an earlier era, but function with some limiting hours. A good automatic washing machine is provided. Day visitors can use the facilities for a nominal charge. Hire dinghies are available. Your friendly hosts Ann and Graeme Dawber offer discounts to pensioners and groups. All sites are $8.50 per person in summer. and $25 for two.

30. Orua Bay Motor Camp
Orua Bay Road, Manukau Heads RD4 Waiuku   (09) 235-1129

Beside a sandy beach on the recreational side of the Manukau Harbour this camp has well groomed level sites, all with power and water. There is no passing traffic and on the Awhitu Peninsula the roading is good, despite its rural location. The camp has an excellent kitchen, although the adjoining laundry has an agitator washing machine and a dryer (both metered) plus ironing board and iron. The spotlessly clean ablutions have toilets and hand basins for each sex, plus metered unisex showers with a separate paraplegic suite. A babies bath is in the ladies facilities. Bring your own provisions as there is no camp store and other shops are some distance away. During the Xmas holiday period fresh supplies are brought in by the milkman. All sites $10 minimum or $8.50 per person 🏠 $70 in season.

31. South Auckland Caravan Park
Ararimu Road, Ramarama RD3 Drury–Auckland (09) 294-8903 (09) 294-8121 (fax 09 294-8122)

Genuinely rural in setting, this camp is easily accessible off the southern motorway at Ramarama. Next door to the camp is a 7-day store and takeaway food. There is an extensive camping area, all virtually flat with around 100 sites plus 8 sleeping-only cabins. Small animal and bird enclosures are a feature and it is a pet friendly place. An active dairy farm occupies the rear of the camp which leads to a recreational pond. A farm tour by trailer is offered to guests. The mini swimming pool is unlikely to attract bathers. The amenities are supplied with a few well-lined showers, plus toilets in good condition. The kitchen has limited cooking with metered appliances, but ample fridges and freezers. The laundry is well equipped with automatic machines (cold wash) . There is a large recreation hall with TV. A self-service dump point is provided. Your friendly hosts are Brian and Rose Thompson. Tent sites $9 per person. Power sites $12 per person 🛏 $35. 🏠 $22.50.

32. Orere Point Holiday Park
Orere Point, Clevedon–Private Bag 11, Orere Point, Papakura. (09) 292-2774 (phone & fax)

Off the main route this park is in a delightful setting at the northern reaches of the Firth of Thames. There is a sparkling river with swimming holes and the sheltered beach is close by. A fine spot for fishing or gathering shellfish. There is plenty of space here with two levels of flat sites and shade if you wish; trees and bush are plentiful. The main amenities block has a spacious kitchen with both small and large appliances,. It includes a full stove, a microwave, a fridge/freezer and a chest freezer, plus tables and chairs. This opens to an attractive paved BBQ area complete with tables and seating. There are generous shower cubicles (metered) and roller towels in the attractive ablution area. The laundry has a good automatic washer and dryer. An indoor games room provides a pool table, table tennis, video machines and a drink-machine. At opposite ends of the grounds are alternative ablutions. Another feature is a porch washing-up area with hot-water and fridge and a filtered drinking-water tap. There is also a second laundry and a cup-of-tea nook with toaster. You can store your boat here between fishing trips and bring your well-behaved pets. Orere Point is a small community with a general store adjacent to the camp. Your hosts Robyn and Kerry Thompson. Tent sites $9 per person. Power sites $10 per person. 🛏 $35 🏠 $45.

33. Tapapakanga Regional Park
Deery Road, Tapapakanga *(09) 292-2799 or* *(09) 366-2166*

On the scenic route south of Orere Point this has recently been opened to campers. It is well signposted throughout and the pou or Maori carved totem poles mark the entry to the park. The camping ground is on an elevated site with lovely water views. Sites are grassy and at present are serviced only by long-drop toilets and taps. The park has good driving roads which also lead to a tempting bathing beach with BBQs and picnic tables. This is a charming spot, with rolling grass and pohutukawa trees. There are toilets and an outdoor cold shower here. Look for further information on page 96.

34. Waharau Regional Park
Kaiaua – Clevedon Road, Waharau *(09) 292-2799 or* *(09) 232-2714 or* *(09) 366-2166*

South towards Kaiaua further along the scenic drive, Waharau Park is a well established multi-purpose park with many walking tracks into the eastern Hunua Ranges. Individual campers may choose between two camps. The closest to the road is **Waikato Tribes Campsite** where there are grassy sites with glimpses of the water. There are 6 power sites and a sturdy ablution block with hot showers and plenty of toilets. To the rear of this building is a verandah-style sink bench facility with hot water and power points. This site is not available between 12 December and 12 February. **Southern Boundary Campsite** is reached past the Park headquarters building; follow the sign posts. The road to the camp passes through a pleasant picnic area with boulder BBQs, a small toilet block and cold-water taps. The camping ground is through the farm gate and is a simple grassy paddock with picnic tables and a bush boundary. There is no power here. If you are planning a group excursion the **Education Camp** is nearby and is totally serviced by hot showers, toilets and a good catering kitchen and communal hall. This will cope with about 90 people. Ideal for school groups. Enquires can be made through Rosehill College, Papakura. No dogs on any camp sites please. Look for further information on page 96.

35. Kaiaua Motor Camp
Coast Road, Kaiaua RD3 Pokeno *(09) 232-2712*

Beside the Firth of Thames; this district is known as the "Seabird Coast" and is. a designated bird-migration area, only 90km from Auckland. The camp occupies a site between the road and the beach and has a stream on one border. At the entrance a new general grocery store and petrol pump service is open daily. The level grounds give access to the beach, which is especially noted for shellfish gathering but not really suitable for swimming. Most of the roomy power sites have taps and there is the occasional willow tree for shade. While the amenities are fairly basic, they are clean, with two smallish ablution facilities for each sex. There is a communal kitchen with gas ring and electric cooking and plenty of fridge and freezer space. The mini laundry has a good automatic washer and dryer. A games hall is provided. If you like camping in a peaceful backwater between the attractions of the Coromandel and the city, this will appeal. No dogs please. The new owners Earleen and Brian Hancock are refurbishing this site. Tent sites are $6 per person or with power $16 for two people. 🛏 $20 for two. Look for the value coupon on page 95.

36. Miranda (Hot Springs) Caravan Park
Coast Road, Miranda RD6 Thames Free phone 0800-833-144 (fax 07 867-3205)

An eye-catching sign directs you to this well known thermal resort. The neighbouring thermal pool complex is open daily. The largest hot mineral pool in the Southern Hemisphere is flanked by 4 private spas and a sauna pool. Around the pools are attractive gardens with excellent picnic and BBQ facilities. The camping ground alongside has 16 power sites in a tree-studded area with room for plenty of tents. Future facilities are underway, but there are minimal amenities for campers. However guests have free access to the open pools, which also provide shower and toilet facilities. A camp store and light-meals service is available every day. Miranda Caravan Park is in a rural area, and not far from a renowned major bird migration sanctuary. You may not bring dogs to this park. Your hosts are Gail and Alan Kidd. Costs for camping are $7.50 per person.

37 Kaueranga Valley
PO Box 78 Thames–Department of Conservation (07) 868-6381

The Kauaeranga Valley is one of the most popular and frequently visited parts of the Coromandel region. The valley contains a wide range of scenery within a relatively small area, from river flats and bushclad hills to more rugged landforms. Families can enjoy picnics, a number of short bush walks and several natural swimming pools in the main river. There are also tracks for horse and pony rides and an historical display at the visitor centre. Access to the valley is by the Kaueranga Valley Road which turns off S Hwy 25 just before entering Thames.

38. Dickson Holiday Park
Victoria Street–PO Box 242 Thames (07) 868-7308 (phone & fax)

Nestled into a garden setting with a backdrop of bushclad hills (offering bush walks) this park offers interesting nooks and crannies amongst its variety of sites. The main amenities block has a homely kitchen with refrigeration and freezer space, microwave and conventional cookers and the adjoining dining room has wonderful bush views and a noticeboard for information. Outside there is a good rubbish-recycling system. There is an excellent laundry with automatic equipment. An outdoor tub, wringer and clothesline may also be useful. The ablutions are roomy with metered showers, a babies bath and roller towel provided. Below this block is an attractive outdoor entertainment area with large solar-heated swimming pool, tennis court, mini golf and an attractive communal BBQ. The children have baby swings, trampoline and seesaw. For those who prefer indoor relaxing there is an "adults only" comfortable lounge for TV and reading. The neighbouring games room provides video games, TV and pool and table tennis tables. If you want to be tucked away at the other side of the camp there is a "pioneer kitchen" you may like to try, or the other BBQs. If campers have no other transport, bicycles can be provided here. The camp is close to the township of Thames and the beaches, but very secluded. Your hosts are Anne, Jack, Geoff and Jenny Hawthorn. Tent sites $7 per person. Power sites $18 for two. 🔳 $28 🚐 $30. 🏠 $54 Look for further information on page 94.

39. Boomerang Motor Park
Te Puru, Thames Coast–Private Bag Thames, (07) 868-2869

A garden setting enhances this mainly community-based camp. There are very few power sites available for casual campers, but these are neat with hard stands for vans, and tent sites are available. The central amenities block has 10 cent metered showers (with dressing space for skinny people) or communal dressing. There are two other toilet blocks provided. The kitchen has island sinks, with plenty of cooking equipment, including microwave, plus fridge. The laundry is well equipped with automatic equipment. A nice gas BBQ has table and chairs in a sheltered breezeway. Dump points are provided. An easy place to find, only 11km from Thames on the road to Coromandel. Your hosts Kim and Bryan Cresswell and Denise and Gary Bevins. Tent sites $16 for two. Power sites $17 for two. 🔳 $28 for two. Tram $32.

39. Waioumu Bay Holiday Park
Waioumu Creek Road, PO Box 556 Thames (07) 868-2777

This is a holiday complex within a well groomed park, attractively maintained. Beside the central play area is an inviting swimming pool. To the rear of the main amenities building is a tree-shaded BBQ radiating from a central chimney and an adventure tower/tree house for the youngsters. There is a hard tennis court also. The ablutions have tiled floors and metered showers and a separate toddlers bathroom is provided. There is an indoor recreation complex with a competition-style table tennis hall and a pool room alongside. The TV room is rather spartan, but the whole area is served by a roomy kitchen with coolroom space by arrangement. This should be a good venue for groups. The laundry has automatic equipment and a metered iron. There is a bait freezer provided. Clothes lines are handy, as are the two separate toilet blocks to supplement the central amenities. There is a dump station here. Your hosts Barbara and Ernie Jackson will accept pets here, but not dogs. Shop at the local store. The office is open 8am to 6pm. All sites are $9.50 per person 🔲 $20 for two 🔲 $51.50.

41. Tapu Motor Camp
Main Highway RD5 Thames Coast   (09) 868-4837

Almost midway between Thames and Coromandel this motor camp is opposite the local hotel and has a good stock of provisions at the camp store. The sites are level, some with shade, and there are plenty of accommodation units within the camp. At the rear is a shallow water inlet for the youngsters to enjoy. There are two kitchens, compact but tidy with metered appliances and fridge/freezers. The TV room is cosy and carpeted with easy chairs and books. A variety of ablutions (some metered) are provided with two very attractive paraplegic suites. There are plenty of toilets for campers. Two laundries with reasonable automatic equipment are provided. All the communal areas are very clean and tidy. There is a "no dogs" policy here. Your hosts Margie and Ray Humphrey. Camping is $7 per person with a power site charge of $2. 🔲 $29 for two. 🔲 $35.

42. Tapu Creek Farm
PDC Tapu. (07) 868-4800

Turn inland for 5km up the sealed Tapu Road. This snug little camp is surrounded by bush and with a creek on one border. There are 20 sites with power, water and sewerage. It has limited amenities with only a shower and toilet provided. This is a retreat from the urban jungle. You will have bush walks, swimming and hunting at your doorstep. A farm trip can be arranged. Interact with the animals. Your hosts Marjolein and Berry Jondag.

43. Long Bay Motor Camp
Long Bay RD1 Coromandel (07) 866-8720

This popular camp occupies a lovely stretch of foreshore with a backdrop of bush. There is no passing traffic; the road terminates at the camp, which is only a short drive to Coromandel township. At the camp you will find an on-site shop for basic supplies and a card phone. There are two distinct waterfront areas, **Long Bay** and **Tucks Bay**. The latter has only long-drop toilets and no power, but is quietly appealing. The Long Bay site has clean, if rather basic amenities. The showers are metered, and there appear to be ample toilet facilities. The kitchen has a full stove. The laundry is complete with dryer. Ideally suited for the boatie, the boat ramp is a busy place beside the lovely sheltered beach. Fish-cleaning and smoking facilities are provided. Delightful bush walks ramble through the perimeter of both camps. There is also a dump station here. 100 sites are available, 65 with power. Lacking only a reasonable supply of rubbish tins, but there are plenty of taps for campers. The boating-fishing set will enjoy this location. Your hosts Ngaire and Dennis Irwin. Sites are $8.50 per person with a $1 surcharge for a power site. ⌐⌐ add $15 to the $8.50 site charge.

44. Coromandel Motels & Holiday Park
Rings Road, Coromandel–PO Box 86 Coromandel (07) 866-8830 (fax 07 866-8707)

There is a prominent old colonial homestead at the entrance to this camp, which is a short walk to the Coromandel township. There are level sites for campers, but only 12 with power. Willows and hedges give shelter. Two kitchens are provided and the ablutions are not metered. The laundry has automatic machines and ironing equipment. A brightly decorated pool and table tennis room, plus a separate TV room are in the main building. Motels and cabins offer alternative accommodation. The hosts here are Marie and Don and they will discuss bringing you pets. Tent sites $8 per person. Power sites $9 per person. ⌐⌐ $26 per person. ⌐⌐ $36 for two.

45. Shelly Beach Motor Camp
Colville Road–PO Box 24 Coromandel (07) 866-8988

Another opportunity for campers to have direct access to the sheltered Coromandel waters. The camp sites do not have water views, but are level and roomy. There is room to park your boat and a boat ramp. Centrally situated is a good amenities block with free showers, nicely lined. For the young family a separate lockable room provides babies bath, shower and toilet. Paraplegic facilities are also provided. The kitchen is large with microwave and hot plates. There is TV and table and chairs, a compact fridge/freezer, in a rather barren style. The laundry has only agitator machines and tubs, plus ironing board, but plenty of space. Young trees are growing in the grounds and a special area has been set aside for campers with dogs. There are 51 power sites, plenty of tent sites and some on-site caravans. New cabins should now be available. For supplies there is a market garden next door and the office-shop carries some items, while at Xmas a vendor store operates from here. Your friendly hosts are Larry and Joan Knudsen. All camp sites are $7.50 per person, with a site charge of $3 extra for power. 🎦 $75 for two.

45. Oamaru Bay Tourist Flats & Caravan Park
Colville Road, Oamaru Bay (07) 866-8735

Set against a bushclad hill, this camp is across the road from the beach. Most sites are leased long-term, leaving only 3 or 4 available for casual campers. There are two amenities blocks; one is past its prime. The new block has a rather curious layout in the ablutions, but has paraplegic toilet facilities. There are good automatic machines in the laundry. The kitchen has a somewhat primitive aspect, a freezer is available. Your hosts Pai and Rihitoto Te Whaiti. There may be a site to spare; please phone for information.

47. Papa Aroha Holiday Park
Colville Road, RD Coromandel (07) 866-8818

A beachfront camp 11km north of Coromandel, this is a water lover's retreat with an extensive beach and tidal creek bordering the camp. There is a boat ramp and parking for boats. The land is level and liberally dotted with tidy cabins and communal buildings. For campers there are some lovely pohutukawa trees for shade. A fully stocked camp store, card phone and petrol pump is on-site and open daily. The showers are in metered cubicles and in a separate area from the toilets. The kitchen has plenty of cooking equipment, but no fridge. A porch-style laundry has good automatic machines. There is a games room, a children's play area and dinghies for hire. Your hosts Bob and Cynthia Cudby. All sites $8.50 per person. 🎦 $30 for two. 🏠 $42.

48 Anglers Lodge Motel & Motor Park
Amodeo Bay, RD Coromandel (07) 866-8584

This holiday resort presents a manicured image to the traveller along the Colville Road. Tastefully presented buildings are the main option here, but there are some sites for campers. A lovely sea vista is available from the park which has access to the beach and boat ramp, and there is a swimming pool and a spa pool on the site. All the amenities are on a small scale, but immaculately clean. The kitchen has 2 full stoves and fridge/freezer. Just a little bathroom with free showers is provided, plus laundry with automatic washer. A pool room and a TV lounge are available, as is a tennis court. The central gazebo with gas BBQ is a feature in the grounds. There are 23 sites available, 15 with power, and a sewerage dump point. No pets here please. Your hosts Lois and Merv Grocott. All sites $10 per person with a $3 surcharge for power sites. 🎦 $59 for two. 🏠 $89 for two.

49. Otautu Bay Motor Camp
Port Jackson Road, Colville (07) 866-6801

Extensive camping sites spread over a working farm. Some areas have a water frontage with riparian rights to the beach, and a metal boat ramp plus jetty is available. The large sweep of beach and the paddock sites are serviced by long-drop toilets and a token number of cold-water showers. Most camping is on level sites with a well tree'd border, and the water supply is abundant. Apart from a freezer being available for campers, there are no other facilities. There are currently 36 power sites and 200 for tents. Your hosts Peg and John Goudie send their campers an annual newsletter. Dogs are allowed in a special area, except in peak season. Caravan yearly storage is available and two on-site caravans may be booked. Camping is $4 per person, plus $3 extra for power.

50. Coromandel Farm Parks
Cape Colville, Department of Conservation PO Box 19 Coromandel
(07) 866-6869

At the northern end of the Coromandel Peninsula, **Waikawau Bay Farm Park** and **Cape Colville Farm Park** give visitors the opportunity to observe a farming lifestyle while enjoying the remote setting for camping. There is no vehicle access between Fletcher Bay and Stony Bay but a 3 to 4 hour tramp along the walkway is worth experiencing. The two farm parks include 5 camping areas **Waikawau** and **Stony Bays** on the eastern side, **Fletcher Bay** and **Port Jackson** on the northern coast and **Fantail Bay** on the western side. Coastal bush and farmland combine to provide an attractive setting. Fantail Bay is great for fishing and the pohutukawa grove provides good shade. Waikawau Bay has a sweeping sandy beach nearby. To reach both sides of the peninsula north of the Colville settlement requires patient driving on narrow unsealed roads. These are the only permitted camps in this region. Most charges will range from $2 to $6 per adult, with a family maximum of $10.

51. Akapoua Bay
Great Barrier Island. Department of Conservation, Port Fitzroy (09) 4290044
or (09) 307-9279

Adjacent to the Department of Conservation headquarters on Great Barrier Island, this campground lies on the water's edge of Akapoua Bay, Port Fitzroy. The Port Fitzroy Harbour hosts a series of sheltered bays suitable for most water sports, swimming, diving, sailing, fishing and windsurfing. Visitors enjoy the short walks in the area and the day tramp to the kauri dam, picnic tables and volley ball. With easy access to a shop, postal centre and services, this campground is popular with family and boating groups. During peak holiday season fees are collected by the Duty Ranger, otherwise a self-registration payment system operates. Price per adult is. $4.

52. Awana
Great Barrier Island. Department of Conservation   (09) 429-0044 or   (09) 307-9279

Nestled in the fertile Awana Valley on the east coast of Great Barrier Island this campground lies next to the Awana Stream and close to one of the island's most famous surf beaches. This camping area has basic facilities, toilets, cold shower, solid fuel BBQs and picnic tables, but no shade. During peak holiday season fees are collected by the Duty Ranger, otherwise a self-registration payment system operates. Price per adult is .$4.

53. Mickey's Place Campground
Awana Bay, Great Barrier Island. (09) 429-0140

Without the benefit of visiting this camp you must draw your own conclusions. Despite having no electric power, there are warm showers available and flush toilets., also a cookhouse and a covered BBQ. Solar lighting is provided. Your host is Mickey O'Shea. Camping here will cost you $3 per person and three on-site caravans are also available.

54. Harataonga
Great Barrier Island. Department of Conservation   (09) 429-0044 or   (09) 307-9279

On the west coast of Great Barrier Island at the end of Harataonga Road, this secluded campground offers a quiet and peaceful place to camp in a pastoral setting. Only a short walk from the camping area is beautiful Harataonga Beach which is suitable for swimming, fishing and diving. Mature trees provide sheltered campsites with toilets, fresh water, solid fuel BBQs and picnic tables available. During peak holiday season fees are collected by the Duty Ranger, otherwise a self-registration payment system operates. Price per adult. is $4.

55. Whangaparapara
Great Barrier Island. Department of Conservation   (09) 429-0044 or   (09) 307-9279

Tucked into the inlet of the Whangaparapara Harbour, on the water's edge lies Great Barrier's Whangaparapara campground. Having no vehicle access makes it the quietest camp on the island. Access is gained by boat or by walking the track leading around from the Field Base at Whangaparapara. Much of the early whaling and milling industry on the island was centred around this area, the remains of which can still be seen today. Swimming, fishing and diving are popular activities plus the short walks and day tramps to the nearby Great Barrier Forest. Campground facilities available are toilets, fresh water and BBQs. A shop and other services are within walking distance. During peak holiday season fees are collected by the Duty Ranger, otherwise a self-registration payment system operates. Price per adult is .$4.

56. Medlands
*Great Barrier Island. Department of Conservation   (09) 429-0044 or
(09) 307-9279*

The most southern of the east-coast camping areas on Great Barrier Island,
Medlands campground lies between the small townships of Claris and
Tryphena in the picturesque Medlands Valley. Adjacent to Oruawharo
Creek and Medlands Beach this popular campground offers safe swimming
in the estuary as well as a surf beach. Facilities include toilets, cold-
water shower, solid fuel BBQs, picnic tables and volleyball. During peak
holiday season fees are collected by the Duty Ranger, otherwise a self-
registration payment system operates. Because this campground is popular
during the New Year period, a limit has been set of 170 campers per night
and booking is essential. (Alternative campgrounds are available) . Price
$4 per adult.

57. Whangapoua Campground
*Whangapoua, Great Barrier Island. Department of Conservation   (09)
429-0044 or (09) 307-9279*

A recently designated conservation campsite on the east coast, this
campground offers an open estuarine setting and views of the nearby
mountain and Rakitu Island. It is a good area for wildlife viewing, as
well as being near Whangapoua surf beach and Okiwi airfield, and campers
can access the day tramps in the Hirakimata area. This, the most exposed
campground on Great Barrier, should not be confused with Whangapoua
Camping Ground on Coromandel Peninsula. The campground has toilets,
a cold-water tap, rubbish bins, but no shade. During peak season fees are
collected by the Duty Ranger, otherwise a self-registration payment system
operates. Price per adult is $4.

*Conservation camping means being aware of and respecting the needs of
nature as well as other campers.*
*NOTE: CONSERVATION CODE – All these Department of Conservation
campgrounds are adjacent to important wildlife habitats for endangered
species such as the brown teal and banded rail. Please don't bring your
pets, they are not welcome.*

57. Whangapoua Camping Ground
*Quarry Road, RD2 Whangapoua Beach –Northeast Coromandel (07)
866-6759*

On the mainland this is back-to-basics camping in a country paddock.
Whangapoua is an isolated rural area, but only 5km of sealed road from

S Hwy 25. The main attraction must be the nearby lovely water playground and wharf on Coromandel's upper east coast. There is a sheltered beach which should be great for water skiing. On the beach side of the camp there is a grocery store (open except for Tuesdays) and petrol (super only) . For the pioneer camper there are long-drop toilets, plenty of taps and at intervals a wringer and tub (outdoor) are provided. A freezer is available. There is also a BBQ with lots of wood. Your hosts are Lance and Margaret Adams. The gates close at 10pm. Campers will pay $5.50 per tent site.

 59. Kuaotunu Motor Camp

Bluff Road, West Kuaotunu, RD2 Whitianga (07) 866-5628

The coastal settlement of Kuaotunu is for the escapist who enjoys the lovely beaches, and some facilities to make life comfortable. The camp shop has local fresh fish and chips with possibly some other fast food. A large level camping area of around 100 sites is dotted with shady trees, mainly willows. The amenities block has metered showers, clean and roomy, and the toilets include one for paraplegic use. The laundry is well equipped with automatic machines. The kitchen has the basics, including a fridge. Outside you will find tubs and a fish-cleaning area. A fisherman's freezer is provided. You can hire a boat here and there is a car and boat wash. Well controlled pets (on a leash) are permitted here. Some cottage accommodation is provided and there are 40 power sites. Your host Phil Pratt. All camping is $9 per person plus $3 for a site with power 🔲 $32 for two.

60. Kuaotunu Beach Tourist Park

S Hwy 25, Kuaotunu, RD2 Whitianga (07) 866-5172

Over the road from 4km of delightful sandy beach, this is a family-orientated camp. The grounds are bordered at the rear by a gentle pine tree clad hill. Many of the camp sites have ocean views and sites are terraced. Small enough to be friendly, the camp has 25 power sites, around 30 tent sites and some cabins. At the office you can exchange books, while shopping and petrol is only 1km away. A central amenities block has spacious ablutions with controlled (7 minute) showers. The laundry offers agitator washing, but a drying room is available. The kitchen has the usual equipment, including a microwave and a big freezer, plus fridge. There is a boat ramp, fish-cleaning facilities, boat wash and park. No dogs at this camp please. Your hosts Joe and Janice Jackson and family. Inquire for off-season rates. All camp sites are $9 per person with a $3 surcharge for power. 🔲 $32 for two.

61. Otama Beach Remote Area Camp
Black Jack Road via Kuaotunu (07) 866-2362

Summer-only camping where you will find a wonderful beach beside a pioneering site for campers. There is no power here. Taps are plentiful and there are long-drop toilets. A dump point is provided. Otherwise self- sufficiency is paramount. Explore this dramatic coastline on the eastern extremity of the CoromandelPeninsula. Your hosts Roy and Beverley will accept vaccinated dogs here. Tent sites $4 per person. Campavans $2 per person.

62. Whitianga Holiday Park
Buffalo Beach Road, PO Box 79 Whitianga (07) 866-5896

Family camping at the northern end of Buffalo Beach and just across the road from the seashore. There are good shady trees here and a card phone at the entrance. Some basic supplies are obtainable at the camp shop. There are two blocks of ablutions with free curtained shower cubicles and vanity bench. The kitchen has all the necessary equipment, including microwave and fridge. Also supplied are hot and cold outdoor sinks. You can arrange for lock-up refrigeration too. The laundry has plenty of good automatic equipment and a babies bath. There is a TV and pool room in a utility style for the youngsters. Outdoor swing and trampoline as well. Over 100 camp sites with 70 that have power. There are also a selection of cabins. Your hosts the Thompson family. Except for Xmas, pets may be permitted by prior arrangement. Tent sites cost $9.50 per person with an extra $3 daily for power. 🔲 $25 for two.

63. Aladdin Motor Camp
Bongard Road, Whitianga (07) 866-5834

Not a large camp, this has a scenic reserve on one boundary and is lush with trees. It is close to the beach, but off the main road, with a secluded aspect. Sites are level and the communal area has a homely and friendly ambience. For those summer meals there is breezeway dining outside, sheltered by a pergola draped with kiwifruit vines. Both wood and gas BBQs for cooking. For the indoor cook the pleasant kitchen area has full stoves and fridges and opens to a cosy recreation lounge with TV and fireplace. The ablutions have free curtained showers and an additional children's toilet in the main block. A pagoda style annexe at the rear of the grounds has an extra unisex suite. The laundry is equipped with automatic machines in a reasonable condition, and has iron and board too. There is fish bait available and a few basic supplies at the office/shop. Your hosts here are Dennis and Tina. Pets are allowed here except in the peak season. Tent sites $8 per person. Power sites $8.50 per person. 🔲 $15 per person. 🔲 $20 per person.

64. Buffalo Beach Resort
Eyre Street, PO Box 19 Whitianga (07) 866-5854 (phone & fax)

A generous park in delightful grounds and centrally situated in Whitianga. It is a short walk to the shopping centre, the magnificent beach and the ferry. When the water garden and hot pools are completed it should be a unique environment. All amenities are of a high standard, with two well equipped kitchens with microwave and fridge. There is an excellent range of ablutions, all in sparkling condition. Outdoor cold showers and sinks are provided too. All automatic equipment in the laundry, and refrigerated lockers are available. Camping is easy here on level sites with a choice of shady trees and dump station provided. Backpackers have a substantial building to the rear of the grounds and there is other accommodation. Your hosts Alan and Trudi Hopping will accept well controlled pets, except in the busy season. All sites from $9 per person. 🏠 $40. 🚐 $55.

65. Water's Edge Motor Lodge
84 Albert Street, PO Box 105 Whitianga (07) 866-5760 or (09) 480 3093

On Whitianga's main street, this camp also has a waterfront location and overlooks the new marina. There is a boat ramp for small craft and a plus for boaties is access to a free mooring at the marina while they stay here. There is a reserve next door, plus a card phone at the gate. The gates are locked nightly at 10.15pm in the busy Xmas season. The 66 sites are level, with some shady trees and some on the estuary. In the amenities we found a spotlessly clean kitchen with plenty of refrigeration, microwave and hot plate cooking. The ablutions are corridor style, with well lined showers operated on a push-button system. The laundry is fully equipped with automatic machines and ironing. There is also an outdoor tub. A swimming pool, spa pool and TV room are here too. Dump points are provided. You can hire boats here. Pets may be allowed, apart from in peak periods. Charges for camping may vary seasonally.   Tent sites $8 per person. Power sites $19 for two. 🏠 $29 for two 🚐 $49 for two.

🐕 Pet friendly	🏠 Cabins
	🚐 Tourist flats & Motels
⚫ Dept of Conservation	🚐 On-site caravans

66. Mercury Bay Motor Camp
121 Albert Street, Private Bag Whitianga (07) 866-5579 (fax 07 866-4891)

A lovely level park with an entrance of mature citrus trees. Other trees dot the grounds, providing a good choice of around 100 sites. These are serviced by two ablution blocks immaculately maintained with showers (metered in January only) and babies bath. Particularly plentiful numbers of toilets are provided. A first class lockable paraplegic suite is easily accessible. There are two laundries with automatic machines. The main kitchen provides microwave and gas cooking, hot plates and fridges, and there is a smaller kitchen too. An excellent standard of housekeeping here. Use the indoor heated spa pool, or the new swimming pool. There is a pool table and a TV room. Outside there is a children's play area, BBQ, car wash and fish-cleaning facility. A dump point is provided. No dogs here please. Your hosts John and Christine Stevenson. Tent sites are from $8 per person plus $2 daily for a site with power, water and drainage. 📺 $30 for two. 🏠 $50.

67. Harbourside Holiday Park
135 Albert Street, Whitianga (07) 866-5746 (phone & fax)

Opposite the harbour estuary, this is an immaculate level park with over 100 good-sized sites, some hedged for privacy, and with a variety of trees. There is a lovely new swimming pool. A coin phone is on-site and there are gas BBQs. The amenities include an average communal kitchen with meal space and plenty of fridges. There is a selection of cooking equipment including microwave. The ablutions have both metered and free showers. An excellent laundry is provided. There is a private spa pool, TV lounge and games room. Ask about boat hire, or the complimentary dinghy. There is a "No Pets" policy here. There is a dump station available, fish-cleaning and car wash also. Your hosts Angela and Chris Evans. Tent sites $8 plus $2 daily for power 📺.$27 for two 🏠 $48 for two.

68. Flaxmill Bay Hideaway Camp & Cabins
Flaxmill Bay, RD 1 Whitianga (07) 866-2386 (fax 07 866-5752)

Beachfront camping at a new resort. This has plenty of space for the smallish occupancy it provides. The boundary is defined by large trees and the grounds are level and dotted with new wood cabins. A licensed restaurant is nearby, as is the ferry to Whitianga. There is a well equipped children's playground. The modern amenities include a compact kitchen with hob cooking. It also has fridge and freezer and toasters and jugs. Gas BBQS are provided. The ablutions include paraplegic facilities. There are automatic machines in the laundry. A dump station is on the site.

Visiting ducks patrol the grounds. Your hosts Peter and Janet Clarke. Tent sites $8.50. Power sites $9.50 🏠 $30 for two.

69. Cooks Beach Motor Camp
Cooks Beach, RD 1 Whitianga (07) 866-5469

A family camp scattered over a large area with an abundance of trees, pongas and bush. It is not on the beach, but close by. The bushland environment is enhanced by the use of timber from the old Whitianga wharf to create interesting fences, a tree-shaded arbour for al fresco meals, and an impressive adventure playground for the children. A large kitchen-dining complex has a pleasant bay-window table for meals. There is tons of equipment and benches, but some stoves were not entirely functional when we called. There are two blocks of ablutions, although one is without toilets. Outside you can wash yourself, your car, or your toddler with a variety of cold showers. There are two laundries, with dryer, but agitator machines for washing. A hideaway atmosphere on a large scale with around 170 sites. Your hosts Mark and Cathy Guilford prefer no pets please. Power sites are $8.50 per person or $8 for tents. 🏠

70. Hahei Holiday Resort
Hahei Beach, Private Bag Whitianga (07) 866-3889 (phone & fax)

Park-like grounds invite you to linger at this extensive complex in Harsant Ave. This has a wonderful beachfront site and level landscaped grounds. Supplies and takeaway food are at the handy shopping centre, with restaurant and petrol also. There are 150 power sites here and almost as many for tents. The stretch of beachfront sites reach half a km. A newly installed children's playground is a winner. There is a campers kitchen with fridges and microwave and top-element cooking. The ablutions are in 3 blocks and lavish with facilities including 10 cent metered showers in lined cubicles with seats. There are baths provided too, including babies bath and children-sized appointments. The laundry has excellent automatic equipment and a drying room is available. There is a central covered area with tubs and wringers, providing covered access to some facilities. In another building is a very comfy TV room with easy chairs and writing desks. Fishing is an attraction here and you may be able to arrange a fishing trip from the camp. There is a fish-cleaning and crayfish-boiling area provided. A dump station is provided. There is a choice of other accommodation. Your hosts Noelene, Jim and Ray. Tent sites $8.50. Power sites $9.50. 🏠 $32 🏠 $57.

71. Hot Water Beach Holiday Park
Hot Water Beach Road, RD1 Whitianga (07) 866-3735

Right next to the beach, this camping complex has a lovely setting with level sites dispersed amongst natural barriers of flax and hedges. There are large Norfolk pines and pohutukawas and plenty of shelter. Yes, there is hot water here. Dig you own pool in the sand (subject to tides) and enjoy Nature's spa. The camp amenities include a roomy kitchen, with two levels of benches, cooking facilities, but no fridge. The ablutions have 6 minute controlled showers, plenty of toilets in a rather spartan setting. The laundry has both automatic and agitator machines. At the camp entrance is a shop and card phone. There are also additional public toilets (including paraplegic) alongside. The shop also manages the private thermal pools which are free for campers. In winter the shop is closed. This camp does not permit dogs and has 32 power sites and 70 tent sites plus some on-site caravans. Hot Water Beach attracts many people for the surfing as well as the natural springs. Your host is Geoff Wolfe. All sites $9 per person. $28 for two. Bach $65 for two.

72. Paku Lodge & Caravan Park
The Esplanade, Paku Headland. PO Box 63 Tairua (07) 864-8557

There is possibly still provision for camping on delightful bush-clad sites which are secondary to the more dominant accommodation provided. The setting commands tranquil views of the Tairua-Pauanui inlet, and a gentle water frontage is directly accessible from here. Ask about the free use of dinghies. There is a communal kitchen, laundry and ablutions. The location is superb, but local shopping is some distance away. John and Bev Short are currently charging $10 per person for sites. For other accommodation and off-season rates make enquires direct.

73. Tairua Holiday Park
4 Manaia Road, Tairua (07) 864-8871

Easy camping in a very handy position, this is a centrally located small park. Ideal as a family base, between Tairua shopping centre and the beach, both a mere few minutes walk away. This is a very tidy camp where there are level sites with reasonable privacy in a ribbon layout and 4 cabins. The use of the BBQ and wooden slab tables provide a pleasant choice for summer dining. There is also a good selection of amenities and a TV room. A dump station is provided. Your hosts Ted and Betty Anderson. Power and tent sites range from $8.50 to $9.50 per person. No dogs please.

74. Pine Lea Motor Camp
Pepe Road, Tairua (07) 864-8551

Cradled in a woodland setting, this camp is not isolated, but close to all local services. Citrus trees grow plentifully within the camp and in the orchard alongside. The combined office and camp store are in harmony with their rustic cabin appearance. The feature BBQ has an immense log table sheltered by a palm frond roof. With plenty of shady nooks under the mature pine trees, this camp is better than usual for privacy. 42 power sites and 60 tent sites are supplied, with a token number of cabins. For the youngsters there is a flying fox, adventure playground and safe swimming in the fresh water stream. Spa pool, TV room and pool room are available. The kitchen is compact, in a fairly dated condition, but contains all the usual equipment and the use of a high chair. There are unisex and wheelchair ablution facilities with a new shower installed. The laundry has automatic appliances. All facilities are well kept. A well behaved pet can holiday here too. Your hosts are Chris and Monika Scherrer. All sites $9. ⛟ $32. 🏠 $35 for two.

75. Pauanui Airtel & Auto Park
Pauanui Boulevard, PO Box 87 Pauanui Beach (07) 864-8568 (phone and fax)

Although this looks like traditional camping, you can in fact park your aircraft here! There is also plenty of parking for buses and other vehicles. Serviced by sealed roads, all power sites have sewerage disposal. The grounds are well maintained with level sites, some terraced, and there is shade from tall pines. BBQs and children's play equipment are available. The service blocks have wheelchair facilities and the usual communal equipment. Camping sites all have power. For a weekly rental you can park your unoccupied van here. Your hosts Peter and Betty Erni. Power sites $10. 🏠 $50 for two. 🏚 $78.

76. The Glade Holiday Resort
58 Vista Paku, PO Box 77 Pauanui (07) 864-8559

Primarily a convention centre, this resort is prolific with pine trees and bordered by an estuary beach. There is a variety of accommodation, including a 96-bed facility. Over the summer holidays you can shop at the camp store. The campers kitchen is adequate, but not overly supplied with appliances. The ablutions are satisfactory and the laundry provides automatic machines. There is a games room and TV/video communal area. No pets here please. Catering for groups is a specialty here so inquire for these prices. Your hosts Pat and Ian Hunter. All sites are $10 per person. 🏠 $32 for two. 🏚 $72 for two.

77. Broken Hills
Puketu–inland from Tairua. Department of Conservation (07) 838-3363

South of Tairua, nestled beside the Tairua River at the top of Puketui Valley Road, Broken Hills is becoming increasingly popular as a retreat from the beach. The secluded valley offers trout fishing, canoeing and swimming, while the scenery boasts impressive rock outcrops. The regenerating native bush almost hides evidence of the area's gold mine and kauri logging past, as well as the township which flourished there in the 1890's. Today only water races, the mines and some stamper-battery artefacts remain.

78. Opoutere Park Beach Resort
Ohui Road, Opoutere Road. Rural Bag 4010 Waihi (07) 865-9152

This is within a wilderness area just 5km from the main road and offers varied terrain of large proportions. There is a central lagoon and bird sanctuary and a stream for small boats, contrasting with a magnificently isolated stretch of beach that is accessible below the coastal boundary of the camp. Canoe and dinghy hire is available. Night sky viewing by large telescope in an observatory on the property can be arranged. Space galore here with around 70 sites, 40 with power, and plenty of tenting options, with varying distances to the two amenities blocks. A good ablution block provides showers (with free tokens) and flush toilets. Two cabins may be available this season. The kitchens have nominal cooking equipment but have fridges and portable appliances. There is a covered patio for outdoor dining. The laundry is well equipped with washing and drying facilities. There is a games room for table tennis and TV. While there is a camp store, supplies may be limited so bring your own provisions. For conservation reasons no pets are allowed in the park. In the winter months of July and August this camp is closed. Peter and Diane Dudfield are the managers here. Camping is $8 per person with an extra $2 daily for power

79. Settlers Motor Camp
101 Leander Road, Whangamata (07) 865-8181 (phone & fax)

Ready for action, this camp was opened nearly a year ago. There is a lovely paved approach to each site (with individual clothes lines) . The 22 sites all have power, water and a sump. The communal kitchen has 2 microwaves for cooking and a covered BBQ garden adjacent. There are a fridge and freezer provided. The latest facilities are provided in the smoke-free ablutions, including a state-of-the-art urinal. There is a private paraplegic suite, a modern laundry and a bathroom. All the services of the Whangamata township are close by. Your hosts Henny and Bruce Gibb and family. All sites $18 for two.

80. Whangamata Motor Camp
Barbara Avenue, PO Box 7 Whangamata (07) 865-9128

A long-established beach camp which is also in close proximity to Whangamata's shopping centre. It is well serviced with amenities; the kitchen, ablutions and laundry are well equipped. There is also a good indoor recreation area. You will find organised entertainment here in the Xmas holidays and an on-site general store. Your hosts Ann and Mick Brien. A power site will cost $17 for two persons and a tent site $8 per person. 🏠 $33 for three.

81. Pinefield Holiday Park
227 Port Road, PO Box 72 Whangamata (07) 865-8719 (phone & fax)

Orderly camping on the main route to Whangamata. The flat sites are on varied levels with trees and hedges offering a private aspect. There are two modern ablution blocks and a laundry equipped with automatic machines. The kitchen is well maintained and has a fridge. 110 power sites are available with 40 for tents, plus backpackers accommodation. There is a TV room. For outdoor entertainment a BBQ and wishing well are alongside the swimming pool with slide. Family camping, and there is a dump point here. Robyn and Trevor Snell are your hosts. Power and tent sites are $20 for two persons. 🏠 $30 for two. 🏠 $55 for two.

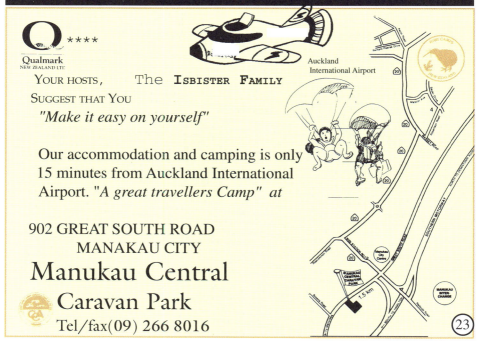

PIHA DOMAIN
MOTOR CAMP

OFFERS YOU **10%** OFF YOUR STAY
BETWEEN 1 FEBRUARY AND 30
NOVEMBER

(WITH THE COUPON FROM THIS BOOK)

TEL 09 812 8815

P O BOX 52, PIHA
AUCKLAND

(9)

STAY A WEEKEND AND
GET **FREE** USE OF A
DINGHY (only from
March to
October)

GET AWAY FROM IT ALL

(1)

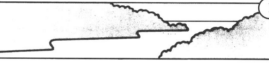

STILLWATER
MOTOR·CAMP

R D 3. SILVERDALE. PHONE   09 424-7518

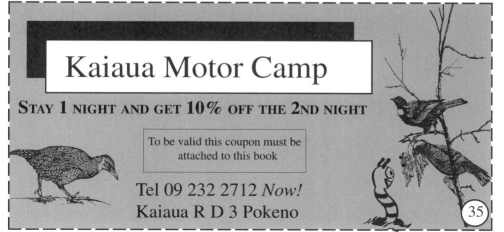

Kaiaua Motor Camp

STAY **1** NIGHT AND GET **10%** OFF THE **2**ND NIGHT

To be valid this coupon must be
attached to this book

Tel 09 232 2712 *Now!*
Kaiaua R D 3 Pokeno

(35)

PARKS INFORMATION SERVICE
"Haere mai"

REGIONAL PARKS
CITY VISITORS CENTRE

Weekdays 8.30am - 5.00pm

(extended times in summer)

Telephone (09) 366 2166

Facsimile (09) 366 2027

FERRY BUILDINGS QUAY STREET

DOWNTOWN AUCKLAND

ARATAKI VISITOR
CENTRE

Everyday 9.00am - 5.00pm

Telephone (09) 817 7134

Facsimile (09) 817 5656

Scenic Drive

Waitakere Ranges

Write to: Auckland Regional Council,
Private Bag 92012 Auckland

Auckland
Regional
Council

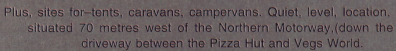

WAIKATO - BAY OF PLENTY - EASTLAND DIRECTORY

Key to locations and maps in Waikato, Bay of Plenty and Eastland districts. Starts at Port Waikato in the west including the coastal settlements of Raglan and Kawhia before returning inland to Huntly and a deviation west to Morrinsville before proceeding south via the main route to Hamilton. Includes Te Awamutu and the Cambridge and Matamata areas. The Bay of Plenty starts at Waihi and mainly follows the east coast until it merges with Eastland, around the East Cape and finishing just north of Gisborne.

Port Waikato	1.	Port Waikato Motor Camp
Raglan	2.	Kopua Camping Ground
Raglan	3.	Raglan Wagon Cabins
Kawhia	4.	Beachside Motor Camp
Kawhia	5.	Forest View Motor Camp
Kawhia	6.	Kawhia Municipal Camp
Huntly	7.	Huntly Camping & Caravan Park
Morrinsville	8.	Morrinsville Camping Ground
Ngaruawahia	9.	Arrow Lodge Motel & Caravan Park
via Ngaruawahia	10.	Waingaro Hot Springs
Hamilton East	11.	Hamilton East Tourist Court
Hamilton	12.	Municipal Motor Camp
Hamilton	13.	Narrows Park Christian Camp
Te Awamutu	14.	Selwyn Park Camping Ground
Cambridge	15.	Cambridge Domain Motor Camp
Lake Karipiro	16.	Karapiro Domain Camp
Cambridge	17.	Rangemoore Farmlands
Cambridge	18.	Finlay Park

WAIKATO–BAY OF PLENTY–EAST COAST

Cambridge	19.	Epworth Retreat & Recreation Centre
Okoroire	20.	Okoroire Hot Springs Hotel Camp
Matamata	21.	Brinkworths Motor Camp
Matamata	22.	Opal Hot Springs Holiday Park
Matamata	23.	Matamata Aerodrome Camping Ground
Te Aroha	24.	Te Aroha Holiday Motor Park
Te Aroha	25.	Dickeys Flat (DoC)
Paeroa	26.	Paeroa Camping Ground
Waihi	27.	Waihi Waterlily Gardens & Holiday Park
Waihi	28.	Waihi Motor Camp
Waihi Beach	29.	Waihi Beach Holiday Park
Waihi Beach	30.	Beachhaven Caravan Park
Waihi Beach	31.	Bowentown Holiday Park
Athenree	32.	Athenree Motor Camp
Katikati	33.	Sapphire Springs Holiday Park
Katikati	34.	Rocky Valley Camp
Omokoroa via Tauranga	35.	Omokoroa Tourist Park
Omokoroa via Tauranga	36.	Noslog Gardens
Omokoroa via Tauranga	37.	Plummers Point Caravan Park
Tauranga	38.	Palms Caravan Park
Tauranga	39.	Mayfair Caravan Park
Tauranga	40.	Silver Birch Thermal Motor Park
Tauranga	41.	Bayshore Leisure Park
Mount Maunganui	42.	Golden Grove Motor Park

Mount Maunganui	43.	Elizabeth Gardens Holiday Park
Mount Maunganui	44.	Mt Maunganui Domain Motor Camp
Mount Maunganui	45.	Cosy Corner Motor Camp
Mount Maunganui	46.	Ocean Pines Motor Park
Papamoa	47.	Papamoa Beach Holiday Park
Papamoa	48.	Beach Grove Holiday Park
Te Puke	49.	Te Puke Holiday Park
Maketu	50.	Beech Caravan Park
Te Puke	51.	Bledisloe Park Motor Camp
Pukehina Beach	52.	Pukehina Motor Camp
Pikowai	53.	Pikowai Domain
Matata	54.	Matata Recreation Reserve
Matata	55.	Murphy's Motor Camp
Thornton	56.	Thornton Beach Motor Camp
Whakatane	57.	Whakatane Caravan & Motor Park
Ohope	58.	Surf' n Sand Holiday Park
Ohope	59.	Ohope Beach Holiday Park
Awakeri	60.	Awakeri Hot Springs
Waimana	61.	Waimana Valley 8 Acre (DoC)
Opotiki	62.	Ohiwa Family Holiday Park
Opotiki	63.	Island View Family Holiday Park
Opotiki	64.	Opotiki Holiday Park
Opotiki	65.	Tirohanga Beach Motor Camp
Opape via Opotiki	66.	Opape Motor Camp

Hawai Bay	67.	Hawai Bay Camping Ground
Te Kaha	68.	Te Kaha Holiday Park
via Te Kaha	69.	Rendezvous on the Coast Holiday Park
East Cape	70.	Maraehako Camping Ground
East Cape	71.	Waihau Bay Lodge
East Cape	72.	Waihau Bay Holiday Park
East Cape	73.	Te Araroa Holiday Park
East Cape	74.	Waiapu Hotel & Caravan Park
Te Puia	75.	Te Puia Springs Hotel & Caravan Park
Tokomaru Bay	76.	Tokomaru Bay
Tokomaru Bay	77.	Mayfair Cabins & Camping Ground
Anaura Bay	78.	Anaura Bay Motor Camp
Tolaga Bay	79.	Tolaga Bay Motor Camp
Gisborne north	80.	Beach Camping

WAIKATO–BAY OF PLENTY–EAST COAST

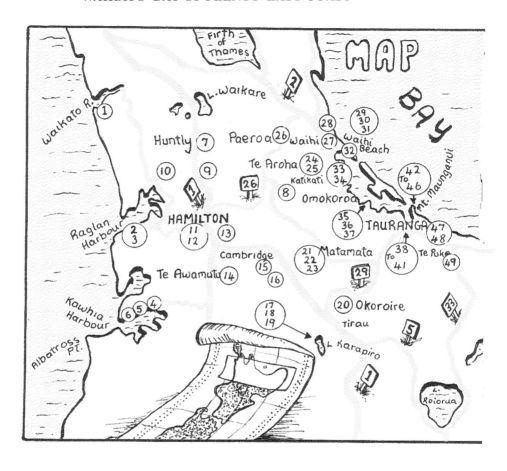

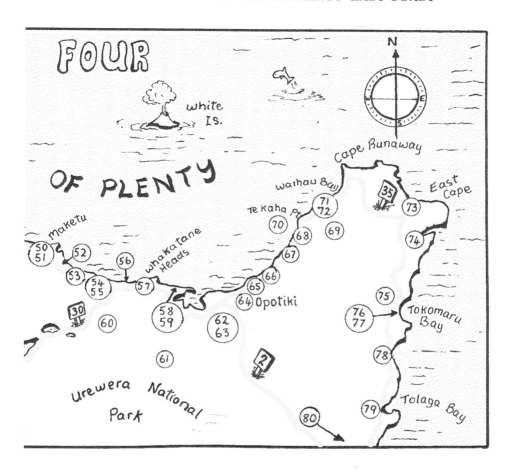

Chapter 4.

WAIKATO–BAY OF PLENTY–EAST COAST

This sweep of land stretches from the Pacific in the east to the Tasman coast in the west. Between these seaside areas lies the rich pastoral countryside of the Waikato. The main north-south highway, State Highway One, bisects the Waikato with an easy drive across the Hauraki Plains. Both coasts are easily accessible with well signposted routes.

For those who love sun-drenched days on a myriad of beaches, the Bay of Plenty to the east has all this and more, with a gentle climate and pockets of thermal pools, it has all the ingredients for a relaxing or invigorating holiday. The major city of Tauranga and the twin resort area of Mount Maunganui offer up-to-the minute facilities, while vast stretches of adjacent beach can provide solitude.

To the north, the sweeping Waihi Beach has some wonderful camping spots. The coastal road connects a chain of superb beaches. Whakatane has quite a significant township and a fishing port. Nearby Ohope Beach offers surfers and swimmers alike a magnificent safe ocean beach.

Out to sea off this coast, New Zealand's most active volcanic island, White Island, continually seethes with thermal eruptions. Regular sightseeing trips can be arranged, including a landing if conditions are suitable. Bay of Plenty motor camps often have natural mineral pools within their boundaries.

There is an outback flavour as you follow the east coast road (State Highway 35) taking in the East Cape. As you leave the Bay of Plenty the road follows the water's edge, prolific with beaches and pohutukawa trees. Look out for the abundance of driftwood, to inspire the creative collector. Camping, country-style, is within easy reach.

From Te Araroa the journey takes you inland. Predominantly Maori settlements are in this region but camping spots continue further along this sun-drenched coast. For about 20km north of Gisborne there is free legal camping right on the beach. These sites are very sought-after in summer.

The westerly perimeter of the Waikato offers a seascape that is more challenging. Here the Tasman Sea creates some spectacular surfing beaches. The Raglan beach has left-hand-break surf plus an adjoining estuary and airstrip. Beachside camping is plentiful.

Rich in variety, this is rural heartland, with each coast providing the region's playground.

WAIKATO–BAY OF PLENTY–EAST COAST

1. Port Waikato Motor Camp
Maunsell Road, Port Waikato–PDC Private Bag 3 Tuakau (09) 232-9857

To reach this west coast camp turn off S Hwy 1 at Pokeno. Signposting to the camp is not very obvious. The pleasant rural drive finishes at Sunset Beach, which is popular for surfing. The camp is in quite a sheltered location with easy access to the sand dunes where the Waikato River meets the Tasman Sea, and in close proximity to Sunset Beach. There are nice level sites here, some amongst groups of trees with plenty of boat parking. There is a congenial BBQ area under the trees with outside lighting. Amenities include a communal kitchen with TV, fridge/freezer and rangettes. Washing-up bench space is minimal. The ablutions have metered showers and include a paraplegic suite, needing some modification. There is a second block of toilets available. The laundry has both automatic and agitator washing machines, a dryer and ironing board. A dump station is provided. A special area has been set aside for people travelling with dogs. There is an office/campstore. Other services in this small seaside community provide grocery items, casual meals and takeaways, and postal agency. There are also cabins and on-site caravans available. A relaxing summer camp where the gates are closed at 9pm. Your friendly hosts John and Margaret Markham. All sites $8. 🏠 and 🚐 $30 for two.

2. Kopua Camping Ground
Marine Parade, PO Box 34 Raglan (07) 825-8283

This camp, about 50km west of Hamilton, is otherwise known as Raglan Camping Ground. It is handily placed for the township, with a footbridge to the shopping centre. Kopua camp is on an estuary with access to a sheltered inlet beach. There are 90 tent sites and 210 sites with power. Some appear to have long term occupation. Sites are all on level and open grounds. Use of an open-air stage in the grounds may be a venue for visiting groups. A very large kitchen is provided but apart from an ample number of sinks there are just some cooking hot plates, but no other appliances. In an adjacent room there is fridge and freezer space. Use the outdoor gas BBQ. A set of tubs in a wash room add to the ablutions which have metered showers in lockable cubicles. There is a second toilet block away from the main building. The laundry is excellent with automatic washers and dryers and ironing boards. A dump point is provided. A central TV/recreation room has carpet and well-used easy chairs. There is a drinks machine and a covered porch outside with seating. The ocean beach nearby is renown for its left-hand-break surf. No dogs please. Your hosts are Kevin and Judy O'Connor. Tent sites $7 per person. Power sites $8. 🏠 from $40 for two.

3. Raglan Wagon Cabins
Wainui Road, PO Box 118 Raglan (07) 825-8268

Rattle on up from Wainui Road to this elevated site with extensive Tasman Sea views. The entrance drive needs careful negotiation for a short distance. The colourful ex-railway carriages are the main accommodation units. These also house a dining car. In the grounds are just a few tent sites, BBQs and picnic decks. Large wood slab tables are a feature. The Railway Station is the communal heart with a homely kitchen that has plenty of cooking options and 3 fridges, adjoining a friendly TV lounge. It is not fussily kept. Ablutions are very limited, but there is a toilet for the disabled. The laundry has one agitator machine. There are other toilet facilities in the Express which sleeps 14. By this summer a new ablution block should be in service. To buy a ticket you must pay a deposit in advance. This appears to be a social gathering spot, with surfing being the main attraction. Your hosts Peter and Miriam Dixon. Tent sites $7 per person. Share 🛏 $12.50 per person. Cottages $25 per person.

4. Beachside Motor Camp
S Hwy 31, PO Box 74 Kawhia (07) 871-0727

This is the first camp on the approach road to Kawhia. The level camping area is to the rear of the communal buildings where there is direct access to the water. There are about 20 sites and half have power and dividing barriers. Another 10 cabins are available. This camp has a "sociability factor" and has a large kitchen with lots of fridges, a coal range, gas and electric cooking and comes complete with pots, pans, crockery, etc. There are lots of tables and bench seating. A cosy, carpeted recreation room has TV and a piano. The ablutions have well-lined showers with towel provided. The laundry has rather archaic machines. There is a flexible policy for pets, please check. Your hosts Tom and Margaret McGuiness. This camp will cater for group bookings at special rates. All sites $14 for two. 🛏 $25.

5. Forest View Motor Camp
Waiwera Street, PO Box 31 Kawhia (07) 871-0858

With a rural rather the "beachy" aspect this camp has mature trees on some boundaries and a backdrop of forest plantation. There are 31 power points, some with hard stands for vans. Tenting space is plentiful and there are some cabins. The kitchen has multi appliances of varying vintages and a small dining bay. The ablutions are functional with curtained showers. The laundry has free use of an automatic washer, an agitator machine and an iron. There is an independent paraplegic suite, complete with all facilities, known as "The Annexe". The TV room is barren but does have easy chairs. A separate community room has pool table, well worn furniture and books. Yes, you may bring Fido here. Just a few play facilities for children, but this includes a sandpit. Your hosts Sheila and Clive Goodley. Tent sites for two people cost $12, or with power $13 🛏 $22.

6. Kawhia Motor Camp
Moke Street–C/o PO Kawhia (07) 871-0863

Very easy-on-the-eye this camp is near Karewa Beach and adjacent to shops and services. It has a cultivated aspect with a lovely lawn underfoot and avenues of willows. There are some 40 power sites and on-site caravans. An old amenities block is at the rear. A small kitchen contains 2 full stoves and 2 refrigerators. The showers are in lockable cubicles of early NZ origin. Separate toilets are provided. The porch-style laundry holds a random collection of appliances. A gas refilling service is on the site. No dogs here please. Substantial improvements are planned by the resident managers Ru and Awhina Toataua. Tent sites $6 per person. Power sites $7 per person. weekly rate on application.

7. Huntly Camping & Caravan Park
Taihua Park Avenue, Huntly (07) 828-7551

This is a small camp, away from the passing traffic, but just a short distance from the main highway at Huntly, north-east of the township. Easy to locate, just follow the signposts. On the shores of Lake Hakanoa (it is not a lake for swimming) there are 42 sites with power, and plenty of tenting space, all well groomed and level. A nearby Domain offers pleasant gardens and an excellent playground for children. The amenities are kept very clean and have unlimited hot water in the showers. There is a well-scrubbed kitchen with minimal cooking equipment, and a refrigerator. The laundry has a good commercial washer and dryer. A dump point is provided. Very handy to break your journey, but not a lot to entertain holidaymakers here. Camp custodian is Noeline. Tent sites $ 6 per person. Power sites $10 per person. One $12 per person.

8. Morrinsville Camping Ground
Cureton Street, Morrinsville (07) 889-7032 (07) 889-6462 (after hours) (fax 07 889-5740)

On the eastern side of the Waikato, the turnoff at Taupiri will take you to Morrinsville. This is part of a large recreation reserve where you can camp close to the football fields, tennis courts and Olympic swimming pool. There is also a polo field, cricket pitch and children's playground and skateboard bowl. There are 24 power sites and 30 for tents in this tree-studded park. It is serviced by a kitchen, laundry, shower and toilet facilities. Keys are issued to campers. There is an effluent discharge point. Administered by the Matamata Piako District Council. In the care of Sue Troy. All sites are $7 per person.

9. Arrow Lodge Motel & Caravan Park
Market Street, Ngaruawahia (07) 824-8360

Just off the main Auckland-Wellington route north of Hamilton, Arrow Lodge caters for just a few campers. There are motel units and a lawn for camping, with 4 power sites. All guests have the use of a swimming pool. No kitchen is available, but a BBQ can be hired and breakfast on a tray can be ordered. There is a small bathroom for campers which is off the laundry, with a free automatic washer and a dryer. There are two entrances. One has a boat ramp just across the road. Boat trips with your host can be arranged. The nearby RSA Twin Rivers offers restaurant and bistro meals. It is just a few minutes walk to the township. Pets may be permitted by prior arrangement. Your hosts Marty and Felicity Kampman. All sites $15.

10. Waingaro Hot Springs
Waingaro Road–Private Bag, Ngaruawahia (07) 825-4761 (phone & fax)

West of Ngaruawahia the road winds out to Waingaro Hot Springs where an inviting thermal pool complex has attractions for day visitors and campers alike. There are 60 power sites on flat terraces above the pools, with shady trees. Each terrace has a tap and most sites are divided by bush and shrubbery. The amenities are clean, with a small but well appointed kitchen and a communal room with kitchenette. The ablutions are in two blocks, and extra toilets are handily placed in the grounds. Two laundries have automatic equipment and clothesline. A variety of pools and "The Big Splash" water slide into a hot-water pool is for the adventurous. There is a bumper-boat lake. There are plenty of BBQs and children's play areas. A dump station is provided. At the entrance is a camp store, but we advise campers to stock up in advance. Please do not bring dogs here. Your hosts Chood and Amro Singh. All sites $12 per person (min $16). ⌂ from $32 ⌐ $70 for two.

11. Hamilton East Tourist Court
61 Cameron Road, Hamilton East (07) 856-6220 (phone & fax)

This is a long established suburban camp about 3km from the commercial heart of Hamilton. The grounds are level with some individual bays for campers and several large trees. They contain 64 power sites, around 10 for tents and some cabins. The kitchen (with washing-up annexe) has good cooking facilities, full stove and microwave, but no eating space. A cool room is also available. A combined TV/pool room is in the same building. There is also a card phone. The two blocks of ablutions are functional with roomy showers. There is a cold wash only automatic washer and dryer, but no tub in the laundry. You can arrange a fast food delivery service at the camp, which also has a few shops adjacent. No dogs please. Your hosts are Greg and Jenny Shipsides. Power sites are $12 per person or $16 for two and tent sites are $8 per person. ⌐ $16 per person.

12. Municipal Motor Camp
1 Ruakura Road, Claudelands–Hamilton (07) 855-8255
(fax 07 855-3865)

Quite a delightful motor camp, thoughtfully laid out but without the glitz of some of the bigger camps. You will find sheltered sites lying well to the sun in avenues of box-hedged sites. There are 36 with power and taps, plus plenty of room for tents. A double-storey playhouse and slide will be a favourite with the children. There is a compact kitchen with gas stoves and gas rings plus an adjoining refrigerator room. There are sturdy ablutions with shower cubicles in a separate room alongside the toilets. The laundry has token-operated automatic washers and a dryer and ironing board. The amenities are well positioned with a BBQ option nearby. Both card and coin phones are on the site. Check first if you want to bring your dog, but other small pets are welcome. The friendly managers here are Richard and Dannielle Simmonds. Power sites $17 for two. Tent sites $14 for two persons. Cabins to tourist flats from $24. 🏠to 🏠.

13. Narrows Park Christian Camp
Airport Road, RD3 Hamilton (07) 843-6862

This is a picturesque camp some 10km south of Hamilton. It was formerly an American Air Force training site during World War Two. It is adjacent to Narrows Golf Club and by the Waikato River. The Presbyterian Church administer this camp and it is used mainly as a group venue. There is cabin accommodation for 120 people but only 30 power sites. There are about 100 other sites in this large park-like setting. The grounds are undulating with groves of shady trees. There are three kitchens available to campers. The main kitchen has just one stove, a refrigerator and table and chairs in dubious condition. The three blocks of ablutions have varying degrees of maintenance. The laundry has an automatic washer and dryer. The camp has unsophisticated outdoor pursuits and a swimming pool (free for campers) . Your host Shirley Murray. Tent sites are $6 per person, or with power $8. 🏠 $15 per person.

14. Selwyn Park Camping Ground
Gorst Avenue, Te Awamutu (07) 871-7478 or (07) 871-7133

This camp is in a transitional phase. Plans are afoot to relocate and this season will probably be changeover time. In the meantime be sure to ring first, or contact the Waipa District Council for information.

15. Cambridge Domain Motor Camp
32 Scott Street, Leamington–Cambridge (07) 827-5649 (phone & fax)

Slightly south of the Cambridge shopping centre, this peaceful camp is off the main traffic routes. Look for the signposts. The land is level and well hedged with rows of large willow trees. There are 88 sites with power and many of these have outdoor lights and taps. There is a good choice of tent sites and 10 cabins too. The amenities include a large kitchen with a small dining alcove. There is good bench space and two full stoves, toast and grill plus refrigerator. Alongside is a laundry equipped with excellent automatic washers and dryers and a drying rack. Apart from the main ablutions there is a separate building which also has paraplegic facilities. All the showers are in nicely lined cubicles. There is a dump point here. A coin phone is provided too. An adjacent tennis court can be used and racquets can be hired. No dogs here please. Tourist outings are organised at the camp office. Your host Pat Bourke. A site with power will cost $8.50 per person. Tent sites are $7.50 🔲 $11.50 per person.

16. Karapiro Domain Camp
Lake Karapiro–C/o Waipa District Council (07) 827-4178

Across the hydro-dam bridge from S Hwy 1 and a mere 8km south of Cambridge, Lake Karapiro is a major venue for time trials, canoe racing and various boating events. The hydro museum is worth a visit. The camp is on terraces above the lake where there are possible views of the water activities. There are 42 power sites and the ground is rather untamed for tents. There is no shopping here and the amenities appear to be minimal. Possibly the regatta facilities are available to campers. While major improvements are planned, they are not in service yet. Environmentally pleasant, but primitive camping. No dogs here please. Your host Alf Bruce. Tent sites are $4 per person and power sites are $5.

17. Rangemoore Farmlands
French Pass Road, Whitehall–Cambridge (07) 827-8995

The small notice at the gate invites you to drive up to a motor home park. Because this is primarily a farm it would be wise to ring first. There is no access if the owners are away. The 2km uphill drive to the farmhouse is fairly challenging as it is winding and unsealed. At the top the views are tremendous. It is a park-only operation with no campers facilities, although access to toilets can be at the house or self-contained flat. There are two accommodation options, bed and breakfast in the house, or rental of the self-contained flat. Campers must be totally independent. Your friendly hosts Ted and Lucy Hulse. Parking is $10 per van.

18. Finlay Park
Hora Hora, RD2 Cambridge (07) 827-8247

Casual camping here is limited by the frequent use of holiday groups. The park is administered by the Baptist Church and is on a lovely site on the banks of Lake Karapiro at the Maungatautari end. It is about 17km south of Cambridge. Accommodation is available in dormitory blocks or cabins. However there are also power sites, plus a variety of tent sites. There is a large communal kitchen, fully equipped, with adjoining coolroom. Group catering can be arranged. There are adequate hot water ablutions and a laundry. There is an emphasis here on outdoor pursuits, with lots of energetic options and plenty of play facilities for the younger set. There is a "no pets" and "no liquor" policy here. Your host Ian Fraser. Camp sites are $7 per person.🏠.

19. Epworth Retreat & Recreation Centre
RD 2 Cambridge (07) 827-2848

Beside Finlay Park, Epworth is a Methodist Church venture. Again 17km south of Cambridge, turn off S Hwy1 into Plantation Road towards Maungatautari. If you are not taking the permanent accommodation (mainly used for groups) you will find the 12 power sites and many tent sites a bit disappointing. There is a delightful picnic area. The ablutions are good, but rather inconveniently located. There are alternative kitchens, but campers may need to use the "basics only" facility if groups are in residence. The laundry has automatic washing and drying machines. Swimming pool, boat ramp, hire boats and sports equipment are on site, also a confidence course. The managers here are Robin and Christine Astridge. Power sites will cost you $12 for two persons and $4 per person on a tent site.

20. Okoroire Hot Springs Hotel Camp
RD 2 Tirau (07) 883-4876

Take a detour to Okoroire where the old style "country pub " is the heart of the community. The hotel administers the neighbouring camp which is nestled behind a glade of trees. Here you will find an oasis of hot thermal pools in a bushland setting. This little pocket of scenery is quite delightful, with the waterfalls of the Waihou River close by. The camp itself has primitive facilities. The shower has hot water but has an "early NZ" corrugated iron exterior. The kitchen offers a sink and a stove. You can probably arrange laundry service through the hotel. Apart from the hotel and an adjacent golf course, it is a fair distance to other services. Your hosts Phil and Tony Belcher. Costs per site are $8 for tents or $10 with power.

21. Brinkworths Motor Camp
195 Firth Street, Matamata (07) 888-7913

With a rural setting of level land, a scattering of trees and some hedges, there are plenty of tent sites here. Power sites are limited to 30. The location is on the perimeter of Matamata, and across and parallel to the railway line. Choose your site if the office/house is unattended. There are no provisions available at the camp. There is a large, rather neglected swimming pool. The amenities are all on a small scale with limited kitchen equipment. The showers and toilets are not fussily kept. The laundry has a dryer, but the washing appliances are disappointing. There is a tiny cubicle with a pot belly stove provided. The grounds are pleasant and with a dump station. Please ask before arriving with your pets, but you will find room for your horse here too! Your hosts Ann and Lewis Brinkworth. All camping is $7 per person.

22. Opal Hot Springs Holiday Park
Springs Road, RD 1 Matamata. Freephone 0800 800 198 or
(07) 888-8198 (fax 07 888-5813)

This camp is 6km from the township and next to the golf course. Follow the signs to the Hot Springs. Camp sites are above the hot pools on terraces. Around 100 sites have power and there are 50 tent sites. There is a wide selection of accommodation here. A TV lounge is provided. Large and small, the pools are all hot mineral water. Apart from golf (hire clubs here) there are BMX and tandem bikes available. Inquire about jet-boat riding and paragliding. The amenities blocks are fairly small. The communal kitchen has a microwave and a fridge/freezer. There is a good auto laundry. A dump point is provided. The camp store has some basic supplies. Rather a functional looking landscape here. Inquire for other prices from your host Ian Hogg. All camp sites are from $9 per person.

23. Matamata Aerodrome Camping Ground
S Hwy 27, Waiharoa–Matamata (07) 888-8386

North of Matamata you will need to watch for the entrance (aerodrome and camp) . Both are hedged from the road. The grounds are pleasant with some shady trees. There are around 40 power sites, abundant tent sites and 12 cabins. The kitchen is generously proportioned and comes with plenty of hot points, rangettes and microwave. The ablutions are functional and double as a laundry. No animals allowed here, but it has excellent potential for clubs and groups. Ideal for the aviation enthusiast. Accommodation booking is essential. Your hosts Pene and Shane. All sites are from $6.50 with an extra $2 to connect to power.

24. Te Aroha Holiday Motor Park
Stanley Road, RD1 Te Aroha West (07) 884-9567 (phone & fax)

The northern Kaimai Ranges with Mount Te Aroha dominating, are to the east of this area. The motor park is just out of town on level fenced grounds with stately old oak trees. Alongside the office is a coffee house for light meals, souvenirs and crafts, open during the holiday season. Enjoy the grass tennis court and swimming pool. There is a children's pool and playground too. A mini-farm area has been created with lambs and other small animals in enclosures. There is an option to camp alongside. A "resident dog and owner" holiday area is provided. All the usual amenities are provided and are well kept. A games room and TV room are here also. Backpackers requiring transport from the township will be collected free of charge. Local bookings can also be made. Prices are from $14 for two persons for a tent site, or $15 with power. Other accommodation is available. Your host Anna Blattler.

 ### 25. Dickeys Flat
Te Aroha–Department of Conservation

Dickey's Flat is part of the Kaimai-Mamaku Forest Park adjoining the Waitawheta River. Easy vehicle access can be gained from S Hwy 2 where it passes through the Karangahake Gorge near Waikino. Additional pursuits include visits to nearby historical gold-mining centres, tramping in the park, swimming and fly fishing in the river and easy walks along the river banks. A swing bridge provides easy foot access in the park. Composting toilets are provided on the site. There is no charge, though a self-registration system will be introduced in the future.

26. Paeroa Camping Ground
Beside Paeroa Information Centre, Paeroa

At the northern end of the Paeroa township (famous for its legendary Lemon & Paeroa, New Zealand's own soft drink) this town is inland from Waihi and the southern Coromandel Peninsula. Weary travellers will find a free camping spot, with toilets, available here. Not intended for long-term stays, it is close to the commercial area and railway line. However there are some power points and shady trees. Donations would be appreciated.

27. Waihi Waterlily Gardens & Holiday Park
Pukekauri Road, RD 2 Waihi (07) 863-8267

This park is on a through road from Karangahake Gorge to Waihi and Tauranga. This is a dual-purpose park, with an amazing range of waterlilies in a peaceful and well cultivated setting. There is provision for camping here with 6 power sites, but plenty of tent sites and one cabin and one on-site caravan, all on attractive level lawns. Access to the waterlily display and the on-site tearooms is limited to between November and April, but campers can stay at any time of year. There is an attractive kidney-shaped swimming pool (open in summer) . A children's play area is provided. We are told there are no mosquitoes here! Campers facilities include a basic kitchen, shower and basins, and separate toilets with basins, plus laundry (no dryer) . Everything is maintained to a high standard. Your friendly hosts Laurie and Liz Ball. All camp sites are at $7 per adult.

28. Waihi Motor Camp
6 Waitete Road, Waihi (07) 863-7654 (fax 07 863-6267)

This camp is not on the main route, so watch for signposting near the hospital. The setting is very sheltered with trees flourishing around the threshold of the camp. A mature garden, with a pond and tame birds to feed, is a feature. Relax in the indoor heated swimming pool. The central amenities include a well appointed kitchen with full stove and fridge. There is an outdoor dining area under a roofed pergola. The ablutions are in good condition and laundry includes a dryer. A dump point is provided. Your host Eunice Smith. There are 50 sites with power and 40 for tents. All sites are $8 per person. 🛏 $20 for two. 🛏 $50 for two.

29. Waihi Beach Holiday Park
15 Main Road, Waihi Beach (07) 863-5504

Although this is a large camp, at the northern end of Waihi Beach, the variety of interesting sites make for individual camping areas that are not overwhelming. There are 130 sites with power and 40 for tents, plus 26 well equipped cabins. The main area is at road level but several sites are above, on plateaus, and some tent sites are virtually right on the beach. Lots of big trees, mainly pohutukawas, enhance the grounds. A stream divides the camp and is spanned by quaint walking bridges. The camp store is open from Xmas to the end of January and other shopping is nearby. There are plenty of ablutions and toilet blocks and a modern camp kitchen, laundry for wash and dry, tidy TV lounge and games room. You can hire surf boards here. Great for summer camping right on superb Waihi Beach. Your hosts Mike and Faye Burston. All camp sites are $9 per person. 🛏 $22.50.

30. Beachaven Caravan Park
21 Leo Street, Waihi Beach (07) 863-5505

More sites here than you would anticipate from the entrance to this camp. Located in a handy residential street, there are 114 sites with power and 40 for tents. There is plenty of additional accommodation including a lodge and new self-contained cottages. Two spa pools are provided. The kitchen includes stoves, microwave and fridge with an adjoining dining/sitting room which has TV. Alongside, a porch houses a table tennis table. A separate room is set aside for video games and playing pool. The ablutions are functional, with metered showers and include a babies bath. There is automatic laundry equipment. A dump point is provided. Bring the family dog in winter only. Your hosts Lindsay and Garry Tapper. Please inquire for tariff of the new cottages. All camp sites are $9 per person . 🖽 $37 for two. Look for further information on page 133.

31. Bowentown Holiday Park
Southern end, Seaforth Road, PO Box 6 Waihi Beach (07) 863-5381 (phone & fax)

Tucked along at the far end of Waihi Beach, this camp offers a choice of surf or sheltered harbour swimming. and has a large capacity with over 140 power sites and 20 for tents. They are on three level terraces, and have sandy, well drained sites. A new mini-market may be in service this holiday season. The facilities are immaculately clean and the ablutions block contains 6 unisex showers, as well as the single-sex variety, and a babies bath. Another toilet block has recently been installed. There is automatic laundry equipment, and open-air tubs and wringer. The kitchen has refrigeration and cooking. Fishermen will find a boat ramp, boat park. Fish-cleaning and fish-smoking facilities (even a mincer) are supplied. No pets here please. Your hosts Dave and Kay Roche. Tent sites are $8.50 per person, or with power $9 per person. 🖽 $18 per person. 🖽 $50 for two.

32. Athenree Holiday Park
Waione Avenue, Athenree, PO Box 33 Waihi Beach (07) 863-5600 (ph / fax)

Picturesque grounds here at the northern tip of the Tauranga Harbour inlet. Lovely level sites are liberally dotted with trees, and some have water views. In season citrus trees provide free fruit for campers. There are 65 sites with power, 100 for tents and a 12-bed lodge plus two cabins. Outdoor dining is in an arbour around the BBQ and there is a spa pool for campers. All the amenities are in spotless condition and include automatic laundry equipment. The ablutions are good and the kitchen has microwave and conventional cooking and refrigeration facilities. Dinghy and canoe hire is available. Pentaque bowling is played here. There is a camp store open during the summer months. This park has a most appealing environment. We enjoyed a warm welcome here from hosts Lynne Adams and Don Mossop. All sites $9 per person. 🖽 $28.

33. Sapphire Springs Holiday Park

Hot Springs Road, RD 2 Katikati (07) 549-0768 (phone & fax)

A rather special environment which should make for a relaxing holiday. There are prominent signposts to this camp on S Hwy 2 just outside Katikati. The camp wanders through a bushland setting and is bordered by a sparkling stream. Sample the warm thermal springs with open-air pools, or the private hot mineral spa pools. There are 180 sites here and 80 have power and taps. Also a 40-bed lodge and unit accommodation is provided. There is a communal kitchen with fridge, good ablutions and a laundry with automatic equipment. There is a dump point here. A social hall is an option for groups and there is a roofed BBQ garden. Takeaway food may be bought here in the holiday season and there is a mini-golf course. The park is looking well maintained under the ownership of Robin and Margaret Carr. Prices are from $8 each for a tent site plus $2 daily for power. 🏠 $30 for two. 🏠 $50.

34. Rocky Valley Camp

Rea Road, PO Box 162 Katikati (07) 549-1696 (fax 07 549-0181)

Just off S Hwy 2, this camp is only 3km from Katikati. There are 16 power sites and some lovely tenting sites for casual campers. The main thrust of this camp is catering for groups which are associated with the Christian youth ministries. School holiday periods could be busy here, with bunkrooms occupied. There is a small camp kitchen with refrigerator, stove and sink. The ablutions have plenty of hot water and private shower-dressing cubicles. The laundry has two washing machines (one automatic) . Both are free, but there is no dryer. The setting is delightful, peacefully enclosed by trees with the entrance through a kiwifruit orchard. If you are planning a group booking there are excellent catering arrangements here. Your host Alan Peary. Up to 126 people can be accommodated in the bunkrooms. Tent site $6 per person. Power sites $7.50 per person. 🏠 $10 per person.

35. Omokoroa Tourist Park

165 Omokoroa Road, RD 2 Tauranga (07) 548-0857 (phone & fax)

An immaculate park in a predominantly rural area. It is 19km from Tauranga city. The level sites are beautifully groomed with flowerbeds and trees. There are 40 sites with power here and another 15 for tents. Other accommodation is available. There is a mini-store at the camp. The children's play equipment is excellent. There are 3 lovely clean outdoor mineral pools for soaking. These are fenced and accessible for the disabled. The kitchen is not large enough for dining, but has plenty of first-class appliances for cooking (including microwave) fridges and freezer. There is a great selection of ablutions, with one splendid paraplegics suite. The recreation rooms offer a separate pool and table tennis room for the youngsters and another with TV and camp library. A high standard of housekeeping here from the hosts Murray and Judy Field. All camp sites are $9 per person. 🔲 $30 🛏 $35 🔳 $49 Look for more information on page 132.

36. Noslog Gardens
468 Omokora Road, RD 2 Tauranga (07) 548-0014

A rural campervan park with provision for 6 vans. Surrounded by an orchard, this little holiday spot is equipped with new facilities. The kitchen-dining has easy chairs as well as dining furniture. There is just a toilet and a shower, both with handbasins. A laundry tub too. Your hosts Peter and Phyl Colsen. Tent sites $7 per person. Power sites $8.50 per person.

37. Plummers Point Caravan Park & Thermal Pools
Station Road, Omokoroa, RD 2 Tauranga (07) 548-0669

Turn off S Hwy 2 at Omokoroa Station Road and where the road ends this long-established park borders the waters of the Tauranga Harbour. There are three levels of camp sites with rows of lovely willow trees dividing the site areas. As a large water boundary forms the edge of the camp, many sites enjoy the quiet inlet view. There are over 100 sites with power here as well as tent sites, and some log cabins. There is a camp store/office with basic supplies. The mineral pools, both large and small, are at comfortable temperatures and are emptied and cleaned daily. There is an adventure playground and free canoes and a boat ramp. The amenities are good, a well equipped kitchen, two blocks of ablutions and auto laundry equipment. Your hosts Christine Shannon and Peter and Gayle Gent. All sites $9 per person . 🔲 $35 for two. 🛏 $38 for two.

38. Palms Caravan Park
162 Waihi Road, Tauranga (07) 578-9337

If you don't want to search for a place to stop, this address should suit you well. It is on the approach road to Tauranga, in the suburb of Judea. Drive in; it is very easy to claim a site, or one of the new cabins. En suite facilities are provided at some sites. All of the 60 power sites have a tap too. The landscape is neat and attractively planted. There is a lovely kitchen with gas cooking and microwave, which opens to an outdoor hedged dining area. The ablutions are particularly nice, with roomy showers. There is automatic laundry equipment. Close by you will find grocery shopping and a service station. Your hosts Jim and Sandra Byrnes. All power sites are $9 per person or $12.50 with en suite. 🔲 $38 for two.

39. Mayfair Caravan Park
9 Mayfair Street, Tauranga (07) 578-3323 (fax 07 578-5910)

The surroundings are sheltered and peaceful and now the holiday atmosphere predominates. You can camp here alongside the waters of the inner harbour, where there is also a boat ramp. There are 70 sites with power, 30 tent sites and a choice of cabins (the new ones are very nice) or on-site caravans. It is a well-tree'd spot, alongside a motel; they are however "not related". You will find the location very central and handy to the hospital. It is an easy drive to either central Tauranga or through to Mount Maunganui. A good standard of amenities are offered here, with paper towels and liquid soap in the ablutions. Out-of-season you can bring your "well mannered" pets. Your hosts Isobell Gibson and Trevor Tapper. All camp sites are $9 per person 🔲 $30 for two. Look for more information on page132.

 40. Silver Birch Thermal Motor Park
101 Turret Road, Tauranga (07) 578-4603

Water's-edge camping where Turret Road crosses the Hairini Bridge. Big silver birch trees identify this park which also has motels and other accommodation. Camp sites are level and mingle with the other units. There are 43 sites with power and 30 for tents. If you choose carefully you can almost fish from your tent. A boat ramp, hire canoes and a dinghy are available. There is a thermal swimming pool. Very good amenities here. The kitchen has fridge, there are good family showers and automatic equipment in the laundry. There is a games room and a camp shop. A warm welcome here from Gary and Norice Jeffery, who will take pets providing previous arrangements have been made. An Eftpos system operates here. Tent sites are $8 per person and power sites are $9. 🔲 $15 per person. 🎛 $30 for two.

41. Bayshore Leisure Park
S Hwy 29, Windermere–PO Box 3189 Tauranga (07) 544-0700

This park is on a spacious site 10 minutes from Tauranga city and adjacent to the Bay of Plenty Polytechnic. There are around 80 power sites here plus a large range of tent sites, some in private bush clearings. To the rear of the park are a choice of cabins and the communal buildings. At the entrance the camp store/office has basic supplies, icecreams and drinks and access to the hot mineral pools, which are open to the public. For outdoor dining there is a gas BBQ and marquee-style eating area. The hard tennis courts are not full size, but well fenced and maintained. The amenities feature a good camp kitchen with separate dining area, glassed in by ranch sliders and with TV. There are adequate ablutions and automatic laundry machines. A dump point is on site. No pets here please. Facilities can be provided for group functions and casual campers may be in a minority here. Your hosts Michael Hills and Marion Palmer. All sites $18 for two. 🗔 $10 per person.

42. Golden Grove Motor Park
73 Girven Road, Mount Maunganui (07) 575-5821 (phone & fax)

In fairly close proximity to the extensive Bayfair Shopping Complex. This camp has convenience shopping alongside. It is not a beachside park, but has a usefully central location. There are 95 sites with power and 20 for tents. A collection of on-site caravans, five cabins and a 20-bed lodge offers other accommodation. The amenities are satisfactory and there is a games and TV room. There is good automatic laundry equipment and a dump point. Your hosts are Max and Deborah Sullivan. All camp sites are $18 for two people. 🗔 $35 for two. 🗔 $42 for two

43. Elizabeth Gardens Holiday Park
5 The Mall, Harbour Road, Mount Maunganui (07) 575-5787

Ideally placed for convenience to the attractions of Mount Maunganui, within walking distance of the shops and ferries., this is a traditionally popular place which seldom has a site to spare. However it is worth making an inquiry. There is accommodation, sites for tents, there may even be a power site. Two motels are offered with bed and breakfast. Campers have communal kitchen facilities and auto laundry. The ablutions combine unisex with segregated showers. This park is dog friendly for campers. Meet the new hosts Dale and Karen Reynolds. Camp sites $9 per person, 🗔 $15 per person 🗔 $75 for two.

44. Mount Maunganui Domain Motor Camp
1 Adams Avenue, Mount Maunganui (07) 575-4471

This camp has a prime site on the slopes of the Mount. It is usually a hive of activity, with the Domain hot salt-water pools sharing the entrance. There is extensive camping with 285 power sites and just 14 for tents, with a choice of either ocean or inner harbour beach aspects. There are three kitchens with cool boxes for hire and plenty of ablution facilities including a brand new block. The laundry has automatic equipment. TV viewing is possible, but there is no TV room now. Almost all the sites have wonderful views and are on level terraces. There is easy access to the local shops from here. Your hosts Marie and Winston Cox. All camping is $8 per person.

45. Cosy Corner Motor Camp

40 Ocean Beach Road, Mount Maunganui (07) 575-5899 (phone & fax)

A favourite spot if you want to share your holiday with friends! This rather intimate smallish camp is within an easy distance of the beach, in a suburban location. All of the 70 sites have power. The camp has a well fenced swimming pool and level grounds. There is an excellent ablution block, tiled, and with individual formica-lined shower and dressing cubicles. The kitchen facilities are good, and the laundry has automatic equipment. For those get-togethers a breezeway BBQ and al fresco dining area is very inviting. Your hosts Donna and Greg Davidson can offer reduced winter rates. All sites are $9 per person. 🏠 $34 for two . 🚐 $40 for two. 🏠 Tourist flats $50.

46. Ocean Pines Motor Park

Maranui Street, Mount Maunganui (07) 575-4265

The coastal drive between the Tauranga Harbour and the open sea of the Bay of Plenty brings you to this camp. The tall pines are a feature. It is 6km from the Mount and offers a less intensely tourist environment. The 211 power sites are very popular and many are continuously occupied, but have a well kept garden look. A solar-heated swimming pool is provided. A dining area is off the kitchen and there are BBQs. The on-site shop has some supplies and there are vendor deliveries daily. There are metered showers in the ablutions. The laundry has automatic washing and drying machines. Please do not bring pets here. Taking good care of this camp are your friendly hosts Margaret and Harvey Cox. All camp sites are $9.50 per person. 🚐 $20 plus camp fees and the self-contained 🏠 $50 for two. Inquire about off season or group rates.

47. Papamoa Beach Holiday Park

535 Papamoa Beach Road, Papamoa (07) 542-0816 (phone & fax) (07) 542-2694

With a broad stretch of pale sandy beach at its doorstep, this park has a superb location. The terrain is slightly banked from the beach with well drained terraced sites. There are 260 sites in all, and 220 have power. The sea views are dramatic. The kitchens supply conventional and microwave cooking, fridge and deep freeze. There are four ablutions blocks with metered showers, a babies bathroom and very well equipped laundries. These facilities are accessible from all areas of the camp. You will find shopping, a restaurant and takeaways adjacent. Sample the BBQ area and sun deck. There are rather special private spa pools, an adventure playground, indoor recreation room and mini tennis too. Please book for space between Xmas and February. Your hosts Bruce and Donna Crosby. All sites $10.50 per person. 🚐 $38 for two. 🏠 $40. 🏠 $55 for two.

48. Beach Grove Holiday Park
386 Papamoa Beach Road, Papamoa (07) 542-1337

A very well manicured park across the road from lovely Papamoa Beach. Nicely landscaped, the camp has 94 power sites plus 50 for tents on level grounds. Site space is generous and there is a camp store and a service station adjacent. An attractive swimming pool and children's playground are provided. There are two modern amenity blocks with metered showers in the ablutions. There is a well equipped kitchen and a laundry with automatic machines. A room is provided for TV. On duty here are Lindsay and Dawn Vallender. All sites here are $9 per person. 🚐, are $32 for two.

49. Te Puke Holiday Park
S Hwy 2, P O Box 10, Te Puke (07) 573-9866

At the northern end of Te Puke, this park presents an attractive road frontage. There are abundant trees and vines and this is one of the few camps along this route that is well away from the beach. There are nice level camp sites here, some reasonably private, with mature trees. The camp contains 54 sites with power, plenty of room for tents, on-site caravans and cabins. There is also a 24 bed backpackers hostel. Long-term occupancy is apparent in some areas. The kitchen and laundry provide adequate appliances (there are automatic washing machines and a dryer) but both are in "tired" condition. The ablutions have a babies bath and there are lockable, formica-lined shower cubicles. The supply of toilets, especially, was rather restricted. There is a private spa room here. The recreation room has video games, TV and a long-suffering pool table. For outdoor relaxation a kidney-shaped pool, fenced and inviting, is available. The camp has a friendly atmosphere and an on-site store. Your new hosts are Kevin and Julie Rau. Tent sites $7.50 per person. Power sites $15 for two. 🚐, and 🏠 $34.

50. Beech Caravan Park
C/o PO, Maketu (07) 533-2165

The little promontory beside the estuary is the site of this camp. Although there are different levels of camping, sites are level, and most have sweeping views. The inner waters provide a wonderful beach playground for the children, with shallow pools and endless sand. Have a picnic under the shady trees. There are 30 power sites, ample tent sites plus on-site caravans and two chalets. All the amenities are modest, the ablutions are reasonable but rather too few in numbers. There is a small kitchen with fridge. The laundry has one agitator machine (metered) and a tub. Despite this, the location is very appealing. Your host Peggy Beech. Prices for two people are $15 for power site or $6.50 per person for tents Some 🚐.

51. Bledisloe Holiday Park
Little Waihi Beach, RD 9 Te Puke (07) 533-2157

This estuary camp is a triangle of level sites bordered by water on two sides with safe swimming and launching for small boats. The land is open; tree planting is on the agenda. There is a shop for basic requirements, now open all year round. Campers have a large kitchen which provides full stoves and fridges. The other amenities are adequate and include washing machines and a dryer. It is an attractive low-key holiday spot with 70 sites with power and 45 for tents. Your new hosts Marie and Winston Cox. Tent sites $5 per person. Power sites are $6 per person. .

52. Pukehina Motor Camp
26 Costello Crescent, Pukehina Beach – RD 9 Te Puke (07) 533-3600

In house-proud order, this is a pleasant camp with a rural atmosphere. The beach is nearby, but not right beside the camp. The well kept level grounds are bordered by trees and offer 50 sites with power and 60 for tents, with plenty of space for the children to run free. There is a nice new BBQ area and a toddlers playground. The kitchen has a full stove and fridge; help yourself to the lemons in season. There are well cared for ablutions, complete with fresh flowers. The laundry has 3 washing machines (no charge) . Gary and Joy are the hosts here. Discount rates may be arranged. Tent sites $6.50. Power sites $7.00. 🏕 🚐 $28 for two.

53. Pikowai Domain
Pikowai

Between Matata and Maketu is a strip camping ground running along the beachfront with direct beach access. On the other side the railway line borders the camp. You can drive straight in from S Hwy 2. The camp is sheltered by nikau palms, giving it a tropical look. There is no camp office here. Although it is well supplied with taps and rubbish bins, there are no power sites. There are two blocks of ablutions. Four unroofed showers have hot water (metered) and there are flush toilets. Two outdoor tubs are provided. Camping here will cost you $5 per site. This camp is tidily kept by your host Jim Marx.

54. Matata Recreation Reserve
Matata Domain–Matata Reserve Board (07) 347-9179

On the central Bay of Plenty coastline, off S Hwy 2 part way between Tauranga and Whakatane, look for the signpost. It is a lovely setting between the sea and the inlet on slightly undulating land. The well-housed amenities have instant hot-water showers (metered) , flush toilets and basins are a unisex facility. There is no kitchen or laundry, but there are BBQs. This reserve is in the care of Pete and Lyn Homan. Tent sites only $5 for two.

55. Murphy's Motor Camp
S Hwy 2, Matata (07) 322-2136

Enjoying a lovely beachfront site with plenty of shelter, this camp has 80 sites with power, 40 for tents plus 6 accommodation units. The land has a rolling contour and a choice of shady or sunny sites. The railway line follows the rear border of the camp. There is an on-site shop open every day with basic supplies, but keeping short hours in winter. A book exchange operates here. The amenities looked clean but were not extensive. A basic kitchen has no tables, but has fridge/freezer, full stove and rangettes. Ablutions and two blocks of toilets are provided. The laundry has two washing machines (one auto) and a dryer. This camp offers holiday and longer term occupancy. Your hosts Terry and Trish Murphy. Tent sites are $6.50 per person and power sites are $7. 🔲 $15 per person

56. Thornton Beach Motor Camp
Thornton Beach Road, Thornton (07) 304-8296

Cast aside your cares and get out the fishing gear. This is an attractive beachfront site where shellfish and line-fishing are rewarding. There is an impressive entrance to this camp, which has terraces of sites. 116 have power and water and 8 on-site caravans are provided. There is a wharf nearby and a boat ramp. Holidaymakers will share with long-term residents here. The amenities include a well kept kitchen, with microwave, fridge and hotplates. The ablutions have good lockable lined shower cubicles (with meters) and toilets. There is a paraplegic suite for each sex. The laundry is well equipped with automatic machines. All the amenities are invitingly well-scrubbed. A well furnished games room has two pool tables. There is a dump point here. Your hosts are John and Gail James, who will accept well-controlled pets by arrangement. Prices are from $5.50 per person for a tent site to $7.50 with power. 🚐 $12.50 per person plus camp fees.

🏢	Tourist flats and motels from
🔲	Cabins from
🚐	On-site caravans from

57. Whakatane Caravan & Motor Park
McGarvey Road, Whakatane (07) 308-8694

No passing traffic here on this riverside camping ground that is level and dotted with willow trees. There is a substantial bank separating the park from the river and there is a fenced "above ground" swimming pool. Children have a play area. There are 80 sites with power and 100 tent sites, a backpackers hostel and other accommodation units. A roomy kitchen provides plenty of appliances, including microwave. The laundry has cold-wash automatic washing and drying, plus an agitator machine. There are three ablution blocks in satisfactory condition. A TV room has fuel-stove heating. Your hosts Alan and Maryanne Gadd. All camp sites are $8 per person. Backpackers beds $12.50. ▭ $20.

58. Surf 'n' Sand Holiday Park
211 Pohutukawa Avenue, PO Box 3001 Ohope Beach (07) 312-4884

A well-named park right on the edge of Ohope Beach this is truly a holiday resort with all the extras. The grounds are thoughtfully planned with borders of Norfolk pines and other shady trees at intervals throughout. There are 175 sites with power and another 50 for tents. There is a range of accommodation units too. Facilities for campers are up-to-the-minute with excellent ablutions, a well equipped kitchen and a laundry with all automatic appliances. There is an "active" recreation room and a separate TV room. The location is ideal for relaxing, but with a convenience store next door. Tennis courts and a dump point are adjacent. There is plenty of hire equipment obtainable at the park. It is walking distance to Ohope Chartered Club (golf and bowls) . This is now an all-year-round holiday venue. Please do not bring pets. Your hosts Maree and Scott Boyle. All sites are $9 per adult. ▭ $30 for two ▭ $52.

59. Ohope Beach Holiday Park
Harbour Road, Port Ohope (07) 312-4460 (phone & fax)

A glorious situation combining the classic holiday beachfront position with well groomed grounds and well appointed amenities. There are 200 sites with power and 100 for tents, plus some other accommodation units. The vista of sparkling sea is only interrupted by the steaming cone of White Island across the water. There is a boat ramp and jetty. The extensive lawn sites are mostly flat with sufficient trees to enhance and provide shady spots. There is a well stocked shop here. The three blocks of ablutions are immaculately kept with metered showers, and have paraplegic facilities. There is an excellent automatic laundry. The kitchen is inviting and opens to a central BBQ garden with tables. A tennis/ basketball hard court is provided. There are two pools here, one for toddlers and a large swimming pool that features a water slide. There is mini golf and an adventure playground. A TV and pool room has an outdoor deck. Boogie boards and wave skis can be hired here. Please do not bring your dogs. Your friendly hosts Gerard and Janene Maguire. All camping is $9 per person. 📞 $36 for two 🏠 $50.

60. Awakeri Hot Springs
Rotorua/Whakatane Highway, RD2 Whakatane (07) 304-9117
(fax (07) 304-9290)

A holiday resort in a park-like setting. The perimeter is well-tree'd with a bush background and mature trees in the grounds. There is a choice of accommodation and 100 power sites plus 50 tent sites provided. The warm outdoor swimming pool attracts many day visitors to the park. Alongside there are BBQ facilities with a covered dining option. This area is well lit at night. The spa pools are for the use of guests only. Other activities available are volleyball and lawn tennis. There is a busy camp store. A good modern kitchen is available. There are two blocks of ablutions, including unisex showers. The main laundry has excellent automatic appliances. No dogs here please. Your hosts Graham and Marguerite Timbs. All camp sites are $18 for two adults. 📞 for two. 🏠 $45 for two.

61. Waimana Valley 8 Acre
Te Urewera National Park–Department of Conservation (06) 867-8531

Where S Hwy 2 wanders inland there is access to this conservation campsite. The setting is very picturesque and Waimana River flows through here. About 10km along the road from the turnoff you will reach 8 Acres, where camping is anywhere you choose. There are flush toilets and cold water on tap. Great environmentalist camping; try tramping, kayaking or mountain biking. There is a $2 fee per adult.

62. Ohiwa Family Holiday Park
Ohiwa Harbour Road, Opotiki, RD 2 Opotiki (07) 315-4741 (phone & fax)

On the eastern tip of Ohiwa Harbour this camp is 5km from S Hwy 2. This is a good prescription to "loosen up" and enjoy a seaside holiday. The spread of level grounds ensure that a sea frontage can usually be found. There are 70 sites with power and 70 sites for tents. A good lawn area has been set aside for outdoor games. The amenities are centrally placed and there is an adequate kitchen which opens to a breezeway dining area, and use of a freezer. There are instant hot-water showers in the ablutions; these and the toilets are on tile floors and function well. There is automatic laundry equipment too. Compost toilets have been installed at the extremities of the grounds. There is a boat ramp. Miles of beach to explore here and great fishing opportunities. Camp sites are from $6 per person, depending on the season. There are a small number of accommodation units. Your friendly hosts Phil and Lana Morgan will accept well supervised pets here.

63. Island View Family Holiday Park
Appleton Road, Waiotahi Beach, PO Box 40, Opotiki (07) 315-7519

A "picture postcard" beach borders this camp which is just 5km from Opotiki en route to Whakatane. Just back from its sandy shores there are 110 sites with power and taps. These are divided by hitching rails and there is a vast amount of tent space. The level land offers extensive views and a choice of open or shady sites. Above the amenities block are some cabins with a panoramic sea outlook. There is a well stocked shop on the site that is open long hours daily. The kitchen has two full stoves and microwave cooking, refrigerator and cool lockers, but no dining space. The ablutions have plentiful hot water and homely touches, with shower cubicles that are starting to show their age. The laundry has both automatic and agitator washing, plus two dryers. A swimming-pool and a children's playground and a fish smokehouse are in the grounds. A games room and TV room are provided. Your hosts are Martie and Garry Sisson. All sites are $9 per person. $30 for two.

64. Opotiki Holiday Park
Potts Avenue, Opotiki (07) 315-6050

This camp has the "presence" of a hotel with its tall palms and stylish buildings. You will find 50 power sites, 20 for tents and a variety of good accommodation here. This well groomed park is not beachside, but close to the township of Opotiki. There is an attractive swimming-pool enclosure. The communal buildings offer great appointments. The kitchen has fridge/freezer, sufficient cooking facilities and a dining area where the ranch-sliders open to a BBQ courtyard. There is a well kept games room for playing pool or TV. The ablutions are first class, although the showers are metered, and they include a babies bath. The laundry is fully equipped with automatic appliances. There is a basic supply of foodstuffs available here, or arrange for a meal to be provided. A sports fishing club is next door and a boat ramp. Your hosts here are Marion and Alan Jamieson. All sites $8 per person, after one night $7 per person. 📞 $28 🏠 $40. Look for further information on page 134.

65. Tirohanga Beach Motor Camp
S Hwy 35, RD1 Opotiki (07) 315-7942 (phone & fax)

It's situation beside a well stocked shop, tearooms, and petrol station makes this an easy place to stop. This extensive camp is divided into separate areas that have barriers of shrubs and trees between them. Sites are level, with good shade and around 50 have power. There is a special area for campers with dogs and this leads through to a vast and lovely beach. Other areas have been set aside for own-your-own residents and there is a feeling that "regulars" dominate this park. The children's play area is rather special with lots of equipment, and there are extra trampolines in the grounds. A terrific confidence course is worth a try. An above ground swimming pool is provided. A fair kitchen is combined with a recreation and TV hall. The ablutions are varied; some have new appointments. There is an outdoor beach shower. Two laundries are provided (one has automatic washers) . Your new hosts are Robert and Glennis McLellan. Tent sites are $13 for two persons and power sites are $14 🖵 $28 for two. 🖳 $32 for two.

66. Opape Motor Camp
East Coast Road, Opotiki (07) 315-8175

A wayside camp around 15km from Opotiki, this has tidy grounds to park on with 120 sites, 40 with power. You can view the sea and White Island from the open sites, which are one paddock back from the beach. A communal building has spartan amenities, but the kitchen does have refrigeration. The laundry is basics only and the hot-water showers are in a rustic condition. You can bring pets here. The camp was unattended when we called, so check for prices.

67. Hawai Bay Camping Ground
Hawai Farms, RD 1 Opotiki (07) 315-6308

A camp undergoing refurbishment and extending its facilities. Open for business at Labour Weekend. Call in and see what is happening here. Your host John Stringfellow.

68. Te Kaha Holiday Park
S Hwy 35, Te Kaha, Private Bag 1096 Opotiki (07) 325-2894 (ph/fax)

As you head towards East Cape, Te Kaha is about 70km from Opotiki. The scenic drive offers great bush and water views. At the entrance to this park is a well stocked shop with takeaway meals available. There is a variety of accommodation here, with camping to the rear, and the whole area has a well cultivated appearance. There are colourful gardens and hedges and trees are prolific in the grounds. You will find 60 power sites and around 100 tent sites, mostly grouped on level lawns. The kitchen has reasonable equipment, with refrigeration and boiling water on tap, some tables and chairs too. There is a bright, clean ablution block with lined showers. The laundry has excellent commercial equipment and a freezer. Fish-cleaning facilities are provided, boats for hire and a boat tractor is available. There is a play area for children. Nearby is a 9 hole golf course and tennis courts. The beach is just across the road from here. Your hosts are Gordon and Cheryle Gallagher. All camping is at $8.50 per adult.🖵 $55 for two. 🖳 $65.

69. Rendezvous on the Coast Holiday Park
S Hwy 35, Whanarua Bay – East Cape, Private Bag 1114 Opotiki (07) 325-2899

Up a gently sloping drive this holiday resort is set in an avocado orchard. There are shelter belts between various sections where you can choose your sites. The tenting options are endless, and there are 40 sites with power. Also serviced rooms and cabin or caravan units are available. At the heart of the camp is a comprehensive shop, with dairy and grocery supplies. Dive and fishing-charter arrangements begin right here. Hire equipment is available too. Behind the shop a large amenities block has a useful kitchen with good cooking appliances, freezers and fridge. There is a TV room with easy chairs and an alternative games room alongside. The ablutions have plentiful hot water in a serviceable setting. There are only basic laundry facilities. The children's play area is well equipped and there is plenty of space for outdoor activities. BBQs amongst the fruit trees must be appealing. Well controlled dogs may be permitted here. Your hosts Darryl and Sue Smith. Power sites are $8 per person. 📺 and 🛁.

70. Maraehako Camping Ground
S Hwy 35, Maraehako Bay, East Cape (07) 325-2685

This is a pretty bay and rivermouth camp off S Hwy 35. The grounds are roughly level and there is camping under the pohutukawa trees beside the beach. There are no power sites here. Amenities are only toilets and cold-water taps, although cold-water showers may be installed. Primitive, yes–but the delight of many for its unspoiled beach atmosphere.

71. Waihau Bay Lodge
Private Bag, Waihau Bay (07) 325-3804

The camping option at Waihau Bay seems to merge with a friendly all-purpose complex with all the requirements for that memorable holiday by the sea. Across the road is a boat ramp and jetty and peaceful waters. There is a fishing club with a weigh-in station. The lodge offers a licensed restaurant and beer garden. There is a level area for campers, only 12 sites in all, and 6 have power. You will find a busy store and Information Centre here, also a petrol station. The amenities are fairly minimal, but there is a nice homely kitchen, with stove and fridge and good views of the bay. Just a couple of showers and toilets are provided. A utility room has automatic washing machines. A variety of accommodation is obtainable at the lodge. Your hosts Bill and Marilyn Hol. The camp ground costs $7.50 for a site with power or $7 for tents. For other prices please inquire.

72. Waihau Bay Holiday Park
Waihau Bay, East Cape, Private Bag 1068 Opotiki (07) 325-3844

This East Cape camp has chosen not to supply details for our book. Please call them for information.

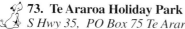

73. Te Araroa Holiday Park
S Hwy 35, PO Box 75 Te Araroha–East Cape (07) 864-4873 (phone & fax)

Discover this oasis midway between the Gisborne and Opotiki centres, nestled into grounds that are lavish with trees and extend right down to the beach. There is a freshwater stream. Sites are level with plenty of taps. In this remote and sheltered area you will find a modern cinema, with table tennis, pool also available. The on-site store has an extensive range of goods and is licensed for liquor sales. There are 80 tent sites here and 38 with power, plus some other accommodation. You can also choose to camp on the more open beachside tent sites. Horse riding is an option in the summer months and the expanse of beach leaves plenty of room to ride, swim, surf, fish or build your bonfire. The amenities offer great appointments, but outdoor lighting is minimal. In the kitchen you will find individual preparation areas, microwave and conventional cooking. The ablutions also have individual vanity areas and excellent showers. The laundry has all automatic equipment and everything is well kept. Choose your TV program from two separate rooms (one for TV1 and one for TV2). There is a dump point here and pets are allowed by prior arrangement. Your hosts Stan and Jocelyn Bryant will accept Eftpos here. Tent sites $7 per person. Power sites $8 per person. 🖵 $10.🖵 $45.

74. Waiapu Hotel & Caravan Park
Tikitiki–East Cape (06) 864-3745

If you don't need sophisticated appointments, pull off the road at the hotel. There are lawn camp sites and clusters of trees (some citrus fruit). Plenty of level tent sites and 6 sites with power are here. The amenities comprise an ablution block with toilets, a shower and an agitator washing machine. There is no communal kitchen, but the hotel will provide meals. This is an easy stopover. Your host Mani Collier. All sites are $8, $2 each extra person.

75. Te Puia Hot Springs Hotel & Caravan Park
S Hwy 35, PO Box 5, Te Puia (06) 864-6861

Beside the hotel you can camp on a large lawn with sheltering trees. These attractive grounds have only 2 power sites, but if you are independent there is a wide choice of camping spots. There is a unisex toilet and handbasin for campers, but when the hotel is open there are other facilities available. A private indoor pool is provided but the main outdoor pool is not functional. Ask your host, Don Fife, for any services you require during your stay. Tent sites $5 per person. Power sites $10. Look for information on page 133.

76. Tokomaru Bay
At the north end of the beach free camping is allowed in summer. No facilities are provided, so campers must be independent.

76. Mayfair Cabins & Camping Ground
PO Box 28, Tokomaru Bay (06) 864-5843

Although this is a small settlement, the Mayfair camp is not immediately obvious. Look for the general store and petrol station on S Hwy 35, across the road from the beach. This is pleasant "low-key" camping; drive in beside the petrol pumps. The land is flat with some nice willow trees for shade. The homely kitchen has a stove, microwave and fridge, with ranchsliders opening to a deck. It merges with a dining-lounge that is comfortable and inviting. A stereo and two TV sets (one at each end) are provided. There are only two showers and four toilets in the amenities building. A roofed porch houses an agitator washing machine. This is a friendly place where you can bring your pets. Cabin accommodation is available here, or 10 sites with power and easy tent space. The store in front is also the office and has light meals for sale. We enjoyed the cheerful welcome by host Lesley Glassford. All camping is $7.50 per person. ▢ $15 per person. Bunkhouse.

78. Anaura Bay Motor Camp
Anaura Bay, East Coast (06) 862-6380

This East Coast bay is between Tokomaru Bay and Tolaga Bay. Although there is a short stretch of fairly steep, unsealed road, the effort is worth it if you want a site at a magnificent beach. Not much shade here for the 94 level sites which include 24 with power, but the well stocked camp store is open 7 days all year round. A nice sheltered verandah stretches along the front and gives access to the recreation hall. There are two kitchens, one very well equipped with plenty of dining space. The shower block is separate from the toilets and a new block has recently been added. There are also outdoor basins and foot bath. The laundry has an automatic washing machine. It is a lovely seaside situation with views to nearby Motuoroi Island. There is excellent diving and crayfishing. Ask about hiring a boat here. Tent sites $8.50 per person. Power sites $9.50 per person. (Lower rates off season and 10% discount for senior citizens.)

79. Tolaga Bay Motor Camp
Wharf Road, PO Box 58, Tolaga Bay (06) 862-6716

On the coast, this camp is 2km from main route and the Tolaga Bay shops. There is a huge jetty out to sea and views of the limestone hills, dotted with caves. There are 50 power sites and 80 tent sites plus some cabins. There is a shop here, but with limited hours and limited stock (no cigarettes for sale) There is a good kitchen with rangettes and full stove and fridge/freezer. Dining space too. There are strictly utilitarian ablutions, although the paraplegic suite is excellent. The laundry has agitator machines. The grounds are level with a protective bank between the sites and the beach. A few shady sites are around the perimeter. No pets here please, and no smoking in the communal buildings. A site with power costs $8 per person, or $7.50 for tents. We got a warm welcome here from the host Mei Thompson.

80. Beach Camping

Note: Follow the coast road south to Gisborne. For approximately 20km north of Wainui Beach there is free camping along this stretch of coast. No facilities exist apart from long-drop toilets. Please keep the area clean.

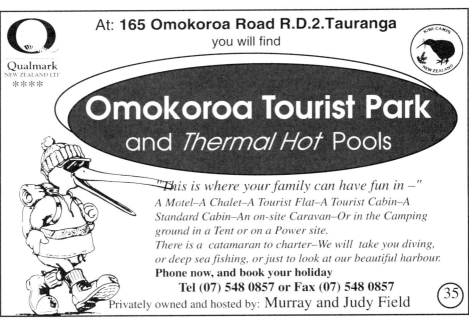

Te Puia Hot Springs Hotel

- Hotel
- Caravan Park
- Backpackers

BOX 5 TE PUIA
EASTCOAST
TEL 06 864 6755

75

Beachaven Caravan Park

21 Leo Street Waihi Beach. Tel (07) 863-5505

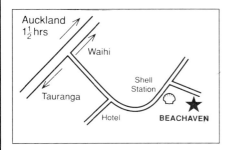

4 Tourist Cabins

1 Tourist Flat

1 Dormitory unit sleeps 16

2 On-site caravans

Spa Pool

Self-contained cottage

School groups welcome

YOUR HOSTS: Lindsay and Gary Tapper

30

Opotiki Holiday Park

Potts Avenue, Opotiki

Tel (07) 315 6050

TOURIST FLATS
TOURIST CABINS
ON-SITE CARAVANS

TENT SITES
POWER SITES

We can arrange
- Fishing trips,
- Horse riding,
- Mountain biking,
- Jet boating,
- White river rafting,
- Kayaking,
- Deer stalking,
- Pig hunting,
  and Tramping,
(All this from the camp)

Walking distance to:
Service clubs
Restaurants
Hotels
Shopping Centre

YOUR HOSTS:
Marion and Alan Jamieson

A short distance to:
◊ Golf Course
◊ Safe beaches
◊ Tennis Court
◊ Squash Club
◊ Bowling Club
◊ Service Station
◊ Surf Casting
◊ Trout Fishing

64

ROTORUA AND CENTRAL PLATEAU DIRECTORY

Key to locations and maps in Rotorua and Central Plateau. Begins at Otorohanga, out to the west coast via Waitomo Caves. Returns to Te Kuiti and then inland to reach Rotorua and the lakes. Leaves Rotorua district en route to Lake Taupo. Skirts the eastern shores of Lake Taupo down to Turangi. Veers west to Taumarunui then south to the mountains of National Park, finishing at Waiouru.

Otorohanga	1.	Parklands Farm
Otorohanga	2.	Otorohanga Kiwi Town Caravan Park
Waitomo Caves	3.	Juno Hall
Waitomo Caves	4.	Waitomo Caves Motor Camp
Marokopa	5.	Marokopa Motor Camp
Te Kuiti	6.	Domain Motor Camp
Pureora Forest	7.	Piropiro Flats (DoC)
Pureora Forest	8.	Ngaherenga Camp Ground (DoC)
Pureora Village	9.	Kakaho Camp Ground (DoC)
Tokoroa	10.	Glenbrook Motor Camp
Atiamuri	11.	Ohakuri Dam
Rotorua	12.	Rotorua Thermal Holiday Park
Rotorua	13.	Autohaven
Rotorua	14.	Kiwi Paka (Thermal) Lodge
Rotorua	15.	Cosy Cottage Intntl Holiday Park
Rotorua	16.	Lakeside Thermal Holiday Park
Ngongotaha (Rotorua)	17.	Rainbow Resort
Ngongotaha (Rotorua)	18.	Affordable Willowhaven Holiday Park

Ngongotaha (Rotorua)	19.	Greengrove Holiday Park
Ngongotaha (Rotorua)	20.	Waiteti Trout Stream Holiday Park
Rotorua Lakes	21.	Ohau Channel Lodge
Rotorua Lakes	22.	Lake Rotoiti Lakeside Holiday Park
Tikitere (Rotorua)	23.	Kiwi Ranch Holiday Camp
Rotorua Lakes	24.	Rotoma Holiday Park
Rotorua Lakes	25.	Merge Lodge Caravan Park
Rotorua Lakes	26.	Hinehopu
Rotorua Lakes	27.	All Seasons Holiday Park
Rotorua Lakes	28.	Holden's Bay Holiday Park
Rotorua Lakes	29.	Cedar Wood Lakeside Holiday Resort
Rotorua	30.	Redwood Motel & Holiday Park
Rotorua Lakes	31.	Blue Lake Holiday Park
Lake Tarawera	32.	Fisherman's Lodge Holiday Park
Lake Tarawera	33.	Te Tapahoro Bay (DoC)
Lake Tarawera	34.	Te Rata Bay (DoC)
Lake Rerewhakaaitu	35.	Lake Rerewhakaaitu (DoC)
Waikite	36.	Waikite Valley Thermal Pool Camp
Reporoa	37.	Golden Springs Holiday Park
Wairakei	38.	Wairakei Thermal Valley Camp
Taupo north	39.	Reeds Farm
Taupo west	40.	Great Lake Holiday Park
Taupo	41.	Taupo Motor Camp
Taupo	42.	Lake Taupo Holiday Park

Taupo	43.	Taupo All Seasons Holiday Park
Taupo	44.	De Bretts Thermal Resort
Taupo	45.	Hilltop Motor Caravan Park
Waitahanui	46.	Windsor Lodge Motel & Caravan Park
Motutere Bay	47.	Motutere Bay Caravan Park
Turangi	48.	Tauranga-Taupo Fishing Lodge
Turangi	49.	Motuoapa Motor Camp
Turangi	50.	Parklands Motor Home Park
Turangi	51.	Turangi Holiday Park
Turangi	52.	Club Habitat
Tokaanu	53.	Oasis Motels & Caravan Park
Taumarunui	54.	Riverhideaway Motor Camp
Owhango	55.	Gardean Goodstead Holiday Park
Tongariro	56.	Eiven's Lodge & Motor Camp
Whakapapa	57.	Mangahuia Campground (DoC)
Whakapapa	58.	Whakapapa Holiday Park (DoC)
National Park	59.	Discovery Motel, Cabin & Caravan Park
National Park	60.	Ski Haus
Raetihi	61.	Raetihi Motor Camp
Ohakune	62.	Ohakune Motor Camp
Ohakune	63.	Mangawhero Campground
Waiouru	64.	Waiouru Welcome Inn

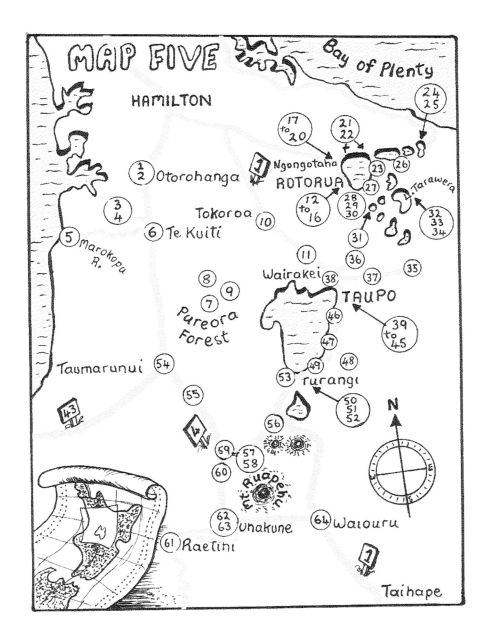

Chapter 5

ROTORUA AND THE CENTRAL PLATEAU

Expect the unexpected. Rotorua lives up to its international reputation for spectacular thermal activity and health spa qualities. It is also a place where Maori culture predominates and visitors can enjoy a close involvement with Maori traditions. At any time of year Rotorua is packed with discoveries for the traveller.

Sample the therapeutic waters of the mineral pools; temperatures vary from the tepid to the almost scalding. To inspect the most breathtaking thermal activity you may need a guide. By contrast there are also tranquil lakes to explore. The city of Rotorua has embraced its unique attractions in so many parks, historic places and complimentary visitor attractions that you will be kept very busy if you want to see them all.

Central to the North Island and within "the volcanic triangle" is Lake Taupo and the namesake picturesque village alongside. As the main highway skirts its eastern shores, panoramic views unfold. The origins of this lake lie in a volcanic eruption of immense proportions that occurred in AD130. It is now a renown recreational lake with a reputation for fine trout fishing. There are lakeside camping spots, and a variety of other accommodation, many offering natural mineral pools. Nearby are river tributaries and more remote lakes that are often sought by serious fishermen. Forestry plantations provide a scenic backdrop, and a thriving timber industry.

The alpine area of the Tongariro National Park is the winter playground of the North Island. This park has three mountains, Ruapehu, Tongariro and Ngauruhoe, which present a spectacular sight rising starkly to the west of the Desert Road, the main link through the centre of the island. Ruapehu is easily accessible to the skier, with gear for hire and chair lifts. Tramping is another option, with many well defined tracks and exhilarating mountain air.

This is adventurous country, from skiing to jet boating, rafting, scenic flights (by many and varied aircraft) and abseiling, to name a few. For the more sedentary traveller the guided trips through the Waitomo Caves, the dramatic scenery, the trout sanctuaries, and the historic sights offer plenty of alternatives.

1. Parklands Farm
S Hwy 3, Kio Kio RD4 Otorohanga   (07) 871-1818 (phone & fax)

Between Otorohanga and Te Awamutu drive in off the main road to a working farm with provision for camping. There are plenty of tent sites and just 6 power sites on a lawn in front of the farmhouse. There is a porch-style mini-kitchen and wringer-washer and tub for campers, with two shower rooms (with toilet and hand basin) alongside. Farm activities can be part of your holiday and you can arrange to share farm meals with the family. There is a conservatory area off the farmhouse where you may be invited to relax. Your host Owen Rountree. Dinner, bed and breakfast can be provided by prior arrangement. Tent sites are $10 for two or $6 per person. Power sites are $12 for two. $10 per person.

2. Otorohanga Kiwi Town Caravan Park
Domain Drive, Otorohanga   (07) 873-8214 (phone & fax)

This well groomed park has a lovely setting with level tree-shaded sites. Around 30 sites, including 21 with power. These sites are all only one deep and some have hard stands for vans. In the immediate neighbourhood is a playing field/reserve and on the other side the Otorohanga Kiwi House & Bird Park is an important conservation and visitor attraction. This camp offers clean amenities and a dump point. The kitchen has two full stoves and fridge. You will find lots of tourist information to peruse and a free phone (for local calls). There are both separate and unisex ablutions. The laundry has automatic washer and dryer. A shuttle bus departs for Waitomo Caves. The local township services are close at hand. No dogs here please. Your hosts Bill and Irene Millar. Two people can have a tent site for $12, or $14 with power.

3. Juno Hall
RD5 Waitomo Caves (07) 878-7649

Just 1km from Waitomo Village, this is primarily a backpackers hostel. Although provision has been made for campers, a power site is probably not available. This is a recently built lodge with a variety of accommodation. The large communal lounge has a TV corner and adjoins a roomy kitchen with 3 sinks, microwave and conventional cooking, where plenty of pots and pans are provided. A limited menu of "fast food" may be available. The laundry has automatic equipment and a drying room. There are modern ablution facilities. If you like a sociable atmosphere with the younger set, this is for you. Tent sites $7 per person. Beds from $14.

4. Waitomo Caves Motor Camp
C/o NZ Supreme Trade Centre. PO Box 14, Waitomo Village
(07) 878-8895

This camp is handily placed for all the attractions of Waitomo Village and Caves. Check in at the NZ Supreme Trade Centre shop across the road. Sites are terraced and there are some large trees for shade. There is a well-used kitchen/dining with assorted furniture or choose the restaurant opposite for meals. The ladies ablutions have a laundry adjoining! Automatic washer provides a cold wash and there is a dryer. Probably your pets can be accommodated. Your new hosts Phil and Christine Caskey. A tent site is $6 per person and a power site is $7 🖼 $12 per person.

5. Marokopa Motor Camp
Marokopa (07) 876-7546

Outback camping for the financially challenged. It's a long winding trail to this coast, but the road is sealed all the way and has a variety of scenery. The camping paddock is separated from the communal building by some very classy tennis courts, which are available for a small fee. There is a small shop for basic supplies in the old school building which also houses the amenities. A large communal room overlooks the courts and leads to a kitchen with adequate equipment for undemanding users. There is an agitator washing machine in the laundry. Ablutions offer 4 unisex lockable showers plus toilets and basins for each sex. Reputed to be a fisherman's camp, although it is not right on the beach. Your hosts Shirley and James Barlow. Tent sites $5 for two people. Power sites $10 for two.

6. Domain Motor Camp
Hinerangi Street, Te Kuiti (07) 878-6223 (fax 07 878-7771)

There is dual access to this camp, with the local school and football ground sharing the approach road. It may be congested at times. However, sites are flat with some nice shady trees and picnic tables; a small stream alongside. Campers are issued with keys to the amenities block. The kitchen has useful equipment, with fridge freezer and coin phone. It combines with dining and TV. There are 2 stoves and toasters. Both ablution facilities have good well-lined showers and toilets. There is an automatic washer and dryer in the laundry. A dump point is provided. No dogs here please. Just down the road is the large local swimming pool. For a tent site the charge is $5.50 per person, or with power $6.50. 🖼 $15 per person. 🖼 $25.

7. Piropiro Flats
West of Pureora Forest Park–Department of Conservation
(07) 838-3363 (fax 07 838-1004)

Piropiro Flats camping area is located on the western side of Pureora Forest Park, near Waimiha. This is a more remote area, especially popular with hunters.

8. Ngaherenga Camp Ground
Pureora Forest Park –Department of Conservation (07) 838-3363
(fax 07 838-1004)

Just one km from Pureora Forest Park headquarters, Ngaherenga is the place to visit if you enjoy seeing tui, bellbirds and kakariki. If you are really lucky, you may also see or hear the rare kokako calling at dawn. BBQs, firewood and toilets are supplied and rubbish is collected regularly. Adults $3 per person. Family concession $8. School children $2.

9. Kakaho Camp Ground
Off S Hwy 32 between Mangakino and Tihoi –Department of Conservation
(07) 838-3363 (fax 07 838-1004)

Located 5km off State Highway 32 between Mangakino and Tihoi, and accessible via the Link Road from Pureora Village, Kakaho is the ideal place for large groups. BBQ areas, firewood and toilets are all supplied and rubbish is removed on a regular basis. There is plenty of room for cricket or volleyball –that is if you ever get sick of the Rimu Walk and the Kakaho swimming hole. Adults $3 per person. Family concession $8. School children $2.

10. Glenbrook Motor Camp
5–7 Sloss Road Tokoroa, PO Box 257, Tokoroa (07) 886-6642

Tokoroa is a central North Island town notable for its production of timber from the surrounding forests. It is not a resort area, but has the advantage of being within an hour's drive of Rotorua. The grounds offer plenty of shady trees and there is a small backpackers lodge with very basic kitchen facilities. The communal ablutions are very "country-style" but have plenty of hot water. An area close to the entrance offers an en suite and tea-making facilities for overnighters. You can walk across a footbridge to the town shops from the camp. A pleasant kitchen, with microwave and fridge, also has TV. The separate games room is not for the fussy. The laundry has automatic machines. There is a dump station. Your pets are welcome here. Your hosts Don and Jo Abbott. Backpackers can stay at $13 a bed, and a tent site is $13 for two persons. Power sites are $15 for two with an extra $1 for the en suite option.

11. Ohakuri Dam
Off S Hwy 1, Atiamuri

Just south of Atiamuri take the signposted short road to Ohakuri Dam. The sealed road gives way to a unsealed forestry road for 3km before you reach Lake Ohakuri. Here you will find a delightful recreational area set amongst the trees around a lovely large lake. This is a free camping spot with a separate picnic area. The only facilities are taps and toilets, but BBQs are plentiful. Tables and rubbish bins are provided. The lake is ideal for swimming and watersports, while the surrounding forest has walking tracks to explore. Dogs are permitted if under control.

12. Rotorua Thermal Holiday Park
Old Taupo Road (south end), Rotorua (07) 346-3140 (fax 07 346-1324)

Opulent camping on a grand scale. Landscaped into suitable areas for every purpose, the park is situated close to Whakawerawera Thermal Reserve (Whaka), opposite a public golf course and adjacent to the local Polytechnic. There are power sites for 150 caravans plus a special 34-site campervan area with covered walkway to the streamlined kitchen bays and inviting indoor recreational area. The campers have efficient cooking facilities, with plenty to choose from, or you may enjoy an open-air meal at the BBQ, or a hangi if you are part of a group. Tent sites are on a picturesque rolling lawn at the rear with their own ablution block. As well as hot mineral pools, there is a heated filtered swimming pool. In peak season a holiday programme is offered (with prizes). All the amenities are first class and hygienically kept. These are also accessible for paraplegics. There is a dump point here. As well as camping you may choose a log cabin or the impressive lodge complex, where breakfasts and dinners are an option. A superb holiday environment with your friendly hosts Carys and Peter Ellery. Camping costs $8.50 per person on all sites. Pathside sites $10 per person. 🔳 $20 per person 🔳 $60 for two. Bunk room $16 share. Look for further information on page 163.

13. Autohaven
137 Pukuatua Street, Rotorua (07) 348-1886 (fax 07 347-6520)

A small-scale camp in a handy position near Kuirau Park, this is centrally situated, but on a busy road. To the rear is an area for around 20 tent sites. Sites with power are adjacent to the other accommodation and are only one deep. A private spa pool is provided. There is a superb kitchen with cutlery, crockery, pots and pans provided, plus good appliances. A bench-high divider separates this from a dining and TV area. There are probably sufficient good ablutions for a small camp and these include paraplegic facilities. Upkeep is good. A compact laundry contains automatic machines. Carol and David Adams are the managers here. Tent sites are $7 per person, or with power $16 for two. There is a range of other accommodation. There is also a surcharge for late arrivals (after 10.30pm).

14. Kiwi Paka (Thermal) Lodge

60 Tarewa Road, Rotorua (07) 347-0931 (fax 07 346-3167)

Rub shoulders with backpackers from all around the world at this complex. Very centrally situated, with a good travel and information centre, there is modern accommodation as well as 12 hedged power sites and 54 tent sites which are fenced from the road frontage. The large kidney-shaped outdoor hot pool is a popular attraction. There are 4 blocks of ablutions with nicely lined shower cubicles and vanity-style basins. A very sociable multi-purpose recreation and services building contains coffee tables and couches, TV and pool table and an efficient kitchen with microwaves, fridges and hot plates in 3 separate bays. There are supplies of cutlery, plates etc. available on request. Both indoor and outdoor dining are alongside. A new en suite cafe and bar has been installed. There are excellent laundry facilities (all automatic) with ironing equipment. The grounds are beside Kuirau Park and it is only 5 minutes walk to the centre of the city, or hire a bicycle here. The new managers here are Joanne and Paul McIsaac. Tent sites are $6 per person and power sites are $8. Dormitory accommodation is from $13 per person.

15. Cosy Cottage International Holiday Park

67 Whittaker Road, Rotorua, PO Box 1598 Rotorua (07) 348-3793 (fax 07 347-9634)

Perhaps the ultimate thermal experience awaits you here! Not only are there "cosy cottages" but the experience of tenting on naturally warmed earth must be tried to be appreciated. Not every tent site is on this thermal carpet, but you will find enough other options to enhance your stay. The al fresco steam oven is a unique cooking experience. For those more conservative cooks there is a handy kitchen with all the usual equipment and dining space. Above this is a large, warm and comfortable recreation room with a TV corner. There is a pool table provided and this area has a smoke-free policy. The ablutions have a plentiful supply of hot water. The laundry provides automatic machines and a drying room is available. A dump point is provided. There is a private hot pool and a warm enclosed swimming pool open to the stars. Inspect the bubbling mud hole (from a safe distance, it is fenced) and the hot-and-cool-water streams. Meet your friendly hosts Claire and Jo Greenwood at the office; they will help you with any enquiries. Some basic supplies are stocked, and local shopping is not far away. Around 35 sites have power. Tent sites $17 for two. Power sites plus $2 per site. ▱ $36. ▦ $48.

16. Lakeside Thermal Holiday Park
54 Whittaker Road, Rotorua (07) 348-1693 (phone & fax)

Bordering on Lake Rotorua, this has a picturesque entrance leading to a level sheltered park of modest proportions. There are 16 power sites with an equal number of cabin/flat accommodation and little provision for tents. The camp jetty and private beach offer a number of holiday activities with free canoes and dinghy or mooring for your boat. There are hot mineral pools and spas for soaking (all free). The camp ablutions are in good order, if a little short on dressing space for the showers. The kitchen features eye-level oven and rangehood, also microwave cooking, toasters and fridge. There is a semi-enclosed area for BBQs with a pool and TV room adjacent. A natural steam cooker is an option. The laundry has excellent automatic equipment. Swans, budgies and ducks reside here, so no pets please! Your hosts Kieron and Liz Casserly. A site with power is $9 per person or $8 for tents. 🔲 $35 for two people. 🔲 $45.

17. Rainbow Resort
22 Beaumont Road, PO Box 23, Ngongotaha–Rotorua (07) 357-4289 (phone & fax)

The well stocked shop beside the entrance is a bonus here. Opposite is a well maintained play area for children and a solar-heated swimming pool alongside. Sites are level, and some are hedged. You may find some power sites have en suite facilities. The cabins have a colourful "dolls house" appearance and other accommodation includes tourist flats, a motel unit and on-site caravan. The kitchen has just the basic requirements, but boasts two refrigerators. Automatic machines are in the laundry. The ablutions offer the usual services and are in a separate block from the toilets. There are free canoes available, but the camp is not immediately lakeside. Your hosts Ron, Beat and Rita. Power sites are $8.50 and tent sites are $7.50 per person. 🔲,🔲, and 🔲.

18. Affordable Willowhaven Holiday Park
31 Beaumont Road, Ngongotaha–Rotorua (07) 357-4092 (fax 07 357-5078)

A picturesque setting right on the lakefront, with a boat ramp and jetty and a safe sandy beach. A new adventure playground is provided for the children. Families have now got a new amenities block. Views of the lake are a feature from many of the 40 power sites, some of which have an unobstructed water frontage. There are tent sites, cabins and chalets and self-contained Lockwood tourist flats. Shady trees dot the grounds. The amenities include a homely compact kitchen with a full stove and microwave. The ablutions are roomy and cater for wheelchairs. Fully automatic laundry equipment is provided. There is a camp store. Your new hosts Daren and Fiona Miller. Tent sites $6 or with power $8 per person. 🔲 $35 for two.

19. Greengrove Holiday Park
Cnr Hall & School Roads, PO Box 57 Ngongotaha–Rotorua
(07) 357-4429

Only 2km from the Agrodome, the entrance to this camp has a tree-shaded aspect with a specimen chestnut tree enhancing the grounds. The central driveway has sites on both sides and seven tourist flats are available. The main amenities are sited to the left of the drive and have rather a "homespun" quality. There is a mini kitchen, and the ablutions are clean with abundant hot water. Automatic laundry equipment is installed, with a small surcharge for the dryer. A basic games/recreation room and outdoor play area with a children's paddling pool is available. An unpretentious camping ground, away from much passing traffic. Your new hosts Glenda and Graham Smith. Tent sites are from $7 per person. $9 with power. Green 🔲. $28 for two. 🔲 $40.

20. Waiteti Trout Stream Holiday Park
14 Okona Crescent, Ngongotaha–Rotorua (07) 357-5255 (phone & fax)

A gentle retreat bounded by the Waiteti Trout Stream. The setting is level lawns dotted with shady trees. Campers can use the free canoe and get their fishing licence and rods here. There is a small store on the site. The kitchen has fridge/freezer and breakfasts can be supplied on request. There is a laundry and ablutions, both fresh and clean. Two recreation rooms supply a TV lounge, or activities room with pool, table tennis and darts. A spa pool is available. There are dump stations here and a bus stop at the gate. Your hosts Eleanor and Gordon, Kim and Dean Munro.

21. Ohau Channel Lodge
Hamurana Road, PO Box 876 Rotorua (07) 362-4761

Fishing? Hunting perhaps? There are competitions held here. A holiday venue with mature level grounds in an appealing setting. The location is 15 minutes from the city on the north-eastern shore of Lake Rotorua where it meets Ohau Channel. You can use the marina, charter boat, boat hire or the launching ramps for your own craft. There are 60 level power sites and ample provision for tents, plus backpacker cabins. An airport or city pick-up (no charge) can be provided for touring backpackers. Reception takes place at the colonial-style general store and tackle shop, where a long verandah features fish-weighing scales. It has a "times past" appeal and overlooks the central playground for children. Amenities include a homely kitchen which opens to a laundry with automatic equipment. The ablutions are satisfactory, with a special children's toilet and basin. Not suitable for disabled people, but there is a unisex bath available. Enjoy the private spa pools (there are two) provided. Your hosts Murray and Irene Brooks. All camping here is $8.50 per person. 🔲 $30.

22. Lake Rotoiti Lakeside Holiday Park
Okere Road, Okere Falls–RD 4 Rotorua (07) 362-4860 (phone & fax)

Watch for Okere Falls turnoff on S Hwy 33 towards Tauranga. This camp has a delightful lakefront perimeter in rural surroundings, great for boaties and fishermen, with jetty, boat ramp, and marina berths. You can get a free row-boat here, or arrange a rafting trip. This tranquil lake is also great for water skiing. There are enjoyable walks to Okere Falls and the Kaituna River. Use the private hot-pool complex, no charge for campers. This is not a large camp, with 40 sites including 10 for tents. There is also cabin accommodation. Amenities are satisfactory, but with a mini-kitchen and an historic recreation hall. There is a dump point here. Your hosts Christine and Wayne Mason. All camping (includes extras) is at $10.50 per person.🖃. Look for the value coupon on page164.

23. Kiwi Ranch Holiday Camp
Rotokawau Road, Tikitere–Rotorua (07) 345-6799

Across the road from Hell's Gate, which seethes with thermal activity, the secluded bushapproach to this camp. Cabins and flats are on the slopes of a spacious valley and on the level floor the camp sites share space with a mini-lake. There are 15 power sites with drainage and some tenting areas, but this appears to be mainly a venue for organised groups using the hostel-style accommodation. In keeping with the main purpose of the camp organised activities are available by arrangement, including riding the many horses that are stabled here. There is also a swimming pool with slide, a spacious outdoor hot pool, and an indoor basketball court too. The kitchen facilities are rudimentary. The rather curious ablutions are subsidised by poolside toilets and changing rooms. The laundry facilities include one with good automatic machines. It is $6.50 per person for a tent site and $9 for a power site.🖃.

24. Rotoma Holiday Park
Manawahe Road, RD4 Rotorua (07) 362-0815

Just off S Hwy 30 this camp has a bush backdrop and level, well groomed sites. It adjoins the Rotoma Scenic Reserve. The camp capacity is not large, with 30 sites that have power, water and drainage, and a similar number of tent sites. There are basic supplies in the camp store. The amenities are functional and include a homely kitchen with full stoves, fridge and table and chairs. A camp library is on hand. There are good ablutions (if you don't mind the minimal windows) and a tiny laundry which has both automatic and manual equipment. In the grounds there are BBQs and 4 private indoor hot mineral pools. Under the care of the Ludovic group. All sites are $8 per person.

25. Merge Lodge Caravan Park
S Hwy 30, Private Bag, Lake Rotoma–Rotorua (07) 362-0880

Use the BP Service Station as your landmark and drive alongside to this lakeside camp right beside Lake Rotoma. This is a clean lake and there is a public jetty next door to the camp. Sites are spread from a grassed terrace which overlooks the lake and boat anchorage. These level sites are often pre-booked so enquire beforehand. The whole aspect is very neat but has a limited capacity of about 35 sites, most with power. All the amenities are of almost domestic proportions, but well kept and complete with all the necessary equipment. There is also a gas BBQ. You can bring your pets to this camp. Try water skiing or fishing here. (There are trout fishing escorted tours in your host's boat.) The native wildlife include the kokako, an endangered bird that still inhabits this area. A personal warm welcome from your hosts Kath and Terry Jones. Tent sites are $8 per person. Power sites are $19 for two.

26. Hinehopu
Main Rotorua–Whakatane Hwy, Lake Rotoiti (07) 362-7641 (phone & fax)

On the eastern shores of Lake Rotoiti, this little level park is an easy place to pull off the road and take refreshments. The spacious and comfortable licensed bar and adjoining restaurant seem to be the prime attraction offered here. However the camp has 28 power sites on level grounds with a shelter belt of trees and a pleasant lakefront aspect. There is a jetty and boat ramp provided, and a 9 hole golf course is adjacent. The amenities are fairly sparse with a tiny kitchen and basics-only ablutions. There are also some fairly primitive cabins available. Your hosts are Merepeka and Theo Sims -Tait. Camping is $8 per person for all sites. 🖮.

27. All Seasons Holiday Park
50-58 Lee Road, Hannahs Bay, Rotorua (07) 345-6240

On landscaped grounds which are dotted with trees this level park has around 74 power sites with hedged borders. There are also 70 sites for tents, and other accommodation. In the spacious grounds is a safe confidence playground. It is an easy distance to Lake Rotorua, local shops and the airport. The kitchen has two full stoves and a fridge. A bath as well as showers is provided in the ablutions and there is no shortage of toilets. Paraplegic facilities are provided. The laundry is huge, with automatic wash and drying machines. A large fenced outdoor swimming pool and a grass tennis court are within the grounds. There is also an attractive private spa pool. Amongst the alternative accommodation is a 28-bed lodge, pleasantly heated. In this building there is a large recreational room with TV and video games for the use of both guests and campers. A good base camp for many activities. Your new hosts are Dave and Adelaide Graham. Tent sites are $8 per person and $9 with power. 🖮 $15 per person.

28. Holdens Bay Holiday Park

21 Robinson Ave, PO Box 9, Rotorua (07) 345-9925 (phone & fax)

A very cultivated complex set amongst mature trees, situated not far from the city, just off S Hwy 30. There is plenty to see and do from here, with Lake Rotorua close by. It is also handy to the airport. There are 90 sites with power and another 80 for tents and most enjoy shelter from shady trees. The accommodation units include a lodge. You can enjoy the private hot pools or a large outdoor swimming pool. A sparkling kitchen with full stoves and hot plates has tiled table and chairs and opens to an outdoor BBQ area. The shower cubicles are nicely lined and there are good mirrors provided. The toilets open off a curved corridor. The laundry has automatic equipment and iron. There is a theatre-style TV room. Beside the office is a shop with basic items, and a sturdy recreation room that the teenagers will enjoy. The younger set have a playground and a small aviary provided. Your hosts Elsbeth and David Liddle. All camping is $10 per person. $25 for two. $55. Look for further information on page 162.

29. Cedar Wood Lakeside Holiday Resort

17 Holden Ave. PO Box 1133 Holden's Bay–Rotorua (07) 345-7773 (fax 07 345-5533)

A proud new resort with all the trimmings. It has a lake-edge boundary and a boat ramp and jetty. Campers have 24 power sites on a lawn with other accommodation around the edges. All the amenities are top-of-the-range and include paraplegic facilities. There is also a dump point. Boat parking and a children's play area are provided. A BBQ is set up in the grounds. This is a well groomed park under the management of Richard Boss. All sites $20 for two. $60.

30. Redwood Motel & Holiday Park

5 Tarawera Road, Rotorua (07) 345-9380,or (07) 345-5421 (fax 07 345-4157)

This easy-to-find park occupies a site on the corner of S Hwy 30 and Tarawera Road. Although only 36 sites are available for camping (24 with power), this has a selection of accommodation as well. The layout separates campers from the units, and the pools are centrally placed for all. Enjoy a soak in the private spa, or use the outdoor swimming pools. There are good amenities here. The kitchen has fridge; modern ablutions and automatic laundry equipment. There is a large play area for children. Your hosts Buster and Shirley Hodges. All sites are $19 for two. $55.

31. Blue Lake Holiday Park
Tarawera Road, PO Box 292 Rotorua (07) 362-8120 (fax 07 362-8600)

Like a picture postcard, magnificent scenery and setting surround this holiday complex overlooking Blue Lake. The lake shores are almost completely bush clad and the park enjoys access to a sandy beach and is sheltered by native bush and mature trees. Several signposted paths lead into the park, which has level sites on gentle terraces. Around 160 sites are provided; about half of these have power. There is a variety of other accommodation. Serviced by two kitchens, metered showers and toilet blocks and two modern laundries (the secondary blocks are open in the busy season only), the whole complex has a well-cared-for appeal. There is a spa pool too. A communal dining room is available with a pagoda-roofed BBQ courtyard outside. From the comfortable TV and recreation room (situated above the camp store) there are lovely lake views. Hire canoes, kayaks, fishing gear and bikes at the park. Your hosts Susan and Jack Timmer. A tent site will cost you $8.50 per person, or $9.50 with power. Other accommodation please inquire.

32. Fisherman's Lodge Family Holiday Park
Te Mu Road, Lake Tarawera–PO Box 692, Rotorua (07) 362-8754

In the "lake district" around 16km from Rotorua, this is a new spot to take the family. The camp has pleasant sloping grounds with clusters of mature trees and ferns. From here you will enjoy views of Lake Tarawera. Sites for tents are abundant, and there are 18 with power. There are well kept ablutions and a good laundry. The kitchen is a modest size with an adjoining recreation room with cosy pot-bellied stove. A separate TV cabin is provided. There is a children's playground. Arrange your fishing or scenic trip at the on-site store. Tent sites $7 per person.

Power sites $8 per person. 🔲 $14 .

🔲 $45 for two.

The following two Conservation camp sites are dog friendly. Permits must be obtained beforehand from The Department of Conservation Te Ikawhenua Visitor Centre, PO Box 114, Murupara.

33. Te Tapahoro Bay
Lake Tarawera–Department of Conservation
Enquiries to The Map & Track Shop, Tourism Rotorua (07) 349-1845
(phone & fax)

"Tarawera Outlet" is the common name for Te Tapahoro Bay at the eastern extremity of Lake Tarawera alongside the Tarawera River. Good car and trailer access is available through Tasman's Tarawera Forest via the township of Kawerau. The site is well suited for tents and caravans and offers excellent trout fishing (fly fishing in season, 1 October to 31 May) and walking. Swingbridge links with the Tarawera Falls walkway which in turn links with the Eastern Okataina walkway. The site is isolated (20 minutes drive from Kawerau). Facilities include composting toilets (one suitable for the disabled) pit toilets, cooking shelter, reticulated water for sites farthest from the lake, and a boat ramp suitable for smaller boats (up to 4 metres). A camp warden may be in attendance during peak holiday periods to assist with information and self-registration matters. Charges are $5 per tent/caravan per night.

34. Te Rata Bay
Lake Tarawera–Department of Conservation
Enquiries to The Map & Track Shop, Tourism Rotorua (07) 349-1845
(phone & fax)

Hotwater Beach in Te Rata Bay is on the southernmost shore of Lake Tarawera. The self-registration campsite here is isolated with only access being a 9km boat trip from the Tarawera Landing at Punaromia. Although a water-taxi service is available, visitors need their own boats in order to enjoy other pursuits such as sightseeing, fishing, water skiing and for access to walking tracks leading to other attractions around the lake. Facilities include lakeshore mooring posts, composting toilets, and a cooking/picnic shelter with tank water. A camp warden may be on site to assist with information and the self-registration system. For further information contact the Map and Track Shop as above. Charges are $5 per tent per night.

35. Lake Rerewhakaaitu
Lake Rerewhakaaitu–Department of Conservation
Enquiries to The Map & Track Shop, Tourism Rotorua (07) 349-1845
(phone & fax)

There are two self-registration campsites with easy vehicle access at Lake Rerewhakaaitu. **Awaatua Bay**, off Brett Road has two composting toilets and the beach is suitable for the launching of light boats. **Ash Pit Road** provides access to the northern extremity of the lake where camp sites are handy to pleasant lake/bush walks, nearby Mount Tarawera access, and a popular fly-fishing bay. A composting toilet is provided on site. Small boats (up to 4 metres) are easily launched off the beach and are ideal for sightseeing and fishing. A camp warden may be present during peak holiday periods. Charges are $5 per tent/caravan per night.

36. Waikite Valley Thermal Pool Camp
Waikite Valley Road, 6km from S Hwy 5, Waikite (07) 333-1861

This thermal pool complex is over the hill from S Hwy 5 and south of Rotorua. Turn off at Waiotapu Hotel. It is approximately 6km from the main road. Camping is set up to compliment enjoyment of the pools. There are some appealing sites on a small scale, and only 8 have power. The pools are divided into an adults main pool with an annexe pool for the children. The mineral water is without sulphur. Campers have free use of these pools. The camp kitchen is equipped with stove, fridge, tables and chairs. BBQ and picnic tables are provided. The ablutions are wheelchair accessible, as are the pools. There is a laundry. On site are tearooms which may be used for campers to get together and relax. There are neighbouring squash courts. Your host Linda Palmer. Camping costs $8.50 per person.

37. Golden Springs Holiday Park
S Hwy 5, RD2 Reporoa (07) 333-8280

This camp is within the thermal belt, midway between Rotorua and Taupo. There are 20 power sites divided by mature boxed hedges and another 10 tent sites. A range of other accommodation is here too. Meals are available at the licensed bistro. There is a thermal stream, a tepid swimming pool (in season) and hot mineral pools. Animal and birds share the park with guests and pony rides can be arranged. Your own pets are welcome. There is an excellent play area for children. A TV room has an adjacent pool room. There is a cosy kitchen with fridge and full oven. The ablutions are not the most recent style but are well maintained. Laundry facilities are automatic. Your hosts David and Jan Taylor were not on hand when we called. All sites $9 per person.. ▱ $33 for two.▱ $40 per person.

▱	Cabins from	▱	Tourist flats and motels from
		☀	Department of Conservation
▱	On-site caravans from	🐕	Dog friendly

38. Wairakei Thermal Valley Motor Camp
1.5 km from S Hwy 1 Wairakei (07) 374-8004

Tucked into a sheltered area and almost alongside the geothermal power project, this camp is only a short drive from the main highway. It has a quaint appeal and offers visitors and campers alike light meals at the cosy tearooms, where a fireplace is inviting. There is now a bar and dining annexe alongside for evening meals, or use the BBQ. Great for a get-together with friends. The camp itself has plenty of privacy and level sites, well tree'd. A pleasantly random style of camping with basic facilities and resident birds and animals. Your pets will be welcome too. On an elevated site overlooking the valley 4 new open-air hot tubs should be ready this season. Explore this interesting natural environment at your leisure. All camping here is $6 per person. There is also a log 🏠 .

39. Reeds Farm
Huka Falls Road, north of Taupo

Just about 100 yards from S Hwy 1 is a turn off to Huka Falls Road. Look for the signpost to Reeds Farm. This is an easy-to-park stopover with plenty of trees for shade. The land is level and on the banks of a swift-flowing river. This a free camping spot with just two toilets supplied.

40. Great Lake Holiday Park
Acacia Bay Road, Taupo, PO Box 171 Taupo (07) 378-5159

Although this is on the rural side of the lake it is just across the bridge from Taupo town centre. Trim and well presented and enhanced by young trees and shrubs, it is a most attractive setting, containing 60 camp sites, most with power. They are level and well kept. This camp is not on the lake edge and has a less commercial environment. There is a welcoming kitchen with dining adjacent and a TV nook to one side. The ablutions are well appointed and have a paraplegic suite. There are automatic machines in the laundry and a dump point is provided. A basement location for the video machines and pool table. Outdoors is a volleyball court and a netball ring. An inviting BBQ garden and a spa pool are provided. Basic supplies are obtainable at the camp store. Please do not bring pets. Your hosts Glyn and Carolyn Rushby and Keith Ericksen. All camp sites are $8.25 per person. There is also other accommodation.🏠 and 🏠.

41. Taupo Motor Camp
Redoubt Street Taupo (07) 377-3080 (phone & fax)

Amongst lots of trees but convenient for the shops of Taupo, this camp has a riverside setting and a boat ramp. The land has a selection of sites due to varying contours. Two kitchens are functional in the busy season. There is a recreation/TV room. The ablutions are rather distant from the water's edge sites, and could be under pressure at peak times. There are good laundry facilities and a dump point. Dogs may be permitted in the off season, by prior arrangement. Your hosts Peter and Jenny Johanson. All camping is $8.50 per person. 🚐 and 🚏 $12 each.

42. Lake Taupo Holiday Park

28 Centennial Drive, PO Box 133 Taupo (07) 378-6860 (phone & fax)

Off Spa Road and next to the Spa Hotel, this camp is opposite Taupo Golf Club (special terms for golfers). There are also thermal pools nearby. This park rambles over large and varied terrain and most sites are terraced, with shade from mature pines. Individual sites are really big and have a tap and sump at each of the 100 power points. There are an equal number of sites for tents. There is a shop and an adventure playground for children. The kitchen has a full size stove and there are modern ablutions and the laundry offers automatic equipment. There is a dump station here. A pleasant TV room and a separate games room are available. School groups are welcome here, also your pets. Your hosts Noel and Chris Topp. All camp sites are $8 per person. 🚏 $35 for two. 🚏 $45 for two. Based on 1994/95 rates.

43. Taupo All Seasons Holiday Park

16 Rangatira Street, PO Box 122 Taupo (07) 378-4272

This is a quiet family park just over 1km from the town centre but not on the "tourist strip". The camp has benefited from plenty of care and attention and has around 100 sites, 65 with power. The amenities are in excellent condition, the kitchen has fridge and lunch bar area. A flagstone quadrangle is attractive with its gas BBQ and picnic tables. Indoors there is a TV room carpeted and cosy, and a games room. There is an outdoor thermal pool and a spa pool. The AC swimming pools are nearby. The ablution facilities include a good functional paraplegic suite and family bathrooms (with bath). There is a dump point here. Automatic laundry equipment is provided. The accommodation here includes a new 40-bed lodge. Small conference facilities are provided. Your helpful host is Virginia Schnauer. All camp sites are $9 per person. 🚏 $15 per person. Look for further information on page 162.

44. De Bretts Thermal Resort
Taupo-Napier Hwy, PO Box 513 Taupo (07) 378-8559 (phone & fax)

Not far from the lake front, De Bretts is long established as both a thermal pool complex and a holiday resort. Within the grounds are private pools at varying temperatures, and an open swimming pool with giant water slide. There is a chip and putt golf course, shopping, takeaway foods and excellent facilities with great showers, although a clothes bench-seat would be appreciated! There are 150 sites (90 with power) and a range of other accommodation. A new all-weather BBQ garden has been created with seating and gas BBQs. A licensed restaurant is available. The camp sites have their own street light and are mostly individually hedged. Taps and sumps are at each power site. 6 en-suite sites should be operational by now. There is a dump point here. If you enjoy a very comprehensive range of tourist trips, from aerial sightseeing to trout fishing, you can arrange it here. This is a busy complex with all the extras. Your hosts Barry and Carol Kirkland. A site with power is $10 per person and a tent site is also $10. 🔲 and 🔳. Look for further information on page 164.

45. Hilltop Motor Caravan Park
39 Puriri Street, Taupo (07) 378-5247

From the lakefront drive south of Taupo township, take the turnoff up Taharepa Road and follow the signposts. This camp has a secluded aspect and is back from and above the lake. Sheltered sites are served by landscaped paths amongst the bush. Most of the 110 sites have power. There are hot thermal spa pools fenced by tree ferns, and a cool swimming pool. We found pleasant amenities with extra-good formica-lined showers. The kitchen has a fridge and extends to patio dining outside. There is a games room. The laundry has automatic machines and ironing equipment. Your hosts Jan and Val Hoogerbrugge. All sites $8 per person. 🔲 and 🔳 .

46. Windsor Lodge Motel & Caravan Park
S Hwy 1, Waitahanui–via Taupo (07) 378-6271

Also serving as the local post office and dairy, this park will appeal to the angler. The Waitahanui River and Lake Taupo are almost within casting distance. There are not a lot of camp sites but there are also eight motel units and two cabins. There is a well-stocked shop/post office with takeaway food available. All the amenities are in excellent condition. The kitchen is compact with metered hot plates and Rototec oven. There are good showers in the ablutions. For the camper the sites are level with shady trees. This is a pet friendly camp. Your hosts Pin and Sandy Tennant. Tent sites $8 per person. Power sites $15 for two people.🔲 $20. 🔳 $45.

47. Motutere Bay Caravan Park
S Hwy 1 Motutere Bay, Taupo–PO Box 338 Turangi (07) 386-8963 (phone & fax)

The eye-catching location, positioned lakeside, is lovely but the provision of amenities falls short of expectations. At the office-shop you can get your fishing tackle. There are also general provisions available. There is a large capacity for campers with around 200 sites, 120 with power. Some other accommodation is available. It is a magnificent setting within a nature reserve with pockets of sites in multi-plateaus that offer privacy. The kitchens are marginal, the main kitchen offering only two single and one double electric rings. There are a number of small ablution blocks with metered showers and wheelchair access, rather "too few and too far" for comfort. The laundry equipment should be adequate. Pretty as a picture for those who can be independent of facilities. Your new hosts Jenny and Brent. Prices vary according to location and range from $6 per person for tents to $8.50 (lakeside) with power. There are some other accommodation units.

48. Tauranga-Taupo Fishing Lodge
S Hwy 1, RD2 Turangi (07) 386-8385 (fax 07 386-8386)

Especially for fishing, but also close to the thermal attractions, this park is 11km north from Turangi and 40km south of Taupo. The camping area is spacious and well laid out with 40 power sites and about 10 for tents. Rubbish bins and taps are plentiful. There is a good camp kitchen which has a TV room extension. Right here you can have a meal at the Ladies Mile steak and ale bar. There is a private spa pool. All the other amenities are also good, with automatic laundry equipment and a drying room. You can shop here, hire small boats and fishing tackle to use on the sheltered river alongside. There is also a children's play area. No pets at this camp please. Your hosts Jenny and Tony Lyons. All sites are $9 per person. 🖼 $15 each, 🖼.

49. Motuoapa Motor Camp
13 Parekarangaranga Street, Motuoapa, RD 2 Turangi (07) 386-7162 (phone & fax)

On the main route and 8km from Turangi, this camp is just across the road from Lake Taupo. There is a total of 56 power sites but probably half of these are occupied by long-term residents. The amenities provide the basics and have recently been refurbished. The kitchen also has TV. BBQs are obtainable. Enjoy the fun bikes (tandem and triandum) or the dinghy that can be hired here. No dogs on the site please. Your hosts Phil and Val Bedingfield. It costs $8 per person for a site with power, or $7 for tents.🖼 $12.50 per person to $17.50 (the de luxe).

50. Parklands Motor Home Park

Cnr S Hwy 1 and Arahori Street, PO Box 142 Turangi (07) 386-7515 (fax 07 386-7509)

This is a glossy complex with provision for up to 22 level mobile home sites. All the amenities are immaculate. The motor lodge has other guest accommodation, including studio units. There is plenty to do here, with tennis court, spa and sauna, swimming pool and putting green. You can arrange other adventures including white-water rafting, scenic flights and fishing trips. There is even a heliport. Parklands has a licensed restaurant and bar. The Turangi shopping centre is opposite. Your hosts Ann and Alan. Tent sites are $15 for two persons or $18 with power. ▦ $65 for two.

51. Turangi Holiday Park

Ohuanga Road, Turangi–PO Box 202 Turangi (07) 386-8754 (phone & fax)

Space and privacy for campers to set up house. There are level single or double sites with flowerbeds and trees. It is serviced by a very functional kitchen and BBQs in the grounds. There is a combined dining and table-tennis hall. The ablution block has good appointments, but some sites may be rather distant from facilities. The laundry also has a drying room. Other accommodation is plentiful, in army-style cabins or on-site caravans. This park has roomy sites and a volley ball court. Your new hosts Phil and Val. Camping is from $8 per person to $9 with power. ⌾ $35. ▭ $15 per person.

52. Club Habitat

Ohuanga Road, Turangi–PO Box 174 Turangi (07) 386-7492 (fax 07 386-0106)

Here is an all-in experience for the younger set. Adventures of all sorts are arranged from the lodge. Plans are in hand for a gymnasium and swimming pool. In addition to the modern camping facilities (22 power sites and 100 tent sites) the lodge itself offers a spacious sunny lounge and dining room/ restaurant. Everything is clean and new with quality appointments. Spa pools and sauna are available for a small charge. The sites are level and well groomed. There is a dump station. Your host Greg Marks. Tent sites are $7 per person, or with power $18 for two. There is a large range of other accommodation, from share rooms to motels, starting at $12 per person.

53 Oasis Motels & Caravan Park

S Hwy 41 Tokaanu, PO Box 266 Turangi (07) 386-8569 (fax 07 386-0694)

This thermal region is at the southern fringes of Lake Taupo and 5km west of Turangi. With all the advantages of hot pools within the park, there is also a general store and restaurant and takeaway meals right here. For campers there are 28 sites with power and 20 tent sites. The sites are flat with a rural aspect and each power site has a tap and a sump. A homely kitchen-dining area is comfortable but not streamlined. The ablutions provide great showers in a new attractive setting. There is automatic equipment in the laundry and a drying room is available. The range of pools, both for swimming and soaking in thermal waters, are popular here. It is also conveniently situated for skiing, fishing and boating. The family pet is allowed here too. Your hosts Tom and Suzanne Wright. Prices are $6.50 per person for a tent site and $8 with power. 🏨 and 🏠.

54. Riverhideaway Motor Camp
Main Road, PO Box 63 Taumarunui (07) 895-5976

Country camping on a small scale just 3km south of Taumarunui. On the bank of the Wanganui River there are some pretty tree-studded sites, 28 with power. Cabins and self-contained units are available. All the usual facilities are provided, plus a dump station. Cost for camping is $8.50 per person, or with power $18 for two persons. This is a Taumarunui District Council camp, which we understand is pet friendly.

55. Gardean Goodstead Holiday Park
CMB 98, Owhango–Taumarunui (07) 895-4774 (phone & fax)

A mini-camp incorporated into a small accommodation complex, the **Field Park** offers 5 sites with power. There is also a hostel and a tourist flat. Placed on the outskirts of the mountain region, it is within commuting distance of the skifields. Here the children have a treehouse, swings, slide and trampoline. The hostel provides amenities. Some have a small charge. There is free use of a drying room. Your hosts Ian and Diana Wellsted offer discounts for group bookings, otherwise tent sites are $5 per person, with power $14 for two. Hostel $12 per person. 🏨 $80 for 6 people.

56. Eivin's Lodge & Motor Camp
S Hwy 47, PO Box 3370 Tongariro (07) 386-8062 (fax 07 386-7659)

For the ski enthusiast who is not afraid to camp all year round! There is also lodge accommodation here. Located between Turangi and The Chateau, it is ideally placed for alpine holidays. Camp sites are not large and there are only 12 power sites and a similar number for tents. There are adequate amenities plus a drying room. Meals are available at the cafe/restaurant and there is a pleasant lounge. On the site there is a store and a petrol station. Ski hire and boat hire are offered here, where a nearby lake promises great trout fishing. No pets please. Your hosts Lorraine and Eivin Lynghaug. Tent sites are $8 per person and power sites are $9. 🛏 $30 for two. Share rooms are available in the Lodge.

57. Mangahuia Campground
S Hwy 47, Whakapaka–Department of Conservation (07) 892-3729

Located approximately 4km past the turnoff to Whakapapa Village, on the left-hand side, Mangahuia is a self-registration campground. Toilets and cold water are available. No dogs are permitted here. The cost to camp is $4 per night per adult.

58. Whakapapa Holiday Park
Tongariro National Park, Private Bag Mount Ruapehu–Department of Conservation (07) 892-3897 (phone & Fax)

Right on the mountain (follow Bruce Road), slightly below The Chateau, this park is nestled among mountain beech forest. Sites are very appealing, with ample space and privacy and soothed by the waters of an alpine stream. With 45 power sites, plenty of tent sites plus a range of other accommodation there are good services here for your comfort. The amenities building is centrally located with good kitchen and dining facilities, a well appointed laundry and a drying room. The ablutions have provision for paraplegic use. There is a dump point here. The Whakapapa Store is open daily. Because this is a National Park and holiday resort area, no pets are permitted. You may take mountain excursions, trips to the crater lake or enjoy bush walks or golf. This is the winter playground of the North Island. Meals and other services are in close proximity. Your hosts Jane and John Solly. Tent sites will cost you $8 per person, or with power $10. 🏠 $33 for two. 🏠 $50 for two. Lodge $16.50 per person.

59. Discovery Motel Cabin & Caravan Park
S Hwy 47, PO Box 55 National Park (07) 892-2744 (fax 07 892-2603)

Another link in the chain serving the adjacent alpine area. Only 7km from The Chateau this is on National Park Road. There is a basic services block with a rather curious layout that almost encircles a lovely swimming pool and two spa pools. There is a laundry and two drying rooms. Ski hire is available and a licensed restaurant and lounge bar are part of this complex. Your host John Campbell. Choose from a range of accommodation or camping at $8 per person. There are tent sites or gravelled sites with power .🏠.

60. Ski Haus
Carroll Street, PO Box 29 National Park (07) 892-2854 (phone & fax)

This is mainly lodge accommodation with a token number of sites for campers who can share the facilities available in the lodge. Supplies and takeaway meals can be purchased just across the road. Your host Murray. All camping is at $7 per person or $12 in the backpacker lodge.

61. Raetihi Motor Camp
S Hwy 4, Raetihi (06) 385-4176 (fax 06 385-4059)

On pleasantly sheltered grounds dominated by the manager's house, here are 34 power sites and plenty of tent sites. The amenities are not for the fussy, being rather vintage and forgotten, but hot water is plentiful and there is use of a drying room. There are quite a few sporting options here. Your hosts Bob and Mary Grave. We were unable to get prices.

62. Ohakune Motor Camp
5 Moore Street, Ohakune (06) 385-8561

On the other (southern) side of Mount Ruapehu the country town of Ohakune is an alternative gateway to the ski areas. Only 20 minutes from Turoa skifield, this camp is also just a short bush walk to the town centre. The grounds are very appealing, with a babbling stream on one border and a new mini golf to try. The BBQ garden has a hand-made table that will cater for 12 people. There is a good kitchen, plus a new dining/TV room, heated and cosy, or use the verandah or BBQs. There are well kept ablutions and a dump station. An automatic laundry is provided. Children have a play area. An inviting camp where there are no seasonal price changes. Your friendly hosts are Noel Sheppard and Sue Davis. Tent sites are $7 per person. Power sites are $18 for two. and costs $16 per person.

 ### 63.   Mangawhero Campground
Ohakune Mountain Road, Ohakune–Department of Conservation
(06) 385-8578

Mangawhero is a self-registration campground, located on Ohakune Mountain Road, approximately 1.5km past the Dept of Conservation Ranger Station, on the left-hand side of the road. Toilets with wash basins and cold water are available. No dogs permitted. The cost for camping is $4 per night per adult.

64. Waiouru Welcome Inn
2 Ngauruhoe Street, Waiouru (06) 387-6247 (fax 06 387-6395)

At the Waiouru-Ohakune junction this spot offers a choice for the travel weary. Cabins, motels and a pleasant well-hedged lawn setting for your mobile home. You will appreciate "The Fast Lane" restaurant here which serves meals from breakfast to dinner with efficient courtesy. This mid-North Island town is on the fringe of Volcanic Plateau with dramatic landscapes unfolding along the Desert Road. There is an interesting military museum here and the town services a military base camp. No pets here please. Your hosts Barry and Frances Hodgson. Costs range from tent sites $7 per person, power sites $8 per person or $9 per person for extra-large vans. $15. $65 for two.

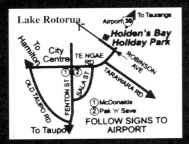

GISBORNE AND THE HAWKES BAY DIRECTORY

Key to locations and map of Gisborne and Hawkes Bay. Starts in Gisborne, leaving the coast and going inland to encompass camping in the Urewera National Park then returning to the coast and the vicinity of Mahia Peninsula. At Wairoa continues on S Hwy 2 until reaching the junction with the Napier-Taupo Road. Goes inland on this road as far as Tarawera. Back to the coast and the resort areas of Hawkes Bay, then heading south to finish inland at Woodville.

Gisborne	1.	Showgrounds Park Motor Camp
Gisborne	2.	Waikanae Beach Holiday Park
Inland from Gisborne	3.	Donneraille Park
Whirinaki Forest Park	4.	Mangamate Falls (DoC)
Lake Waikaremoana	5.	Waikaremoana Motor Camp (DoC)
Lake Waikaremoana	6.	Lake Waikaremoana (DoC)
Tuai–Waikaremoana	7.	Kokako Camping Ground
Morere	8.	Morere Camping Ground
Mahia Beach	9.	Mahia Beach Motor Camp
Opoutama	10.	Blue Bay Motor Camp
Wairoa	11.	Riverside Motor Camp
Northern Hawkes Bay	12.	Tutira Recreational Reserve
Napier north	13.	Waipatiki Beach Motor Camp
Eskdale	14.	Eskdale Holiday Park
Tarawera	15.	Tarawera Tavern & Caravan Park
Inland from Napier	16.	Riverlands Outback Retreat
Napier	17.	Westshore Holiday Park

GISBORNE–HAWKES BAY

Napier	18.	Kennedy Park Complex
Taradale	19.	Taradale Holiday Park
Clive	20.	Clive Motor Camp
Hastings	21.	Hastings Holiday Park
Hastings	22.	Raceview Motel & Holiday Park
Havelock North	23.	Arataki Holiday Park
Te Awanga	24.	Sullivans Motor Camp
Clifton Beach	25.	Clifton Beach Domain Motor Camp
Waimarama	26.	Waimarama Holiday Park
Tikokino	27.	Tikokino Hotel & Caravan Park
Southern Hawkes Bay	28.	Kairakau Beach
Southern Hawkes Bay	29.	Pourerere Beach
Aramoana	30.	Aramoana Beach Camp
Aramoana	31.	Two Macs Seaside Camp
Aramoana south	32.	Blackhead Beach
via Waipukurau	33.	Porangahau Beach Camp
via Dannevirke	34.	Herbertville Seaview Holiday Park
Akitio	35.	Akitio Motor Camp
Waipawa	36.	Waipawa Motor Camp
Waipukurau	37.	Waipukurau Holiday Park
Dannevirke	38.	Dannevirke Motor Camp
Woodville	39.	Woodville Caravan Stop
Woodville	40.	Coppermine Caravan Camp

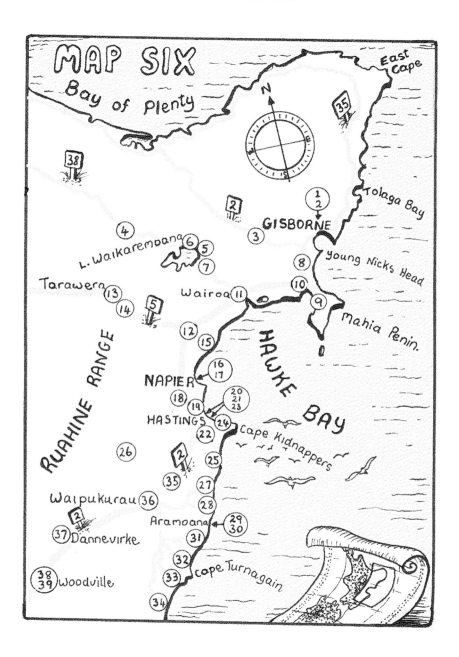

Chapter 6

GISBORNE AND HAWKES BAY

Nature was very kind to the neighbouring regions of Gisborne and Hawkes Bay. The sunny, equable climate combined with easy terrain and good soils were quickly recognised as very productive for horticulture. Both areas produce fruit and now have well established vineyards.

Gisborne, to the north, is a city with a busy atmosphere and a wonderful surf beach but five minute's easy stroll from its heart. It lays claim to be the most easterly city in the world, and the first to see the sun rise each day. This sunny coast has less humidity than the north of New Zealand and is ideal for outdoor living.

Lake Waikaremoana or "The sea of rippling waters" is inland from the coastal town of Wairoa, within the Urewera National Park, the largest unspoiled native forest in the North Island. A perfect destination for those looking for tranquillity and the chance to explore the many walking tracks or fish the clear waters. Yes, you can camp here too.

The hub of Hawkes Bay are the twin cities of Hastings and Napier. The sunshine hours are considerable, with high summer temperatures. Although the cities are only about 20km apart, each has a personality of its own. Napier, with its Marine Parade and avenue of stately Norfolk pines is an entertainment centre for locals and visitors alike. Almost completely rebuilt after the devastating earthquake of 1931, it now also attracts attention for its art-deco architecture dating from that era. It has a busy port and the smart shopping centre is just a stone's throw from the Pacific coast with its glorious beaches.

Probably the foremost orchard area of New Zealand, Hastings appeals with its abundance of flowers and trees. Enjoy the vineyards, with wine tasting and perhaps a meal at an adjoining restaurant to compliment the delights of the wine. The "Fruit bowl of New Zealand", the Hastings district offers fresh fruit in season direct from the neighbourhood orchards.

For a change of scenery, take a trip to Cape Kidnappers. This is one of the main gannet sanctuaries of the world where you can view the giant birds at close range, so include this in your holiday plans.

Coastal, bushland, urban and wayside–this is an area well endowed with camping spots. Enjoy your place in the sun.

GISBORNE & HAWKES BAY

1. Showgrounds Park Motor Camp
20 Main Road, S Hwy 2, Makaraka–Gisborne (06) 867-5299

Administered by the Poverty Bay A & P Association this is an extensive level park with a rural atmosphere. Every January there is a weekend of Dog Trials at the park, and other regular events may also occur. Apart from on these occasions there should be plenty of space. A truck park is available. There is a huge kitchen, and rather utilitarian ablutions provided. The toilets are in a separate area. There are automatic washing and drying machines in the laundry. A phone booth is in the grounds, but no shopping. Country camping just inland from Gisborne city. The managers here are Willy and Nicola Rogers. Camp charges $10.50 for two persons. 📠 $11.25 per person.

2. Waikanae Beach Holiday Park
Grey Street, PO Box 747 Gisborne (06) 867-5634 (fax 06 867-9765)

The traditional Kiwi family holiday. Sunshine, surf beach and sociability. This is a holiday complex directly accessible to beautiful Waikanae Beach and within a few minutes stroll to the commercial centre of Gisborne. Sites are level with most enjoying a shady aspect and securely fenced and hedged around the perimeter. There are open spaces for volley ball or similar pursuits. With over 170 sites (most with power) this is a popular venue. The amenities blocks function well, with plentiful hot water and vanity areas in the ablutions. The kitchen and laundry are well equipped. Hard tennis courts are provided and there are bikes, surfing and boogie boards for hire. There may be entertainment in summer. Trampolines, TV and video games are here too. No pets please. Your stand-in manager and host is Lesley Greaves. Tent sites are $14 for two people, or $16 with power . 📠 and 🏧.

3. Donneraille Park
Off S Hwy 36 southwest of Gisborne

Not for long-term camping, this is a freedom site in a tranquil valley. Look for the signpost about 35km inland from Gisborne. Approached from over a bridge, this has the feel of a canyon with the Hangaroa River on one border. Environmentally delightful, the sites are level and grassy with a choice of shady trees. Cold water and flush toilets are the only amenities.

4. Mangamate Falls
In the Whirinaki Forest Park, near Minginui (07)366-5641

 A self-registration campsite off the road to Minginui via S Hwy 38, east of Murupara. Secluded sites adjoin the confluence of the Whirinaki and the Mangamate Stream. Facilities include BBQs and composting toilets. Excellent fly fishing in season and easy access to magnificent bush walks and sightseeing in the Park. For further information contact the Dept of Conservation, Te Ikawhenua Visitor Centre in Murupara (where you can apply for a permit to bring your dog), or The Map and Track Shop, Tourism Rotorua, (07) 349-1845 (phone & fax) can provide details of this and other local conservation attractions.

 ### 5. Waikaremoana Motor Camp
Lake Waikaremoana, Private Bag 2058 Wairoa–Department of Conservation (06) 837-3826

A modern serviced camping ground on the shores of Lake Waikaremoana with caravan and camp sites, cabins and ample parking. There are petrol pumps here and a boat-launching ramp. A shop has a good range of foodstuffs. Visit the nearby Dept of Conservation Visitor Centre at Aniwaniwa. See at first hand threatened species such as the kereru (native pigeon). The area abounds in superb bush and waterfalls. The camp amenities are bright and airy with attractive kitchen divided into bays. There is an adjoining dining area with great views. Some of the appliances are metered. There are excellent ablutions with paraplegic suites. The laundry provides automatic equipment and some freezer space. A covered verandah gives access and has a card phone. There are 25 power sites and 25 tent sites plus other accommodation. No animals here please. A tent site is $6.50 per person, or with power $7.50. Booking is advisable in the busy season but extra charges and restrictions may apply for the use of credit cards and cheques.

 ### 6. Lake Waikaremoana
Department of Conservation (06) 867-8531

Lake Waikaremoana is a focal point for boating, fishing and the "great walk". The winding road which reaches Ruatahuna is unsealed but the glorious bush and glimpses of the lake are a bonus. The Department of Conservation has a number of campsites along the road including **Te Taita, Omakora, Mokau Landing, Aniwaniwa** and **Rosie Bay.** Those wanting strenuous activity can find many satisfying climbs, or more relaxed short walks. Hunting is available all year round with some restrictions. There are many picnic spots around with easy access to the lake edge where swimming, boating, kayaking and fishing can be enjoyed.

7. Kokako Camping Ground
S Hwy 38 Tuai–Waikaremoana (06) 837-3777

On the approach road to Lake Waikaremoana, this is a roadside camp with reasonably private camping bays and picnic tables. The grounds are nominally flat and a bit uncultivated. There are 11 power sites available and Fishermans Hut will sleep five people. The toilets and showers are in separate rooms, nicely lined. The office/tearooms are open daily. Your hosts the Traill family and Angela Coleman. Tent sites are $4 per person, or with power $6.

8. Morere Tearooms Campground
S Hwy 2 Morere (06) 837-8792

Between Wairoa and Gisborne this little tree-dotted area is alongside the tearooms, which also have a NZ Post agency. Predominantly this has bed and breakfast or tourist-flat accommodation. The amenities are minimal. Across the road the Morere Hot Springs and Scenic Reserve are well worth a visit. All sites $16 for two.🏠 $12 per person.

9. Mahia Beach Motels and Motor Camp
Moana Drive, RD 8 Nuhaka–Mahia Beach (06) 837-5830

The hub of Mahia Beach, with a general store and office which can provide takeaway meals. The camp is level and adjacent to a beach with an open aspect. The accommodation buildings may be better served than the campers for amenities. The veteran ablutions are well painted and tidy. There is a large games hall and the laundry has automatic washers and dryer. You can hire bikes here. Your hosts Allan and Joyce Cox have reduced rates out of season.

10. Blue Bay Motor Camp
Main Road, Opoutama RD 8 Nuhaka (06) 837-5867 (phone & fax)

A popular pine tree clad camp with a large capacity and a secluded aspect. The underfoot carpet of pine needles and sand leads directly through to the large sweep of Opoutama Beach. At the entrance there is a general store, well stocked and specialising in fresh baked hot bread. There is a card phone available. The amenities come under heavy use in the holiday season and there is a communal kitchen with freezer and fridge. A rather spartan TV room is alongside a hall for table tennis and playing pool. The ablutions and toilets are in separate buildings with 5 minute showers, plus an outdoor hot/cold shower. The laundry has automatic machines. Those who enjoy a shady site and a sociable atmosphere should find this appealing. It might require some alternative cooking and toilet facilities when the camp is busy. Your hosts Roy and Thelma Baxter. Around 120 tent sites are $8.50 per person and 125 sites with power are $8.80 per person. 🏠.

11. Riverside Motor Camp
19 Marine Parade, PO Box 54 Wairoa (06) 838-6301 (fax 06 838-8874)

Gateway to beautiful Lake Waikaremoana in the Urewera National Park, Wairoa is also a pleasant coastal town within the "sunshine belt" of Hawkes Bay. Very pleasant camping awaits you here on level grounds alongside the river (great for water skiing), yet conveniently close to all shopping and alongside a public swimming pool. A play area is provided. This is very good fishing territory and fishing tours can be arranged. The communal lounge is inviting, smart and comfortable with carpet and a TV/stereo nook. There is a sheltered balcony outside to enjoy the summer evenings. A spacious kitchen has microwave and fridges and there is a BBQ garden under shady trees. The clean ablutions have metered showers. The laundry is well equipped with automatic machines, washbasket and ironing facilities. This well maintained camp offers a welcome from your new hosts Caty and Barry Gay. Tent sites are $7 per person, or with power (and taps) $8. 🖾, and 🖾 .

12. Tutira Recreational Reserve
Off S Hwy 2 north of Napier

A popular free camping spot around a lake. Power boats may not be used here, but sails or oars are OK. The lovely setting has resident swans and willow trees. There is tap water, flush toilets and long-drop toilets on the far side of the lake.

13. Waipatiki Beach Motor Camp
6 Moray Place, Tamatea–Napier (06) 836-6075 (fax 06 844-4806)

Away from mainstream camps, this is a coastal camp some 40km north of Napier. Access is by way of a secondary road and unsealed for most of the journey. The camp is set on a low plateau overlooking the bay and lagoon and has only 13 power sites, though there are plenty for tents. It is a most attractive beach, golden sand and fairly sheltered. This is a summer season camp, which is closed after Easter until Labour Weekend. The amenities are not lavish, but are well kept. There is a big freezer in the kitchen, but minimal cooking elements. There is a dump point here. Your hosts Bill and Anne Perry. All camping is a$8 per person for one night. There are discounts for longer stays. 🖾.

14. Eskdale Caravan Park
Yule Road, Eskdale, PO Box 170 Bay View (06) 836-6864 (phone & fax)

This soothing site with the Esk River forming a boundary is just a short distance from S Hwy 5 as it winds inland to Taupo. The grounds are sheltered and have lovely poplar and willow trees for shade. There are some roomy sites for motorhomes here. The park itself is fairly modest, with an adequately equipped kitchen, cooking by hotplates or microwave and a fridge/freezer. The ablutions are not extensive, but feature a separate paraplegic unit. Use of the washing machine is free and there is a dryer. A coin phone is available. Your host Leonie Gale.

15. Tarawera Tavern & Caravan Park
S Hwy 5 Tarawera–Private Bag, Taupo

Almost midway between Napier and Taupo on the connecting road this camp has a tearooms as well as restaurant meals in the tavern and a camp store. There is a hot springs area nearby. The setting is rural with shady trees and flat sites. There are modern ablutions and laundry, but no kitchen. A BBQ and a trampoline are available. Adventure trekking trips can be arranged here. Your hosts Dave and Moeawa Hall. Two people can camp here for $8. It is $10 for campervans and ⬛ $12 (per two people).

16. Riverlands Outback Retreat
McVicar Road, RD 2 Napier (06) 834-9756 (fax 06 834-9724)

Seek this out for something different in a holiday experience. Country activities offering here include white-water rafting, horse trekking, excursions for the adventurous are provided, or just escape to this working; sheep, cattle and deer farm. The location is about 55km from Napier, off the Napier/Taupo Road. Be prepared to negotiate a 4km stretch of rather difficult road, rising steeply to the little plateau that houses the office and the stables. The camping area is another 1km on and occupies a sheltered valley site. The amenities are grouped in one block with a good kitchen plus plenty of indoor recreation options. There is a games room with table tennis alongside a large, carpeted and comfortably furnished lounge. This has a pot belly fireplace, TV, video and piano. The showers are not the most modern, but in clean condition. You can enjoy a sauna and a spa here too. The laundry has automatic machines. An on-site shop is provided and the grounds are attractively landscaped with swimming pool and plenty of BBQs. Choose lodge accommodation, a self-contained unit or camping, all beside the Mohaka River. You can obtain a package deal for the "adventures" on offer. Enquire for prices. This camp is dog friendly. Your hosts Pauline and Bruce McVicar.⬛

17. Westshore Holiday Park
1 Main Road, Westshore–Napier (06) 835-9456

The swimming beach for Napier is nearby. This modest-sized camp is also a good spot to take time out in a friendly setting. You will find about 70 sites (46 with power) and these are grouped in small sections with hedges and trees providing privacy. This is home base to some regular occupants with individual gardens and a penchant for fishing. You might also like to try your luck. An indoor spa pool and a TV room are provided. Children have a play area. There are good amenities with fridges and freezers available. The ablutions are well kept and the laundry has automatic machines. A takeaway food outlet, a tavern and petrol supplies are opposite the camp. Wine trails and local activities can be arranged here. During the holiday season it is preferred that you do not bring pets. Your hosts Brian and Shirley and Ann. A family rate of $22 may apply to tent sites, which cost $7.50 per person. Power sites $8 per person. 🔲 $25 for two people. 🔲 $40 for two.

18. Kennedy Park Complex
Storkey Street, Napier (06) 843-9126 (fax 06 843-6113)

Holiday with all the extras. This combined camp, conference facility and accommodation complex features a BYO restaurant complete with outdoor balcony. There are over 200 camp sites, most with power. The setting is beautiful with shelter trees and shrubs and an extensive rose garden. Very well provided with facilities, the camp also includes paraplegic appointments. There is a TV lounge, recreation room and an inviting new swimming pool, trampolines and a "Krypton Factor" course for the youngsters. Something will always be happening here, and it is close to central Napier. Your host Terry Cairnes. Prices range from $16 for two persons for a tent site to $18 with power. There is a large range of other accommodation.

19. Taradale Holiday Park
470 Gloucester Street, Taradale–Napier (06) 844-2732 (phone & fax)

If you want to divide your time between Hastings and Napier and enjoy a well serviced location, Taradale is a desirable spot. There is excellent local shopping and the Hawkes Bay Polytechnic is opposite. This is a spacious camp with a public park and river adjacent. A golf course is nearby. Two kitchens provide lots of tables and big refrigerators as well as the usual cooking equipment. Some basic items can be bought on site. There are very good unisex bathroom facilities. The laundry has automatic washing and dryer. A coin phone is available. The grounds are well laid out with abundant pepper trees and gardens settled by long-term residents. Your host Norm Hard. Around 100 sites in all, there are 60 with power. Tent site $14 for four. Power site $15 for two. There is other accommodation, including a 48-bed lodge at $15 each person.

20. Clive Motor Camp

Farndon Road, Clive (06) 870-0609 (fax 06 870-0292)

A pleasant dormitory-style camp between Hastings and Napier. For the camper there is good shade and level sites for tents. There is a slightly "busy" aspect due to the well established long-term occupants. Bring your own provisions as there is no shop on site, but excellent facilities are available in the kitchen. There is also an outdoor BBQ area with tables and seating. The ablutions could be under pressure at busy times. Tennis courts and public swimming baths are available in the adjacent Farndon Park. A good place for the fruit gatherer in the heart of orchard country. Your hosts Jim and Sandra Thorne. All camping is $8 per person or $13 for two.

21. Hastings Holiday Park

Windsor Avenue, Hastings (06) 878-6692

A thoughtfully planned park to make holidays easy for the disabled. Facilities are of the latest "wheelchair friendly" design, both for campers and with purpose-built chalets to rent. Families will enjoy the adjacent Fantasy Land, skating rink, tennis courts and swimming pool, a highlight for the children. With around 180 spacious sites (over 100 with power) and dotted with lovely trees this is a charming setting. A special winter camping area is located at the rear of the services block, and most sites have a sump, tap and rubbish bin. There are excellent kitchen facilities with individual cold boxes. The ablutions are attractive and practical, for easy paraplegic use. There are automatic laundry machines. Quite a special place, with hosts Norma and Vin Unverricht. A dump point is provided.🔲 and 🔳 . All camping is $8 per person. Other accommodation ranges from $35.

22. Raceview Motel & Holiday Park

307 Gascoigne Street, Hastings (06) 878-8837

This is the closest camp to central Hastings and is adjacent to the racecourse. Not a large camp, but with a big swimming pool and toddlers pool. All the usual services plus waste disposal in a rather functional setting. The games room has table tennis tables. This camp is pet friendly. Some restorative work here would not go amiss. Your hosts Muriel and Ivan Mapson. All camp sites are $13 for two persons. 🅿 and 🔳.

23. Arataki Holiday Park
139 Arataki Road, Havelock North (06) 877-7479 (phone & fax)

Sweet as honey for the family in holiday mood. So many things to do without leaving the park. There is a covered swimming pool (heated in winter), crazy golf, and a hive of activities for children. The office/shop area has a camp library and phone. There are 100 power sites and 30 for tents. Most sites have trees and shrubs, with fruit trees to harvest in season. There is a good kitchen with cool lockers and plenty of BBQs in the grounds. The ablutions include paraplegic facilities. Automatic laundry equipment is provided. As well as camping, a 72-bed lodge and other accommodation units are available. There is a dump station here. Modern conference facilities are also on site. Camping's a breeze here with hosts Brian Phillips, Joy and Fred Mildenhall. Tent sites $9 per person. Power sites $9.50 ⛺ and 🚐 $40 for two.🏠 $57 for two.

24. Sullivans Motor Camp
52 Kuku Street, Te Awanga–Hastings (06) 875-0334

A coastal camp east of Hastings and great for the surfcasting fisherman. There is safe swimming in the lagoon. Around 100 level sites have sealed roads and reasonable privacy. There are wonderful spots adjacent to the beach. Dining and BBQ facilities are provided, but the camp store is only open during the Xmas holidays. The camp is well laid out and has a jetty. Ample parking is provided for boats and trailers. There are 75 sites, but not a lot of kitchen equipment. Other facilities include an automatic laundry. Your hosts Toby and Peggy Sullivan. Tent sites $12.50 for two. Power sites $14 for two. ⛺ and 🚐 $25.

25. Clifton Beach Domain Motor Camp
Clifton Beach, RD2, Hastings (06) 875-0263

En route to the gannet colony at Cape Kidnappers this is a popular spot notable for its sheltered beach and panoramic views. An offshore reef harbours green-lipped mussels. There is room for 180 campers, most with power, plus some water's-edge cabins. Boating facilities are provided. In addition to a good ablution block (with reasonable disabled facilities) there are outdoor showers. The kitchen has four full size stoves. Laundry equipment is plentiful, both washers and dryers. On site is a camp store and a pay phone, plus a camp library. Within 20 km of Hastings and Napier this coastal route is away from main thoroughfares. Book first if you plan to be there between Labour weekend and Easter. Your hosts here are Mike and Majorie Gaston. 🚐. Tent sites $12 for two. Power sites $12.50. Check out the backpacker rates.

26. Waimarama Holiday Park
Airini Road, PO Waimarama (06) 874-6836

Please contact direct for further details.

27. Tikokino Hotel & Caravan Park
S Hwy 50, Tikokino (06) 856-5881

12 power sites at $10 per person. Tent sites $6 per person. Hotel and bed and breakfast accommodation.

28. Kairakau Beach
South– Hawkes Bay

Beach camping, pioneer style. Access via Elsthorpe.

29. Pourerere Beach Caravan Park
P.O Box 88 Waipawa. ph (06) 857-8802

New owner, Dick Grenfeld. There are 30 power sites, $13 for two people. Details came in too late to include more data."Watch this space!"next year.

Note: The connecting road from this coast to Waipawa is to be avoided at sunset. Visibility is very difficult at this time of day. Otherwise the road is an easy pastoral drive.

30. Aramoana Beach Camp
Aramoana (06) 857-8651

On the coast north of Porangahau there is a stretch of shoreline with a number of spots to camp. Aramoana is about midway between these camps. There are no power sites and no kitchen, but hot showers and flush toilets are available. This is a small camp of level sites between the surrounding hills. Please phone Betty Scott at number listed above for further details.

31. Two Macs Seaside Camp
Aramoana, RD 1 Waipawa (06) 857-7830

The dominant camp at Aramoana, this is a generous sized camp with a central "village" of caravans with mini gardens and boat shelters. Casual camping is separate from this area   and has a lovely wilderness appeal with sea views and plenty of sunshine. Around 100 sites have power. It is not lavishly endowed with amenities, but there are metered showers, four extra toilets have recently been installed and there is a limited paraplegic facility. You will find a sweets, icecream and drinks store here and you can buy a newspaper. Other supplies and petrol should be brought with you. The approach road through this rural area has only 7km of unsealed surface. Your hosts Neville and Pauline Green. Tent sites are $10.50 for two people, or with power $12.50.

32. Blackhead Beach
South– Hawkes Bay, south of Aramoana

There are a few power sites here, but otherwise almost no facilities.

33. Porangahau Beach Camp
via Waipukurau

For the pioneer who wants a stretch of uninhabited golden sandy beach. Free camping here. Civilisation has brought you toilets and cold water, otherwise be self-sufficient. North of Cape Turnagain.

* Beacon Road Holiday Park, Porongahau–see p 182.

34. Herbertville Seaview Holiday Park
via Dannevirke (06) 374-3558

On a sealed road 68km east of Dannevirke and north of Akitio, this is also a hotel. The camping area has a typical rural look, with a flat paddock and some hedges and trees. The 'country pub' will serve meals and has a beer garden. There is a basic kitchen for campers, with plenty of fridge space. The showers are comfortable with 20 cent meters. No dryer is supplied in the laundry. Although this is close to the coast it is not right on the beach. There are tennis courts nearby. Your hosts Dave and Val Sunnex. A plentiful supply of power sites, and tent sites are all at $5 per person. 🏕️ and 🏚️, plus a cottage.

35. Akitio Motor Camp
Southern Hawkes Bay (06) 374-3524

Just a dot on the map, Akitio is almost in the Wairarapa and right on the coast. It is a long drive from Dannevirke, some of it on metal roads. There is no coast road in this area. If you want a fairly isolated spot this is right on the beach. There is no kitchen or laundry, but the ablution block is a recent addition. A Tararua Council camp with resident caretakers. Few power points, but all camping is $4 per person.

36. Waipawa Motor Camp
Harker Street, Waipawa (06) 857-8976

A well groomed country setting with plenty of space to enjoy. The camp is friendly with a warm welcome, but minimal facilities. If you are reasonably self sufficient the few amenities provided will be adequate. Just a clean, quiet, rural spot in close proximity to a trout-fishing river, swimming baths and tennis courts. There is shopping conveniently near to the camp. Your hosts Norman and Nora Ward. Tent sites are $8 for up to two people, or $9 with power.

37. Waipukurau Holiday Park
River Terrace, Waipukurau (06) 858-8184

In a typically rural New Zealand township, this camp offers nice level sites adjacent to the Tukituki River for fishing and swimming. Hand feed the deer. There is a shop and service station, which also has supplies. Visit the historic cottage. The kitchen has TV and includes microwave cooking; this opens to a dining area with comfy seating. The ablutions are clean and tidy, but are not over supplied. There are adequate laundry facilities and a dump station. Your hosts are Anne and John McDermott. Tent site $7 per person. Power site $8 per person . 🗔 $28 for two. 🖩 $48 for two.

38. Dannevirke Motor Camp
29 George Street, Dannevirke (06) 374-7625

Not for hunters! This little nature reserve has camping amidst friendly animals and birds. Outdoor dining and BBQ facilities are in the Bird Park. All the usual amenities are provided with a good kitchen (no microwave) but other useful equipment. The ablutions and laundry were in average condition. TV is not supplied. There is a dump station here and shopping, petrol and banking are just five minutes away. Tennis, croquet and bowls are options here. The aspect is peaceful and well shaded. Pets may be accepted by prior arrangement. The new owners here are Deane and Jayne Garvey. Both power and tent sites are $12 for two people. 🗔 $18 for two.

39. Woodville Caravan Stop
Woodville Rugby Club, Main Road South, Woodville

Park in the car park of the local Rugby Club. There are 4 power sites in an open paddock. There is a toilet block kept locked. The key is available at the Woodville Motordrome.

40. Coppermine Caravan Park
Coppermine Road, RD 2 Woodville (06) 376-4863

Feeling frayed around the edges? Relax in the country where this caravan park is 15km from Woodville. The camp is also a farm where the shearing quarters have come into use as bunk rooms. It is simple, homely camping with level grassy sites and a natural swimming hole in the creek. You will find adequate appliances in the kitchen, including fridge and freezer. There are clean ablutions with new toilets and showers. The laundry has a free washing machine. Light the chip heater for your hot water. This is a nice tidy low-key holiday spot with both power and tent sites and a bunk room. No dogs here please. Your host N.Galloway. All sites and share accommodation are $6 per person.

Beacon Road Holiday Park
RD3 Porongahau (06) 8555-281 (Phone & fax)

New camping ground set in a park of mature trees, 50km from Waipukurau on the East Coast. A couple of minutes walk to the beach and adjacent to the golf course and bowling green. The facilities include a disabled suite.There are just 50 sites, which cost $7 per person for power or $6 per person for a tent site. $25 per night.

TARANAKI AND MANAWATU DIRECTORY

Key to locations and maps in Taranaki and Manawatu. Starts at Mokau and follows the coastal route through New Plymouth and the seaward side of Mt Taranaki. At Hawera goes inland east of the mountain to Stratford. Continues up S Hwy 43 as far as Tahora. Returns to Hawera, with a deviation to Lake Rotorangi. Continues south along the coast to Wanganui going inland to Marton and Bulls. Veers north on S Hwy 1 to the Taihape district. Back to the mouth of the Rangitikei River at Tangimoana. Returns inland to finish at Palmerston North.

Location	No.	Camp
Mokau	1.	Seaview Motor Camp & Tearooms
Mokau	2.	Riviera Motor Camp
Urenui	3.	Wai-iti Beach Camp
Urenui	4.	Urenui Domain Motor Camp
Waitara	5.	Onaero Domain Camp
Waitara	6.	Marine Park Motor Camp
New Plymouth	7.	Gateway Motel Campervan Park
New Plymouth	8.	Princes Tourist Court
New Plymouth	9.	Fitzroy Beach Motor Camp
New Plymouth	10.	Hookner Park Motor Camp
New Plymouth	11.	Belt Road Seaside Camp
New Plymouth	12.	Aaron Court Motel & Caravan Park
Oakura	13.	Oakura Beach Camp
Opunake	14.	Opunake Beach Resort Camp
via Manaia	15.	Kaupokonui Beach Camp
Oakiawa	16.	Oakiawa Domain Camp
Ohawe	17.	Ohawe Beach Camp
Hawera	18.	King Edward Park Motor Camp
Eltham	19.	Presbyterian Camp
Stratford	20.	Stratford Top 10 Holiday Park
via Stratford	21.	Te Wera Camp

via Stratford	22.	Whangamomona Village Motor Camp
via Stratford	23.	Bushlands Farm Camp
Lake Rotorangi	24.	Lake Rotorangi Hydro Camping Ground
Patea	25.	Carlyle Beach Camp
Waverley	26.	Wairoa Domain
Waiototara	27.	Ashley Park Tourist Resort
Mowhanau	28.	Mowhanau Motor Camp
via Kai Iwi	29.	Bushy Park Homestead
Wanganui	30.	Aramoho Holiday Park
Wanganui	31.	Avro Motel & Caravan Court
Wanganui	32.	Castlecliff Motor Camp
Wanganui	33.	Bignell Street Park
Turakina Beach	34.	Turakina Beach Camp
Marton	35.	Marton Municipal Motor Camp
Marton	36.	Duddings Lake Holiday & Picnic Park
Bulls	37.	Bridge Motor Lodge & Caravan Park
Hunterville	38.	Queen's Park Camping & Picnic Ground
Hunterville	39.	Vinegar Hill Reserve
Mangaweka	40.	Mangaweka Domain
Taihape	41.	Abba Motor Camp
Bells Junction –Taihape	42.	Titoki Point Garden
Tangimoana	43.	Tangimoana Motor Camp
Sanson	44.	Sanson Motels & Caravan Park
Feilding	45.	Greenmeadows Holiday Accommodation
Pohangina–Ashhurst	46.	Totara Reserve
Ashhurst	47.	Ashhurst Domain
Palmerston North	48.	Palmerston North Holiday Park

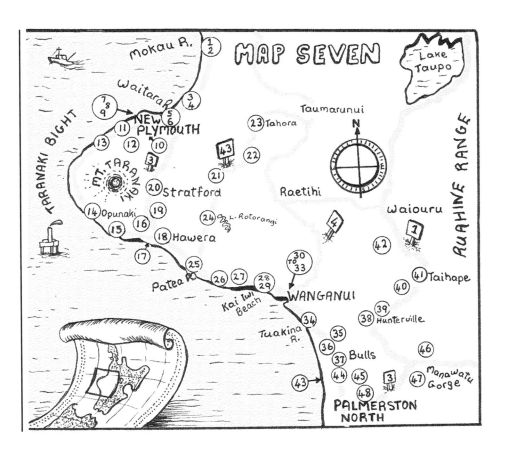

Chapter 7

TARANAKI AND MANAWATU

The classical cone shape of Mount Taranaki dominates the western extremity of the North Island and is within a National Park. A photographer's delight, the lower slopes are thickly forested, while its snow-topped peak is also a popular skiing venue in winter. Stratford is the alpine village of this area.

New Plymouth is the main centre of Taranaki, with beaches and beautiful Pukekura Park, which is only 10 minutes' walk from the main commercial district. The neighbouring areas, notably Waitara and Kapuni, are now producing some of New Zealand's recent energy resources, petroleum products and natural gas. You can arrange to visit these projects.

The Pukeiti Rhododendron Trust is located in the foothills inland from Oakura. The park is world famous for its collection of rhododendrons and azaleas and is open all year round. The spring months of September through to November are recommended for the most spectacular floral display.

South of New Plymouth, on the seaward side of Mt Taranaki are some recreational seaside resorts. Experience the sparkling black sands (due to their iron content) that are a feature of these beaches.

This coastal route leads down to the river city of Wanganui. The Wanganui River was once a trading route to the inner North Island. Today, trips along this river are as popular for the scenic attractions as much as for the significant history. It could take you five days to explore the upper reaches at your leisure, and there are wonderful stopping places along the way.

Palmerston North is an inland city on the northern banks of the Manawatu River. At its hub is The Square, which is an oasis of attractive gardens. The city serves both the students attending Massey University and the permanent population of the surrounding districts.

The wilderness ranges of the Ruahine State Forest, northeast of Palmerston North, are a natural barrier between the Manawatu and Hawkes Bay regions, and the Manawatu Gorge is a masterpiece of early roading. This forest of some 93,000 hectares attracts recreational trampers and hunters. Kiwis can still be found on the forest slopes.

Taranaki and Manawatu are not always sought out as tourist regions, being basically pastoral, but there are still beaches, forests and rivers of unspoiled beauty to enjoy here.

TARANAKI– MANAWATU

1. Seaview Motor Camp & Tearooms
S Hwy 3, RD1 Mokau (06) 752-9708

On the main route north of Mokau enjoy this stretch of coastline. This beachfront camp is neat and smart and sheltered from the ocean by sand dunes and shrubbery. Offering a choice of fishing, both river and sea, this is a spot with a reputation for whitebaiting. At the restaurant/cafe you can get takeaway food too (with a whitebait fritter specialty). Other supplies are obtainable at the on-site store. The amenities are clean and freshly painted but definitely not lavish. Most appliances are metered, as are the showers. There are 60 power sites here and plenty for tenting, with some other accommodation options. Pat and Earl Forman and Warren and Maryanne Loveridge are your hosts. Tent sites $6 per person. Power sites $7 per person.

2. Riviera Motor Camp
S Hwy 3, Mokau (06) 752-9713

A well-tree'd camp set on two levels in a circular layout, this is a simple little holiday spot in close proximity to the beach. The setting is pretty and includes shopping, post office and meal facilities. Some of the amenities are being refurbished. These include a toilet for the disabled. The kitchen is being improved, but laundry facilities remain rather primitive. Your hosts N.H. and L.H. Johnson. A power site will cost $13 for two people, or $9 for a tent site.

3. Wai-iti Beach Camp
Pukeruke Road, RD 44 Urenui (06) 752-3726

For a holiday just above the black sands of a Taranaki ocean beach this camp has 83 power sites with tenting and other accommodation. The sites are terraced and hedged and some enjoy seascape views. This is an unsophisticated spot where the beach (fishing and swimming) are probably the main attractions. A shop may also provide takeaway meals. Although the kitchen is adequate, and has a microwave, other facilities are minimal for the capacity of the camp. There is a dryer in the laundry and a TV/pool room for indoor entertainment. Hall hire for groups (with the use of a kitchen) can be arranged. Inquire from the resident managers for up-to-date tariff.

4. Urenui Domain Motor Camp
PO Box 25, Urenui (06) 752-3838

Making the most of a waterfront location, this "holiday village" has access to both sea and river directly from the camp. Right on the sea boundary are about 100 holiday homes with a 'village green' centrally placed. There are golf links right alongside. The atmosphere and appearance is most attractive with a large choice of sites, 120 with power. There is a good playground for the children and a volleyball court. Takeaway food is available at the general store. A boat ramp is provided. There are good, useful amenities, plus an outdoor shower. A well located resort north of New Plymouth. No dogs here please. Your hosts Karen and Ken Shorter. Tent sites are $14 for two people. Power sites are $16 for two.

5. Onaero Domain Camp
S Hwy 3, RD 43 Waitara (06) 752-3643

Reasonably close to Urenui, this camp straddles both sides of the river in an estuary situation. There are around 70 sites with power, which are hedged and level. Paddle boats can be hired here and fishing and whitebaiting are attractions. There is an adjacent store. The amenities are good and the newest block was designed to accommodate paraplegic facilities. The layout of the camp is user friendly but please do not bring your pets. Your new hosts are John and Pam Rochester. Tent sites are $13 for two people, or with power $15 for two. ⌷ $27 for two. ⌷ $15 per van.

6. Marine Park Motor Camp
Centennial Avenue, Waitara (06) 754-7121

Surrounded by a perimeter of large trees, this camp is adjacent to Ocean Beach and at the river mouth. Grouped sites are a feature, with hedged borders, while the main grounds are uncluttered and open. The BBQ area is complete with an interesting herb garden. There is a boat ramp here. The amenities include stoves and microwave in the kitchen, but the ablutions are not of the most recent variety. There is an adequate laundry and a dump point provided. You can play a 9 hole chip & putt golf game here. A handy spot to explore our alternative-energy projects, and local shops are just over 1km away. This is a pet friendly camp. Your hosts Dawn and Jack Chard will make you welcome here. Tent sites $8 per person or $10 for two. Power sites $8 per person or $12 for two.

7. Gateway Motel Campervan Park

Cnr S Hwy 3 & Mangati Road, Bell Block–New Plymouth
(06) 755-0978 (fax 06 755-0624)

New and different. On the northern approach to New Plymouth this park offers a number of special extras for travellers. If you want to put your feet up, order your meals, use the spa pool or the baby-sitting service, or even have your vehicle valet serviced, it is available here. The views are rural, the location handy to the golf course and Airport and campers can enjoy the motel facilities. There are both power and tent sites here. Your hosts Bonnie and Gary Stewart. Look for further information on page 202. 🖭.

8. Princes Tourist Court

29 Princes Street, Fitzroy–New Plymouth (06) 758-2566 (phone & fax)

With a charming "continental" air this camp has sprouted flowers in abundance and the "new glowworm" of coloured lights enhance the grounds at night. This is an inviting spot with a moderate capacity of 40 power sites, 5 tent sites and some other accommodation. There is a lovely walled-in swimming pool and a spa pool too. Camp sites are attractive and level with dividing ponga fences. There is an on-site store. The amenities are first class with all the appointments kept in immaculate order. The dining area was cosy and combined with a recreation centre for indoor entertainment. For the European traveller you will find Dutch and German spoken here. Your friendly hosts are Mieke, Monika and Holger Hasselman. Tent sites $14 for two. Power sites $17 for two.🖭.

 ### 9. Fitzroy Beach Motor Camp

Beach Street, Fitzroy–New Plymouth (06) 758-2870

Beachfront camping on two levels at Fitzroy Beach where the surf rolls in. Just 2km north of New Plymouth city centre you will find 80 sites with power and 60 for tents in a well maintained environment that has privacy plantings on some sites. There is a golf course and a children's playground adjacent. The kitchens have plenty of cooking appliances, including microwave and gas rings. There are good showers in the ablutions. Automatic equipment is provided in the laundry. There is an on-site store for basic supplies and takeaways. Pets may be permitted by prior arrangement. Your host Ruth Goodall. Tent sites $14 fortwo.Powersites $16 for two .🖾 and 🖼 $32.

10. Hookner Park Motor Camp
551 Carrington Road, No 1. RD New Plymouth (06) 753-9506
(fax (06) 753-9168)

This is in a rural situation some 10km from the heart of New Plymouth. There are 20 camp sites, 16 with power here on this working dairy farm combined with a motor home park. The campers appointments are superb! The attractive kitchen and adjoining lounge both have access to a patio and then to a cobblestone courtyard with picnic tables. The bathroom, (with shower rooms), separate toilets and handbasins, has a fully functional paraplegic suite. The laundry has all automatic machines. There is a dump point here. Bring your own provisions, for this is a quiet, non-commercial area close to the Pukeiti Rhododendron Trust. Your hosts Nancy, Kevin and David. All camp sites are $16 for two people. 🛏 $30 for two. 🛏 $26 for two.

11. Belt Road Seaside Motor Camp
2 Belt Road, New Plymouth 0800 804-204 (FREE phone)
(06) 758-0228 (phone & fax)

A special place with the sea below green, level, cliff-top sites that give you ringside seats overlooking the harbour and are sheltered by mature pohutukawa trees. There are around 90 sites with power, plus 43 for tents and some cabins. Well serviced with amenities, these are in first class order and include a kitchen with gas, electricity and microwave cooking. You will find plenty of showers in the ablutions. The laundry is equipped with automatic machines. A dump point is provided. Game fishing is an option in this area, as well as just boating, and swimming. The attractions of New Plymouth are nearby. These include an aquatic "wave" pool, unique in New Zealand and just a short walk from the camp. A very appealing environment here, but please do not bring your pets. Your hosts Chris and Cordelia Parkes. Tent sites $14 for two. Power sites $16 for two. 🛏.

12. Aaron Court Motel & Caravan Park
57 Junction Road–S Hwy 3 New Plymouth 0800 101-939 (FREE phone & fax)

This complex presents a very orderly appearance and accommodation takes precedence here. There may be power sites and level tent sites in the grounds but these are being phased out. Placed just south of the city and quite close to Pukekura Park, this resort has plenty of play equipment for the children. A large swimming pool and a private spa pool are also provided. There are good amenities with automatic laundry equipment. There is a dump point here. Your hosts Graeme, June and Andrew McCluskey.

13. Oakura Beach Camp
PO Box 55, Oakura (13km southwest of New Plymouth) (06) 752-7861

There are two levels of camping here, beachfront, following the long line of the shore. The sites are large with a border of flax on the seaward side. It should be no problem to find a site here,;both power and tent sites are plentiful. We had an "informal" reception here so information was sparse. The ablutions (with 10 cent metered showers) and toilets were of a good standard. The kitchen was meagre. A couple of challenging agitator washers are provided in the laundry, and there is a dryer. There is an on-site store with food available here. Check with Peter Cavey, the camp manager, for prices. This camp closes after Easter and opens again after Labour Weekend.

14. Opunake Beach Resort Camp
Beach Road, PO Box 72 Opunake (06) 761-8235

Travel the coastal route (S Hwy 45) around Cape Egmont to experience this beach camp. It is a traditional holiday venue for many local families and enjoys a lovely coastal beach frontage. The grounds are level,with 100 power sites and 50 tent sites in a ribbon layout. Use the boat ramp or try surfcasting. Water skiing is also popular. There is lots of adventure play equipment for the children. The camp kitchen is good, and there are plenty of toilets and excellent showers. The laundry has automatic machines. There is a large camp store and a wet-weather pavilion. Nearby Opunake has a number of services, including a heated pool. No pets here please. Your hosts Brian and Maureen Vincent. Tent sites are $7 per person, or with power $8.

15. Kaupokonui Beach Camp
3km west of Manaia (06) 278-8134 or (06) 274-5131

If you don't mind camping without the frills, this beachside camp offers some interesting sites. Some are on the cliffs overlooking the beach and there are some nice lower sites on the banks of the river boundary. There are meagre facilities here, although there is a fairly new porch-style kitchen alongside the shop (which is seasonally open). M.J. Dudley is your contact here. Tent sites are $8 for two persons and power sites are $10.

16. Oakiawa Domain Camp
Due north of Hawera

Spartan camping on large open grounds which are totally surrounded by thick high foliage and only have 4 power points. BBQs and picnic tables are provided. There is a token kitchen with sink and Zip boiler. A large open porch with sturdy tables and benches serves as a dining area. There are 3 toilets (one with disabled access) and no showers. Cold water is on tap.

17. Ohawe Beach Camp
Ohawe, Hawera (06) 728-6939

Look for the AA sign between Hawera and Manaia. The Ohawe Beach Camp is on a pretty cliff-top setting. There is a children's pool and the coast is noted for fishing and whitebaiting. The camp store is open in season. Get permission to camp from the Maori Trust C/- Ngaere Brogden, Tawhiti Road, Hawera. Only basic facilities here. Camp sites include 20 with power. All camping here is $9 for two persons.

18. King Edward Park Motor Camp
70 Waihi Road, PO Box 39 Hawera (06) 278-8544 (fax 06 278-8757)

Ease and privacy for the mobile camper at Hawera in south Taranaki and handy to the mountain. Drive in to your individually hedged site, which has generous space for your vehicle. There are 28 power sites, self-contained cabins and on-site caravans, but not much provision for tents. The service block is centrally situated. The kitchen has 2 full stoves plus hot-plate cooking, fridge and TV. The ablutions are of an average standard and the laundry is well equipped. There is a dump point here. This camp adjoins King Edward Park, with play area and Olympic-standard swimming pool. There are tennis courts here and an ornamental lake. Your new hosts are Wayne and Margaret Wilson.Tent sites $8 per person. Power sites $9 per person. and

19. Presbyterian Camp
30 Bridger Place, Eltham (06) 764-8201

This camp functions as a gathering place for groups but there are some lovely tenting areas on the lower level, with river border. There are also some very high density bunkrooms. The kitchen facilities are of catering proportions with auto dishwashing etc. The ablutions and laundry are reasonably adequate. The recreational attractions here include a demanding confidence course, trampoline and table tennis. Only 12 power points available. Tent sites are $5 per person, or with power $6. Six-bed and eight-bed bunkrooms are by arrangement.

20. Stratford Top 10 Holiday Park
10 Page Street, Stratford (06) 765-6440 (phone & fax)

A really polished park with the backdrop of Mount Taranaki dominating the skyline. Around the perimeter large, high hedges protect the grounds. There are 40 sites with power, most in sheltered, individual bays. Another 40 or so sites are available for tents. There is a combined kitchen/TV/ dining area. The ablutions are by key access and have copious supplies of hot water. There is also a spa pool. The laundry has automatic appliances. The 'Rimu Lodge' has an inviting recreation room, beautifully appointed and with pool table,

TV and self-catering kitchen. It is centrally heated. A dump point is provided. You may need to check for availability of sites. Your new hosts, Richard and Wendy Hill and family, offer discounts to NZMCA members and others. You may qualify. Tent sites $8.50 per person. Power sites $9.50 per person. 🏠 $30 for two. 🚐 $51.50. Backpackers from $15 per person.

21. Te Wera Camp
S Hwy 43, RD 25 Stratford (06) 762-3859

Keep this in mind if you are organising a group experience. There is a good road taking you inland for 37km from Stratford. The original camp was for forestry workers and has extensive sites, including 70 with power. A cluster of basic huts provides other accommodation. Low-key camping in an unsophisticated setting. There is a hall and a catering cookhouse with stoves, fridge and freezer and utensils for a crowd. Two blocks of ablutions are provided and there is a laundry with a drying room. Your hosts Ross and Dixie Farley. Get quotes for groups. Tent sites $5 per person. Power sites $4 per person.

22. Whangamomona Village Motor Camp
RD 26 Stratford (06) 762-5823,or (06) 762-5822

A very rudimentary campsite on an open paddock close to the village and the local hotel. On one side a former school house does duty as an amenities block. An "early NZ" kitchen and laundry are provided. The solitary shower is well lined with formica and the toilets (one for each sex) are in fair condition. Although there is a swimming pool and a tennis court, neither would prove very inviting. 🏠 and power sites will be available.

23. Bushlands Farm Camp
S Hwy 43, Tahora, RD 27 Stratford (06) 765-5546

Midway between Taumarunui and Stratford. Be prepared for a long winding road, some of which is unsealed, if you want a farm experience you will find it here. The camp is above the river in a green valley dotted with willow trees. There are 8 sites with power, tent sites to choose, and two cabins and a tourist flat. One large holiday house will sleep 12 people. The kitchen is limited in cooking equipment but has tables and chairs and a large deck overlooking the river. A minimal quantity of showers and toilets are provided. The laundry has "old faithful" agitator machines and tub. This area has bush ranges to tramp and huts for those trampers to stay in overnight. Your hosts Joan and Bruce Herbert. Inquire for prices. 🏠 and 🚐.

24. Lake Rotorangi Hydro Camping Ground
27km inland from Hawera–Lake Rotorangi

Retreat into the hinterland of Taranaki for this new discovery. Part of your journey (8km) is on unsealed road through native bush and farmland. There are limited facilities, but a hot shower is available ($1). There are toilets. Otherwise campers should be independent, but a fridge and wood burning BBQs are provided. This is the site of a large hydro dam with a concrete boat ramp. There is lake swimming and bush walks. A caretaker is at the dam with a phone available. The land is somewhat uneven but has a tidy aspect. There is rubbish disposal. No pets please. All sites only $4.

25. Carlyle Beach Camp
Beach Road, Patea (06) 273-8705

If you like a little, more intimate camp which has a snug seaside aspect, this could appeal. At the mouth of the Patea River it is pleasantly sheltered and has a golf course next door. The kitchen is in "apple-pie" order and has good appliances and TV. Although there are not many ablutions, they are modern and spotlessly clean and paraplegic facilities may be available. The laundry offers one agitator machine. There is a dump point here. A modest but appealing and well kept small camp. Tent sites $10 for two. Power sites $12 for two.

26. Wairoa Domain
Waverley Beach Road, PO Box 28 Patea (06) 346-5277

This appears to be one of those part-time operations that provide for camping mainly in the holiday season. The 28 power sites are in a paddock which has rather an uneven base, but has ample tenting space. To the rear of the camp a nice playground is provided for the children. There is a shop too, but only open mid-summer. Apart from a useable kitchen the other amenities were locked. It is $10 per night per site to camp here.

27. Ashley Park Tourist Resort
S Hwy 3, PO Box 36 Waiototara (06) 346-5917 (fax 06 346-5861)

Between Patea and Wanganui, this complex covers the needs of campers, with bunkrooms, and farm-stay guests as well. The camping area is level and densely planted with camellias and rhododendrons and has 24 power sites, unlimited tent sites, plus other accommodation. The facilities are quite luxurious, many of them in the comfort of a house. A new dining room adjoins the pleasant kitchen. There is a wood-fired BBQ too. Apart from a picturesque lake which you can explore by boat, there is a swimming pool for holidaymakers. An antiques and craft shop and a tearooms invite you to linger. You share your environment with the deer, donkeys, farm animals and visiting birds. There is also an aviary. Your hosts Barry Pearce and Wendy Bowman. Tent sites $6 per person. Power sites $14.50 for two. Shared accommodation is $11 per adult. 🏠 and 🖾.

28. Mowhanau Motor Camp

RD 4 Mowhanau (06) 342-9846 or (06) 342-9658

The little settlement of Mowhanau is just 9km off S Hwy 3 towards the coast. The road is sealed. It is less than 5 minutes to the beach where there is a boat ramp. The camp has anon-site store with food available. There is a fee for use of the swimming pool. The grounds are level with some shade and shelter and outdoor taps are plentiful. There are grassy sites, 51 with power and another 100 for tents. The ablutions are clean and include a babies bath. An outdoor cold-water shower is provided too. The kitchen has electric cooking, small appliances and a fridge and freezer. There are tables and chairs. The laundry has free agitator washers and ironing equipment. This is low-key family camping for those who like fishing and country walks. Your host Sue Fellingham. Tent sites $12 for two. Power sites $14 for two.

29. Bushy Park Homestead

via Kai Iwi–Rangitatau East Road, RD 8 Wanganui (06) 342-9879

With only a very tiny capacity for campers (2 power sites) this is better known for guest accommodation and day visitors. There are toilets and showers for campers and automatic laundry equipment. There is use of a kitchen. No visiting cats please. Your hosts Paul and Pam Trail. Power sites $6 per person.

30. Aramoho Holiday Park

460 Somme Parade, Upper Aramoho–Wanganui (06) 343-8402 (phone & fax)

For the connoisseur of camping, this park must rate as one of the best. On the city side, and right beside the Wanganui River, this park spreads itself between the road and the river banks. The landscaped grounds delight the eye with many gracious trees. There are a variety of sites on slightly different levels divided by a raised berm. 59 sites have power and there are 12 hard stands for caravans. Wonderful tenting space, with 100 sites. There is a well appointed bunkhouse, some delightful chalets (with balconies) and cabins. The amenities block is centrally situated. The kitchen has gas cooking, fridge/freezer and opens to a large, comfortable recreation room. The ablutions are generously proportioned with a well-scrubbed look. There is a separate paraplegic bathroom. The laundry has automatic equipment. A dump point is provided. Although this is on the outskirts of the city, it offers many holiday attractions. There are plenty of river cruises, or launch your boat from the boat ramp. Across the road a general store also has takeaway food. It is advisable to book in the holiday season. Your hosts Les and Linda Richdale.

All sites $16 for two. 🏠 $32 for two. Tourist flats $47.50 for two. Look for further information on page 202.

31. Avro Motel & Caravan Court
36 Alma Road, Wanganui (06) 345-5279 (fax 06 345-2104)

Tailor-made for the mobile home or caravan traveller. If you like to "hit the road" but hate communal facilities, the Avro complex offers you an individual en-suite bathroom/toilet at your site. The van park is on level lawns behind the motels, and tents are welcome, but there are no kitchen facilities (except for a freezer). The laundry has automatic equipment, plus iron. The grounds are level and have a large enclosure with swimming pool and picnic tables. There are also private spa pools. The camp is adjacent to a 7-day dairy and licensed restaurant. There are two nearby golf links and you can hire equipment. It is also very handy to the racecourse. Your van site, including bathroom, costs $12 per person, or $18 for two. Inquire for other prices.

32. Castlecliff Motor Camp
1A Rangiora Street, Castlecliff–Wanganui (06) 344-2227

On the coastal side of Wanganui this camp is close to Castlecliff Beach and next door to 7-day shopping. Around 100 sites are available, 57 with power, plus some cabin accommodation. The sites are level and some are hedged. A children's playground and tennis courts are provided. There is a swimming pool as well as good swimming at the beach. Fishing can be successful here and fishing rods can be obtained at the camp. This camp is well appointed with amenities, particularly for paraplegics. The kitchen has ramp access and has gas, electric and microwave cooking; there is a dining room (with TV) alongside. Fridge and freezer are available. There is free use of a gas BBQ. The ablutions are modern, with a paraplegic suite. The laundry is fully equipped with automatic machines and iron. A dump point is provided. Pets can be accommodated by arrangement. Your hosts Fred and Tineke Frericks. Discount group bookings can be negotiated. Tent sites $7.50 per person. Power sites $16 for two. 🚐 $30. 🏠 $32. 🏘 $35.

33. Bignell Street Motels, Cabins & Caravan Park
Bignell Street, Wanganui (06) 344-2012

Formerly the "Friendly Motor Camp", the new name indicates a change in emphasis. Yes, they are still friendly! However, this is more suitable for the overnight stopover, with a dominance of long-term residents. You can bring your pets. Somewhere economical to break your journey. Your host Peter One. Both power and tent sites are $8 per person. There are on-site vans for $25 for two people. 🏠 and 🏘 $40.

34. Turakina Beach Camp
21km south of Wanganui, RD 11 Turakina (06) 327-3770

This is a west coast beach between Wanganui and Bulls where an open camping site is enclosed on three sides by a wooden fence. There is also a cluster of holiday baches. Mastery of the showers will be a challenge. The hot shower was locked. The available showers are cold water operated by foot treadles! One flush toilet for each sex is provided. The kitchen porch has a sink. There is a tank labelled "drinking water". Gutsy campers will pay $5 for a power site plus 50 cents per person. Your host T. Dooney. Tent sites are $3 plus 50 cents also.

35. Marton Municipal Motor Camp
30 Maunder Street, Private Bag 1102 Marton (06) 327-8174 (fax 06 327-6970)

A signpost on S Hwy 1 invites you to detour to Marton. It is just a short level drive to this rural township. Marton Motor Camp is well placed, with the town shops just around the corner. The camp has tent sites, 3 cabins and 18 power sites. Camp sites form a semi-circle around the central lawn and BBQ. The kitchen is well appointed, including a deep freeze. There are ablutions and laundry, but no dryer. These facilities are protected by issuing keys to campers only. There are several old trees bordering the camp and alongside is a well groomed community park. Enquires to the Rangitikei District Council. Power sites are $15 for two people and tent sites are $10. The 3 🏠 $25 for two.

36. Duddings Lake Holiday & Picnic Park
S Hwy 3, RD 3 Marton (06) 327-8127 (phone & fax)

Day trippers and campers alike are catered for at Dudding Lake Reserve between Turakina and Bulls. It is 11km from Marton. The centrepiece of this park is the lake, with shady trees, picnic tables and playgrounds scattered around the edge. There is a boat ramp and lots of gentle water craft for hire. The water slide offers action for the younger set. There is a well stocked store here with groceries and hot and cold drinks, icecreams and snack food. The grounds offer 20 power sites and unlimited tent sites in a pleasant recreational environment. The kitchen and dining area are functional with a fairly small capacity. The ablutions have good showers and toilets There are laundry facilities. No dogs at this park please. Your hosts Sharon and Adrian. Power sites $7.50 per adult. Tent sites $6.50 per adult. 🚐 $12.50 per adult and caravan storage at $5 per week.

37. Bridge Motor Lodge & Caravan Park
2 Bridge Street, Bulls (06) 322-0894 (fax 06 322-1957)

Directly off S Hwy 1 just south of Bulls township, this complex includes a roadside tearooms. There are level grounds with plenty of parking. The Rangitikei River is on one border. It is a rural setting with 12 power sites located to the rear of the Motor Lodge. There are plenty of sites for tents. There are good facilities, plus a TV lounge, spa pool and swimming pool. Beside the camp the river offers alternative swimming and fishing. Pets are welcome here. An easily identifiable stopover quite close to the Ohakea Air Force Base and Museum. Your hosts Anne and Bevan Brown. All sites are $9 per person. ⌷ $15. ⌷ $65.

38. Queen's Park Camping & Picnic Ground
Hunterville

If you want to enjoy the benefits of a free camp site in a pretty park, look out for this one. It is beside the main road. At the back of the grounds is a swing bridge. This is a Lions project and has no on-site power or amenities. However, a nearby motel has toilets and showers (nominal charge) for camper's use.

39. Vinegar Hill Reserve
Hunterville

Just off S Hwy 1, 6km north of Hunterville, this reserve has access from the Feilding-Taihape Road, and offers sites (without power) in an unspoiled setting. The flat land borders the Rangitikei River and is abundant in trees and native bush. The only facilities here are toilets. An honesty system operates for your ground rent. Please observe the rules! Apart from at New Year, you can "go bush" here anytime.

40. Mangaweka Domain
Mangaweka (06) 382-5730

Mangaweka is between Hunterville and Taihape. It is blossoming into a playground for outdoor adventurers. This camping spot is for those with a pioneering spirit. There are lovely trees and level terraced sites, some beside the river. The scenery is dramatic and gaunt, rather than beautiful. A"stage-coach-days" kitchen and similar other facilities are provided. Great for self-suffiient campers. A tent site will cost you $5 for two people, or with power $7.50.

41. Abba Motor Camp
Old Abbattoir Road, PO Box 73 Taihape (06) 388-0718

Originally developed as a railway town, Taihape (or Gumboot City) retains its central North Island popularity as a refreshment stop. The Abba Motor

Camp is about 2km north of town off S Hwy 1. Although the "through the timber mill" approach is less than ideal, the actual camp is pretty and pleasantly spacious. Camp sites are on two levels on the banks of the Hautapu River. There are some shady trees and the whole camp is screened by hills. There is a good well appointed kitchen (high chair provided). The laundry facilities are modern. Ablutions are adequate (unless they are temporarily closed!) The weary traveller will find this a helpful location. Pets can stay by arrangement. Your hosts the Bradley family. Power sites are $15 for two people, or $13.50 for a tent site. 🖻 $16 per person.

42. Titoki Point Garden
Koukoupo Road, Bells Junction–RD 1 Taihape (06) 388-0242

Inspect one of New Zealand's finest gardens and you will also find there a site for your campervan. It is a 20-minute drive to the west from S Hwy 1, about 22km south of Waiouru. Visit this for the beauty of the gardens, and the rare plants to be found here; don't expect a holiday camp. Limited provision has been made for mobile homes and the garden is sometimes closed. For further information contact Cynthia Collier, as above. Tent sites are $6 per person, or $7 with power.

43. Tangimoana Motor Camp
Private Bag, Tangimoana (06) 324-8208

The road to Tangimoana follows the Rangitikei River to the sea. This camp is only 1km from both the river and the sea. The area is noted for whitebaiting. The grounds are of the level and basic variety. There are 30 sites with power, serviced by a new ablution block which has facilities for the disabled. A washing machine is available but no kitchen appears to be provided. Campers are issued with keys to the ablutions. Both regular residents and holidaymakers will find this a quiet but friendly spot. Your hosts Helen and Ross Cormack. Budget camping at $5.50 for two on a tent site or $7 for two with power.

44. Sanson Motels & Caravan Park
Main Road, PO Box 106 Sanson (06) 329-3839 (fax 06 329-3580)

Weeping willows fall gracefully all round this camp, wonderful in summer, perhaps not so good in the rain. Situated at the junction of the Shannon/Wellington/Palmerston North highways, the access road to the left just before the corner, for north-bound travellers is very convenient. A pleasant little stopover with only minimal facilities for campers. You can arrange for meals to be supplied. Gordon and Zella Donaldson are your new hosts. The sites with power are $12 for two people, or tent sites $8. 🚐 $15 per person and a hut $12.

45. Greenmeadows Holiday Accommodation Park
5 Arnott Street, Feilding (06) 323-5623

Just 3km from the town centre (off Kimbolton Road) is a pleasant family camp in a semi-rural location. Basically a farming community, Feilding has good local shopping and is only a 15-minute drive to Palmerston North. This is a taste of the country, without being remote and isolated. Yes, it has a camp store and food is available on the site. There are good level sites with a choice of gravel or grass and plenty of taps. A modest kitchen with a full stove and extra hotplates also has fridge and freezer. There is a dining room, and communal TV. The ablutions are clean and have facilities for the disabled. There is a laundry with an automatic washing machine and a dryer. A dump point is provided. There is a "no animals" policy here. Your hosts Lyn and Rob Waterson also have bunkrooms and on-site caravans. Tent sites $8 per person. Power sites $9 per person. 🏚 and bunkrooms $20 per person.

46. Totara Reserve
Pohangina Utuwai Rural Delivery, Pohangina–Ashhurst (06) 329-4708

The surrounding hills and valleys are well wooded, with bush-walking trails. Level camping and picnicking spots are beside the river. This is an interesting area to explore, with a wide range of mature NZ native trees in the lovely reserve. There are 12 power sites and ample tent sites with BBQs for cooking. Toilets and showers are provided. Children have a play area, but please do not bring dogs to this reserve. The Manawatu District Council administers this park, which is in the care of Kevin Brown. Ecologically correct camping for bush lovers. Tent sites $9.50 for two adults. Power sites $11 for two adults.

.

47. Ashhurst Domain
Napier Road, Ashhurst (06) 326-8203

Some 14km from Palmerston North is the tiny township of Ashhurst. Here you will find a pleasantly tree-shaded camp adjacent to the local Domain where there is a children's playground. The facilities are modern and adequate. It is doubtful whether this camp would ever be crowded. Enjoy the bush walks, and river with trout fishing. Its greatest claim to fame may be that it is at the western entrance to the Manawatu Gorge. In the care of R.S. Sproull or K.G. Pratt. Tent sites $4 plus $2 per person. Power sites $6 plus $3 per person.

48. Palmerston North Holiday Park
133 Dittmer Drive, Palmerston North (06) 358-0349

State-of-the-art camping. There are 75 power sites, 30 with double hard-paved stands and waste and sewerage drop points. Around 85 tent sites, and sleeping accommodation for over 100 people. This is a manicured park, enhanced by avenues of mature trees and up-to-the-minute facilities. In the kitchen you will find gas stoves and even a dishwasher. There are refrigerated lockers, television and video. Alongside is a major recreation area for Palmerston North bordered by the Manawatu River. Sports fields, indoor and outdoor swimming pools and mini golf course are some of the attractions. This holiday park is not far from The Square, via Fitzherbert Avenue. There is a "no animals" policy here. Your hosts Stuart Fisher and Sue Davis. Tent sites are $7.50 per person and power sites are $16.80 for two. Other accommodation ranges from $23.

WELLINGTON AND THE WAIRARAPA DIRECTORY

Key locations and map,begins on the west coast just south of Palmerston North. Follows the coastal route south to Wellington. Leaves Wellington to go north through the Hutt Valley and across the Rimutaka Ranges to the Wairarapa. Goes as far north as Pahiatua returning to Masterton to link the beach resorts of Castlepoint and Riversdale to the east, then to the remote southernmost camps of Palliser Bay.

Himatangi Beach	1.	Himatangi Beach Motor Camp
Foxton Beach	2.	Foxton Beach Motor Camp
Foxton Beach	3.	Manawatu Caravan Club Inc.
Levin	4.	Waiterere Beach Motor Camp
Levin	5.	Hydrabad Holiday Park
Levin	6.	Playford Park Motor Camp
Levin	7.	Tatum Park
Manakau	8.	Waikawa Stream (DoC)
Otaki Beach	9.	Otaki Beach Motor Camp
Otaki Beach	10.	Capitol Seaside Resort
Otaki	11.	Otaki Forks (DoC)
Paraparaumu	12.	Lindale Motor Park
Paekakariki	13.	Batchelors Holiday Park
Pauatahunui	14.	Battle Hill Farm Forest Park
Porirua	15.	Aotea Lodge
Porirua	16.	Camp Elsdon

WELLINGTON–WAIRARAPA

Lower Hutt	17.	Hutt Park Holiday Village
via Wainuiomata	18.	Rimutaka Forest Park (DoC)
Upper Hutt	19.	Harcourt Holiday Park
via Upper Hutt	20.	Kaitoke Regional Park
Martinborough	21.	Martinborough Camp Ground
Featherston	22.	Leeway Motel & Caravan Park
Greytown	23.	Greytown Motor Camp
Carterton	24.	Howard Booth Caravan Park
Carterton	25.	Waiohine Gorge (DoC)
Masterton	26.	Mawley Park Motor Camp
via Masterton	27.	Holdsworth Lodge (DoC)
via Masterton	28.	Kiriwhakapapa (DoC)
Eketahuna	29.	Eketahuna Motor Camp
Pahiatua	30.	Carnival Park Motor Camp
Castlepoint	31.	Castlepoint Motor Camp
Riversdale	32.	Riversdale Beach Motor Camp
Lake Ferry (Palliser Bay)	33.	Lake Ferry Motor Camp
Te Kopi (Palliser Bay)	34.	Putangirua Scenic Reserve (DoC)

Chapter 8

WELLINGTON AND THE WAIRARAPA

The capital city of Wellington is at the foot of the North Island. There are two road links to the north–plus airport, rail and shipping terminals to take you to the South Island and elsewhere. Interisland ferries will take you and your vehicle across Cook Strait. This regular service should be booked in advance, especially at holiday times.

Northwest of Wellington the main route follows the coast, where pleasant seaside settlements are favourite weekend retreats. A visit to Southwards Car Museum along the way is an interesting diversion. It has one of the largest private motor-vehicle collections in the Southern Hemisphere.

The centre of New Zealand's Government, Wellington has a character all its own. Overlooking the deep-water harbour, the houses of the city dweller seem to cling precariously to the surrounding hills. The "Windy City" offers many vantage points. The most accessible, a ride in the cable car to the suburb of Kelburn, should not be missed. At the summit are Wellington's Botanical Gardens and the Observatory.

Wellington is an easy city to explore on foot. Over the years the old wharf area has been transformed into a virtual entertainment centre. The East-West ferries will whisk you across the harbour to the beaches of Days Bay and Eastbourne which have a particularly tranquil charm.

Wellington's Marine Drive has some 39 kilometres of seafront to explore. Almost in the heart of the city, Oriental Bay is a popular beach for bathing or people watching. The Freyberg tepid baths are alongside.

The alternative route from Wellington takes you to the rich farmland of the Wairarapa. Pass through the level Hutt Valley floor until you reach the foothills of the rugged Rimutaka Ranges. The road winds steeply before descending into the Wairarapa.

The Wairarapa is dotted with a series of small "character" towns, each with it's own motor camp. There are coastal resort areas too. Both Riversdale and Castlepoint have impressive ocean beaches and camping facilities.

Taste the exhilaration of Wellington and its environs. You will be pleasantly surprised.

WELLINGTON –WAIRARAPA

1. Himitangi Beach Motor Camp
Koputara Road, Himitangi Beach (06) 329-9575

The beach settlement of Himitangi is located 6km from S Hwy 1 and on the fringe of the Manawatu area. It is a 30-minute drive to Palmerston North, while the beach is popular for whitebaiting (in season), surfing and swimming. The camp presents a tidy appearance although there is a dominance of long-term van occupation. Sites are level with both grass and gravel parking. Entertainment for children is on the agenda in the summer holidays, also there is play equipment in the grounds. A games room has video machines and TV. There are adequate amenities, including automatic laundry machines (no charge for the washers). The local store and the beach are close by. This is a dog friendly camp, with a special area set aside for those families with dogs. Your friendly new hosts are Margaret and Pone Utumapu. The camp is spacious with around 100 sites. Tent sites $6 per person. Power sites $7 per person. 🏠 $18.

2. Foxton Beach Motor Camp
Holben Parade, Foxton Beach (06) 363-8211

A pleasant coastal camp with a large capacity for holidaymakers. It is not quite on the beach, but adjacent to the mouth of the Manawatu River. There are 100-plus power sites, 60 tent sites and 5 cabins. There are tennis courts next door. The land is slightly undulating and has a screened BBQ area with big old pine trees for shade. There is excellent play equipment for youngsters. The amenities appear clean and functional, with paraplegic facilities in the ablutions and automatic machines in the laundry. Shopping is nearby and in summer a fruit and vegetable vendor calls with produce. Your pets are allowed here too. Your hosts Margaret and Ginger Street. Tent sites $6.50 per person. Power sites from $7 per person. 🏠 $28 for two.

3. Manawatu Caravan Club Inc.
Nash Parade, Foxton Beach

As the name suggests, this is a limited camp for travellers. There is no provision for tents. Casual visitors may park here for a maximum of 21 days, and there are 126 power sites. The camp has some shady trees and hedges but looks rather regimented. There are good clean facilities, a children's playground and a lovely BBQ. It costs $12 for two persons to park here.

4. Waiterere Beach Motor Camp
Park Avenue, Waitarere Beach–Levin (06) 368-8732

This small camp has a cherished appearance. It is adjacent to sweeping Waitarere Beach and has 34 sites with power, plus tent sites and two cabins. The kitchen, which has two full stoves and a dining area, adjoins a TV room. This has a warm and friendly atmosphere, with homely touches. All the amenities are of a good standard, well kept and clean. Shopping is just around the corner and a walk through the sand dunes will bring you to the beach. No dogs here please. Your hosts Shirley and David Ramsbottom. Family camping here is $13 for two persons on a tent site, or $16 with power. ▭.

5. Hydrabad Holiday Park
Forest Road, Waitarere Beach, PO Box 563 Levin (06) 368-4941

In a rural/coastal area, take the turnoff from S Hwy 1 about 8km north of Levin. This is not a beachfront camp but offers an attractive setting for the 55 power sites and around 30 tent sites here. The grounds are level with sites grouped and sewerage disposal at the power sites. Ideally placed to work off some energy at the skating rink, tennis courts and swimming pool next door. The children's play equipment is imaginative and challenging and there is a skateboard ramp. Well serviced with amenities, the little kitchen has all the necessary equipment including a microwave. An attractive ablution block has hand towels and soap provided and looked clean and tidy. Together with the laundry, the standard of upkeep is high. Resident host is George Burdan. Power sites are $16 for two people. Tent sites are $14 for two. ▭ $31 and ▥ $40 for two.

6. Playford Park Motor Camp
38 Parker Avenue, Levin (06) 368-3549

Appealing and orderly, this camp is within the pleasant community of Levin. The grounds are well laid out in a circular fashion. Both the perimeters and the sites are lined with sheltering hedges and one tree to each site. There are 36 sites with power, at least 50 tent sites and 10 cabins. In the centre an open area leads to the amenities block. The kitchen is spacious with a dining option. There is a TV room. The ablutions are tidy with both unisex and wheelchair-access showers. There is automatic laundry equipment. Picnic tables and children's play area are provided, as well as a dump point. Your new hosts Joy and Murray Graham. Prices range from $8 for tent sites to $10 with power for two persons. ▭ $17. ▥ $35 for two. Look for detailed directions on page 218.

7. Tatum Park
S Hwy 1, Manakau. Private Bag 4006 Levin (06) 362-6799 (fax 06 362-6502)

Right on the main north-south route, this camp is for public use, and is only a one-hour drive to the Cook Strait ferry terminal in Wellington. However the emphasis is more on training and conference facilities, or as a venue for functions. The grounds are magnificent; level parkland sheltered by native bush and mature trees. There is generous space for the 28 power sites, 13 tent sites and a few cabins. This is an "activities" camp with swimming pool, golf-paddock, volleyball courts, bush walks and confidence course. A recreation room is provided. For the casual camper there is use of the porch-style kitchen with a fridge/freezer, or an adjacent restaurant with budget-priced meals. A new ablution block provides showers and toilets. There is satisfactory laundry equipment, including dryer and ironing facilities. Your hosts Nigel and Aaron Hopkins. Tent sites $7 per person. Power sites $8.50 per person.⬛, $12.50 per person. 🔲 $35 for two. 🔲 $50 for two. Look for further information on page 218.

8. Waikawa Stream
North Manakau Road, Manakau–Department of Conservation

Waikawa Stream is a pleasant self-registration campground adjacent to an exotic forest. There is shelter, picnic and rubbish facilities and pit toilets. Water is available from the stream. The campground is large and is not heavily utilised, so there is plenty of choice of camp sites. There are short walks as well as longer tramping routes back into the heart of the Tararua Forest Park. A permit is required for recreational hunting in the park, and there are also some mountain biking tracks in the area. For further information contact the Dept of Conservation, PO Box 141 Waikanae.

9. Otaki Beach Motor Camp
40 Moana Street, Otaki Beach (06) 364-7107

Sheltered but "beachy" with a rather token holiday atmosphere, although it is adjacent to both the river and the beach. There appears to be some long-term occupancy here. The camp capacity is reasonably large offering around 70 sites with power plus almost as many for tents. There is a swimming pool, BBQs and a children's play area in the grounds. You can buy takeaway food at the on-site store. The kitchen has old stoves and limited space. By contrast the showers are king-size with similar sized dressing rooms. A TV/recreation room and also a laundry are provided. Your host Grant Richardson. A power site is $13.50 for two people, or $11 for tents.6 ⬛, are from $20.

10. Capitol Seaside Resort
20 Tasman Road, Otaki Beach (06) 364-8121 (fax 06 364-8123)

There are some fine alternatives here for those wanting to use the licensed restaurant and bar, the gym and sauna, the conference room or the tennis and squash facilities and swimming pool. It is nicely placed and handy to the beach. Amenities for campers are rather forlorn by contrast. There are plenty of sites and most have power. There is a dump station here. Your friendly hosts are Gavin Case and Cindy O'Brien.Tent sites $15 for two. Power sites $18 for two. are an option.

11. Otaki Forks
Otaki Gorge Road, Otaki–Department of Conservation

Otaki Forks is the main access point to the western side of the Tararua Forest Park and the area has been extensively developed in recent years to offer excellent family camping facilities near the road end. Camp sites are well drained and are served by water and toilet amenities. Rubbish facilities are centralised. There are attractive walks to suit all ages and fitness levels, leading to a network of tracks throughout the Forest Park. The area is also popular for day trippers, canoeing, rafting and trout fishing. For further information contact the Dept of Conservation, PO Box 141 Waikanae.

12. Lindale Motor Home & Caravan Park
S Hwy 1 Paraparaumu North, PO Box 274 Paraparaumu (04) 298-8046

Good neighbours. While the Lindale Farm Park next door is an innovative tourist and refreshment stop, the adjacent motor park enjoys direct access. Try the hearty breakfast. Camping conditions are quite luxurious with 45 fully serviced sites with shrubs and a lawn giving individual privacy. All the amenities will come up to your expectations, and include an appealing and comfortable TV room. There is a paraplegic suite in the ablutions. The well equipped kitchen also has a phone. Fully automatic laundry equipment is provided. There is also a dump point. A handy situation on the outskirts of Wellington city, but with plenty to see and do right here. Your hosts Mick and Audrey Orr. Tent sites $9 per person. Power sites $17 for two. $40 for two. $50 for two.

13. Batchelors Holiday Park
Wellington Road, Paekakariki (04) 292-8292 (phone & fax)

Alongside Queen Elizabeth Park (access by way of Wellington Road) take the railway crossing off S Hwy 1 at Paekakariki. The extensive grounds can accommodate 170 sites, 150 with power. There is also a 30-bed lodge and 9 🏠 . This is a mature park with pohutukawas and other shady trees. All sites are generous and individually hedged. Just north of the local township this Golden Coast area offers a lovely beach adjacent to the camp. There is a high standard of amenities here, which include a big laundry with commercial machines. There is a TV room and a private indoor spa. The playground for smaller children is a feature. There is a dump point provided. Pets are welcome here. Your hosts Karol and Gary Kurukaanga. All camp sites are $9 per person and the Lodge is available for group booking. 🏠 $28.

14. Battle Hill Farm Forest Park
Paekakariki Hill Road, Pauatahanui (04) 237-5511 or (04) 526-4133

A Wellington Regional Council park inland from the Golden Coast beaches, and signposted on Paekakariki Hill Road. There is a mixture of recreational activities, farming and forestry here, where camping is unsophisticated on sheltered paddocks. The park is available for walking, and swimming (in a fresh-water stream). Cyclists and horse riders can use designated tracks. There is cold water and wheelchair-access toilets only. Because of the livestock and wildlife here no dogs are permitted. This park is closed at night. Normal camp fees are $4 per site. Larger groups should make enquiries from the ranger.

15. Aotea Lodge
Whitford Brown Avenue, PO Box 50373 Porirua (04) 237-4257

For those looking for a temporary refuge from the rigours of the road there is parking for your mobile home here. There are 18 power points provided, as a sideline to the motel accommodation. Use of the motel units (except the bed and the kitchen) is yours for $20 for two persons. There is a small fee for the use of the laundry, but a swimming and spa pool are at your disposal. A conservatory and an indoor swimming pool have recently been installed. There is a good restaurant service here too. Porirua is a short motorway journey from Wellington city. Your hosts Patricia and Peter Chinnery.🏠.

16. Camp Elsdon
PO Box 50-023, Porirua (04) 237-8987

Here is a stop over to the east of Porirua city. Although this complex is purpose-built for groups,it may be a useful venue for school or other youth organisations. A smaller area offers 4 power sites and tent sites for individual campers. The managers are Garry and Helen Cooper. Check out the availability before arrival. Visitors are charged a minimum fee of $4 per day or tent sites from $6

17. Hutt Park Holiday Village
95 Hutt Park Road, Lower Hutt (04) 568-5913 (fax 04 568-5914)

A long-established camp on mature, level grounds. There are both grass and hard sites for mobile homes. A change of emphasis has resulted in more high-density fixed accommodation, although there are 52 sites with power and 40 for tents. However it is very handily placed for convenient access to Wellington city and the beaches of Petone and Eastbourne. There is a shop for basic supplies with takeaway food within the camp. Also good indoor and outdoor recreational facilities, which include a well equipped confidence playground. There are excellent kitchens with cool boxes. The ablutions include paraplegic facilities and there is automatic laundry equipment. Two large dining halls make this a useful venue for groups. There is a dump point here. Pets may be permitted by prior arrangement. A booking service is provided. Your hosts Noel and Jane, Debbie and Ross. Sites with power are $18 for two people, or $16.50 for tents.

18. Rimutaka Forest Park
Coast Road, Catchpool–Department of Conservation (04) 564-8551

There are excellent camping areas in the large Catchpool Valley which is 10km south of Wainuiomata. Many camping sites are secluded and most are well drained and some have gas-fired BBQs. Toilets and water supplies are conveniently sited. There is a 24-hour telephone and limited supplies available from the Visitor Centre at the bottom of the valley. There are several small swimming holes in the Catchpool Stream. As forest fires are a constant threat, please only use the cooking facilities provided. There are walks to suit all ages and fitness levels in very attractive native bush. For further information contact the Department of Conservation, Private Bag 43 902 Wainuiomata.

19. Harcourt Holiday Park
45 Akatarawa Road, Upper Hutt (04) 526-7400 (phone & fax)

Just north of Upper Hutt, turn off S Hwy 2 at the junction of Akatarawa Road. This camp is a short distance from the corner and is adjacent to the upper reaches of the Hutt River. The approach is abundant in flowering shrubs and trees and has a rural atmosphere. There are 18 sites with power here, and 10 for tents. There is also tourist flat accommodation, with one unit totally suitable for paraplegic use. The surrounding area features a children's playground and paddling pool and river swimming. The grounds are easy drive-on, but not completely flat. Apart from a power pylon, the outlook of surrounding hills and the valley below is most attractive. Amenities include a kitchen with microwave cooking, fridge and dining space. The ablutions have a lovely paraplegic suite and seats in the showers. There are automatic laundry machines. There is a dump station here and Harcourt Park is conveniently situated for shops and petrol and a nearby tavern. Well behaved dogs are welcome. Your new hosts Gordon and Vicki Bennett. All sites $9 per person. 🖵 $48.

20. Kaitoke Regional Park

Off S Hwy 2, Te Marua–PO Box 40 847 Upper Hutt (04) 526-7322 (phone & fax) or (04) 526-4133

Another Wellington Regional Council park, north of Upper Hutt, where there is a wonderful site full of lovely trees. Lots of sheltered space for campers, with clear pools and a sparkling river, great for fresh-water swimming. Not too far to drive from the city, either for a day trip or to camp on the grassy flats, this area is sheltered by surrounding hills. There is a newly created BBQ/dining area, roofed and adjacent to a smart toilet block. Facilities are cold water only. Apart from the coin operated BBQs, and sinks, no facilities exist for campers who need to be independent. It costs $4 per site. For group bookings inquire from the ranger.

21. Martinborough Camp Ground

Cnr Princes and Dublin Streets, Martinborough (06) 306-9518

Quite a pleasant little camp, with a number of trees for shelter. The camp is behind the swimming pool and is administered by the Borough Council. The kitchen has two full size stoves and the laundry has an auto washer but no dryer. Only one of each in the ablutions, but with few power sites here it may not be a problem. There is room for about 30 tents. Contact the caretaker Paul Armstrong for details. Power sites $12 for two. Tent sites $10 for two.

22. Leeway Motel & Caravan Park

8 Fitzherbert Street, Featherston (06) 308-9811

The first town "over the hill" from Wellington and in to the Wairarapa. This is a mini-camp with 12 power sites, motel units and some sites for tents. Although there are no cooking facilities, a new kitchen is soon to be added. The local shops and services are across the road. The ablutions are very nice, if slightly limited in numbers. There is a fully equipped laundry. The sites are on a level lawn, tidy and well groomed. Your new hosts Paul and Bernice Robinson. Tent sites and power sites $12 for two. 🖵 $68 for two.

23. Greytown Motor Camp
Kuratawhiti Street, Greytown (06) 304-9837, after hours (06) 308-9891

Just off S Hwy 2, this is a lovely level park in the heart of market-garden and orchard country. Trees, ferns and shrubbery enhance the grounds, which have 32 sites with power and some tent sites. In the centre there is a picnic and BBQ garden. Two tennis courts and a wonderful children's playground are provided. The facilities were locked when we called, but are provided in two groups. There is a swimming pool adjacent. This camp may be closed in winter. Contact the Martinborough District Council for details.

24. Howard Booth Caravan Park
Belvedere Road, Carterton (06) 379-8267 or (06) 379-8112

Conforming to the neat, quiet aspect of its surroundings this is a desirable small camp, not far from the main road and the village shops. There are 16 power sites divided by shrubs into very private individual bays. There is room for 20 tents, also on tidy attractive sites. The kitchen provides stove and microwave cooking and fridge. A glassed-in dining area has TV and opens to a covered terrace. There is free use of the washing machine and a dryer is provided. A well appointed ablution block includes full paraplegic facilities. These amenities are central in the camp and there is a dump point. Your hosts Mike and Beryl Newport. Sites with power are $13 for two people and tent sites are $11. Other accommodation is from $12 for two. 🏠 (sleeps six).

25. Waiohine Gorge
Waiohine Gorge Road, Carterton–Department of Conservation

The Waiohine Gorge Road is another popular access point to the eastern side of the Tararua Forest Park. Camping areas are still being developed, but existing sites are private, and centralised rubbish facilities, flush toilets and water-supply points are handy. There are steep banks down the Waiohine River and children must be well supervised. This is a popular area for rafting and canoeing, and it is a major area for outdoor education, with 1800–2000 students visiting each year. There is also good brown trout fishing. One of the country's longest swing bridges leads to attractive bush walks up the Waiohine Valley. Totara Flats can be reached in 3– 4 hours. There is also a day picnic area with BBQ facilities and a shelter, short of the road end. Again children must be supervised because of the steep banks down to the river. For further information contact the Department of Conservation, PO Box 191 Masterton.

26. Mawley Park Motor Camp
Oxford Street, PO Box 444 Masterton (06) 376-6454 (phone & fax)

If you are looking for a holiday spot to explore the hub of the Wairarapa, Masteron should be on your itinerary. Mawley Park is close to the northern end of the township and occupies an attractive location on the banks of the

Waipoua River. The grounds are level and well maintained with large trees and plenty of space for the 100 or so tent sites and 60 sites with power. The camping areas are grouped in separate sections with sealed road access and ablutions serving each area. These include paraplegic facilities and a ladies bath. There is good kitchen and auto laundry equipment too. Access to all amenities is by way of a punch number system. A dump point is provided. There is a TV and recreation room. This is an attractive Masterton District Council camp in the care of Brian and Alma Speers. Tent sites are $7 per person and power sites are $15 for two. ⌼ at varying prices.

27. Holdsworth Lodge
Mt Holdsworth Road, Masterton–Department of Conservation

Located 15km west of Masterton, this is a popular well serviced camping area set in bush at one of the main access points to the Tararua Forest Park. The road is sealed to within 1km of the camping area and secluded well-drained sites are available near the river and up on bush terraces. There are centralised rubbish facilities, convenient water supply points and both flush and pit toilets. Holdsworth is suitable for families, with good BBQ amenities (wood supplied) and the Atiwhakatu Stream has good swimming holes for children. A resident caretaker has information on the great array of park walks which cater for all levels of fitness. Mount Holdsworth Lodge (20 beds) at $8 per night, has basic cooking facilities. For further information contact the Dept of Conservation, PO Box 191 Masterton.

28. Kiriwhakapapa
Kiriwhakapapa Road, Masterton–Department of Conservation

The road is sealed to within 2km of the campground, which has flush toilets, a convenient water supply and good picnic facilities. This is a popular area for families and provides good access to the Tararua Forest Park, with walks to the Blue Range and along the Mikimiki Track. For further information contact the Dept of Conservation, PO Box 191 Masterton.

29. Eketahuna Motor Camp
Stanly Street–PO Box 23 Eketahuna (06) 375-8242

Possibly not always in use (the gate may be locked), this is a "backwoods" camp but neat and well-tree'd. Situated on the banks of the Makakahi Stream it offers lots of pleasantly private tent sites with masses of pine and gum trees. Choose from shady and sunny areas. Minimal amenities, but there are 20 sites with power and two ⌼.

30. Carnival Park Motor Camp
Glasgow Road, Pahiatua (06) 376-7583

Surrounded by a high macrocarpa hedge, this camp is just south of the township of Pahiatua, not notable for any major holiday attractions but having a good selection of shops and services. There is a children's play area provided. The grounds are level, open sites of quite a generous size, with some large shady trees. 22 sites have power. The kitchen has a stove, but lacks tea-making facilities. There is a dining area, glassed-in and inviting. Outside the kitchen an automatic washing machine is provided on a patio. All camp sites are $8. There is a new 🔳 available.

31. Castlepoint Motor Camp
Jetty Road, PO Box 413 Castlepoint, via Masterton (06) 372-6705

This is quite a dramatic seaside environment some 64km from Masterton. The road is long and winding, through the rural Wairarapa countryside. An avenue of tall palms leads into the camp which is alongside a safe beach sheltered from the south by the outcrop of Castlepoint Rock and lighthouse. There are 110 power sites with taps, plus 40 for tents, 14 cabins and a backpackers lodge. The land is terraced and sites are varied, grouped and with shady trees. There are great sea views. All the amenities are modern and clean, with push-button showers. The kitchen combines with dining and there is a separate TV lounge. The laundry has a cold-water automatic wash and a dryer. There is even a swimming pool. A dump point is provided. Nearby is a store and service station (with LPG). Swimming, surfing and fishing are very rewarding here. Ask about the beach horse-racing, a popular attraction held in March. No pets please. Your hosts Sue Martin and Tom Wilton. Tent sites are $8 per person and power sites are $9.🔳 $35 for two.

32. Riversdale Beach Motor Camp
Riversdale Beach, via Masterton (06) 372-3482

South of Castlepoint, this is a sweeping ocean beach with sand dunes and rolling surf. The journey from Masterton is around 54km. The whole area is a seaside resort, with a 9 hole golf course an alternative attraction. With 45 power sites and 55 for tents, the camp is divided by the coast road although most of the seaward side may be occupied by leasehold caravans. The other side is less appealing, but possibly more sheltered. There is a children's play area. The necessary amenities are provided, to a fairly basic standard. Fishing is an attraction here; put out the crayfish pots. There are also surf boards for hire. You can shop at the camp store and also get a fish and chip meal. Pine trees and beach aspect. All camp sites are $8 per adult and free for "under 5's". Your host Daniel Shearer.

33. Lake Ferry Motor Camp
Lake Ferry Road, RD2 Featherston (06) 307-7873

This interesting area is bounded by Lake Onoke and the open sea. It is 45km south of Featherston and is separated from the "urban sprawl" of Wellington by the Orongorongo Ranges. There are 30 power sites, limited tenting and some cabins on level ground, with a dense border of trees at one end, and direct access to the lake. Alongside is a rugged stretch of coast separated from the lake by a stony spit. There is a boat ramp and a playground for children. This is a sparsely populated area and provisions should be brought with you, although there is a general store and petrol supplies 5km away. Across the road is a country pub where you can get meals and icecreams. The fishing opportunities are endless. Well worth a trip to explore and blow the cobwebs away. The amenities are modest, but include a kitchen with two full stoves, fridge/freezers and TV. A covered deck and picnic tables are outside. Basic ablutions and laundry facilities are provided. It is $8 per person for a site with power, or $7.50 for tents. Other accommodation is from $15 per person. Your friendly hosts Jan and Geoff Bell may take pets here by arrangement .��.

34. Putangirua Scenic Reserve
Whatarangi Road, Te Kopi–Department of Conservation

This campground lies roughly between Cape Palliser and Lake Ferry and access is by way of the coast road. Trampers and recreational hunters can enter the Haurangi Forest Park from here. There are short walks to the unique geological formations—the Putangirua Pinnacles. The camp is well drained, has pit toilets, and water is available from a nearby stream. The campground is well used by people fishing around the coast, and near Cape Palliser Lighthouse is a seal colony, usually with 200 to 900 seals. For further information contact the Dept of Conservation RD2 Featherston.

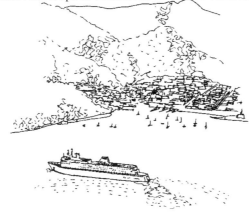

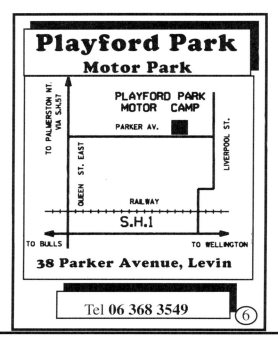

Playford Park
Motor Park

38 Parker Avenue, Levin

Tel **06 368 3549**

⑥

⑦

Tel 06 362 6799 Fax 06 362-6502

TRAINING & CONFERENCE CENTRE
State Highway 1, Manakau, Private Bag 4006 Levin

- ♦ **Tourist Flats**
- ♦ **Tourist Cabins ****
- ♦ **Restaurant**
- ♦ **Swimming Pool**
- ♦ **Confidence Course**
- ♦ **Tramping in the hills**
- ♦ **Within an hour's drive to the ferry**

Qualmark
NEW ZEALAND LTD

SOUTH ISLAND
TIME/DISTANCE MAP

Takaka

2·20
(111)

NELSON

2·10
(116)

Picton

0·30
(28)

2·30
(130)

2·50
(163)

Blenheim

Westport

0·55 1·00
(47) (48)

Murchison

0·35
(32)

Inangahua

1·25
(84)

2·20
(129)

2·30 (101)

Reefton

0·50 (45)

Springs Junction

Greymouth

1·20
(79)

2·45
(154)

Kaikoura

2·05
(82)

3·35 (179)

Otira

2·20
(131)

Waipara

Franz Josef Glacier

0·50 (24)

Fox Glacier

2·50
(167)

1·05
(58)

CHRISTCHURCH

2·10 (118)

Mt Cook

Haast

0·50
(58)

2·40
(154)

2·20
(163)

Akaroa

3·50
(145)

Pukaki

Milford Sound

0·35 (37)

Omarama

Timaru

Wanaka

2·10
(114)

2·00
(119)

1·20
(84)

2·10 (117)

Queenstown

2·55
(171)

2·50
(121)

Cromwell

1·05
(62)

Alexandra

Oamaru

1·00
(60)

Te Anau

1·55
(106)

2·20
(143)

Palmerston

1·15
(80)

Lumsden

1·05
(64)

1·00
(56)

DUNEDIN

1·20
(80)

Gore

1·40
(98)

1·00 (58)

Invercargill

1·00
(66)

Milton

(194)

Bluff

NELSON AND MARLBOROUGH DIRECTORY

Key to locations and maps in Nelson and Marlborough. Starts on the western side of Golden Bay. Follows S Hwy 60, except for minor roads leading to Abel Tasman National Park. At Motueka goes inland as far as Motupiko. Returns to the coast and camping between Motueka and Richmond. Continues on S Hwy 6 with a deviation to Okiwi Bay and French Pass, then around Queen Charlotte Sound. Leaves Picton travelling south on the main route via Blenheim to Lake Grassmere. Finishes at the inland area of Nelson Lakes National Park.

Collingwood	1.	Pakawau Beach Motor Camp
Collingwood	2.	Collingwood Motor Camp
Takaka	3	Golden Bay Holiday Park
Takaka	4.	Golden Bay Caravan Park
Takaka	5.	Pohara Beach Camp
Abel Tasman National Park	6.	Totaranui Camping Ground (DoC)
Marahau	7.	The Barn
Marahau	8	Marahau Beach Camp Ltd
Kaiteriteri	9	Kaiteriteri Beach Motor Camp
Kaiteriteri	10.	Bethany Park Christian Camp
Motueka	11.	Motueka Vineyard Tourist Unit
Motueka	12.	Fearon's Bush Motor Camp
Motueka	13.	Fernwood Holiday Park
Tapawera	14.	Crossroads Holiday Park
Motupiko	15.	Quinney's Bush
Mapua	16.	McKee Memorial Reserve
Mapua	17.	Ruby Bay Backpackers Lodge
Mapua	18.	Mapua Leisure Park
Richmond	19.	Richmond Holiday Park
Richmond	20.	Waimea Town & Country Club
Nelson	21.	Tahuna Beach Holiday Park
Nelson	22.	Nelson Cabins & Caravan Park
Nelson	23.	Brook Valley Motor Camp
Nelson	24.	Maitai Valley Motor Camp

via Rai Valley	25.	Okiwi Holiday Park & Lodge
French Pass	26.	French Pass (DoC)
Rai Valley	27.	Pelorous Bridge Motor Camp (DoC)
Canvastown	28.	Pinedale Motor Camp
Canvastown	29.	Wakavale Farmstay
Havelock	30.	Havelock Community Park
Havelock south	31.	Chartridge Park
Wairau River	32.	Onamalutu (DoC)
Portage Bay	33.	Cow Shed Bay (DoC)
Picton	34.	Queen Charlotte Holiday Park
Kenepuru Sound	35.	Te Mahia Bay Holiday Resort
Picton	36.	Momorangi Bay Motor Camp (DoC)
Port Underwood	37.	Whatamonga Bay (DoC)
Port Underwood	38.	Whites Bay (DoC)
Picton	39.	Picton Campervan Park
Picton	40.	Alexanders Motor Park
Picton	41.	Blue Anchor Holiday Park
Picton	42.	Parklands Marina Holiday Village
Picton	43.	Waikawa Bay Holiday Park
Spring Creek	44.	Spring Creek Holiday Park
Blenheim	45.	Blenheim Motor Camp
Blenheim	46.	Grove Bridge Holiday Park
Blenheim	47.	Grenfelt Caravan Park
Blenheim	48.	Duncannon Caravan Park
Seddon	49.	Seddon Motor Camp
Lake Grassmere	50.	Marfells Beach (DoC)
Wairau River	51.	Kowhai Point (DoC)
St Arnaud	52.	Kerr Bay Camping Ground (DoC)
St Arnaud	53.	West Bay Camping Ground (DoC)
Nelson Lakes Parks	54.	Lake Rotoroa (DoC)

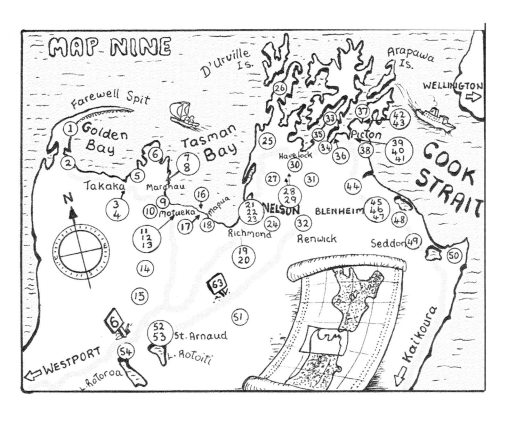

Chapter 9

NELSON AND MARLBOROUGH

The delightful jigsaw of contrasting bush-draped bays and sparkling waters are your invitation to the Marlborough Sounds. The almost land-locked waters are often first seen from the deck of the Interisland Ferry. Immediately it evokes the holiday feeling and the desire to see more of this intriguing area, some of which can only be reached by boat. The Cook Strait ferries are the only means to transport your vehicle between the North and South Islands. Picton, at the head of Queen Charlotte Sound, is a little town with a busy port. As well as being the southern terminal for the arriving and departing passengers, Picton has water taxis, fishing and pleasure craft plying its waters. A good range of camping spots lies on the fringes of Picton and in the Sounds.

Across the Wairau River towards Nelson the village of Havelock is an attractive spot to break your journey. From the Rai Valley the road traverses some picturesque ranges before descending to Nelson, on the fringe of Tasman Bay. Various communities flourish around the bay, popular for the climate, fruit growing and especially as holiday destinations. You will find a wide choice awaits you along this coastal route, culminating in traffic-free Abel Tasman National Park. The Park itself offers camping and tramping to those who want to "get off the beaten track".

More remote, but just as delightful is Golden Bay, protected from the Tasman Sea by Farewell Spit. Check out the Takaka and Collingwood districts. Some wonderful sandy beaches line this large bay.

Travelling east and joining the main route south, after a short journey one arrives at Blenheim. Because it regularly records New Zealand's longest sunshine hours, and enjoys a low rainfall, the surrounding fertile areas have increasingly developed a reputation for producing many fine wines.

If you want the contrast of forest camping, head inland to the township of St Arnaud, gateway to the Nelson Lakes National Park. This region attracts the independent camper who can also ski the Rainbow and Mt Robert ski fields. Various wilderness camps are accessible and enjoyed by the more energetic traveller.

The neighbouring Marlborough and Nelson regions, noted for both mild weather and superb scenery, are worth a lengthy visit. It would be a pity not to put them on your itinerary.

NELSON – MARLBOROUGH

1. Pakawau Beach Motor Camp
RD 1 Collingwood (03) 524-8327

At the Farewell Spit end of Golden Bay and facing the sunrise, this biscuit-coloured sandy beach seems to stretch forever. Most sites are protected from the beach by a border of shrubs and trees. The camp store also serves the local community with grocery items as well as petrol pumps. You can arrange tours here and Eftpos is available. A range of good accommodation is an alternative. Clusters of camping sites are divided by shrub and flax borders and the camp has its own boat ramp. A children's play area is around the BBQ garden and close to the kitchen, which has hot-plate and microwave cooking. The ablutions are roomy with large dressing rooms off the metered showers. The laundry has excellent automatic washers and a dryer. TV is not provided here. It might be a nice change! This is a tidy camp and your host is Glenys Forster. Tent sites are $14 for two, or with power $15 for two. 🖻 and a 🖼.

2. Collingwood Motor Camp
William Street, Collingwood (03) 524-8149

A camp with a sense of humour. (As you come in look for the invisible kiwi, as you leave look for the moa remains.) This camp has an attractive location on a little promontory with views to Farewell Spit. There are a variety of sites, slightly uneven and rather crowded in the main camping area, with some cabins and self-contained accommodation as well. Along the water's edge there are more private and tree'd sites. Outdoor taps were just a little under supplied. A most appealing kitchen-dining and adjoining sitting room has French doors to your table and chairs under the beach umbrella. There is an extra sink and tea-making facilities in the sitting room. The kitchen is also supplied with pots and pans. The ablutions include a paraplegic suite. The laundry has washer, dryer and iron. There is a hard tennis court in the centre of the camp and you can hire racquets. Also canoes, bikes and gold pans are offered for hire. There is a boat ramp. Very handy to Collingwood village on this sunny coast. Your host Shelley and Bill Climo.Tent sites are $7 per person, or with power $8 for two. Backpackers share $13 per person.🖻 and 🖼.

3. Golden Bay Holiday Park
Tukurua Beach, RD2 Takaka (03) 525-9742

A seaside park with an immaculate presentation, offering a variety of sites for campers. Perhaps the prime areas are each side of a tree-lined avenue almost beside the beach. There is also "Campervan Court" which is grassed and separated from the sea only by shady trees. A large services block is close to the beach and an extensive dining hall, with telephone supplied, is off the kitchen. The laundry (with automatic machines) adjoins the women's showers, and all are in spotless condition. Besides providing 100 tent sites and 75 power sites the park has a backpackers lodge and cabins. An outdoor shower and a children's play area are provided. There is a dump station here. Remember that this camp is closed in mid-winter (June/July) but for a golden summer this is a choice spot. Your hosts Peter and Johanna Crockett.

All camp sites are at $17 for two persons.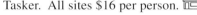

 ### 4. Golden Bay Caravan Park
718 Abel Tasman Drive, Takaka (03) 525-9046

Probably you will have to pass this one by. It is a small park almost totally occupied by long-term residents. There usually are lawn sites available for tenters. All the facilities are small scale but nice and immaculately clean. To find out if there is a casual site, contact your host Colin Pettit. There may be a spot here for your dog. Sites are $8 per person.

5. Pohara Beach Camp
Pohara RD1 Takaka (03) 325-9500 (fax 03 525-8689)

Footprints in the sand, with a horseshoe of sandy beach beside the camp. Come here for peace and quiet amongst the shady trees on well groomed sites. There is a cook-friendly kitchen with a hedged al fresco dining area alongside. The other amenities are plentiful and well kept, with all the usual appointments. There is a good supply of outdoor taps. On the site is a 7-day store and petrol pump. There is a restaurant and bar directly across the road. People without pets are welcome. Your friendly hosts are Judith and Selwyn Tasker. All sites $16 per person.

 ### 6. Totaranui Camping Ground
Totaranui Road, Abel Tasman National Park, via Motueka Department of Conservation (03) 528-8083 or (03) 525-8026

The Abel Tasman National Park's warm and temperate coast means it is a pleasant area to visit all year round. Camping at Totaranui is at a well-spread -out site some 33km from Takaka at the northern end of the National Park abutting a golden sands beach. Tents, campervans and caravans are catered for at the Totaranui campground and in summer (between Labour Weekend and Easter) a shop is open which sells basic food items and ancillary goods as well as tickets for various trips. There is also a coin phone. However, power and hot water are not available at any of the facilities, so it is a "back to basics" experience. Excellent swimming, fishing, boating, diving, walking or picnicking opportunities exist in the area. No pets please. Good public transport to and from Totaranui is available and bookings are essential in mid-summer. There is a boat-launching facility. Please book through the Department of Conservation. Tent sites $7 per person.

7. The Barn
Near Marahau, Abel Tasman National Park, RD2 Motueka
(03) 527-8043

Primarily catering for backpackers with the closest hostel to Abel Tasman National Park (the Park headquarters and cafe are next door), this has plenty of tent sites too. In fact you can hire a tent here and also cookers. There is a small camp store plus fresh fruit and vegetables for sale. Pick up your DoC passes, and make water-taxi bookings here. Camping is in an open paddock with a border of gum trees. The amenities are not lavish, but are clean and new. Buses from Nelson make this an easy destination, and ideal for trampers. All tent sites are $8 per person, with a bed in the hostel for $13. Your hosts Dave and Gloria.

8. Marahau Beach Camp Ltd
RD2 Motueka, 18km north of Motueka (03) 527-8176

It's a long trail a-winding to this camp, but the road is sealed. Although the camp is close to the shore, it is not alongside, nor flush with attractions for the holidaymaker. The amenities are large, but not lavish. There is a dining room with open fire. The showers and dressing rooms are spacious. The laundry is well equipped. Sites here are $16 and your host is Leonie Dymock.

9. Kaiteriteri Beach Motor Camp
Kaiteriteri–Motueka (03) 527-8010 fax (03) 5278031

On a picture-postcard sheltered bay, this camp has a popular following. The village-type layout offers many extras. There is a licensed restaurant and takeaway shop within the camp. A post box and petrol are next door. Sporting enthusiasts have tennis and volleyball while there is a golf course alongside. There are plenty of amenities blocks here, all very sturdy and clean. This is camping on a large scale with a multitude of power sites, 🏠 and chalets. Your hosts Daphne and Neville Stretch.

10. Bethany Park Christian Camp
Martins Farm Road, Kaiteriteri (03) 527-8123

A most attractive destination in a sheltered valley with a tree border. It is not right on the beach, but combines a farm-seaside location. The sites looked appealing and the amenities are excellent. Once again there has been no new information available. It is possibly more geared for groups.

11. Motueka Vineyard Tourist Unit
328 High Street, Motueka (03) 528-8550

An urban stopover where camping is a sideline to the main accommodation. The few sites available are on grass with shelter and shade. The communal kitchen is fairly small, but does have a fridge. There is a good laundry with automatic machines. The ablutions are well kept and include a babies bath. There is hostel accommodation, otherwise there are only 8 camp sites provided, 2 with power. Tent sites $8. Power sites $20 single ($30 double). 🏠 accommodation

12. Fearon's Bush Camp
10 Fearon Street, Motueka (03) 528-7189 (phone & fax)

The lovely environment of this park is not obvious from the entrance. Within there are smooth lawns and a myriad of mature trees. There are 200 sites here and most have power. An almost new amenities block has given the camp some great facilities. The kitchen opens to a covered BBQ area with seating. Banks of refrigerated lockers are provided. There are most attractive ablutions, tiled and tastefully presented. The laundry has automatic equipment. There is a dump point here. This camp is close to the shopping and services of Motueka. Michael and Angelia Miles are your hosts. Camping is $8.50 per person. 🏠 $14 per person.

13. Fernwood Holiday Park
519 High Street South (S Hwy 6), Motueka (03) 528-7488

A fledgling park on the main road to Abel Tasman National Park. There are lovely views of Port Motueka from the grounds which have 30 power sites and an attractive landscaped area for tents in a garden setting. Facilities are on a small scale, but with the essential equipment. Your hosts Sharlene and Bruce Primmer. Tent sites $6.50 per person. Power sites $8 per person. 🏠 $30.

14. Crossroads Holiday Park
Tadmore Road, PO Box 67 Tapawera (03) 522-4334

On S Hwy 61 and inland from Nelson and Motueka, this is a well wooded park with random camping. There are 15 power sites and 20 for tents. The land is level and there is a dump station here. Drop in to the kitchen for the whole gamut of indoor recreation. There is also a fuel burning stove. There are good modern ablutions with unisex showers. The laundry is basic, with old machines. Upkeep is just a bit on the ragged side, but comfortable for general purposes. Pets can stay by prior arrangement. Use noticeboard for advice if camp is unattended. All camping is $10 for two people. 🏚 and 🚐.

 ### 15. Quinney's Bush
Motupiko, RD2 Nelson (03) 522-4249

What camping is really about! The owner/manager here has operated this farm camp over the past decades. Focusing on the youngsters, he has an amazing variety of experiences awaiting them. Try the sack rides, the 10 flying foxes, the roundabout. There is also good river swimming. Spread across 6 hectares of open spaces and native bush, this camp operates all year round. There are only 5 sites with power, but tons of tenting space. This is a pet friendly place. You will have to be an independent cook, but there is wood supplied for fires. There are flush toilets and plenty of hot water in the free showers. An agitator washing machine and basins are the laundry facilities. Your host Ray takes a personal interest in his campers and asks for donations on behalf of Christian charitable work. The expected charges are $4 per adult and 50 cents for children.

16. McKee Memorial Reserve
Ruby Bay, Mapua (03) 540-2685

Right at the water's edge of a pebbly beach, this has plenty of space and good new play equipment for the children. There are lots of taps here but no power, no kitchen and no showers. There are long-drop toilets. The road is paved and trees are plentiful. BBQs are provided at intervals. This is a Tasman District Council camp with no on-site office. It will cost you $4 per person or $6 for two to camp here.

17. Ruby Bay Backpackers Lodge
S Hwy 60, Ruby Bay, Mapua (03) 540-2542

Between Motueka and Mapua, Ruby Bay is not right on the beach. It is a budget way to break your journey between the many resorts of Tasman Bay. There are cabins and both power and tent sites. The amenities appear to be satisfactory, with a nice recreation room. Inquire direct for further information. 🏚.

18. Mapua Leisure Park

Toru Street No 33, Mapua–Nelson (03) 540-2666 (phone & fax)

For the non-conformist camper, you will find this camp easy to bare! The policy is clothes optional. As well as this, the location is superb with a water boundary on three sides and for the sea lovers a new waterside camp area has been established. There are around 200 sites available. The kitchen appointments are excellent with gas and microwave cooking and a dining patio, plus BBQs. Light meals are available at the popular on-site cafe which has a large deck for outdoor dining and water views. Get in a lather in the community shower, without door, for the uninhibited. The children's play area is imaginative. "Custers Fort" is a feature and there is plenty of equipment. The park contains a swimming pool, sauna/spa, tennis and volleyball courts. The large, comfortable TV and recreation room opens to an extensive deck with pavement chess and backgammon tables. A boat ramp and boat hire is offered. Your hosts Dave Hutton and Kathy Trott. All tent sites are $8 per person or $9 with power. 🖳 and 🖳

19. Richmond Motel & Holiday Park

29 Gladstone Road (S Hwy 6) Richmond, Nelson (03) 544-7323

or (03) 544-5218 (fax 03 544-4597)

This park offers a range of accommodation on well manicured grounds with a reasonable capacity for campers. There is also an inviting swimming pool with outdoor furniture for poolside relaxation. The kitchen is spotless, small but well equipped and a separate fridge room is available. There is a carpeted TV room. The ablutions are well kept, with both unisex and separate sex facilities There is a dump point here. There is automatic equipment in the laundry. It is an easy place to stop for the traveller, and the Richmond Information Centre is across the road. Your hosts Nita and Paul Borcovsky. All camping here is $17 for two persons.

20. Waimea Town & Country Club Caravan Park

345 Queen Street, PO Box 3183, Richmond (03) 544-6476

More of a "members only" facility and entertainment centre. You can enjoy a drink and a meal and play the machines. It is very close to the commercial centre of Richmond. Sites for camping are somewhat of a sideline here, but they are available, as are hire caravans. There are other sports facilities (a bowling green and squash court) within the park. There are standard service blocks for campers. Inquire direct for more information.

21. Tahuna Beach Holiday Park
70 Beach Road, Tahunanui–Private Bag 25, Nelson (03) 548-5159

(fax 03 548-5294)

A large scale holiday park with an incredible number of sites and other accommodation. The 22-hectare park is delightful with lovely trees and a variety of terrain. Despite an enormous capacity for campers there is good privacy here. Camp sites tend to be grouped in little clusters, well serviced with amenities. Name it – you should find it here! There is even an on-site supermarket. This complex is just about self contained and is adjacent to Tahuna Beach. There are dump points provided. Amongst the accommodation options are paraplegic accessible motels. Your new host is Geoff Grocott. Camp sites (around 550 with power) are at $12 per person or $17 for two. 🏠 $30 for two.🏚

22. Nelson Cabins & Caravan Park
230 Vanguard Street, Nelson (03) 548-1445

Ideal for the mobile camper looking for just a handful of sites, which are generous and quite private with a garden aspect., this small park has no provision for tents. It is very centrally situated, with Nelson Hospital opposite and a good selection of services nearby. The facilities are well kept and the ablutions have a paraplegic suite. The kitchen offers individual cool boxes and an adjacent outdoor meal area. TV, automatic washing machines and a dryer are provided. The 20 power sites are tucked into the rear of the tourist flats, and offer comfortable private parking with a dump station. Your host James Dunne. Power sites $16.🏠 and 🏚

23. Brook Valley Motor Camp
Brook Valley, PO Box 294 Nelson (03) 548-0399 (phone & fax)

An extensive camp that stretches along the banks ofThe Brook, in an area which is rich in bird life and has a naturally secluded setting. The "botanical garden" appearance is very appealing, enhanced by many mature trees. The sites are flat, but on varying levels and rather scattered, with taps throughout. Several interesting walks are in the vicinity and you can walk beside the stream to a local dam. There is also a swimming pool, recreation room and TV lounge. Well serviced by reasonable facilities which include automatic laundry equipment. There is an adventure playground for the children. Shop at the camp store, but please don't bring pets. Your new hosts Harold and Diane Osborne. A power site is $15 for two people, or a tent site $14. There are other accommodation units. 🏠.

24. Maitai Valley Motor Camp
Maitai Valley, Nelson (03) 548-7729

Environmentally a delightful spot, reached along a 5km scenic drive, this has a woodland setting with a river swimming pool. The sites are wonderful for the tenter, spacious, yet private. The land is undulating with access by sealed roads, but possibly a bit restricted for large mobile homes. There is a children's playground and a tiny TV room. The facilities are generally good for campers, unless it is the busy season. You will also find an on-site shop. The valley is sunny, but sheltered. Bush camping at its best. There is a dump point here. Your new hosts are Barbara and Allen Cochrane. Tent sites are $14 for two people, or $15 with power. 📺 $20.

25. Okiwi Holiday Park & Lodge
Okiwi Bay, RD 3 Rai Valley– Marlborough (03) 576-5006 (phone & fax)

A recently created park for the traveller on the road to French Pass. Although it is at Okiwi Bay the camp itself is not right on the beach, but there is a boat ramp about 400 metres away. This little camp has only 12 sites, all with power and water. There is a shop for everyday supplies. You can fill dive bottles here and also get petrol. The first class, spacious facilities are wheelchair accessible and most attractive. Bunkrooms are available in a small lodge, well appointed and with a delightful communal lounge/dining room. Meals can be provided for lodge guests. To enjoy the local attractions, mainly fishing, diving, boating and mountain biking, charter or guided trips can be arranged here. Your welcoming hosts Pam and Ian Montgomery advise that booking for trips is essential. Camp sites are $8.50 per person. Lodge beds from $20, with discounts for family groups and longer stays.

26. French Pass
French Pass Road, Department of Conservation (03) 546-9335

Located at the end of French Pass Road. Facilities include showers, toilets and water supply. There is limited parking. A shop is opposite for supplies. A good location for exploring the outer Pelorous Sound. Good boating and fishing. Tent sites are $4 per person.

27. Pelorous Bridge Motor Camp
Pelorous Bridge, RD2 Rai Valley – Department of Conservation

(03) 571-6091

Since last century Pelorus Bridge has been a popular stopover point for travellers between Marlborough and Nelson. The camp is situated in the heart of a magnificent lowland forest reserve dominated by kahikatea trees.

The Pelorus River sweeps through the reserve, making the camp ideal for swimming, picnicking, trout fishing and canoeing. Bush walkers, botanisers and bird-watchers will also profit from a visit to the area. No pets please. A shop, card phone, 14 power sites, 23 tent sites and 5 cabins plus separate, low-budget backpackers accommodation is available. There are kitchen, shower and laundry facilities. Tent sites are $7 per person and power sites are $8.🖼.

28. Pinedale Motor Camp
Waikamarina Valley, PO Box 36, Canvastown (8km from the main road) (03) 574-2349

Encouraging signs lead you to this pioneer camp, which is almost midway between Blenheim and Nelson. There is a 3km stretch of unsealed road before you reach the tree-studded valley. Right at the entrance is a new 9 hole golf course, and club hire is available. Camp sites are terraced above the river, which is a popular spot for gold panning and for "tubeing" in the summer. The kitchen has very few appliances (bring your own cooker) but there is a recreation room with pot bellied stove, dart board, table tennis and TV. The ablutions are good with free showers and a shub. There is a camp store for all your basic supplies and the local hotel has meals available. Inquire about the kennels, if you want to bring your dog. A camping retreat that adequately provides for simple relaxation. Your hosts Grant and Julia Craig. Tent sites are $7 per person, or with power $8 .🖼 $12.50 per person.

29. Wakavale Farmstay
6 km up the road (behind Trout Hotel), Canvastown

Lots of options here if you want to try Kiwi ingenuity in a farming location. There are many wandering animals, meet George and Mildred the resident pigs (with piglets in tow on our visit). Apart from the "normal" ablutions you might like to try the open air bath! There is a privacy fence. Stoke your fire, warm the water and contemplate the stars. The outdoor showers are heated by a coal range. There is a kitchen complete with pots and pans, crockery and cutlery and microwave and rangette. The outdoor summer chef can use a sheltered gas-cooking alternative. Campfire evenings are great for socialising. There is an adequate laundry. Apart from two cabins and a caravan, the Tree House honeymoon suite may appeal. Something different for the adventurous camper. Your hosts are Arlene and Graeme Couling.Tent sites $7(with bed $10).Tree House $15.🖼 🏕.

30. Havelock Community Park
24 Inglis Street, Havelock (03) 574-2339

This camp is close to the attractive village of Havelock. Each power site is well supplied with a tap and rubbish tin and on nice level ground with some large shady trees. Plenty of tent sites too. All the amenities are clean, with metered showers and a disabled-access toilet in the ablutions. There is TV in the kitchen and an extra outdoor oven provided. The laundry has automatic equipment. Administration is by Phillip and Janette Steel. Tent sites are from $7 per person, with power plus $2. $13 plus $2 surcharge for two.

31. Chartridge Park
S Hwy 6, 8km south of Havelock (03) 574-2129

Presenting a most appealing image, this camp has a lovely orchard/garden setting. There is a well fenced swimming pool here. Practice your golf on the 6 hole course and make friends with the pet sheep. The ablution facilities are first class, with a paraplegic unit. The kitchen is excellent and a big brick BBQ garden is a feature, surrounded by a high sheltering fence. There is a good laundry. A comfortable TV and games room is provided. The local river is good for trout fishing and eeling. The camp was unattended when we called. Your hosts here are Murray and Norma Sanders. All camping is $8 per person.

32. Onamalutu
Onamalutu Road, North bank Wairau River–Department of Conservation (03) 527-9100

A self-registration Department of Conservationcamp with few facilities. For the escapist this is rather remote camping and you need to be self sufficient. There is a water supply and 6 power points here. Great botanist country, and pleasant for walking. For details contact DoC at PO Box 51 Renwick. It is $4 for a tent site or $6 with power.

33. Cow Shed Bay
Portage Bay, Kenepuru Sound–Department of Conservation (03) 546-9335

A self–registration conservation camp in Portage Bay. Basic facilities are toilets and water supply. A good place for boating and fishing. A good location if you wish to walk or mountain bike the Queen Charlotte Walking Track. Tent sites $4 per person.

34. Queen Charlotte Holiday Park
The Grove, RD1 Picton (03) 574-2251 (phone & fax)

On Queen Charlotte Drive, this park is midway between Picton and Havelock and 18km from both. This picturesque spot is sited beside but above the waters of the Sounds. The grounds are prolific with trees of every description and the whole impression is of a tranquil haven. You can hire dinghies and canoes here. There is a shop on site for basic needs. Just a small capacity here, with homely but well kept amenities, including a brand-new kitchen, with everything; pots and pans as well as the kitchen sink. You will find both auto-washer and dryer in the laundry. There is a gas BBQ. There is a TV and games room. The 4 power sites are $18 for two people and tent sites are $7 each person. $50

35. Te Mahia Holiday Resort
Kenepuru Sound, Picton (03) 573-4089

One of those delightful bays which are part of the charm of the Sounds. It will take you about an hour's drive from Picton; watch for the Linkwater turn-off. The road is sealed all the way. This a motel and camping ground with all the usual services, mostly unisex. The native bush slopes down to the beach and boat landing. Unobstructed water frontage. There are a moderate number of sites, some with power. $35 per person. Your hosts Trevor and Jann Hook. Camping here is $8.50 per person for two people.

36. Momorangi Bay Camping Ground
Queen Charlotte Drive, RD Picton–Department of Conservation
(03) 573-7865

The Momorangi Bay camp is found in picturesque Queen Charlotte Sound and just 25 minutes drive from Picton. Its sheltered location at the top of Grove Arm is great for boating, swimming, walking and picnicking. Accessible by sealed road from Picton and Blenheim or turn off onto Queen Charlotte Drive if travelling from Nelson. No pets please. Full facilities are available. (Possibly suitable for disabled; please inquire). There is a shop, 80 power and 80 tent sites and a boat ramp. It costs $7 per person to camp here or $8 with power.

37. Whatamonga Bay
Port Underwood Road, Picton – Department of Conservation (03) 573-7582

A self–registration conservation camp with a water supply and toilets. This coastal camp provides excellent bird watching opportunities in an estuarine setting with wilderness values. Contact DoC PO Box 161 Picton. Tent sites $4 per person.

38. Whites Bay
Port Underwood, Picton – Department of Conservation (03) 527-9100

A conservation self-registration reserve at the Pukatea Stream. For the nature lover, as well as walking in the area, there is sea fishing, swimming and small boating. No power and the only facilities are toilets and cold water, but there is disabled access. For enquires write to DoC PO Box 51 Renwick. Tent sites $4 per person.

39. Picton Campervan Park
25 Oxford Street, Picton (03) 573-8875

Somewhere soothing for motorhome drivers to gather their strength. This brand-new park is ideally situated for ferry travellers. You will find hard court parking with all the extras on each site. There are dump point facilities and a car wash. The communal amenities are superb with an elegant lounge, dining and kitchen to a high standard. The showers and toilets are equally impressive. There is even a spa bath. A fully equipped laundry is provided. This park only caters for recreational vehicles. There is no provision for tents. Your hosts Pam and Barrie Lane. Power sites are $9 per person.

40. Alexanders Motor Park
Canterbury Street, Picton (03) 573-6378

Choose your site here from a diverse selection. The park has open sections and others that are heavily wooded. Within the native bush area is the Waitohi Stream for swimming and there are glow worms in the valley. A trampoline and play area is provided for the children. There is an office/store and two kitchens with full stoves and fridges. Both laundries have automatic machines and irons. There are plenty of ablutions. The main amenities block is a little past its prime, but everything is well maintained. There is a dump station here. You may hear passing trains occasionally, but there is no access to the rail line. This park is well located for the Cook Strait ferry terminal and the Picton shops. No dogs here please. Power sites are $17 for two persons. There are tent sites. ▯ $25 for two people and ▯ $25. Welcome back to hosts Liz and Bob Reid.

41. Blue Anchor Holiday Park
70–78 Waikawa Road, Picton (03) 573-7212 (phone & fax)

With a backdrop of bushclad hills, this is a resort offering cabins and camping options and a motel. In the heart of Picton, it is opposite the marina with boat launching facilities. The land is terraced and has a very orderly aspect, with the ablutions in the centre and amply supplied with taps. All facilities were excellent and plentiful. Try the focal-point gazebo offering BBQs, tables and chairs and TV. There is a swimming pool and children's play area and a good range of indoor entertainment. Shopping and services are handy. As a courtesy to late arrivals on the Cook Strait ferry this camp stays open at night (except for Sundays). There is a dump station here. No dogs here please. Your hosts are Lyn and Brian Kirwan. Prices are from $9 per person for tents or $18 for two with power. 🔲 $28. 🔳 $48.

42. Parklands Marina Holiday Village
10 Beach Road, Waikawa Bay, PO Box 237 Picton (03) 573-6343

Just 2.5km from Picton this camp is near the marina but does not have a water frontage. There are 200 sites on level, tree-dotted grounds, perhaps slightly lacking in privacy. An excellent mini-market is on the site. The amenities include two excellent kitchens back to back, with a generous range of appliances. There is an extensive dining area, both indoor and out, strung with coloured lights in the evening. Meals can be supplied in summer by arrangement. The ablutions contain curtained showers and there is a paraplegic unit. There are automatic machines in the laundry. A TV/games room has extra toilet facilities. There is a playground for children. Your hosts are Margaret and Bill Morice. All camp sites are $9 per person. Other accommodation is available.

43. Waikawa Bay Holiday Park
302 Waikawa Road, Picton (03) 573-7434 (phone & fax)

On the eastern coastal fringe of Picton this camp has a wonderful outlook. There are level sites on gently rising land with trees growing between the campsites. With a garden theme there is a plesant outdoor eating area, its BBQ sheltered by trellis and pergola. The tables and chairs invite you to relax. There is a children's play area and a swimming pool. The amenities include a well equipped kitchen with island hobs, microwave and fridge, plus small appliances. There are good ablutions, well kept and with plenty of hot water . The laundry has automatic washing machines, a dryer and irons. It is a gentle stroll to the local shopping, beach and marina. This is a peaceful rural setting with a mini store on site. Your friendly hosts are Kerry, John, Zoe and Doug. All sites $16 for two. 🔲 $29 and 🔳 $45. For further details see page 241.

Marlborough Sounds

The Department of Conservation manages various other campsites in the Marlborough Sounds. These provide an ideal base to explore the area. The inner Sounds provide excellent swimming water, free from rips and warmer than the average coastal waters. Some of the best boating waters in New Zealand are found here. There is a range of walking tracks and there is still much evidence of areas rich in history. For further information on these campsites please contact the Department's Havelock or Picton offices. Present charges are $4 per person.

44. Spring Creek Holiday Park
Rapaura Road, PO Box 47 Spring Creek (03) 570-5893 (fax 03 570-5889)

In the heart of vineyard and fruit-bowl country, this camp is 6km from Blenheim and a short distance from the main highway to Nelson. Along one boundary there are camp sites beside a lazy stream and shaded by willows. Some sites have hard stands for vans and there are 75 with power. The sites are spacious and varied. A special area is set aside for the children's playground and a swimming pool. At each end of the camp there are BBQs. Of the two smallish kitchens provided, one has minimal equipment. A pleasant TV room invites relaxation. There are two blocks of excellent ablutions and all automatic equipment in the laundry. Your congenial hosts are Dave, Val and Geoff and Katherine Bowen. Both power and tent sites are $18 for two people. A lodge and ▥.

45. Blenheim Motor Camp
27 Budge Street, Blenheim (03) 578-7419

A central camp in a more urban situation. The perimeter of the grounds is fringed with willows and there are 24 sites here for campers. There is a swimming pool and a camp store. The cabin accommodation seems to predominate here. There is a good communal kitchen with stoves and microwave cooking. A TV room too. Satisfactory ablutions and a laundry with washing and drying machines. The grounds are in close proximity to the rail line and other services. Prices for all sites are $16 for two people.▥.

46. Grove Bridge Holiday Park
78 Grove Road, Blenheim (03) 578-3667

This is a large park which straddles S Hwy 1 and has a river border with a landscaping project in progress. The grounds are level and spacious with plenty of dividing trees and some picnic tables. There are about 190 sites here, both tent and power. A tavern and fast food outlet are nearby and there is a shop next door. This should be a favourite spot for the children, for entertainment options include swimming pool, trampoline, jungle gym, roller coaster. Yes TV is here as well. There are two well equipped kitchens with plenty of table space, electric cooking, with fridges and toasters as well. Modern ablutions and automatic laundries. In the centre of this park are clusters of other accommodation, two with paraplegic facilities. Your new hosts are David and Elizabeth Lange. All sites are $9 per person. A brand-new lodge is from $30 for two, or ▥ $35.

47. Grenfelt Caravan Park & Motels
173 Middle Renwick Road, Blenheim (03) 578-1259 or (03) 578-1258

Despite a promising appearance from the road, there is little to attract the holidaymaker here. The park has become home base for long-term residents, leaving little for the casual camper. It offers the usual camp facilities and video games, TV and pool table. There are both camp sites and other accommodation, when available. Pets are allowed by arrangement. A swimming pool and a spa pool are provided. Tent sites are $6 per person, or $14 with power for two.

48. Duncannon Caravan Park
St Andrews, Main South Highway, Blenheim RD4 (03) 578-8193 (phone & fax)

Easy access at St Andrews on the newly sealed S Hwy 1, just 2km south of Blenheim. Camping is on attractive lawns with large trees reminiscent of an old garden. An original-style homestead contains the amenities with home comforts in the kitchen and dining areas which are very well appointed and open to an outdoor dining patio. The showers are metered, and rather too compact for comfort, but there is a high standard of cleanliness. The laundry has both washing and drying. There is a riverside area with BBQs and although this is some distance from the amenities it must be a choice site for the tenter. You can hire boats and use the boat jetty. As well as a camp store there is a licensed restaurant next door. Your hosts the Crispin family. The 20 power sites are $9 per person and the 20 tent sites are $8. and $26 for two. For further information see page 241.

49. Seddon Motor Camp
17 Nursery Lane, Seddon (03) 575-7150

A rural retreat just an hour's drive from the Picton ferry and 24km south-east of Blenheim. Amongst the sites are some with bush and reasonable privacy and tame birdlife reside here too. The kitchen is well provided with appliances and includes a table, comfortable seating and TV. You can order a meal for $6. The ablutions are in good order and clean. The washing machine use is free. There are just 17 power sites and 7 on-site caravans, plus around 40 sites for tents. A children's play area and a small library are provided. This is "low key" camping with village services within easy reach. Country camping and country hospitality from the host Denise Corden. Power sites are $18 for two people and tent sites are $10 for two. $18.

50. Marfells Beach
Marfells Beach Road, Lake Grassmere–Department of Conservation
(03) 527-9100

A self-registration conservation campground on the coast. This beachfront camp has only toilets and cold water. Make enquires through DoC, PO Box 51 Renwick. Site fees are $4 per person.

51. Kowhai Point
S Hwy 63, Wairau River–Department of Conservation (03) 527-9100

A self–registration conservation camp. Trout fishing is the main attraction here. There are 2 pit toilets and fresh water only. No power, but there are open fireplaces. No pets please. Make enquires at DoC, PO Box 51 Renwick. Site fees are $4 per person.

52. Kerr Bay Camping Ground (St Arnaud)
Eastern Bay of Lake Rotoiti, Nelson Lakes National Park – Department of Conservation (03) 521-1806

If you are looking for wilderness camping, this is for you! With infinite camp sites on attractive mountain country, the facilities are somewhat primitive and not really operational in winter. There is easy access to this outpost camp on the shores of Lake Rotoiti, with jetty available. There are 10 power sites and 17 tent sites here. Contact Park HQ C/o PO St Arnaud for details. No pets please. Power sites are $8 per person and $7 for tents.

53. West Bay Camping Ground (St Arnaud)
Western shore of Lake Rotoiti, Nelson Lakes National Park–Department of Conservation (03) 521-1806

West Bay camping ground is another wilderness camp with sites formed by natural landscape features of boulders and shrubbery. Easily accessible to motorists, and facilities include hot water showers. There are 19 power sites and 43 tent sites here. A delightful spot in summer, it is on the lake shore. Contact Park HQ C/o PO St Arnaud for details. No pets please. Power sites are $8 per person and $7 for tents.

54. Lake Rotoroa
Nelson Lakes National Park–Department of Conservation (03) 521-1806

A self–registration conservation camp. A number of water sports are attractions on the lake. There are gas BBQs available. Other amenities are 4 toilets and fresh water. It is interesting for walking and tramping too. No pets please. Make enquires at Park HQ DoC, Private Bag St Arnaud. Tent sites are $4 per person.

Waikawa Bay Holiday Park

302 Waikawa Road Picton

(43)

Phone/Fax 03 573-7434

- ☼ Quiet and relaxed with views over looking Waikawa Bay, close to swimming beach, boat ramp and shops.
- ☼ Quality motel, tourist flats,cabins on-site caravans.and camping facilities.
- ☼ We offer a courtesy van to and from the ferry terminal for motel, tourist flat, and cabin dwellers.
- ☼ You are assured of a warm friendly welcome by Kerry, John and family.

Present this coupon for a 10% discount

Duncannon Caravan Park

(48)

PRESENT THIS ADVERT AND GET **10%** OFF BOAT HIRE OR A BOAT TRIP

Main Highway
2 km South of
Blenheim

THE CRISPIN FAMILY
WELCOMES YOU

PH/FAX 03
578-8193

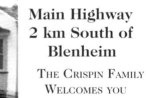

√ Quiet relaxed atmosphere

√ River access for boaties & fishermen

√ BBQ, large lawned area

√ Cabins & on-site caravans

NORTH AND MID– CANTERBURY DIRECTORY

Key to locations and maps in North and Mid Canterbury. Begins on the east coast just north of Kaikoura and continues south with the majority of camps along the coast. Here and there an inland route is necessary to reach mostly forest-based camps. The region finishes at Ashburton in the south.

Waipapa Bay	1.	Waipapa Camp Ground
Kaikoura	2.	The Esplanade Holiday Park
Kaikoura	3.	Kaikoura Motels & Caravan Park
Kaikoura	4.	Searidge Holiday Park
Kaikoura	5.	Peketa Camping Ground (DoC)
Kaikoura	6.	Boat Harbour (DoC)
Kaikoura	7.	Omihi Reserve (DoC)
Kaikoura	8.	Goose Bay Motor Camp (DoC)
Kaikoura	9.	Paia Point (DoC)
Cheviot	10.	The Staging Post
Cheviot	11.	Cheviot Trust Caravan Park
Cheviot	12.	Cheviot Caravan & Camping Park
Gore Bay via Cheviot	13.	Gore Bay Camping Ground
Gore Bay via Cheviot	14.	Buxton Camping Ground
via Cheviot	15.	Nape Nape (DoC)
Waiau	16.	Waiau Motor Camp
Rotherham	17.	Rotherham Hotel
Hanmer Springs	18.	Hanmer River Holiday Park
Hanmer Springs	19.	Mountain View Holiday Park
Hanmer Springs	20.	A.A. Tourist Park
Hanmer Springs	21.	The Pines Motor Camp
Culverden	22.	Culverden Domain
Greta Valley	23.	Greta Valley Caravan Park
Waikari	24.	Waikari Reserve Camping

Amberley	25.	Amberley Beach Camp
Amberley	26.	Delhaven Motels & Caravan Park
Leithfield	27.	Leithfield Beach Camp
Loburn	28.	Loburn Leisure Park
Mt Thomas	29.	Mt Thomas (DoC)
Oxford	30.	Ashley Gorge Motor Park
Rangiora	31.	Waikuku Beach Camp
Woodend	32.	Woodend Beach Motor Camp
Rangiora	33.	Rangiora Holiday Park
Springfield	34.	Kowhai Pass Domain
via Kaiapoi	35.	Pineacres Holiday Park
Kaiapoi	36.	Brooklands Motor Camp
Kaiapoi	37.	Blue Skies
Kaiapoi	38.	Kairaki Fishing & Holiday Park
Christchurch	39.	Spencer Park Holiday Camp
Christchurch	40.	South New Brighton Motor Camp
Christchurch	41.	Amber Park Motel Caravan Park
Christchurch	42.	Showground Motor Camp
Christchurch	43.	All Seasons Holiday Park
Christchurch	44.	Meadow Park Holiday Park
Christchurch	45.	North South Airport Park
Christchurch	46.	Russley Park Motor Camp
Christchurch	47.	Riccarton Motor Camp
Christchurch	48.	Prebbleton Holiday Park
Christchurch	49.	Alpine View Holiday Park
Little River	50.	Little River Holiday Park
Duvauchelle	51.	Duvauchelle Reserves Board Camp

NORTH AND MID CANTERBURY

Akaroa	52.	Akaroa Holiday Park
Banks Peninsula	53.	Le Bons Bay Motor Camp
Banks Peninsula	54.	Okains Bay Motor Camp
Banks Peninsula	55.	Pigeon Bay Motor Camp (DoC)
Banks Peninsula	56.	Purau Motor Camp
Glentunnel	57.	Glentunnel Holiday Park
Rakaia	58.	Rakaia River Holiday Park
Rakaia	59.	Rakaia Gorge
Methven	60.	Methven Caravan Park
Methven	61.	Kohuia Lodge
Ashburton	62.	Hotel Ashburton Motorhome Park
Ashburton	63.	Coronation Park Motor Camp
Ashburton	64.	Tinwald Domain & Caravan Park

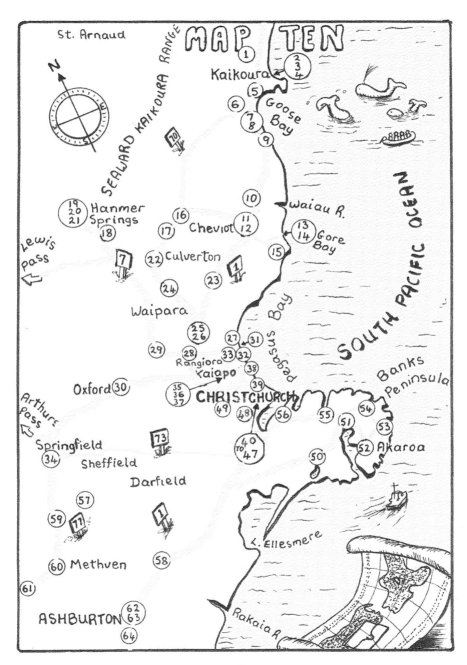

Chapter 10

NORTH AND MID CANTERBURY

The main route south passes the landmark pyramids of salt at Lake Grassmere and then returns to the coast. This is a rugged seascape, peppered with rock formations that encroach on the road. Kaikoura combines majestic scenery with the character of a fishing village. Whale-watching here is an experience not to be missed.

By contrast, Nature has provided an inland oasis at Hanmer Springs, where the largest thermal spa waters in the South Island have become a popular resort area. The stunning vista of snowy mountains provides a backdrop while the hot mineral pools draw both locals and visitors alike for their therapeutic qualities, or just relaxation. There should be no difficulty in finding a camping spot here.

Canterbury is enclosed by the Southern Alps to the west and the Pacific Ocean to the east. The Canterbury Plains are New Zealand's largest area of flat land.

The urban area of Christchurch is the South Island's largest city, noted also for its gardens, a sight to behold, especially in Spring. Because of its flat terrain and the tranquillity of its Avon River, it is known as the most "English" city in New Zealand. Cathedral Square dominates the central city. Street performers, markets and the Christchurch Wizard draw many people to the Square.

It is certainly worth a trip to the charming settlement of Akaroa, which takes you back into hills of Banks Peninsula. As you descend towards Akaroa Harbour there are some captivating views. Historically this area was earmarked for French settlement in the 1840s, but only a nominal number stayed. However, this delightful fishing village has preserved its Gallic connections with street names and memorabilia.

Try the jet boats of the Rakaia River or the skiing experience, perhaps heli-skiing or hot-air ballooning at Pudding Hill, if you prefer more adventurous pursuits. At Ashburton you may like to take the alpine trail inland or continue south along the Canterbury Plains.

The Canterbury region is on the dry side of the South Island, although it is subject at times to dramatic temperature changes. The land is sprawling, so in this one region you will find alpine, coastal and river environments and space to enjoy all the recreational activities they offer.

NORTH AND MID–CANTERBURY

1. Waipapa Camp Ground
Waipapa Bay (03) 319-4307

A small facility where you will probably not be tempted to linger. There are tent sites and 18 sites with power plus ablutions that have seen better days. A kitchen is in the planning stages and may be in service this summer. All sites $5 per person.

2. The Esplanade Holiday Park
128 The Esplanade, Kaikoura (03) 319-5947

Far-reaching views from a "close up" camp. Of the 25 sites here there are 20 with power. Situated just across the road from the marine playground of Kaikoura, the environment is briskly seaside. There are also cabins and on-site caravans provided. At busy times this could be a rather crowded location. The facilities are up-to-date and include paraplegic access in the ablutions. There is a TV/recreation room and a spa pool. The laundry contains all automatic equipment. There is a dump point here. Your host Georgina Woolley. Tent sites are $7 per person, or with power $16 for two. 🖻 and 🚐

3. Kaikoura Motels & Caravan Park
11 Beach Road, Kaikoura (03) 319-5999 (phone & fax)

Very close to the township of Kaikoura is this well groomed small camp. There are pleasant level sites bordered with trees and hedges. There is a small swimming pool with a tiny sundeck and a trampoline. The amenities are almost new. Two very smart kitchens have tables and chairs. There is an outdoor alternative dining/social breezeway area. The ablutions have basic showers, with all facilities in their prime. A laundry offers automatic equipment. There is a dump point here. There is a large range of other accommodation. When you check in, enquire from your new hosts Glynis and Stuart Windle. Tent sites are $15 for two people, or with power $16. 🖾

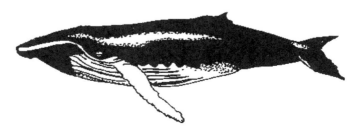

4. Searidge Holiday Park
34 Beach Road, Kaikoura (03) 319-5362

A well landscaped park on the seaward side of Beach Road, this is a handy camp for Kaikoura's attractions (the Whale Watch depot, and the shops). There are grassy areas, well planted with young trees, around the 140 sites. There are 40 with power. The kitchen/dining complex is attractive and well equipped but also well used. The ablutions are excellent and include a paraplegic suite, needing a slight modification. The laundry has fully automatic equipment. A dump point is provided. Inquire from your hosts Lynne and Gerald Nolan about bringing your pets. Tent sites are $15 for two. Power sites are $18 for two. $30. $50.

5. Peketa Camping Ground
RD 2 Kaikoura –Department of Conservation (03) 319-6299

Located on S Hwy 1 in South Bay, 8km from the centre of Kaikoura. There is a shop on site and the camp is well equipped. It is an ideal base for diving, whale-watching, fishing, Kaikoura Peninsula walks, tramping in the seaward Kaikoura range, seal and coastal bird watching. There are also tennis courts here. All the usual amenities including a dining area and a public phone.

This is a conservation camp where no dogs are permitted. may be available. There are over 100 power sites here, plus even more for tents. These cost $7 per person with an additional $2 for power.

6. Boat Harbour
Kaikoura–Department of Conservation

This and the following camping grounds are collectively known as Kaikoura Camping. This camp has a boat ramp and 28 power points. Basic camping with metered showers, kitchen and a washing machine available.

7. Omihi Reserve
Kaikoura–Department of Conservation

Check in at Goose Bay. There are 36 power points, toilets and fresh water. Tent sites $5 per person.

8. Goose Bay Motor Camp
RD 2 Kaikoura–Department of Conservation (03) 319-5348

This fully serviced conservation campground is located just 18km south of Kaikoura on S Hwy 1. There are ablutions, kitchen and laundry here. There are 5 cabins here as well as plenty of tent sites and around 90 with power. This and the other conservation camps are mostly right on the coast.

The rocky and spectacular shore offers great fishing and diving, superb coastal walks and is close to whale-watching opportunities. 🖼.

9. Paia Point
Kaikoura–Department of Conservation

Check in at Goose Bay. Few facilities, but toilets and fresh water available. Contact the Department of Conservation for full details of these last four sites. Tent sites $4 per person.

10. The Staging Post
S Hwy 1, Hawkswood, RD Parnassus, Cheviot (03) 319-2898

Historically a sheep station, this is currently also an adventure camp. Only 16 power sites here, but with over 1800 ha of land, great tent sites The approach is through a glade of gum trees. While you are here there are various outdoor pursuits to indulge your "free spirit". Try the flying fox (not for the timid) Go pig hunting. There are also rabbits and opossums to pursue. Horses are available, either for a sedate ride or a two-day trek to the coast. There is an interesting selection of buggies too; a ride in those may appeal. Try the sporting options with cricket equipment, a golf practice range (with golf clubs available) tennis, volleyball and croquet all on challenging courses. You can fish the Conway River. Feeling creative? There is a woodworking shop, a smithy and a pottery wheel and kiln. There are two kitchens, one with free-standing fire and all the modern appliances too. There are a host of BBQs including an outdoor brick oven for baking bread. Both ablutions supply free soft-water showers. There are two laundries, one has the "mod cons". Yes there is an indoor recreation room and even a new museum. Although you are a fair distance from any shopping, a delivery of goods can be arranged. Meals are available here at budget prices. All camping is at $7 per person. Handmade adobe🖼. Your host 'JD'. Look for further information on page 267.

11. Cheviot Trust Caravan Park
(behind Cheviot Hotel) PO Box 58, Cheviot (03) 319-8616

Enjoy a travellers respite at this pretty little campground with clusters of sites. The grounds are well kept and landscaped for good privacy. Not a lot of facilities.The kitchen/laundry does not have cooking appliances. Extra amenities at the hotel, where you can buy a good meal. A quiet spot at very reasonable rates. Your hosts Scott and Margaret Robertson. Tent sites are $8 for two people or $12 with power.

12. Cheviot Motel Caravan & Camping Park
Ward Road, Cheviot (03) 319-8607

A quiet, sheltered little park with a rural aspect. It is adjacent to the motels, but entirely separate. There is a swimming pool, BBQ and children's play area, but there are only 8 power sites. The amenities are well kept, with excellent appointments, but not extensive. The kitchen-dining has TV. Peaceful camping, yet close to town and off the main highway. Your hosts Bob and Joan MacFarlane. Tent sites are $6 per person, or with power $8. ⛺ $13 per person. 🛖 $20. 🚐 $38 per person.

13. Gore Bay Camping Ground
Gore Bay (03) 319-8364

Economical camping, with sites on two sides of the dividing road. The water's edge side has access to a stony-sand beach. Across the road you will find some sites with shady trees. There are some stately pines and shrub hedges for shelter. Old-style facilities are provided, with metered showers, but there is a paraplegic suite. A combination kitchen/laundry has minimal equipment. Tent sites are $8 for two people or with power $10 for two.

14. Buxton Camping Ground
RD3 Gore Bay (03) 319-8695 or (03) 319-8364

Just a little coastal camp with a banked border all round, 8km from Cheviot. Basic camping on a flat paddock with a new BBQ house to serve as a kitchen. There are also newly installed hot showers and toilets. Beside the stopover site is a children's playground. Only 6 sites with power here. No dogs please. Camping fees $10.

15. Nape Nape Camping Area
Blythe Road, 20km southeast of Cheviot–Department of Conservation

A conservation camp for those wishing to take advantage of what the North Canterbury coast has to offer. There is over 12km of unsealed road to reach this camp which has only a water supply and toilets. No fires and no dogs here please. Charges are $3 per adult.

16. Waiau Motor Camp
S Hwy 70, north of Culverden (03) 315-6193

Although the camping ground looks uninspired, there are pleasant facilities here for comfortable camping. A roomy and well appointed kitchen and dining plus a large comfy TV lounge has a homely "feel". The ablutions include a paraplegic unit (only lacking a grab handle). There are laundry facilities. The caretaker here is B. Nelmes. 12 power points here. All sites are $5 per person with a surcharge of $3 for power. 🛖 $10 for two persons.

17. Rotherham Hotel
Rotherham (03) 315-6373

A little spot for camping beside and behind the hotel. The surroundings are pretty. Only 2 power points, some tent sites and cabins. There are good toilets and showers provided. You can buy an appetising meal here at a reasonable price. Your hospitable host is Keith Fenwick.

18. Hanmer River Holiday Park
6km before Hanmer Springs (03) 315-7111

A mini camp located in a large private garden. There are only 6 sites, 4 with power, with another 6 cabins and a tourist flat all connected by a gravel path and with good privacy. Because this also has the nucleus of an animal park, pony rides, tame goats, pig and fowls, the children will enjoy the experience. They have a play area too. Campers have a good kitchen with stoves and fridge and dining table. There is a homely lounge too. Newly installed ablutions and laundry. Your host Alison Chalmondeley may be able to accommodate your pet, but check beforehand. Tent sites $7 per person. Power sites $7.50 per person. ▤ $12 per person. ▦ $42 for two.

19. Mountain View Holiday Park
Main Road, PO Box 169, Hanmer Springs (03) 315-7113 (phone & fax)

This is the closest camp to the village and mineral pools of Hanmer Springs. There are options for the camper; within the busy area or more secluded sites, all are level. The women's ablution block is particularly nice, tiled and with a bath. The men's showers are not as plentiful. A dump point is provided. There is an adventure play area for the children. You may play squash, or there is a TV and pool room for the less energetic. Dominant mountain views as the name suggests. Your hosts Gordon and Alison Collister. Tent sites are $16 for two, or with power $18.

20. AA Tourist Park
Jacks Pass Road, Hanmer Springs (03) 315-7112 (phone & fax)

Just 2km from Hanmer village and at the end of a road with mountain views this is an extensive park with spacious sites for campers. Well serviced with sealed roads and superb amenities, it offers excellent lodge accommodation, cabins and flats and over 100 camp sites. There is an adventure playground and BBQs in the grounds. In addition to the first class facilities with paraplegic unit, there is a drying room opening off the laundry. A dump point is provided. There is a TV room and a separate games room for pool and table tennis. Quite a luxurious holiday resort. Your hosts Dayle and Laurie North. (These prices are reduced for AA members). Tent sites $14 for two. Power sites $16 for two. ▤ $37 for two. ▦ $55 for two.

21. The Pines Motor Camp
Jacks Pass Road, PO Box 193, Hanmer Springs (03) 315-7152

Located in the Hanmer Springs Domain where there are a variety of sporting options. The hot pools are also in close proximity. The camp has its own mini golf. The grounds are moderately smooth. The amenities are very modern but not profuse. There are metered showers in the ablutions which also have a paraplegic suite (lacking only a grab handle). The communal kitchen has fridge and freezer. A laundry has automatic machines. There is a backpacker dormitory, cabins and on-site caravans. Pets can be accommodated here and there is a dump point. There are 34 sites with power plus some for tents. Your hosts Linda and Russ Waitokia. Tent sites $6 per person. Power sites $7 per person. ▭ $30 for two.

22. Culverden Domain
Culverden

Roadside camping by a pocket of trees. The facilities all look forlorn and unkempt. There are 4 power points here. Useful for an emergency stopover.

23. Greta Valley Caravan Park
S Hwy 1, PO Box 7 Greta Valley (03) 314-3874

A camp in the older style with pleasant surroundings though in close proximity to the main highway. There is a licensed family restaurant for 7-day meals. It is also convenient for shopping and petrol. Camp sites are on different levels and there are around 22 with power. There is a spa pool. The kitchen doubles as a TV lounge and there are the usual amenities provided. Not a busy camp. Guests will check in at the tavern next door. Tent sites $7. Power sites $14 for two. ▭ $30.

24. Waikari Reserve Camping
Princes Street, Waikari

Simple camping without fuss. There are level grounds well protected by a large macrocarpa hedge and adjacent to a playing field. Only 4 power points, but reasonably good showers and toilets. A tiny kitchen has some tables and chairs and a covered porch.

25. Amberley Beach Camp
Amberley (03) 314-8816 or (03) 314-8192

Rather more of a parking place than a camp. 12 power points are supplied in an open grassed area which is not on the beach. Toilets and handbasins appeared to be the only facilities. Tent sites are $6 for two people, or with power $8.

26. Delhaven Motels & Caravan Park
124 Main North Road, Amberley (03) 314-8550

This is a corner site with two levels of camping. The motels are prominent but there are plenty of tidy sheltered sites, in a choice of positions. The road frontage area is more convenient for the amenities. Each of the 40 power sites has water and lighting. There is a dump point here. The kitchen is well appointed with cooking appliances and fridge. The ablutions have plentiful hot-water showers. Everything you need for the laundry is provided. There is a covered swimming pool and a carpeted TV lounge for the "stay-at-homes". Your hosts Bill and Jeanette. Tent sites are $12 for two, or with power $14. There is a range of other accommodation.

27. Leithfield Beach Camping Ground
PO Box 1, Leithfield Beach (03) 314-8518

This camp is just 2km from the main road and is a rambling seaside park with sand dunes dividing the camp sites from the long Pacific beach. The sites are defined by pine hedges. Ideal for the camper who enjoys a '"laid-back" atmosphere without being crowded. In the grounds are a camp store, tennis courts and an inviting children's paddling pool. There are good, clean, basic beach amenities here. The use of the washing machine is free. No dogs here please. Your hosts Anne and David Herd. Tent sites are $12 for two. Power sites are $14 for two.

28. Loburn Leisure Park
Loburn–6km from Rangiora (03) 312-8872

Escapist camping among 12 hectares of level sites, well sheltered by a perimeter of trees. There are endless tracks to explore on foot, or with a mountain bike. A combat course is a challenge. The amenities offer a huge community lounge with two woodburning stoves. There is also a TV room. The kitchen, ablutions (with paraplegic facilities) and laundry equipment are all free. Activities include table tennis, pool, water slide and splash pool and flying fox. Your new hosts are June and Ken Buchanan. Tent sites $5 per person. Power sites plus $3. Share 🏠 at $9 per person. Look for the value coupon on page 264.

🏠	All grades of cabins from
🏚	Tourist flats and motels from
🚐	On-site caravans from

29. Mt Thomas
Hayland Road, 30km northwest of Rangiora–Department of Conservation
(03) 379-9758

Adjacent to Wooded Gully Stream and approximately 50km northwest of Christchurch, this camping and picnic area is administered by the Canterbury Conservancy. This is the gateway to North Canterbury's foothill forests and there is abundant hunting, tramping and other recreational opportunities. The camp has water supply, toilets, picnic tables and BBQs (otherwise no fires). We advise a map. Detailed directions are available from the DoC office. No dogs please. Charges are $3 per adult.

30. Ashley Gorge Motor Park
Glentui, RD Oxford (03) 312-4099 (fax 03 312-4926)

Alongside an extensive picnic area leading down to the Ashley River this park is 8km from Oxford. Amongst the infinite number of tent sites and power sites there are plenty of shady trees. There is a fenced play area for children and a recreation room for pool and TV. Bush walks, fishing and canoeing are other options. High-country horse-trek adventures can be experienced. Inquire about these and also jet boating and skiing. This is part of a scenic reserve, now leased out for holiday and recreational purposes and with resident peacocks. The kitchen is newly refurbished and includes a fridge. The ablutions have metered showers. There is automatic laundry equipment. Two substantial bunkhouses are here, plus cabins and an on-site caravan. You can pay by Eftpos. Your new hosts Lyn and Ken Buttling. Tent sites are $7 per person, or with power $8. Bunkhouse $10 per person. ⛺ $36 for two. 🏠 $40 for two.

31. Waikuku Beach Camp
Waikuku Domain, PO Box 417, Rangiora (03) 312-7600 (phone & fax)

A truly oceanside camp some 33km north of Christchurch. The layout of meandering sealed roads and grouped camp sites makes for a community atmosphere. There are avenues of mature trees. The grounds are extensive and have an interesting layout. At the entrance is an office /camp store. The kitchens are adequate and there is a gas BBQ. Dispersed in local areas are four ablution blocks. There are two good laundry rooms and a toddlers and babies wash and changing room. Whitebaiting in season, or fishing and swimming to enjoy. Well suited for a seaside family holiday. Your hosts Cliff and Lyn King. Tent sites $13 for two. Power sites $15 for two. 🏠 $20 for two.

32. Woodend Beach Motor Camp
3km from S Hwy 1, Woodend (03) 312-7643

Taking just a short deviation through farming country, you will find this seaside camp. The grounds have sealed roads and are reminiscent of a rolling golf course.

There are masses of camp sites, large trees and a relaxed atmosphere. Amenities blocks are scattered throughout the camp. There are a number of clean and tidy kitchens and a TV room with an open fire. There is an on-site shop open all weekends from November to the beginning of February. A drink dispensing machine is provided. There is mini golf and an adventure playground and a safe swimming beach. A well patronised camp with Katrina and Ian on duty. Tent sites are $13 for two persons or with power $14.

33. Rangiora Holiday Park
339 Lehmans Road, Rangiora–Off S Hwy 72, RD 1 Rangiora (03) 313-5759

This holiday park is 2.5km west of Rangiora and only a half-hour drive from Christchurch. Not far from the Ashley River it has some lovely tent sites amongst the pine trees and 30 power points for vans. There is a range of activities nearby at the Rangiora Indoor Sports Centre, as well as the racecourse. In the grounds you can play beach volley ball or mini golf. A very attractive conservatory is a focal point, with TV and phone available while you relax. The ablutions have a luxurious appearance. There is automatic laundry equipment. A kitchen with stove, microwave and fridge is provided, or you can arrange to get a continental breakfast. There are a number of walkways from the camp. Your hosts Raewyn and Allan Campbell. Two people can have a tent site here for $16, or with power $17.50. 🏠 $28 for two. Bunkhouse $36 for two.

34. Kowhai Pass Domain
Springfield (03) 318-4864

Country-style camping 30 metres from S Hwy 73 at the east end of Springfield. There are 16 power sites looking attractive under mature trees. Facilities are on the other side of the tennis courts and these are nominally clean and not lavish. There is an adventure playground for children and lots of room for tents. Only $2 per person for a tent site. Power sites are $7 per vehicle.

35. Pineacres Holiday Park
Main North Road–near Kaiapoi (03) 327-5022 (fax 03 327-7421)

This park comes complete with a licensed restaurant where you can enjoy music and entertainment. A very pleasant place, combining motels and motor park and a local Information Centre. Within its boundaries are a swimming pool, children's play area, flying fox, BBQs and a resident donkey. The amenities offer a good kitchen with full stove and microwave cooking, also a communal fridge. There is a TV lounge and games room. Video films can be hired. The ablutions and laundry are clean and modern. There is a dump point here. 100 sites share the park with a range of other accommodation. There is provision for pets. Your hosts Caroline and Ted Marris. There are 50 power sites. All camping with power is $16 for two. 🚻 and 🏠 $27.50 for two.🏚 $40.

36. Brooklands Motor Camp
Kaiapoi (03) 329-8867

The entrance is uncluttered now, but towards the rear this camp has succumbed to the pressure of latter-day gipsies. Although the grounds are long and hairy around the edges, the amenities are small but well scrubbed. There is a shop on site and a good meal to be had at the BYO restaurant. There is a phone available. A friendly welcome awaits campers.

37. Blue Skies
12 Williams Street, Kaiapoi (03) 327-8007 (fax 03 327-5210)

This is a combination camp and community facility, known as a Training and Conference Centre. However the camp sites are well maintained in a park-like area. The development is designed to cater more for lodge accommodation and group courses. The camping area does not have a kitchen but meals can be arranged. It has a new conference hall, disabled facilities and a swimming pool. This is used as a Scout training camp, but other groups are welcome. Equipment includes a confidence course and abseiling tower. Pets are permitted by arrangement. Enquire for details.

38. Kairaki Fishing & Holiday Park
Kairaki Beach, Kaiapoi (03) 327-7335

Although there is a village of well settled caravans here, the presentation is attractive, with mini-gardens, and there are some lovely big hedged sites available for casual campers. The location is by the mouth of the Waimakariri River with a walkway from the camp. Salmon fishing is a priority here. A bright cheerful kitchen and average amenities are provided. Your hosts are Bronwyn and Alan Waters. A tent site will cost you $9 for two people, or with power $14. ⌨

39. Spencer Park Holiday Park
Heyders Road, Spencerville, Christchurch 9 (03) 329-8721 (phone & fax)

This holiday camp is situated in a large regional park bordered by wetland reserve with walking tracks to the beach. Magnificent landscaped grounds are level with shady trees. The paths are sealed and there are BBQ facilities, mini golf, tennis courts and a spa pool. For children the activities include trampolines and flying fox. There is a huge capacity for campers with close to 500 sites, 300 with power, but some of these will be a long way from the amenities. The ablutions are well appointed and include a bath and paraplegic facilities. There is a good kitchen with fridge and cool lockers available. There is a dump point here. Your new host Trevor Inwood. Power sites are $9 per person and tent sites $8. ⌨

40. South New Brighton Motor Camp
Halsey Street, South Brighton, PO Box 18-591 Christchurch
(03) 388-9884

This park offers appealing level sites and many are screened by hedges and shrubs. It has an estuary frontage where there are opportunities for water skiing, fishing and boating. This appears to be a peaceful spot, just off Marine Parade, with some big trees for shade. Check out the wonderful play fort with horse-drawn dray and tepee for the children; they have a paddling pool too. The kitchen is particularly nice with a conservatory-style dining corner. The ablutions are well kept and there is automatic laundry equipment. There is a dump point here. A shop with basic food supplies is within the camp and other shopping is nearby. There are over 100 power sites here plus 40 for tents and some cabins. Your hosts Ivan and Sandy Williamson. Power sites are $17 for two persons, or $15 for tents. $15 per person.

41. Amber Park Mini Motel & Caravan Park
308 Blenheim Road, Christchurch (03) 348-3327

A gentle environment for the mobile camper. There is limited provision for tents. It has a settled, orderly air with level sites divided into blocks and laced with sealed roads. There are 52 sites with power, dotted with trees, with a BBQ set up in its own garden. A dump point is provided. The fussy traveller will enjoy the superb amenities, immaculately presented with a bath and hair dryer available and pristine showers. In the laundry there is automatic equipment including iron and board. There is an inviting carpeted TV lounge. There is a bus stop at the gate. Your hosts John and Sharron Lee. All sites are $19 for two people. Self-contained units from $35. Look for further information on page 266.

42. Showground Motor Camp
Whiteleigh Ave, Addington–Christchurch (03) 338-9770

If it's a holiday you want, give this complex a miss. Camping and the provision of accommodation for events at the sale yards, Winter Show or Addington Raceway is the priority here. The camp is a central venue and can be a hive of activity, so don't look here for privacy. There are times when it is closed to the public, due to events at the Showgrounds. It is the closest camp to central Christchurch and on the bus route. There is a big functional kitchen, two ablution blocks with good showers and laundry equipment. There are several phones available and you can get a daily paper plus milk and soft drinks. There is a dump station here. A tent site will cost you $6.35 per person. Two people can have a power site for $14.65 Lots of s.

43. All Seasons Holiday Park

5 Kidbrooke Street, PO Box 19765, Christchurch (03) 384-9490
(fax 03 384-4110)

With only a 5km drive to Christchurch this little camp is usefully placed. The sites are level and there is a spa pool. The forts in the children's playground are sure to appeal, and there is also a trampoline. There is a pleasant kitchen opening to a courtyard BBQ garden. Other facilities are good with automatic laundry equipment, and the usual ablutions. A dump point is provided. There is 7-day shopping adjacent to the camp. Your hosts Colin and Claire Park. Power sites are $15 for two people. There are only 5 tent sites at $7 per person. ▢ and ▢ from $15 per person. ▢ $35 per person. .

44. Meadow Park Holiday Park

39 Meadow Street, PO Box 5178, Christchurch (03) 352-9176
(fax 03 352-1272)

Possibly the ultimate in camping luxury. This park has an incredible range of entertainment for the children. Everyone will enjoy the heated indoor pool. Try the curling water slide and the tube.There is a toddlers pool alongside, also a private spa and sauna. The adventure playground is an imaginative experience. Within the park "village" you will also find a gym and games room. In fact the list is endless. Choose from sites of all types on lovely level land with plenty of shady trees. The amenities are in the top class too. There are paraplegic facilities and everything is provided for the comfort of campers or those using the lodge or other accommodation. Yes it is a large complex, with wide roadways linking it together, and no shortage of room. Please do not bring pets. Your hosts Ian and Daphne Gamble. Camping is at $20 for two persons or $13.50 each. ▢, ▢ and ▢. Look for further information on page 268.

45. North South Airport Park

Cnr Johns and Sawyers Arms Road, PO Box 14017 Christchurch
(03) 359-5993 (fax 03 359-5614)

Enter through an avenue of trees. Mix and mingle with the cabins and other accommodation. This is a budget way to stay and have easy access to the airport and the city. An excellent children's playground is provided and there is a tennis court and a swimming pool. There is an on-site shop and a restaurant adjacent. Kitchen items, linen and TV can be hired here and car storage is obtainable. There are good amenities provided including kitchen with fridge. A feature here is a courtesy van for free airport connections. Your friendly hosts Keith and Shelley Ellis. Power sites are $16 for two, or tent sites $6 per person. ▢.

46. Russley Park Motor Camp
372 Yaldhurst Road, Christchurch 4 (03) 342-7021 (fax 03 349-4681)

On S Hwy 73 this camp is opposite Riccarton Racecourse. There is an attractive approach to this well tended camp, which has chalet accommodation too. Not large, but offering 40 power sites and plenty of tarseal. Kitchen equipment is good quality and plentiful, and the ablution area is fresh and clean with tiles and a bath. Additional features are spa pool and TV room. There is automatic equipment in the laundry. A car wash is available. There is a children's play area and video games and pool table for indoor entertainment. This has a neat, orderly aspect that is inviting. Your host Craig Tewnion. Power sites are $19 for two people or $16 for tents. ⌨

47. Riccarton Motor Camp
Riccarton–Christchurch (03) 348-5690

No extra touches here. This supplies the basic camping requirements on a rather ragged ground. There is a small area that offers lawns and flower beds. The dominance of the hut accommodation around the amenities block, and the long term clientele do not inspire confidence. There is an average kitchen and a TV room. The ablutions are satisfactory. There is a porch-style laundry with an automatic washer. Your hosts Mr and Mrs Main. Tent sites are $7 per person or $16 for two with power.

48. Prebbleton Holiday Park
18 Blakes Road, Prebbleton, Christchurch (03) 349-7861

A semi-rural camp of smallish proportions, sited 12km south of Christchurch. All the standard camping facilities are here, small blocks, but handy throughout. At the rear of the camp the sites were open, but pleasant and level. Holiday makers and long-term occupants share the facilities. There is also a TV/pool room available, and a swimming pool. This camp is modestly appointed but well kept and on an upgrading program. Your new hosts Ellen and Gordon Mockford. Prices were from $13 to $15 for two persons. ⌨ and ⌨

49. Alpine View Holiday Park
S Hwy 1, 650 Main South Road, Christchurch (03) 349-7666

A pleasantly maintained entrance leads into this park with flower borders, about 2km from Hornby. Further into the camp the sites are grassed and a little ragged round the edges. Some home-base buses have taken up residence here. There are 18 power sites serviced by a small kitchen and ablution block. The laundry equipment is modern. There is a dump station here. All the power sites have sewerage and taps. Across the road is a garage, also takeaway food outlet and an hotel. Your hosts Bob and Carol Christie. Tent sites here are $6 per person or $14 for two with power.

50. Little River Holiday Park
4km from S Hwy 75, off Okuti Valley Road, Banks Peninsula (03) 325-1141

Take the Okuti Valley Road through the attractive hilly countryside of Banks Peninsula. The park is also known as Birdlands Sanctuary; here campers can wander (no charge). There are waterfalls, lily ponds and resident peacocks throughout the park, which is accessible for wheelchairs. A small shop offers wildlife souvenirs. The facilities have wheelchair access. There is a well appointed kitchen and BBQ area. Some basic foods are available here, or use the general store in Little River. Your pets will be allowed, but must be restrained to protect bird life. Tranquil camping in appealing surroundings with a bonus for ardent fishermen. Get the fishing secrets from your hosts Pat and Margaret Robson. Tent sites for two people are $15, or with power $16. 🏠 and backpackers accommodation. Look for further information on page 265.

51. Duvauchelle Reserve Board Motor Camp
Seafield Road, Duvauchelle (03) 304-5777

On a spectacular location on the inner reaches of the Akaroa Harbour, this camp is directly off S Hwy 75 . Two large terraces of sites give superb views of the bay. There are tennis courts adjacent. You may water ski and use the boat ramp. Neighbourhood shopping and hotel is about 1km away. The kitchen and indoor recreation area are spacious. There is a new ablution block and the other has been restored to include a paraplegic suite. The sites are generous and there is a dump station. Some sites are leased long term to weekend visitors. No pets here please. All camping is $7 per person.

52. Akaroa Holiday Park
Morgan's Road, PO Box 71, Akaroa (03) 304-7471

Directly off Old Coach Road and above Akaroa village, this park has an enviable location. The camp enjoys a picture-postcard view of Akaroa village, harbour and lighthouse. Carefully maintained, the terraced sites have easy access and trim flowerbeds at each level. About 150 sites are available here and all have a sweeping outlook. Most have power, stormwater drains and taps. There are multiple dump points. An area is available for boat parking. There is a big in-ground swimming pool. A TV room is provided. The amenities include push-button showers, good kitchen and automatic washers and dryers in the laundry. The children's play area rambles through a naturally tree clad setting just below the camp. Just down the hill to the township for shopping. Your hosts Marie and Kevin Pope. All sites are $9 per person. 🚐 $32 for two.🏠 $42 for two.🏚 $56. Look for further information on page 265.

53. Le Bons Bay Motor Camp

Valley Road, Le Bons Bay, Banks Peninsula (03) 304-8533 (phone & fax)

Serviced from Akaroa; many small bays line the perimeter of Banks Peninsula. Le Bons Bay has a sheltered beach reached by a rather tortuous access road. A new comfortable-pace walk goes to Akaroa and back with an overnight stopover at Le Bons Bay. This is fairly remote hill-farming country, where it would be prudent to stock up on petrol and food beforehand. The camp sites here are spread across a paddock that does double duty for grazing sheep. On one side there is a recreation room with table tennis, pool table and TV. A fort and playground for the children are provided as well as an in-ground heated pool. There is an on-site shop, sometimes unattended. The ablution block is good, with unisex showers. Less attractive is the kitchen, although it is fairly well equipped, with fridge/freezer. The laundry provides washing and drying. There are 16 power points here, plus room for at least 40 tents, and a dump point. This will suit those looking for a rural escape, with horse trekking, pony rides and mountain biking. Your hosts Doug and Pam Hueston. Tent sites are $7 for two people, or $8 with power.

54. Okains Bay Motor Camp

Off S Hwy 75, Banks Peninsula (03) 304-8646

Towards the northeast coast of Banks Peninsula, this bay is 19km from Akaroa. Look for the turnoff along the scenic drive. There is a general store here. Camping is within an untamed pine plantation spread over a large area, that has a rugged appeal, with many waterside sites. There is a small playground for children. A new amenities block houses a kitchen with hot -plate cooking, fridge and freezer and meal space. There is also an automatic washer in the laundry/cool room. There are two ablution blocks, which have a paraplegic toilet. Contact the Domain Board for further details.

 ### 55. Pigeon Bay Motor Camp

Off S Hwy 75, Banks Peninsula–Department of Conservation

This is a conservation camp on the north coast of Banks Peninsula. Half the camp opens onto a wide sandy estuary and the other to a beautiful sheltered bay. Petrol is available at the store 2km away. There is only water and toilets here and no power. Vistas of coast and rugged hills open out all the way along the ridge road from which the three previous camps branch off. Please do not bring dogs here.

56. Purau Motor Camp
Diamond Harbour Road, Banks Peninsula (03) 329-4702 (phone & fax)

Although this camp is only about 31km from Christchurch and near the entrance to Lyttelton Harbour, it has a get-away-from-it-all aspect. Big old trees shelter the grounds and it is across the road from the bay. There is a boat ramp and a boat and car wash. An adventure playground awaits the children, plus a swimming pool. A TV room is provided. There are two kitchens and two blocks of ablution amenities plus full laundry facilities. You can buy basic supplies at the camp store and also hire canoes. If you want to visit Christchurch ferry terminal, a bus or a ferry service is available. Nearby kennels will look after Fido, or you may be able to bring him here by prior arrangement. Diamond Harbour is 2km away and your hosts Dick and Diane Wallace will collect you on request. There are plenty of sites here and all are $8 per person. 🔲 from $30.

57. Glentunnel Holiday Park
S Hwy 72 (Homebush Road), Glentunnel (03) 318-2868

The combination of an environment-friendly location with up-to-the-minute facilities is very appealing. This camp is 13km from Darfield. A delightful choice of tent and caravan sites with lots of nooks and crannies are in very spacious grounds. Mature trees give shelter, while four natural swimming holes have been created in the river. There are tennis courts, a shop and a hotel with meals available nearby. A golf course is next door. The amenities are paraplegic accessible. Horse riding is available from the camp. Salmon fishing in the lakes and river is open all year round. Your hosts Noel and Robyn Langridge. Tent sites $6.50 per person plus $2 for power.

58. Rakaia River Holiday Park
Main South Road, Rakaia (03) 302-7257 (phone & fax)

Just over the Rakaia River Bridge, travelling south, is this well established camp with an abundance of conifers. An on-site store for your basic supplies is here. Many sites are individually hedged and sheltered and there are 62 with power. A swimming pool and a well equipped playground are provided. There is a modest small kitchen with a covered porch outside for meals. There is automatic laundry equipment. The ablutions are nice, with shub. All the facilities are well kept. There is a dump point here. Primarily a park for the fishing enthusiast. You can also jet boat the Rakaia River. You will find everything you need here for fishing, and perhaps smoking or canning your catch. Philip and Robin Harrex are the owners here and have lots of local knowledge. Tent sites are $7 per person, with power $7.50. 🔲 $16 for two. 🚐 $42 for two.

59. Rakaia Gorge
Rakaia

Nestled into the base of Rakaia Gorge is a stopover point where toilets and a basin are provided. The area is very sheltered with an abundance of trees. Our unverified information is that campers make a donation to cover costs.

60. Methven Caravan Park
Barkers Road, PO Box 68, Methven (03) 302-8005

This park is carefully maintained on rather open grounds. It is the A & P Showground Park. There is a lot of level space for campers. The kitchen is large and functional, with useful stoves and a long communal table. There is a carpeted TV room, cosy with a chip heater. There are metered showers in the ablutions and automatic equipment in the laundry. A simple camp, nicely kept. Your hosts Nola and John Duff. Tent sites $10 for two people. Power sites $15 for two. ⬛, $10 per person .⬛ $12 per person.

61. Kohuia Lodge
S Hwy 72, PO Box 69, Methven (03) 302-8416 (phone & fax)

To find this holiday spot at Pudding Hill, go inland from Rakaia via Methven. The location has a raw majesty, nestled at the base of the Alps. There are 32 power points with water, adjacent to the lodge resort. The camp ground offers an area of grassed sites for both caravans and tents. The major accommodation provided has precedence, but campers can enjoy the fringe benefits. Geared for the "apres ski" there is a huge lounge with boulder fireplace, and often mulled wine to warm you. There is also a bar and TV here. Another TV room has beanbag furnishings and table tennis. There are two spas and saunas (small fee). A parachuting experience awaits you right next door. The campers amenities are interesting. There is a cosy, carpeted kitchen. Three hands would be useful in the unique showers (one hand is needed to control the water flow by way of a pull handle). There is automatic laundry equipment and a drying room. There is a sewer dump point. Meals are obtainable at the on-site licensed restaurant. Your host is Don Gorrie. Tent sites are $6 per person, or with power $7. Look for further information on page 266.

62. Hotel Ashburton Motorhome Park
Racecourse Road, PO Box 70, Ashburton (03) 308-3059 (phone & fax)

This is a very small, serviced van park area where all sites have taps and privacy walls. The hotel complex provides meals, use of laundry equipment, games room, sports venues. No cooking or BBQ facilities. There are en suite amenities for your motorhome. Not really geared for the camper as there are no tent sites. There is a dump point. The 12 power sites are $17 for two persons.

63. Coronation Park Motels & Motor Camp
778 East Street, Ashburton (03) 308-6603 (phone & fax)

A most inviting park in a sylvan setting. The attractive entranceway is typical of the rest of the grounds. There are plenty of lovely large trees for summer shade. The layout of sites is only one deep. There is a well equipped and fenced play area for children. Both swimming and spa pools too. Lots of space here for the 90 sites provided (70 with power). As well as two kitchens, there are four BBQ areas dotted about the camp. The ablution block also has baths. All automatic equipment in the laundry and there is a dump point. An easy place to stopover or linger awhile. Your friendly hosts Dave and Gay Luke. Tent sites $14 for two. Power sites $18 .⛟ $28 for two. ⛺ and ⛺ $46 for two

64. Tinwald Domain & Caravan Park
Maronan Road, Tinwald, Ashburton (03) 308-6805

This camp is built around a man-made lake, often abundant with ducks. You can hire a row boat. Centred in the lake is a mini-island. There are plenty of level sites, with old trees for shade. The adjacent domain swimming pool and tennis courts may be used. There is a convivial kitchen with ample equipment and complete with table and chairs, plus two comfy couches and a stack of magazines. There are functional ablutions and laundry equipment is free. This has a pleasant setting, perhaps lacking some outdoor taps and rubbish bins. Your hosts Sandra and Colin Sinclair. All sites are $5 per person with an extra $3.50 per site for power.

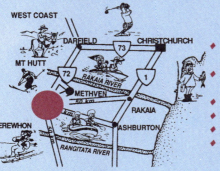

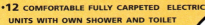

MEADOW PARK
Holiday Park
Tel (03) 352 9176   Fax (03) 352 1272

YOUR HOSTS
DAPHNE AND IAN GAMBLE

* *4.8 kilometres to the square*
* *Walking distance to Northland shopping centre and hotel*
* *36 cabins with carports*
* *15 graded cabins with own toilets and showers*
* *11 new self-contained "Kosy-Kiwi" units*
  Some with paraplegic accommodation
* *100 sheltered, powered caravan sites (40 with water and drains)*
* *Motel (4 berth)*
* *22 room Lodge, with conference facilities*

* *Refrigerators and fully automatic laundries*
* *Colour TV, lounge and recreation room*
* *Heated indoor pool, spa pool, sauna*
* *Barbeque and outdoor dining*
* *New adventure playground, trampolines*
* *Table tennis, Video games*
* *Indoor play equipment*
* *Gym*

While in Christchurch
'Ride a tram'

39 MEADOW STREET (OFF MAIN ROAD NORTH)
PAPANUI
CHRISTCHURCH 5 (P.O. BOX 5178)

SOUTH CANTERBURY DIRECTORY

Key to locations and maps in South Canterbury district. Starts at Mount Somers, west of Ashburton, taking a southeasterly direction towards the coast and Timaru, then diverting inland to Lake Tekapo. Back to the main road and coastal route to Glenavy. It follows the path of the Waitaki river inland, where there is camping beside the lakes. The final destination is Mount Cook in the northwest extremity of South Canterbury.

Mt Somers	1.	Mt Somers Holiday Park
Mt Somers	2.	Mt Somers Domain
via Geraldine	3.	Peel Forest Camp (DoC)
via Geraldine	4.	Orari Gorge Camping Area (DoC)
via Geraldine	5.	Waihi Gorge Camping Area (DoC)
Geraldine	6.	Geraldine Motor Camp
Geraldine	7.	The Farmyard Holiday Park
via Geraldine	8.	Pioneer Park Camping Area (DoC)
Winchester	9.	Winchester Domain Motor Camp
Temuka	10.	Temuka Holiday Park
Timaru north	11.	Seadown Holiday Village
Timaru	12.	Selwyn Holiday Park
Timaru	13.	Glenmark Motor Camp
Timaru	14.	Pleasant Point Domain Motor Camp
Fairlie	15.	C.J. Talbot Memorial Motor Camp
Lake Tekapo	16.	Lake Tekapo Motor Camp
St Andrews	17.	St Andrews Recreation Reserve
inland from Timaru	18.	Otaio Gorge Camping Area (DoC)
inland from Timaru	19.	Mt Nimrod Camping Area (DoC)

Waimate	20.	Victoria Park Motor Camp
Waimate	21.	Knottingley Park
Glenavy	22.	Glentaki Holiday Camp
Glenavy	23.	Gateways Caravan Park
Lake Benmore	24.	Haldon Arm Motor Camp
Lake Benmore	25.	Sailors Cutting
Lake Ohau	26.	Lake Middleton Reserve
Lake Ohau	27.	Lake Ohau Lodge
Lake Ohau	28.	Temple Forest Camping Area (DoC)
Twizel	29.	Ruataniwha Motor Camp
Mt Cook	30.	Glentanner Park
Mt Cook	31.	White Horse Hill Camping (DoC)
Waitaki Lakes	32.	Waitaki Reserves

Power site → Strom anschluß

SOUTH CANTERBURY

Chapter 11.

SOUTH CANTERBURY

Space–stretching into the foothills of the Southern Alps, with fingers of glacial lakes interrupting the landscape. this is inland South Canterbury. Originally much of this region was tussock country where the early settlers created sheep stations of enormous size. There are landmarks such as Erewhon and Mesopotamia, impressive names given to pioneer stations on a scale that has no equal anywhere else in New Zealand.

The abundance of lakes seems to be around every corner as you travel inland. At Lake Tekapo the landscape is enhanced by larch trees forming a welcome relief from the starkness of the hill country. The lakes of Tekapo and Pukaki are a breathtaking milky turquoise colour. This is caused by the suspension of finely ground glacial particles from their source in the ever-moving backdrop of glaciers.

There is a range of lakeside camping in the Lake Benmore and Lake Ohau region. This is unsophisticated camping with few facilities. However, the environment is sheltered and unspoiled, while the charges are very moderate. Inspect the hydro developments of the upper Waitaki as an alternative to the mountain playground that surrounds this area.

Because South Canterbury is an uncrowded place with inland skifields, numerous lakes, gorges and rivers spilling down to a more gentle coast, it is well suited to the environmentalist camper. Of course the coastal settlements have their own charm. See the special street of Victoriana architecture in Oamaru.

Dividing the unique West Coast from the western extremity of Canterbury are the Southern Alps. Highest among these mountains is Mount Cook which rises 3764 metres. This is within a National Park and you will find skiing, sightseeing flights, mountaineering or bush walking among the many pastimes that are available here.

There are endless opportunities for leisurely exploration and the roads are good. The lakes and rivers provide the fisherman with wonderful opportunities to bag that trophy salmon or trout. Dramatic in winter, serene in summer and spectacular when autumn brings balmy days, crisp nights and brilliant foliage to the trees.

SOUTH CANTERBURY

1. Mt Somers Holiday Park
Hoods Road, Mt Somers (03) 303-9719 (fax 03 366-0214)

On the fringe of the Southern Alps, this park is 49km inland from Ashburton. Meet your friends here for that skiing trip. The Mt Hutt skifield is nearby. On attractive grounds with level sites, this small-scale camp has 12 sites with power and 10 tent sites, plus cabins and on-site caravans. It is a sociable group venue which also provides a hot-dog and takeaway food outlet. The amenities include a cosy kitchen with a thermowave oven and microwave cooking. There is also a BBQ. The recreation room has a pot belly stove for comfort and space to watch TV or play pool in homely surroundings. The ablutions include paraplegic facilities. This is a country village venue, with plenty of services nearby. Your new hosts are April and Graeme Davey and Colleen and Ivan Kirk. Tent sites $10. Power sites $15. ▭ $30 for two .▭

2. Mt Somers Domain
Hoods Road, RD1 Mt Somers (03) 303-9717

This camp is almost next door to Mt Somers Holiday Park. Sited in pretty Domain gardens, it has plenty of trees and picnic tables. There is no kitchen, but toilet, showers and power points are available. There is an adventure tower and tennis courts available for campers. Sites are $6 with power and $4 for tents. Your host Mrs Glesson.

3. Peel Forest Camp
Peel Forest Park, RD22 Geraldine. Department of Conservation (03) 696-3826

Birdsong beside the river. This camp is a conservation area just past Peel Forest (approximately a 1-hour drive from Timaru). It is an environmental delight and easy to camp here too. There are 34 power sites and 46 sites for tents. There are groves of trees and open sunny spots. The kitchen is also a recreation room with open fire and is well appointed. There are good ablutions and laundry. A public phone is available. No shopping here, but you can fish the Rangitata River. There are a number of cooking fireplaces around the grounds. Earth-care camping and very popular. No dogs please. Book through the Department of Conservation, with a $10 deposit. Sites are $6.50 per adult, with an extra $2.50 for power.

4. Orari Gorge Camping Area
Yates Road, 12km northwest of Geraldine. Department of Conservation (03) 379-9758

Road access is from Tripp Settlement Road to Yates Road. Orari Gorge campsite is set in 80 hectares of native bush in the low foothills between Yates Road and Station Stream opposite the Glenburn Youth Camp. Open the gates (closing them after you enter). There is a relatively easy forest walk of about three hours partly along the line of an old bush tramway and passing through several quite distinct forest types. The high point gives good views out across surrounding countryside. The campsite is close to the Orari River which has good fishing. There is usually a water supply, (but not for drinking), toilets, picnic tables and BBQs, otherwise light no fires. Dogs are not permitted. Charges are $3 per adult.

 5. Waihi Gorge Camping Area
Waihi Gorge Road, 14km northwest of Geraldine. Department of Conservation (03) 379-9758

This conservation campsite adjoins Waihi river in the South Canterbury foothills. There is a water supply (but not for drinking), toilets, picnic tables and BBQ. (No other fires please) A strip of steep bush on the north side of the Waihi River extends almost 5km up river from the campsite. Waihi means "water gushing forth" and the backdrop of bush and hills are the main attractions. There are, however, no tracks through the bush. Waihi Gorge is close to a range of recreational opportunities in the South Canterbury foothills, including fishing, tramping and hunting. No dogs please. Charges are $3 per adult.

6. Geraldine Motor Camp
Hislop Street, Geraldine (03) 693-8860

In picturesque setting with well spaced sites among huge specimen trees, this camp adjoins a public park in the heart of Geraldine. There are some hard stands for vans and the gardens are delightful. In this neighbourhood there are plenty of leisure options, even an art gallery. There are 70 power sites, up to 30 for tents and seven cabins. Taps are plentiful and there is a dump station available. There is a bright roomy kitchen, not lavishly equipped with cooking appliances. The TV room is non-addictive. There are satisfactory ablutions and automatic equipment in the laundry. Park in the camp for $7.50 per person. ▭ $15.

 7. The Farmyard Holiday Park
Coach Road, Geraldine (03) 693-9355

This camp is handy to S Hwy 1, and 8km south of Geraldine. Watch for the turnoff at Orari. Brimful of people when we called, it also has a host of four-footed friends to make your acquaintance. Your pets are welcome here too.

Spread over a 40 acre farmlet, it has 30 power sites, innumerable tent sites and a few cabins available. Free treats for the children include donkey rides every morning. Small motorised bikes are available. The BBQ area is delightful and generously supplied with wood fuel. You won't have to compromise with facilities, as they are in first-class order. The kitchen is particularly well appointed and opens to a very inviting TV and dining area. The ablutions are good and there is automatic equipment in the laundry. There is a dump point here. A great experience for city folks. Your hosts Bob and Shirley Guthrie. Tent sites are $13 for two people, or with power $14. 🖻. Lots of other accommodation. (see page 282 for further information.)

8. Pioneer Park Camping Area
Gudex Road or Middle Valley Road, 14km west of Geraldine.
Departmentartment of Conservation (03) 379-9758

On S Hwy 79, this camp is 18km north of Fairlie. This conservation camp includes water supply, toilets, BBQs, picnic tables and rubbish facilities. Please use no fires except for BBQs. The site is the Canterbury foothills and over a river bed, very handy to numerous recreational opportunities in the bush and on the rivers. Contact as above. Charges are $3 per adult.

9. Winchester Domain Motor Camp
S Hwy 1, Winchester (03) 615-7564

Economical camping north of Temuka. There are 32 power sites and lots of room for tents on this camping field. It is open from Labour weekend and is closed after the May holidays. A nice flowerbed graces the middle of the camp and there is a border of trees. The amenities are of a limited quantity, one shower and four toilets for each sex. (Unless you count both the ladies and men's "washroom" which has an agitator washer, a tub and sinks each) There is a small kitchen. In the care of Paula Cooper. Just a modest little stopover at $8 for two persons for a tent site, or $9 with power.

10. Temuka Holiday Park
1 Ferguson Drive (Domain Ave), Temuka (03) 615-7241

This is a Domain camp which has a large capacity for campers with around 245 sites. The sites are large and level and adjoin a football field. A model Maori whare and the local baths are here. As well as the sporting facilities an adventure playground is provided. A canteen-style shop is on site and milk and bread are delivered. There are two kitchens but no indoor recreation (TV) room. The ablutions are on an upgrading program. The laundry has automatic machines. There is a dump point here. Julie and Stuart Rose and family are your hosts. Tent sites are $7 per person, or with power $7.50. 🖻 $13 per person.

11. Seadown Holiday Village
S Hwy 1 Timaru (north) PO Box 2035 Washdyke (03) 688-2657
(phone & fax)

The entrance to this complex is off a side street from S Hwy 1, which makes for very easy access. The setting is rural but state-of-the-art camping appointments are provided. You can order breakfast here too. The kitchen, complete with pots and pans, has all the trappings for an enthusiastic cook. Adjoining this is a lovely TV lounge opening to a patio. Great ablution facilities, soap and paper towels provided, or your personal en-suite at some of the power sites. The laundry provides the latest automatic machines. There are 40 sites here, 30 with power and taps. An on-site store will take care of your basic provisions. Your hosts George and Anne Crump. Tent sites are $7 per person and the en-suite power sites are $18 for two. 🏠 $12 per person.📷 Look for further information on page 282.

12. Selwyn Holiday Park
Selwyn Street, Timaru (03)   684-7690 (fax 03 688-1004)

This is a large camp with a border of sheltering trees. On the northern outskirts of Timaru, it is particularly handy to the golf links. A visit to the attractive beach at Caroline Bay is just a short trip east.. Of the 150 sites available, most have power and are in an almost garden setting. There are multi-service blocks of amenities, and in the main ablution block liquid soap and hand towels are supplied. Three kitchens provide cooking and fridges. French doors opening to a patio are a feature. There is a large, comfortable TV lounge. The laundry is also large and has automatic machines.   A bus stop is at the gate and local shopping nearby. There is also a playground for children. Your hosts Tracey and David Horrell. Tent sites are $8 per person, or with power $17–$18 for two. 🏠 and 📷 $28 to $45.

13. Glenmark Motor Camp
Beaconsfield Road, RD2 Timaru (03) 684-3682

An easy- to-find rural camp at Saltwater Creek, just south of Timaru. The grounds are level with easy access to all sites which are landscaped with trees and shrubs. An attractive kidney-shaped pool is in a fenced enclosure. The amenities are centrally placed and are of a high standard. The kitchen is a beauty, together with a TV lounge that overlooks the children's play area. The ablutions are functional and very clean, as is the automatically equipped laundry. Of the 110 sites here, 70 have power. There is a dump point here. As well as a camp store for basic requirements, bread, milk and papers are delivered daily. Despite its country atmosphere this is only a short journey to central Timaru and lovely Caroline Bay. Site of an annual carnival over the Christmas holidays. Your hosts are Dot and Len Booth. Tent sites are $7 per person, power sites $8 with a minimum charge of $10.🏠 $25 for two people.🚐. .

14. Pleasant Point Domain Motor Camp
S Hwy 8 Pleasant Point–PO Box 522 Timaru (03) 614-7300

On the road to Lake Tekapo and inland from Timaru, this camp is thick with trees, with around 30 power sites, and 20 tent sites in a sheltered grove of oaks and conifers. This camp may be closed in winter. The public park alongside has playing fields, a stadium, golf and tennis available. The communal kitchen has a fridge and the ablutions have disabled facilities. There is a laundry. No pets here please. Tent sites are $6.50 per person, or with power $7.50. There are four 🏠 $13 per person.

15. C.J. Talbot Memorial Motor Camp
Allandale Road, Fairlie (03) 685-8375

Formerly known as Fairlie Motor Camp, this is a Domain camp on S Hwy 79. In a park-like setting, yet handy to town, it offers large level sites big trees . The camp has 50 power sites, a few tent sites and cabins. There is a farmhouse style kitchen with log burning heating and electric cooking. Outside a BBQ garden with rustic seats is set under a canopy of willows. The three blocks of amenities include paraplegic facilities and a well equipped laundry. There is a dump station. Good all -round camping in well maintained surroundings. Two people can camp here for $12, or with power $14. There are eight 🏠, including one family unit at $9 per person.

16. Lake Tekapo Motor Camp
Lakeside Drive, PO Box 43 Lake Tekapo (03) 680-6825
(fax 03 680-6824)

Shoreside camping by a crystal lake and sheltered by pine trees. There are 80 power sites, 100 for tents, and alternative motel and cabin accommodation. Camping areas are terraced slightly above the lake, on ground that has some boulders. There is a boat ramp. From around June to September you can ice skate here. Well endowed with amenities, the showers (shub type) are in two modern blocks, with a step-up version for the children's bath. An excellent laundry too. There is a good kitchen equipped with three full-size stoves. There are plenty of mountain attractions and you can arrange flights and hire bikes. Your hosts Peter and Anne Brass. You can pay by Eftpos here. All camping is $8 per person, 🏠 $24 and 🏢 $58.

17. St Andrews Recreation Reserve
S Hwy 1–1km south of St Andrews (03) 612-6519

Administration is by the St Andrews Domain Board and this reserve is not predominantly used by casual campers. There are 12 sites with power and over 20 for tents. The level sites are on grass and next door is a greyhound-racing track. Campers should be alert for the railway line which runs between the nearby beach and the camp. Keys to the amenities are obtained from the Highway Diner. There are basic ablutions here and a laundry with agitator machines. There are cooking facilities and a fridge in the kitchen but only one sink. BBQs are provided and an adventure play area for children. Tent sites $3.50 per person. Power sites an additional $3 for power.

18. Otaio Gorge Camping Area
Back Line Road, 29km southwest of Timaru–Department of Conservation (03) 379-9758

This conservation camp offers water supply, toilets, BBQs, picnic tables and rubbish facilities. It is another campsite close to Hunters Hills, Waitaki River and their abundant recreational opportunities. Please light no fires (except for BBQ) and do not bring dogs. Charges are $3 per adult.

19. Mt Nimrod Camping Area
Back Line Road, 32km southwest of Timaru–Department of Conservation

Another conservation campsite with similar facilities to Otaio Gorge. Make your enquires to thesame phone number. Charges are $3 per adult.

20. Victoria Park Motor Camp
Naylor Street, PO Box 122 Waimate (03) 689-8954

Beside the Domain gardens, this has an attractive setting fully hedged round the perimeter. Under a canopy of oak trees this camp has good sealed roads to serve the 39 power sites, but not all of these may be available due to longer term leases. The aspect is restful on the eye, with cultivated gardens alongside and the park is well groomed. There are a choice of sporting and play areas adjacent. The annual Xmas holiday carnival and evening entertainment is probably still continuing here. The central amenities block contains spacious and luxurious showers and toilets. The kitchen is also good and there is a communal TV/sitting room. The laundry provides automatic washing and drying. Plenty of taps and a dump point are in the grounds. Power sites are $14 for two people. There are also tent sites and 🏪.

21. Knottingley Park
PO Box 122 Waimate

The environment is delightful, with landscaped grounds in a beautiful setting, around 3km from Waimate. There are level sites within the park and 20 have power. Recent improvements have been newly installed showers and toilets (partially suitable for paraplegic use). The kitchen has a rustic, rather than efficient, quality with a large open fire, TV and comfy chairs, but few appliances. There is a nominal laundry. Powers sites are $5 per person and tent sites are $4.

22. Glentaki Holiday Camp
S Hwy 1 Glenavy (03) 689-3888

Personal, warm and friendly, this camp near the northern banks of the Waitaki River is possibly part of a bygone era. While the facilities are humble and of a rare vintage, it is a welcoming place to stop. There are 45 power sites, room for some tents and some army style cabins. The kitchen has three full stoves and tea-maker. The grounds are level with some dividing trees. Fishing is an option here. It could be of interest to day visitors as well as campers. Your friendly hosts are Barbara and Graeme. Tent sites are $10 for two people, or $14 with power. Basic 🛏 $10 per person and there is other accommodation.

23. Gateways Caravan Park
McLean Street, Glenavy (03) 689-3875

Alongside S Hwy 1 and beside Glentaki Camp, another 38 power sites and plenty of tent sites are available. Although the grounds are open, there are shelter belts of trees and some shrubs between the power sites. The kitchen is modern, sturdy and fairly small, but there are several BBQs. Very nice ablutions, immaculately kept, quality but not quantity. There is a basic laundry. You will find a Railway Carriage Restaurant and takeaway food right here. There is a large play area for children. Claude and Bev Scott are in charge. It costs $6 per person for a tent site, or $13 for two, with power. One flat is available at $25 and an 🚐 (with awning) at $28.

24. Haldon Arm Motor Camp
Lake Benmore

The turnoff to this camp is at the mountain end of Burkes Pass hill. The journey is around 50km of unsealed road, but worth it if you want a large lakefront camp with a boat ramp and fishing and boating to your hearts content. This is not luxury camping, and you need to be reasonably independent. There is a dump point here. Food vendors call in holiday time. More information is available from Waitaki District Council,. Private Bag, Oamaru.

25. Sailors Cutting
S Hwy 83 Lake Benmore (03) 434-8060 ext 8658 or (03) 434-1658

Lake-edge camping without the frills. There is a boat ramp and a jetty and 100 tent sites. There are showers and toilet with disabled access. One sink and a power point are provided.. Environmental camping. Inquire from Doug at Waitaki District Council. Tent sites are $6. or by season ticket.

26. Lake Middleton Reserve
Lake Ohau Road, Lake Ohau

Another lake-edge option with a choice of sites on various levels. There is no power here, but plenty of firewood and use of BBQ pits. This reserve has at least 20 tent sites in a pleasant, well-tree'd location. There are a couple of tables and ample rubbish bins on hand. The only amenities are toilets and taps, plus a sump. The honesty box is for your registration.

27. Lake Ohau Lodge
Lake Ohau (03) 438-9885 (phone & fax)

In the heart of the ski country is this resort with provision for camping. There are 14 sites with power and plenty of space to pitch a tent. The sites are level but have no special communal facilities. The Lodge is comfortable, with amenities that campers can share with guests. There is no self-catering kitchen provided, but meals can be purchased. There is use of a spa pool and a drying room. This is alpine camping where you can also hire ski equipment. Your friendly hosts are Mike and Louise Neilson. Power sites $5 per person.

28. Temple Forest Camping Area
Lake Ohau Road, 50km northwest of Twizel. Department of Conservation (03) 379-9758

This conservation camp includes water supply, toilets, BBQs, picnic tables and rubbish facilities.It is close to Ohau ski area, Lake Ohau and the Ohau Forests Recreation area. On offer are a wide variety of outdoor pursuits, to cater for the needs of all interests and abilities. No fires here please. Charges are $3 per adult.

29. Ruataniwha Motor Camp
PO Box 83, Twizel (03) 435-0613 (phone & fax)

If you enjoy space to spread yourself, there is no problem here. The camp is lakeside and on the southern side of Twizel. You can share the large sites with a conifer or two and you won't feel fenced in. There are 92 sites with power and endless room for tents, plus some cabins. The kitchen has microwave and conventional cooking and cool boxes for campers. A games room is provided. The ablutions are satisfactory, in two blocks, hopefully soon to be repainted. The laundry has adequate equipment and there is a dump point here. There is a well stocked general store which is licensed to sell liquor. Hire equipment includes fishing equipment, aquabikes and canoes. This is a national rowing championship venue. Fishing is always an option. For winter sports this is handy for skiing. Your host Stephen Rhodes. Tent sites here are $8 per person or $8.50 with power . $17.50 per person.

30. Glentanner Park
PO Box 23, Mt Cook (03) 435-1855 (fax 435-1854)

An alpine playground at the base of the Ben Ohau mountain range, offering views to Mt Cook over Lake Pukaki, this park is on S Hwy 80 and 20km from Mt Cook village. There are 60 large power sites, very private and cut into bays. A multitude of tent sites are here, plus some cabins. There is also a licensed restaurant. A comfortable dining and TV room is spacious and has a freestanding fireplace and a stack of firewood. This room opens to a boulder patio with glorious views. The kitchen adjoins and has a good array of equipment. The two chimneyed BBQs are a feature in their own special garden. Good laundry facilities. Although the ablutions appear to be somewhat inconveniently placed, they have recently been upgraded. This park is a base for tourist attractions including arranging a scenic flight or hiring mountain bikes. It can also supply your shopping and meal requirements. Your hosts Ian and Pat Ivey. Tent sites here are $6.50 per person, or with power $7 . bunkrooms and $30.

31. White Horse Hill Camping Area
Mt Cook National Park. Department of Conservation

This minimal facility camp is 3km from the Hermitage. There is no power and less than 20 sites for tents. However, they are level with a variety of shade and shelter. Toilets and water taps are provided. A simple outdoor structure with tables and chairs and rubbish bins are on site. This is only suitable for summer camping. Contact Stu Drake at the Department of Conservation office at the Hermitage.

32. Waitaki Reserves Lakeside Camping
Private Bag 50058 Oamaru (03) 434-8060 (fax 03 434-8442)

A range of environmentalist camp sites are clustered on the edge of the hydro lakes. They are in magnificent positions, but they lack facilities, except for toilets. Most have boat ramps and effluent disposal. Inquire through the Waitaki Lakes Reserves. Camping is at $6 per family or $115 for a season ticket. These camps are open from 1 October to 6 May.

The **Farmyard** Holiday Park

Coach Road.Geraldine Tel **03 693-9355**

"Hey! kids. How about a holiday on a real farm?
There are donkey rides, mini-motorbike rides, Bar-B-Q, and lots and lots of animals to make friends with.
Mum and Dad will love the nice clean modern showers and toilets, the kitchen is just like home, and there is a bright , friendly lounge to curl up in on a wet day, with a TV."

Your hosts, Bob and Shirley Guthrie, have catered for disabled people too.

CABINS AND TOURIST FLATS AVAILABLE

⑦

Hi there cobbers, you will have a bonza holiday at

⑪

Seadown Holiday Village

State Highway 1 P O Box 2035, Washdyke Timaru

Tel/fax 03 688 2657

- ❖ Motels
- ❖ Cabins
- ❖ En-suite power sites
- ❖ Spacious grounds with big shady gum trees
- ❖ Superb modern facilities
- ❖ Shop on site

Continental breakfast available for $7.
Cooked breakfast available for $14.

Your hosts, George and Ann, offer you a warm welcome

WEST COAST DIRECTORY

Key to locations and maps in the South Island's West Coast. Begins just north of Karamea, following the coast as far as Westport. Turns inland as far as Murchison. Returns to the coast along an inland route into Lewis Pass. Returns south towards Greymouth. Continues the mainly coastal route to Haast. Finishes on S Hwy 6, Haast Pass.

North of Karamea	1.	Kohaihai Camping & Picnic Area (DoC)
Karamea	2.	Karamea Holiday Park
Karamea	3.	Karamea Camping Ground
Little Wanganui	4.	Little Wanganui Hotel & Motor Camp
Seddonville	5.	Mokihinui Domain
Seddonville	6.	Seddonville Motor Camp
Granity	7.	Fisherman's Lodge Camping Ground
Westport	8.	Westport Chalet Holiday Park
Westport	9.	Seal Colony Tourist Park
Upper Buller Gorge	10.	Lyell Camping Area (DoC)
Murchison	11.	Riverview Motor Camp
north of Charleston	12.	Jack's Place
Charleston	13.	Charleston Motor Camp
Punakaiki	14.	Punakaiki Motor Camp (DoC)
Rapahoe	15.	Rapahoe Motor Camp
Ikamatua	16.	Ikamatua Hotel & Holiday Park
South of Reefton	17.	Slab Hut Creek Camping Area (DoC)
Reefton	18.	Reefton Domain Camp
via Reefton	19.	Marble Hill Camping Area (DoC)
Lewis Pass	20.	Maruia Springs Thermal Resort Ltd
Lewis Pass	21.	Deer Valley (DoC)
Ahaura	22.	Ahaura Domain Camp
Ngahere	23.	Nelson Creek Camping Ground (DoC)
Greymouth	24.	Greymouth Seaside Holiday Park

Greymouth	25.	South Beach Motels & Motor Park
Moana	26.	Lake Brunner Camping Ground (DoC)
Kumara	27.	Kumara Motels & Caravan Park
Goldsborough	28.	Goldsborough Camping Ground (DoC)
Hokitika	29.	Hokitika Holiday Park
Lake Kaniere	30.	Hans Bay (DoC)
Lake Mahinapua	31.	Shanghai Camping Ground (DoC)
Ross	32.	Ross Motor Camp
Ross	33.	Ferguson Farms
Pukekura	34.	Lake Ianthe Cabins
Harihari	35.	Harihari Motor Inn & Caravan Park
Whataroa	36.	Whataroa Hotel Caravan Park
Okarito	37.	The Forks Bunkhouse
Okarito	38.	Okarito Camping Ground (DoC)
Lake Mapourika	39.	McDonalds Creek Camping Area (DoC)
Franz Josef	40.	Franz Josef Holiday Park
Fox Glacier	41.	Fox Glacier Motor Park
Fox Glacier	42.	Glow-Worm Forest Motor Home Park
Gillespies Beach	43.	Gillespies Beach Campsite (DoC)
south of Fox Glacier	44.	Pine Grove Motels
Lake Paringa	45.	Lake Paringa Camping Area (DoC)
Haast	46.	Haast Motor Camp
Haast	47.	Haast Highway Accommodation
east of Haast	48.	Pleasant Flat (DoC)

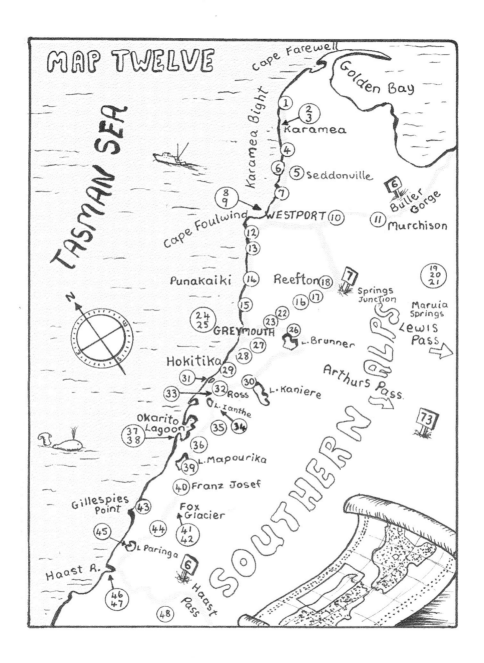

Chapter 12

THE WEST COAST

Outpost New Zealand. A character-filled area where semi-isolation has left its mark – even the climate is different. A journey to the West Coast is like a step back in time. You can relive some of the goldmining, coalmining, timber and greenstone boom times in ghost settlements along the way. Look for the greenstone and pan for the gold; both are still here.

At the threshold of the West Coast and of the Heaphy Track, lies Karamea. With a microclimate that provides unusually mild conditions, the range of plants and trees that thrive here is impressive.

The West Coast drive takes you along a narrow strip of land bordered on the east by imposing mountain ranges and by a rugged coastline to the west. Between Westport and Greymouth the Pancake Rocks at Punakaiki are right beside the road. The surf blowholes can be a spectacular sight (and sound) and worthy of recording with your camera.

Remnants of old towns and rustic relics give testimony to the human struggle of years gone by. Many historic sites and walking tracks help visitors to read the history from the landscape, whilst Coaltown and Shantytown provide working examples of a colourful past.

Surrounded by Westland National Park is the township of Franz Josef. Guided Glacier tours, fishing and canoe trips, horse treks as well as scenic flights operate from here. The Fox Glacier township has similar attractions, with serene views of Lake Matheson and other scenic gems for those prepared to explore on foot. To watch the sun set on the glaciers is a breathtaking experience. Glacier walks are not all strenuous, but you will need a competent guide.

The Glacier highway south to Haast passes through isolated country. Bear in mind that the Southern Alps cover more area than the entire country of Switzerland! As you travel south many kilometres of unspoiled forest will add pleasure to your drive.

Haast, the southernmost town on the West Coast, is renowned for its whitebait. At Haast you will turn inland through the pass. Particularly after heavy rain, (for which the coast is well known) this drive has to be one of the most spectacular in the country.

Linger awhile on the West Coast. You will be made most welcome.

WEST COAST

 ### 1. Kohaihai Camping & Picnic Area
15km north of Karamea, PO Box 47 Karamea–Department of Conservation (03) 782-6852

You will find a sheltered area for camping, with water, fireplaces and toilets at the end of the road. A public telephone is in Shelter Hut. It is right at the start of the Heaphy Track. Activities include sea and freshwater fishing, swimming and scenic walks. Pets must be kept under control at all times and are not allowed in the Forest Park. Further information is available from the above address.

 ### 2. Karamea Holiday Park
No.1 RD, 2067 Karamea (03) 782-6758

Just 3km south of Karamea along a hilly road. The tremendous scenery en route is well worth the drive. This is an attractive camp combining a choice of open sites or those nestled into a sheltered environment lush with trees. The camp itself is not large but does boast two kitchens with up-to-the-minute cooking equipment. The ablutions are past the first flush of youth. There is automatic equipment in the laundry, and the little bit of maintenance required here has probably been done. There is a dump point here. Backpackers accommodation is also provided. This is a peaceful and somewhat isolated spot, where you can enjoy a variety of fishing, particularly for whitebait. Explore the caves, walk the Heaphy Track; transport from here is available. Your hosts John and Margaret Mansell. Tent sites $7 per person. Power sites $15 for two. $18.

3. Karamea Camping Ground & Bunk Room
Behind the school, Karamea.

"Any port in a storm" is our advice for those seeking somewhere to stop for the night. You will find 6 power points at the end of the football field. Forgotten amenities, kitchen with two stoves, two showers for women and an eight-person shower for men! Bring your scrubbing brush. There are two tennis courts here. An honesty system operates and all camping is at $8 for two.

Cabins from		Pet friendly	
Tourist flats and motels from		Department of Conservation	
On-site caravans			

4. Little Wanganui Hotel & Motor Camp
Little Wanganui Hotel, RD 1 Westport (03) 782-6752

Camping country-pub style with 10 power sites plus tent sites behind the licensed premises. There is also an adventure playground for small children. A campers annexe provides two toilets and showers plus a small carpeted kitchen with a full stove and microwave. Otherwise a meal at the hotel is an option. There is a laundry available. Pamela and Ken Greenwell are on duty here. Power sites $10.

 ### 5. Mokihinui Domain
Mokihinui–via Westport (03) 782-1832

On the coastal side of Seddonville this camp is adjacent to a shingle beach, where you can do a spot of fishing, more particularly whitebaiting. The level camping ground is without trees or shelter. A good large kitchen has 3 electric stoves and dining tables and chairs. For a change you could try the local hotel for meals. The ablution block has been upgraded. There are free laundry facilities here. Your new hosts are Barry and Ediner Neale. There are 19 sites with power and other accommodation is obtainable. Tent sites $9.50 for two. Power sites $12 for two.

6. Seddonville Motor Camp
Seddonville (03) 782-1816

Between Karamea and Westport there is a turnoff from the main road to this camp, where you won't be jostled for room. Formerly a school, it has a swimming pool in the grounds and fairly good kitchen and ablution facilities. The cabins and the cosy rooms with pot belly stove could be useful if the weather lets you down. The camp is handy to an hotel, postal service, and other shopping. This area is noted for whitebaiting. The host, Mrs C.Cull was absent when we called. Tent sites here are $6 for two people, or $9 with power. ▱.

7. Fisherman's Lodge Camping Ground
Torea Street, Granity (03) 782-8011

Robust campers may like to tackle this rather challenging camp. It could be useful as a stopover, with hotel facilities and food available. There are a small number of sites, but the obsolete fittings for power should be avoided. Some rather unkempt ablutions are supplied and one agitator washing machine. The hosts Ian and Joy Chambers were not at home when we called. ▱.

8. Westport Chalet Holiday Park
Domett Street, PO Box 294 Westport (03) 789-7043 (fax 03 787-7199)

Somewhere restful in a native bush setting, this is a sheltered camp only 1km from the Post Office and other services. The environment is definitely "green" and wekas patrol the grounds. There is a bright sunny kitchen with stove and fridge, plus a large TV/ social room. The ablutions have roomy showers and dressing space, with a seat. All laundry facilities are automatic. You can do your whitebaiting within the camp grounds. Also there is fishing and goldpanning. The Coal Town Museum is worth a visit. There are 28 power sites here, but 100 for tents, some newly created. A pleasant leafy retreat brimful of bird life. New hosts are probably in residence now. Tent sites $14 for two. 🖥 and 🖥. Power sites are $16 for two.

9. Seal Colony Tourist Park
*Marine Parade, Carters Beach No.2 RD Westport (03) 789-8002
(fax 03 789-6732)*

You will find it hard to fault this West Coast park for facilities and upkeep. The location is just off the main road and close to the beach. The grounds cater for around 140 campers; 38 of the sites have power. Nothing has been spared to make the amenities first class. The kitchen has been thoughtfully planned, with all the latest equipment and a walk-in cold room, with individual lockers for guests. An attractive dining room opens to the recreation room. The ablutions feature two bathrooms as well as showers. There is all automatic equipment in the laundry. There is a dump point here. Outside is an adventure playground and a special fenced BBQ area is supplied with beechwood for your fireside get-together. Handily placed for the golf links and the seal colony, this is a well established AA enterprise. Your hosts Lynda and Ross Eddy. There is an AA members discount here. Tent sites $16 to $18 for two. Power sites $18. 🖥 and 🖥.

 10. Lyell Camping Area
*Upper Buller Gorge–Department of Conservation (03) 732-8391
(fax 03 732-8616)*

A scenic and historic camping area on the site of the town of Lyell, once a thriving goldrush centre. There is a large level grassed area with picnic tables and one tap in the middle. Two "long drop" toilets are the only facilities. The outlook is bush-covered hills. Walkways fan out from the camping area. Beware of sandflies here. Of geological interest, much of the surrounding area has been modified by earthquakes. No pets in this camp please. It is managed by the Reefton Field Centre, Conservation Department.

11. Riverview Motor Camp
Chalgrave Street, PO Box 99 Murchison (03) 523-9315

With Murchison 2km to the south, this camp provides a stopover between Picton, Nelson and the West Coast. Dominated by tall pines, the grounds are neat and the neighbouring area is quiet. There is a nice play area with climbing frames, for children. The amenities provided are adequate, if a little unpreened, and these are handy to the 30 power sites and cabins. There are tent sites beside the Buller River with open fireplaces only. Scenic and white-water rafting is based at the camp. The river is good for swimming or fishing. Goldpanning is another option. Your hosts Shelly and Peter Flintoff. Tent sites $15 for two persons. Power sites $8.50 per person.

12. Jack's Place
S Hwy 6, Little Totara River via Westport (03) 789-6501 (phone & fax)

The colourful road signs direct you to this unique enterprise just 4km north (inland) of Charleston. If you can manage without power you will find plenty of free tent sites here. A tree-planting program is underway. At present the sites are level and grassy and there is a gentle flowing stream on one boundary. Dedicated to rest and relaxation; take time out here. The ablutions are well kept with a rustic appearance and include facilities for the disabled. There is an automatic washing machine and a dryer available. There is no kitchen. Jack wants you to enjoy his beer garden and licensed restaurant. Music too. Try the homemade bread and organic produce. You can smoke here! There is accommodation offered too. Your host Jack Schubert speaks German.

13. Charleston Motor Camp
S Hwy 6, Charleston–Buller (03) 789-6773

This camp is on a scenic coastal highway some 28km from Westport. If adventure is on your agenda, you will find a company catering to your needs almost next door. The camp itself is not large, but has a postal agency, tearoom and shop with card phone on the site. The land is level, with 14 power sites and 30 tent sites. It is quite close to both sea and river fishing. The kitchen says welcome with its coal-burning range set in river boulders. There is also electric and microwave cooking and a fridge. Alongside is dining/sitting nook. The ablutions are average, and the laundry has both washer and dryer. Yes you can bring your pets here. Your hosts Murray and Audrey. Tent sites $15 for two. Power sites $16 for two.

14. Punakaiki Motor Camp

Owen Street, PO Box 12 Punakaiki–Department of Conservation (03) 731-1894 (fax 03 731-1888)

The Pancake Rocks and blowholes are almost within hearing distance of this very accessible Conservation camp. With sealed roads, and the contoured land giving privacy and shelter, this lovely, large coastal camp appears to be well-drained, even in winter. There are hotplates in the mini-kitchen (but no room to linger) and a dining and recreation room provides a fireplace. The ablutions are somewhat under-supplied and there is a laundry. There are excellent drying facilities, and a card phone is available, with shopping just up the road. No pets please. A great base to explore the spectacular West Coast. Your hosts Gary and Carol. Tent sites here are $7 per person. Power sites $7 per person plus $1 for power.

 15. Rapahoe Motor Camp

10 Hawker Street, Rapahoe (03) 762-7025

This tiny settlement is just a dot on the map some 11km north of Greymouth. Here you will find West Coast hospitality in a small camp with high standards of housekeeping. There are 10 power sites, plus some tent sites and two cabins in a garden setting and well sheltered by mature trees. The beach is adjacent. Children are provided with a variety of play equipment and pets are welcome here. Complete with a coin phone, the kitchen is well appointed with 3 full stoves, and invitingly clean. This opens to a social/recreational hall with masses of pot plants and a cosy fuel burner. There is no shortage of toilets and handbasins, but showers are limited. Your hosts Peter and Jan Fletcher. Tent sites $6 per person. Power sites $6 per person plus $2. 🏪

 16. Ikamatua Hotel & Holiday Park

Ikamatua--Grey Valley, Westland (03) 732-3555

You can get railroaded here! There is just a small camp with 6 power sites and tent sites on a large back lawn with cabins and backpackers accommodation available. The recycled Railway Station is now a services block with platform "sun deck". There is a multi-purpose room for cooking, dining, TV/ stereo and a comfy chair. There are a couple of showers and toilets including paraplegic facilities. Laundry facilities are provided. This is a dog friendly location. Your hosts Nette and Brian & Greg and Deedee can provide all meals at the hotel. Inquire for these prices. Tent sites $5 per person. Power sites are $12 for two people. 🏪

17. Slab Hut Creek Camping Area

Victoria Forest Park, via Reefton–Department of Conservation (03) 732-8391 (fax 03 732-8616)

This conservation camping area is a golden treasure–literally. Located south of Reefton in Victoria Forest Park, it is within easy driving or cycling distance (8.5km) of the town. Bounded by a stream and forest, it offers a small number of secluded and well-drained campsites. Basic facilities with disabled access are provided, but campers should be relatively self-sufficient. Slab Hut is extremely popular, particularly in summer, so it may be difficult to find a campsite. One reason for its popularity is gold. The camping area fronts onto a large gold-fossicking claim where good "colours" can often be found. Gold pans only please. The Slab Hut camping area is managed by the Reefton Field Centre.

18. Reefton Domain Camp

S Hwy 7, Broadway, Reefton (03) 732-8477

With a perimeter of tall fir trees, this has a lovely sheltered aspect and a river alongside. The sites are level with plenty of room, and well kept. The kitchen has new hot plates but apart from new dining tables and chairs, is not lavish. The ablutions have variety! While there are large showers and dressing rooms in the women's section, this area is close to its "use by" date. The men have newer, formica-lined facilities. The laundry provides both washer and dryer. There are BBQs outside and a children's play area. The Reefton shops are close by. This is an area of historic interest, where coalmining has been commemorated in the museum, and gold can still be panned in the rivers. Beside the camp you can fish or swim as well. Your host is Lyn Roa. Tent sites $12 for two. Power sites $14 for two.⌂ $15 per person.

19. Marble Hill Camping Area

S Hwy 7, Maruia Springs and Springs Junction Department of Conservation (03) 732-8391 (fax 03 732-8616)

A thoroughly "uplifting" conservation camping area. Just east of Springs Junction, Marble Hill lies adjacent to the Alpine Fault–the boundary of two continental plates of the Earth's crust. It was (and still is) the collision of these two plates that formed the Southern Alps! Apart form its geology, the area has much to offer. The popular Lake Daniells Track begins here. An easy three-and-a-half hour walk away, the lake is a superb trout fishery. The camping area is large with many campsites. Picnic tables, fireplaces and toilets are provided. No pets please. Use Marble Hill as a base to explore the scenically diverse Lewis Pass National Reserve. The Marble Hill area is managed by the Reefton Field Centre.

20. Maruia Springs Thermal Resort Ltd
S Hwy 7, Lewis Pass, Private Bag 55-014 Christchurch (03) 523-8840 (phone & fax)

Attention trailblazers! On S Hwy 7 this is central South Island country at the northern end of the Southern Alps. It is surrounded with native beech trees and bush with the Maruia River flowing directly in front of the thermal pools. There are backpacker bunkrooms and hotel units plus unpowered camp sites. However campers have toilets and water, with showers in the adjoining thermal complex. They can also use the thermal open rock pools and bathhouse. Alpine tramping is the other attraction here. It costs $5 per site plus $6 per person to camp here. Discounts are available for groups.

21. Deer Valley
Off S Hwy 7, Lewis Pass National Reserve–Department of Conservation (03) 755-8301

This Conservation camp site is in the upper reaches of the Lewis Valley, surrounded by beech forest and beside the Lewis River. No dogs here please. Toilets, tap water and BBQ facilities are provided.

22. Ahaura Domain Camp
S Hwy 7, Ahaura (c/o Ahaura Postal Centre) (03) 732-3876

Between Reefton and Greymouth, this little camp has a much improved image. The grounds are well tree'd, with new plantings and a tidy lawn for the 4 power points (or tent sites). The amenities are clean, but not lavish. In the tiny kitchen there is electric cooking, a microwave oven and a fridge. Squash and tennis courts are next door. The outdoor sportsman may like to try deer stalking or fishing. Both are in close proximity. Your host is Don. Tent sites are $3.50 per person or with power $5 per person.

23. Nelson Creek Camping Ground
Nelson Creek Road–Department of Conservation (03) 768-0427

This attractive Conservation campground is set in an old goldmining area full of exciting exploration opportunities. The 7km sealed road to Nelson Creek leaves the Grey Valley Road (S Hwy 7) approximately 1km east of Ngahere. The Nelson Creek village, including a store, hotel and pottery shop, sits on a terrace immediately above the camping and recreation area. The campground, which is next to the creek, has numerous sheltered campsites, clean toilets, play equipment, BBQs, picnic tables, running water and a swimming hole. A track leading through a tunnel and over a swing bridge provides access to a number of interesting short bush walks through an intensively mined landscape with tunnels, tailraces and hand-stacked tailings. A high-grade wheelchair track is easily reached by road and a goldpanning area is signposted. Enquires to Greymouth Field Base, Department of Conservation.

24. Greymouth Seaside Holiday Park
Chesterfield Street, Greymouth (03) 768-6618 (fax 03 768-5873)

Not the most expansive entrance to this camp, although the grounds have little surprises (fresh herbs, if you choose your site carefully). Some of the 50 power sites have hard stands for vans and there are 50 tent sites, on level but indifferent grounds. This camp is at the southern end of Greymouth with a walkway to the beach and a playground for children. There is a camp store and food is available here. Of the two kitchens provided, one is decidedly more attractive and opens to a pleasant TV room. There is a roller towel and liquid soap provided in the ablutions, which have paraplegic facilities.. There is automatic equipment in the laundry. A private spa pool is available. There are a wide variety of camp sites plus cabins and a backpackers bunkhouse. A dump point is provided. The managers are Doug and Rhonda Levien. Tent sites $17 for two. Power sites $19 for two.

25. South Beach Motels & Motor Park
318 Main South Road, Greymouth (03) 762-6768 (fax 03 762-6748)

A thriving smaller complex just 5km south of Greymouth. The trees are growing too and the lawns are well sheltered. Camping and motels merge here and there are hard stands for vans around the service block. A modern kitchen has a comfortable TV/recreation room adjoining. The ablutions are well appointed, with bath and an excellent paraplegic suite. There is automatic laundry equipment provided. Try the spa pool. Children have a selection of play equipment and there are BBQs and picnic tables in the grounds. There is a dump point here. Your hosts Eric and Sandra Powell and Jodee and Graham Smith. Tent and power sites $18 for two people.

26. Lake Brunner Camping Ground
Moana (03) 738-0543

Views of the lake are a feature of this camp. The village of Moana is off the Reefton Road, 39km from Greymouth. There is an impression of rather ungroomed grounds for campers, despite some flowers in season. The kitchen is roomy and has plenty of appliances and a lovely lake outlook. The ablutions looked a little forgotten. There is an adequate laundry. Together with the TV/recreation room the communal buildings look sturdy, but stark. There is a dump point here. The site, with Lake Brunner at its doorstep, offers trout fishing, water taxi and boat hire. Tent sites are $12 for two. Power sites are $16 for two people.

27. Kumara Motels & Caravan Park
63 Greenstone Road, Kumara (03) 736-9847

A pot pourri of motels with a small lawn for a few power sites in front. A gas BBQ is provided but there is no kitchen. A little play equipment is provided for the children. The ablutions have good showers and toilet. Use of a pioneer washing machine for the laundry. Your host Jack Cooper. All sites are $5 per person.

28. Goldsborough Camping Ground
Stafford–Dillmanstown Road, 17km from Hokitika–Department of Conservation (03) 755-8301

This Conservation campground is on the site of the old mining town of Goldsborough. The many tracks in the nearby Waimea Forest provide the opportunity to explore a genuine West Coast goldmining area. Goldsborough can be reached by signposted roads from the main highway (S Hwy 6) 9km and 12km north of Hokitika, or by the Stafford Loop Road which leaves Arthurs Pass highway 3km east of Kumara. The campground offers pleasant, sheltered campsites with clean toilets nearby. Picnic tables, fireplaces and a shelter shed are available for both picnickers and campers. Goldpanning is allowed in marked areas of the creek which flows past the campground. An honesty box is provided for suggested nightly tariff of $4 per person. Managed by Arahura Field Centre, Conservation Department. Hokitika.

29. Hokitika Holiday Park
242 Stafford Street, Hokitika (03) 755-8172 (phone & fax)

Situated close to the centre of this individualistic town, this park offers great facilities. The kitchen has a high standard of equipment and plenty of tables and chairs. If you want to relax there is a comfortable TV lounge, where there is also a dining annexe. The ablutions are excellent and comfortable and have wheelchair access. There is automatic equipment in the laundry. Some play equipment is provided for the children. There are 35 sites with power and some have hard stands for vans, with sumps and taps. There are 40 tent sites and a selection of 🏠. Inquire from your host Ron Heward for current prices.

30. Hans Bay
Stafford Street ext. East, Lake Kaniere–Department of Conservation

A new camp some 22km inland from Hokitika. There are several levels of camp sites with panoramic views of Lake Kaniere. Toilets, cold water taps and BBQs are the only facilities.

31. Shanghai Camping Ground
Lake Mahinapua, S Hwy 6–Department of Conservation (03) 755-8301

Sited on the shores of beautiful Lake Mahinapua and surrounded by lush West Coast rain forest, this Conservation campground is an ideal spot for all types of passive water recreation in a pleasant and relaxed setting. The campground provides a range of sheltered campsites with picnic tables and fireplaces for campers use. The recreation area also has a playground, fresh running water and clean toilets. No pets please. Bush walks radiate from the campground, with more further afield. A 10-minute walk past the well known Mahinapua Hotel takes you to a classic West Coast beach with magnificent views. For an unforgettable experience try exploring Mahinapua Creek at the northern end of the lake in a canoe. An honesty box is provided for a suggested nightly tariff of $4 per person. Managed by the Arahura Field Centre, Hokitika.

32. Ross Motor Camp
Ross (03) 755-4005

Looking for a West Coast experience? Try the little settlement of Ross, some 30km south of Hokitika. This camp has 20 sites across from 14 cabins and adjacent to a hotel and store. There is not an abundance of grass for parking. The services include a smallish kitchen/ dining room with a full stove plus hot plates. The ablutions are supplied with curtained showers. There are good automatic washers and dryers in the laundry. Information on local attractions is obtainable at the hotel. In charge here are Doug and Colleen King. Tent sites $7 per person. Power sites $8 per person. 🏠 $14.

33. Ferguson Farms
Fergusons Bush, Ross (03) 755-4125

Between Ross and Harihari this West Coast farm-stay is at the south end of Ferguson's Bush Scenic Reserve, on the fringe of the Mikonui State Forest. It also caters for campers although there are only 6 sites with power, a level garden area for parking and just single toilet and shower facilities. There is a laundry available. Your hosts Jim and Jocelyn Ferguson. Tent sites are $5 per person and $5 is the charge for vehicle and occupants, with power.

34. Lake Ianthe Cabins
Lake Ianthe Tavern, Pukekura (03) 755-4032 (fax 03 755-4002)

As the name suggests, this is mainly cabin accommodation, with some tent sites and 4 power points provided by Lake Ianthe Tavern, where you can also buy some basic supplies. There are communal unisex ablutions and a washing machine and dryer available. There did not appear to be cooking facilities, but there is use of a fridge. Your hosts Carol and Rod Mulholland. Check first on availability and prices. 🏠

35. Harihari Motor Inn & Caravan Park
S Hwy 6, Harihari (03) 753-3026 (fax 03 753-3109)

A choice of accommodation here includes bunk rooms, hotel rooms or you may hitch your wagon to one of the 16 power sites. Harihari is in the State Forest area and reasonably handy to the alpine region. The grounds are level and open with fairly average maintenance. There is a children's play area. Campers may use the hotel facilities, but there is no kitchen. Laundry and ablutions are available and there is a dump point. A westerly camp, but not on the coast. Your hosts Heather and Steve. Tent sites $5 per person. Power sites $12 for two.

36. Whataroa Hotel Camper Caravan & Car Park
S Hwy 6, Whataroa (03) 753-4076

What it lacks in camping facilities this park makes up for in atmosphere. No provision for tents, but drivers have 12 gravel-based power sites for easy parking. A well kept selection of ablutions for your comfort and all the facilities of the hotel are at your disposal. Golfers may want to linger. You can hire clubs and the golf course adjoins the park. There is a friendly welcome here and an evening at the character-filled bar is not to be missed. Many other services are within walking distance. Jim and June Lancaster will take care of you here. Power sites $15 for two. Bed and breakfast $50 for two.

37. The Forks Bunkhouse
Okarito
This little camp has only 3 power sites and plenty of shady tent sites plus bunkhouse accommodation. It is 2km from the main highway. This is wild country with a river alongside and untended grounds. Not really suited for motorhomes, in fact not really suited for anyone who is fussy about facilities. However this may be about to change. There is new host at the helm. Watch this space.

38. Okarito Camping Ground
Okarito–Department of Conservation, Hokitika (03) 755-8301

Once a goldmining centre, this township is but a cluster of houses now. However, the white heron (kotuku) is very much at home here. A cute little camp, it is across the dunes from the beach and nestled cosily amongst some trees. There are fireplace sites, picnic tables and grassed campsites. Two showers and a paraplegic toilet are here, but no power. An interesting lagoon and lowland rainforest are worth a visit. Maintenance is done by the local Community Association. Donations for these purposes are expected.

39. McDonalds Creek Camping Area
S Hwy 6, south end of McDonalds Creek Bridge–Department of Conservation

Adjacent to S Hwy 6 at the northern end of Lake Mapourika, this is a basic camping area with a toilet and picnic tables. Attractions include Lake Mapourika, which is 15km north of Franz Josef township on S Hwy 6.

40. Franz Josef Holiday Park
Main Road, Franz Josef, PO Box 27 (03) 752-0766

Just south of Franz Josef, this is a delightful mountain park providing a good number of holiday options. There are 34 power sites, 80 tent sites, and a choice of other accommodation. It enjoys an attractive setting, with level sites surrounded by alpine bush and ferns. The sealed areas between power sites are useful for motorhomes, but may be a little restricting for tents. A new recreation complex now includes a writing room, pool and table tennis tables, video machines and leads to a spacious sunny lounge with patio, overlooking the stream. Other amenities are first class with a convenient kitchen and excellent commercial laundry. The modern ablutions are squeaky clean and include paraplegic facilities and a babies bathroom. These facilities are shared with the cabin residents, which makes for some congestion at times. There is a dump station provided. The park is 5km from the foot of the glacier, with a bus stop outside. Your hosts Marion and Roy Clarke. Tents $7.50 per person. Power sites $17 for two. 🏠.

41. Fox Glacier Motor Park
Lake Matheson Road, PO Box 37 Fox Glacier (03) 751-0821 (fax 03 751-0813)

This is a complex with well serviced accommodation, but the camping facilities are less attractive. There are around 130 camping sites, with half of these on power. A general store is on site and a licensed restaurant with takeaways is close by. There is a functional kitchen/dining and fairly nondescript ablutions provided. There is automatic laundry equipment and a dump point. However campers may share the amenities provided in the pleasant environment of the Lodge. Most camping sites are on gravel, without privacy, but there are some with a border of greenery. There is a small playground for children. Your new host Mike Gibson. Tent sites are $16.50 for two persons, or with power $18.

42. Glow-Worm Forest Lodge & Motorhome Park
Main Road, PO Box 22 Fox Glacier (03) 751-0888 (phone & fax)

Sorry, no tent sites here. For the others this is a charming alpine park on the southern fringe of the Fox Glacier township with a boundary of West Coast bush. The 24 power sites form a two-tier radius around the centre of the camp. The lodge buildings are virtually new, but blend attractively with their environment. The ground floor provides the amenities, which are superb. Enjoy a shower with plentiful hot water and all the basins have liquid soap and hand towels. The kitchen has gas and microwave cooking and is a convivial place to discuss the day's events. You will find all the other utensils, including crockery, here. There is even a supply of tea and coffee. There is also an outdoor dining area and BBQ. A well equipped auto laundry too. Yes, check out the glow worms and perhaps opossums after dark. You can hire bikes here or use the services of a professional fishing guide for that trout or salmon. Your hosts Fran and Laurie Buckton. The lodge has rooms available. Power sites are $18 for two people.

 ### 43. Gillespies Beach Campsite

Gillespies Beach, PO Box 9 Fox Glacier–Department of Conservation (03) 751-0807

This is a small campsite at the north end of Gillespies Beach, 22km from Fox Glacier. The approach is by a narrow, winding road not recommended for towing caravans. There are walks to historic goldmining sites and seal colony nearby. Toilet and water supply on site. Further information from the above address.

44. Pine Grove Motels

PO Box 26, Fox Glacier (03) 751-0898

On S Hwy 6, 35km south of Fox Glacier, there are now 2 power points supplied beside the motels. The grounds have a bush surround, but sites are on a gravel base. The kitchen has gas cooking, fridge and TV. Some basic pots and pans are provided. There is a combined ablution/laundry facility for campers. Whitebaiting and fishing are popular here. Your hosts Carol and David Scott.

 ### 45. Lake Paringa Camping Area

Lake Paringa, PO Box 9 Fox Glacier–Department of Conservation (03) 751-0807

An accessible campsite on the bushclad shore of Lake Paringa with beautiful lake and forest views. Excellent boating, fishing and swimming with boat ramp facilities. Just "long drop" toilets and urinal, but paraplegic access. Cold water on tap (or in the lake). It costs $4 per person for a power site here. Further information from the above address.

🚐	On-site caravan from	🐕	Dog friendly
🏠	Cabins from		
🏨	Tourists flats and motels from	⌒	Department of Conservation

46. Haast Motor Camp
Jacksons Bay Road, PO Box 8, Haast (03) 750-0860 (phone & fax)

Haast township is a tiny oasis in South Westland. The motor camp is 15km off the main road. The grounds are on a peninsula where you can enjoy both sea and river fishing and whitebaiting. This may be your best opportunity to enjoy the clean sweep of beach before heading through the mountainous terrain to the east. Although this is pleasingly remote you will find a general store here, garage service and petrol. There are 70 sites here on fairly level ground divided by shelter belts. Around half of these sites have power. Generously supplied with amenities, the camp has two good kitchens and a spacious mezzanine dining-living room with huge open fire, good furnishings and TV. The ablutions are plentiful and formica-lined. Excellent laundry equipment too. There is a boat ramp here and a dump point. A card phone is available. Your friendly hosts Brian and Phillipa Glubb. Tent sites $14 for two. Power sites $17.

47. Haast Highway Accommodation
Marks Road, PO Box 11 Haast (03) 750-0703 (fax 03 750-0718)

Watch for the turnoff from S Hwy 6 just 3km east from the Information Centre. This offers motels and budget accommodation and services together with 14 power sites and tent sites by arrangement. Asphalt parking and water on tap is on each power site. An inviting up-to-the-minute kitchen has everything supplied, including pots and pans. This adjoins open plan dining and attractive step-up lounge, pleasantly furnished. The ablutions are also good with metered showers. Automatic equipment (plus iron and board) are in the laundry. There is a good range of supplies obtainable here and a public phone. There is also a dump point. Your hosts Peter and Jenny Barrett. All camping is $16 for two people. ▦.

 48. Pleasant Flat
S Hwy 6 –45km east of Haast, Department of Conservation (03) 755-8301

Adventurous campers may like to explore the rugged beauty of remote alpine country from this campsite. Toilets and tap water are provided.

SOUTHERN LAKES–FIORDLAND DIRECTORY

Key to locations and maps in the Southern Lakes and Fiordland. Begins at the head of Lake Wanaka. Continues between Lakes Wanaka and Hawea to Wanaka township. Goes south to Queenstown and around Lake Wakatipu District. Across to Te Anau, then south to Manapouri. Returns via S Hwy 94 to finish at Milford.

Lake Wanaka	1.	Boundary Creek Reserve (DoC)
Makarora	2.	Makarora Tourist Centre Ltd
Lake Hawea	3.	Kidds Bush Camping Area (DoC)
Lake Hawea	4.	Lake Hawea Motor Camp
Wanaka	5.	Penrith Park
Wanaka	6.	Wanaka Motor Park
Wanaka	7.	Wanaka Pleasant Lodge Holiday Park
Glendhu Bay	8.	Glendhu Bay Motor Camp
Arrowtown	9.	Arrowtown Camping Ground
Arrowtown	10.	Arrowtown Caravan Park
Queenstown	11.	Frankton Motor Camp
Queenstown	12.	Kawarau Falls Lodge & Motor Camp
Queenstown	13.	Queenstown Creeksyde Campervan Park
Queenstown	14.	Queenstown Motor Park
Queenstown	15.	Arthurs Point Camping Ground

SOUTHERN LAKES–FIORDLAND

Queenstown	16.	Closeburn Alpine Park
via Queenstown	17.	Moke Lake Reserve (DoC)
via Queenstown	18.	Skippers-Mt Aurum Reserve (DoC)
Glenorchy	19.	Glenorchy Holiday Park
Routeburn	20.	Lake Sylvan Roadend Campsite (DoC)
Kinloch	21.	Kinloch Campsite (DoC)
via Queenstown	22.	Kingston Stream Holiday Camp
Mavora Lakes	23.	Mavora Lakes Conservation Campsite (DoC)
Te Anau	24.	Fiordland Holiday Park
Te Anau	25.	Te Anau Mountain View Cabin & Caravan Park
Te Anau	26.	Te Anau Motor Park
Manapouri	27.	Lakeview Motels & Motor Park
Manapouri	28.	Manapouri Glade Motor Park & Motels
via Te Anau	29.	Hollyford Valley Camp (Gunns Camp)
Te Anau-Milford	30.	Milford Road Conservation Campsites (DoC)
Milford	31.	Milford Sound Lodge

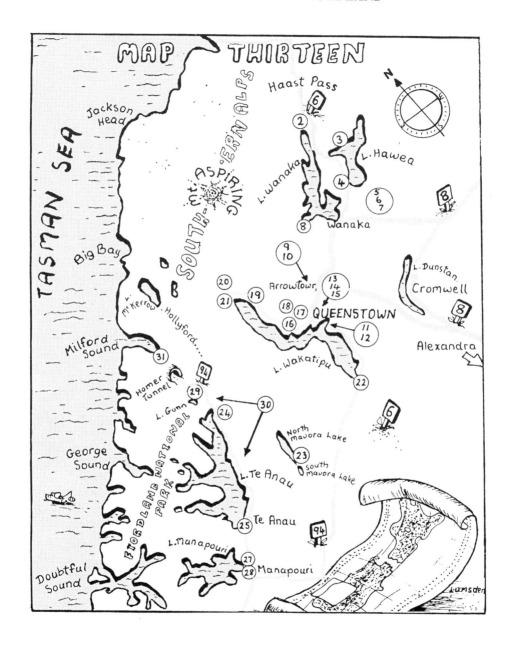

SOUTHERN LAKES–FIORDLAND

Chapter 13

SOUTHERN LAKES AND FIORDLAND

Leaving the Haast Pass behind, your journey will take you alongside Lake Hawea, and on to the holiday town of Wanaka. Amongst this alpine country the many lakes float images of their neighbouring mountains.

For the camera or video buff the scenery is truly breathtaking. The colours, particularly in autumn, are indescribable. Peppermint-blue lakes contrast against snowy mountains and the deciduous trees that edge the lakes are the colour of barley sugar at this time of year.

For the energetic try bungy jumping, rafting, jet boating, horse riding, parapenting, alpine walks and skiing. For those who prefer less nerve-racking activities, a trip in the gondola to view Queenstown and the surrounding area, a game of golf on a world-class golf course, a gentle cruise on the historic steamer *SS Earnslaw* or a visit to the pedestrian shopping mall will give you days of relaxation.

Living history is part of the charm of nearby Arrowtown. A day spent here is an entrancing experience.

Te Anau is set on the shores of the South Island's biggest lake. It has a quieter tempo than Queenstown and is the gateway to Fiordland National Park. At the head of Lake Te Anau the Milford Track beckons. It is a world famous walk and booking ahead is essential.

The drive to Milford is relatively short and has dramatic vistas along the way. The road climbs steeply to the Homer Tunnel and then descends its winding path to sea level and Milford Sound. If walking the various tracks (the Milford, Routeburn and Kepler), do not appeal, try one of the launch trips into this almost landlocked lonely sound. Fantastic scenery and voracious sandflies are to be expected. Pack your insect repellent, sit back and enjoy the majestic landscape.

While you are in this region it would be a shame to miss a visit to the Manapouri Power Station. This includes a cruise, a tour of the power station and a lunch at a very reasonable cost. In spite of the sparse population in this area, you will find it well served for comfortable holiday-making.

SOUTHERN LAKES–FIORDLAND

1. Boundary Creek Reserve
S Hwy 6, Head of Lake Wanaka–Department of Conservation (03) 443-8365

A new camping area with an alpine flavour. Recently developed with access for the disabled, this is still a remote spot with few facilities. There are flush toilets, tap water with BBQ and picnic tables provided. Inquire for details.

2. Makarora Tourist Centre Ltd
Makarora via Wanaka (03) 443-8372 (fax 03 443-1082)

In a picture-book setting with a mountain backdrop, this complex is 65km from Wanaka. The camping area is sheltered and attractive and there are A-frame chalets dotted through bush clearings in the grounds. The communal facilities do not match up to the landscape. Built of galvanised iron they have a shabby appearance and offer rather unkempt appointments. In addition to the camping area there is a tourist shop and general store, postal agency, tea rooms and petrol supplies, plus a card phone. A large swimming pool is an attraction. There is an emphasis on backpackers accommodation and camping may be phased out. Camp sites are from $7.50 per person plus a $2 power site charge. 🔲.

3. Kidds Bush Camping Area
Hunter Valley Road, Lake District. Department of Conservation (03) 443-8365

This is a popular Conservation campsite in a sheltered area on the shores of Lake Hawea, although the nearest creek is 400 metres away. It is 6km from the main road. The sites have a mountain beech tree backdrop and have rowan, beech and oak trees for shade. There is space for up to 40 "family" groups to camp. There are only token facilities with 3 flush toilets, including one with disabled access (own paper required!) basin, and a drinking water tap. In winter there is no tap water because of frozen pipes. A picnic shelter with information bulletin is provided. Eight BBQs are here and a boat ramp is 400 metres away. There is a grassed area suitable for volleyball etc. For a "back to nature" experience this has interesting walks. No dogs here please. Contact the Otago Conservancy for details. A self-registration system applies with a small fee per site.

4. Lake Hawea Motor Camp
S Hwy 6, PO Box 46, Lake Hawea (03) 443-1767

A large undulating camp on the Wanaka-Haast Road, nicely sited for access to Lake Hawea, with roads and tracks leading to the water and a boat ramp. The sites are varied and randomly laid out and there are 80 with power, plus plenty of tent sites. The kitchen will be a bonus for those "travelling light" with all the usual appointments plus pots and pans and a campers pantry box (help yourself or donate), and a TV. There is also a fish smoker. Two separate ablution blocks, with shub, include a paraplegic unit. The laundry has good equipment. This is a family orientated camp which also has a self-contained cottage to rent and cabins. Your hosts Mike and Michele Cotter and family. It costs $7 per person for tent sites or $8 per person for power. 🔲

5. Penrith Park
Beacon Point, PO Box 111 Wanaka (03) 443-7009

This camp occupies a lovely position with views over Lake Wanaka   Very sheltered sites offer privacy in an attractive layout. The basic amenities are poorly maintained and do not complement the setting. There is a shop open here at busy times, and casual meals may be provided in the ski season. The hosts were absent when we called. Check for prices.

6. Wanaka Motor Park
212 Brownston Street, PO Box 33 Wanaka (03) 443-7883 (phone & fax)

You can walk to the Wanaka township from here, yet this is an extensive complex with close to 300 sites, 190 with power. Well placed for sampling the ski fields in winter, and to enjoy lake views. The main amenities block has excellent cooking appliances in the kitchen, and a fridge. A recent renovation of the men's ablution block, and improvements in the women's are appreciated; the showers are first class. There are other amenities blocks too and a well equipped laundry with a drying room. There is an on-site store and a post box. A tiered TV room is provided. Dump points here and squash courts next door. The cabins and tourist flats are possibly better placed for access to the main amenities than are the camp sites. Your hosts are Gordon and Joan Martin. All sites $9 per person. 🔲

7. Wanaka Pleasant Lodge Holiday Park
Glendhu Bay Road, PO Box 125 Wanaka (03) 443-7360 (phone & fax)

Alpine or lake attractions are accessible from this park 3km west of Wanaka township. In this rural setting there is a choice of accommodation as well as 100 camping sites, 70 with power. Pick up a ski bus at the gate. It is 18km to Treble Cone ski fields. There is plenty for the children within the park which has an adventure playground, a swimming pool with 3-lane water slide and a balancing beam. There is also an indoor spa pool, plus a TV room. All the amenities are of a high standard, the kitchen having good appliances including fridge and ranch sliders to outdoor recreation. Very plentiful ablutions include a children's bathroom. All automatic equipment in the laundry. The camp, which has an on-site shop, is open all year round. There is a dump point here. Your new hosts are Rudi and Aggi Sanders. Tent sites are $8 per person. Power sites $17 for two.

8. Glendhu Bay Motor Camp
Glendhu Bay, PO Box 33, Lake Wanaka (03) 443-7243 (phone & fax)

Traditionally one of the landmark camping spots in this region, with a magical situation, the camp stretches along 1500 metres of tranquil lakefront with the Southern Alps rising steeply in the background. Stately trees enhance the sites and a flying fox should keep the youngsters busy. There are kayaks for hire and a concrete boat ramp. A camp store, post box and petrol station are right here. There are plenty of outdoor taps and a dump point. The ablutions are in good order, with metered showers. There is a good range of laundry equipment. A mountain-house style kitchen has a big pot belly stove in the middle with a sociable amount of tables and chairs. The park-like grounds have a large capacity for camping with 150 power sites and plenty for tents plus some cabins and a backpackers unit. Your hosts Herbie and Chris Illingworth. Tent sites $7 per person. Power sites $8 per person. 🏠.

9. Arrowtown Camping Ground
11 Suffolk Street, PO Box 61 Arrowtown (03) 442-1876 (phone & fax)

An unpretentious camping ground with plenty of open spaces and its own shop, yet also handy to the Arrowtown shops. The camp buildings are of the older style, but clean and tidy. There are separate blocks of showers and toilets plus a good laundry. In the kitchen are a new microwave and TV. There are BBQs and a children's play area in the grounds. Your hosts Faye and Gordy Gibb. Tent sites are from $8 per person or $9 with power.

10. Arrowtown Caravan Park
47 Devon Street, Arrowtown (03) 442-1838

Delightfully sited in an orchard, this is a thoughtfully planned little park with 95 power sites and a few tent sites. You will enjoy the fruit harvest if you time your trip correctly! The amenities are great, with two particularly nice ablution blocks, formica-lined with paraplegic facilities. The kitchen is spic and span and has meal space, plus an adjoining dining/lounge with TV. There is freezer space for all your needs. Excellent laundry equipment. No pets here please. This camp closes in April and reopens in October. Your hosts Trish and Jim Wilcox. Tent sites $8 per person. Power sites $9 per person.

11. Frankton Motor Camp
Yewlitt Cresc, Frankton, PO Box 798, Queenstown (03) 442-2079 (phone & fax)

An all-purpose camp with some lovely lakefront sites for casual campers. These sites go to the edge of a gravel beach, but require some self sufficiency by campers as they are not well serviced by amenities. Long-term residents occupy a fair proportion of the camp. There is an on-site store and also the Remarkables Hotel alongside, plus another shop. Although there are three ablution blocks and two kitchens, they are in rather "tired" condition. The laundry is adequate and a drying room is available. There is also a TV room. Tent sites are $7.50 per person or with power $8.50.

12. Kawarau Falls Lodge & Motor Camp
Frankton RD1 Queenstown (03) 442-3510 (phone & fax)

A magnificent setting on the edge of the Kawarau River where the ducks mingle with the picnickers enjoying water's edge BBQs and the outdoor tables and chairs. This camp has 100 sites, 20 with power and it is only 7km from Queenstown. It is a sheltered situation with mountain views and lovely trees. There is a jetty and a golf course nearby. Among the amenities provided here is a fantastic kitchen with everything for the cook, plus pots and pans and other equipment. This opens on to a spacious social room with dining, comfy chairs, TV and piano. In the ablutions a babies bath is provided. Use of a good laundry too. The buildings are "smoke free" zones. The Lodge has capacity for 40 guests and there is other accommodation. No pets please. The managers here are Jan and Eddie Wilkinson.Tent sites $8.50 per person. Power sites $9.50 per person.

13. Queenstown Creeksyde Campervan Park
54 Robins Road, PO Box 247 Queenstown (03) 442-9447 (fax 03 442-6621)

Do you want all the luxuries of a continental-style resort at your fingertips? This is camping with class! The superb ablutions include a spa bathroom and paraplegic facilities. You can gather in the comfort of a splendidly furnished lounge with TV or the sunroom with dining bay. A separate lounge-bar is provided. The kitchen has all the latest appointments and is bright and sunny. The laundry facilities are excellent. A complimentary supper is offered nightly. We recommend you book ahead as this does not have a huge capacity for campers. Most sites are on concrete strips. There is also Lodge accommodation, plus motels and a flat. There are dump points here and a mail box. It is only a stone's throw from the heart of Queenstown. Your hosts Toni and Erna Spijkerbosch and family. Tent sites $11 per person. Power sites $22 for two. 🖳.

14. Queenstown Motor Park

Main Street, PO Box 59 Queenstown (03) 442-7252 (fax 03 442-7253)

Generous camping which is terraced, with space on a grand scale, and overlooking Lake Wakatipu. There is a centrepiece of trees and it is so close that you can walk to almost all of Queenstown's attractions. Catering for holidaymaker's, there are tons of things to do from this handy base. You can book your trips here. There are two kitchens and all the amenities are also of large dimensions. There is a bath provided in the ablutions which have provision for the disabled. All the facilities are well maintained. There are automatic machines in the laundry. A homely and comfortable TV room is a nice feature. There is a dump point here and a shop at the gate. Your host Greg Hartshorne also has lodge accommodation. Tent sites are $9 per person and power sites are $10.

15. Arthurs Point Camping Ground

Gorge Road, PO Box 352 Queenstown (03) 442-9306 (phone & fax) or (03) 442-9311

While this camp has a rural atmosphere, it is only 5km from Queenstown. There is plenty here for active campers to enjoy. A swimming pool and a children's playground are in the camp. You can also try the bungy jumping, horse trekking, river rafting, Shotover jet boat or skiing in this vicinity. The camp has 45 power sites, ample tent sites, a backpackers lodge and some cabins and is adjacent to an hotel and restaurant. There will be no problem cooking for campers in the large, well equipped kitchen combined with recreation hall. The amenities complex also has a drying room plus a high standard of plentiful ablutions and laundry. Your hosts are Graham and Pamela Cooper. All camping is $9 per person. 🏪.

16. Closeburn Alpine Park

Glenorchy Road, PO Box 384 Queenstown (03) 442-6073

Along the high road heading west this park is 7.5km from Queenstown, situated above Lake Wakatipu. You will get extra long summer evenings here. The property is undergoing redevelopment, leaving a limited choice for holidaymakers. Some power sites and chalets may be all that is available. There is a basic campers kitchen with a perimeter of outdoor dining space, also a gas BBQ is provided. The TV lounge is cosy with a solid fuel stove. Communal ablutions and a good laundry are available. Mountain bikes can be hired and you can get your fishing licences here, but shop for your provisions in Queenstown. There is a dump point. Your new host is Barry Ford. Inquire for further information.

17. Moke Lake Reserve

via Queenstown–Department of Conservation (03) 442-7933
(fax 03 442-7932)

A Conservation campsite 20km from Queenstown. Moke Lake provides fishing and canoeing or explore the shores by mountain bike or tramping. Water and toilets are the only facilities.

18. Skippers–Mt Aurum Reserve

via Queenstown–Department of Conservation (03) 442-7933
(fax 03 442-7932)

A Conservation campsite of historic interest. It is 34 km from Queenstown. Tramping and hunting in the area. Water and toilets are the only facilities.

19. Glenorchy Holiday Park

2 Oban Street, PO Box 4 Glenorchy (03) 442-9939 (fax 03 442-9940)

Explorers territory amongst the mountains at the head of Lake Wakatipu. This is a challenging drive for most of the way, along a winding, partially sealed road, and some 50km from Queenstown. It is virtually the entrance to Fiordland here and at the base of the Southern Alps. A handy "Backpackers Express" bus service provides a daily link to Queenstown and to the many walking tracks. The park has level grounds for campers and a self-contained communal lodge. There is a general store at the entrance to the camp. Complete with all the usual facilities, the kitchen-TV-dining room is inviting and has a piano. Cooking equipment is good and includes a supply of pots and pans. Children have an interesting playground provided. There is a dump point here, a postal agency and a nearby Information Centre. A base for alpine trampers with secure vehicle parking. Your hosts Glynn and Liz Kemp. Tent sites $7 per person. Power sites $8 per person. 🏠 $14. Bunkroom $12.

20. Lake Sylvan Roadend Campsite

off Routeburn Road, Mt Aspiring–Department of Conservation
(03) 442-9937 (fax 03 442-9938)

Within the Mt Aspiring National Park, this camp is 22km from Glenorchy. Easy reach to the Routeburn Track from here. The sites are on the bush edge on the bank of the Routeburn. It is also close to Lake Sylvan Walk. The only facilities are toilets. There are fireplaces and picnic tables. No dogs here please. Self-registration fees are $2 per adult.

21. Kinloch Campsite
Kinloch–Department of Conservation (03) 442-9937 (fax 03 442-9938)

A lakefront site at the upper reaches of Lake Wakatipu. It is 27km from Glenorchy. The only facilities are toilets. Stone-age camping with boating, fishing and canoeing on the lake. Self-registration fees are $2 per adult.

22. Kingston Stream Holiday Camp
S Hwy 6, PO Box 85 Queenstown (03) 248-8501 (phone & fax)

On the southern tip of Lake Wakatipu, this camp is in a peaceful valley with a bubbling stream and nicely tree'd. Half of the 122 sites have power and there are also cabins here. The community centre, with tennis courts and swimming pool, is right next door and shopping, postal services, tavern and meals are nearby. The amenities are adequate, the kitchen having fridge/freezer and microwave cooking plus gas rings and a rangette. There is also a BBQ. The ablutions are fair, while the laundry porch has table and chairs. Kingston is the terminus for the *Kingston Flyer* steam train, and the *SS Earnslaw* calls occasionally. Your hosts Sylvia and Graeme Donaldson. All sites are $17 for two people.

23. Mavora Lakes Conservation Campsite
Off S Hwy 94, Mavora Lakes Park–Department of Conservation (03) 249-7921

A popular campsite over the summer within the Mavora Lakes Park. The Mavora Lakes are set among picturesque mountains, beech forest and tussock grasslands. The park is a great place for walking, tramping, fishing (brown and rainbow trout), mountain biking, boating, sailing, canoeing and horse riding. Good populations of bush robins are found in the forest and NZ falcons are often seen above the bush line. Toilets, BBQs, picnic tables and rubbish collection is provided. Water is collected from the river. There are no bookings. Sites are $4 per adult.

24. Fiordland Holiday Park
Milford Road, No.1 RD. Te Anau (03) 249-7059

Along the S Hwy 94 route to Milford, this is a delightful spot with many comfortable amenities. The site has great views of the mountains and lake. Hedges divide some of the sites, which have at least 16 with power. A wonderful confidence playground is a bonus for the children. The kitchen has plenty of equipment. It opens to a delightful dining room with TV opening to a patio. There is a games room, also with TV, and volley ball in the grounds. The ablutions and laundry offer excellent facilities. The camp store features home-grown honey. Track transport is arranged here and a courtesy vehicle is available. Your hosts, the Saunders family. Tent sites are $7 per person, or $7.50 with power.

25. Te Anau Mountain View Cabin & Caravan Park
Mokonui Street & Te Anau Tce–PO Box 171 Te Anau (03) 249-7462 (phone & fax)

In a pristine setting, neat level and dotted with trees, this park is almost in the heart of Te Anau. Neat sealed roads divide the sites. There are 50 power sites, a few tent sites and cabin accommodation. The kitchen has limited capacity, but boasts a fridge, while there are excellent ablutions with paraplegic facilities. There are fully automatic machines in the laundry. There is also a TV room. These amenities are well located in the centre of the park. A children's play area is provided, as are picnic tables. The new owners here are Ken and Heather McCleary. All sites are $10 per person.

26. Te Anau Motor Park
1 Te Anau-Manapouri Road, PO Box 81 Te Anau (03) 249-7457 (fax 03 249-7536

This large park is on the fringe of Fiordland. The grounds are terraced up from the lake with 150 power sites and 100 tent sites plus a variety of other accommodation. Local shuttle services operate from here to other holiday destinations. Mountain bikes are for hire. There is a bar and grill. A well planned service block offers kitchen, ablutions and laundry just steps apart. There are, in all, three blocks of ablutions, formica lined and with a paraplegic unit. The laundry has excellent commercial equipment. There is a dump point here. There are tennis/volley ball courts and an adventure playground for the younger set and the lake options of boating, fishing and swimming. A boat ramp is available. As hosts Jill and Clint Tauri had no time to spare for us. We were unable to verify prices.

27. Lakeview Motels & Motor Park
Manapouri-Te Anau Road, PO Box 3 Manapouri (03) 249-6624

An innovative camp in an alpine setting, just 1km north of Manapouri. There are 35 power sites offering privacy in an informal setting, nicely sheltered and with beautiful mountain and lake views. Amongst the fruit trees you will also find two-storey chalets. Two great playgrounds are provided. There is a nice homely kitchen, opening to a dining room and a compact TV room. The well equipped laundry adjoins this social/dining spot where many games machines are provided. There are plentiful ablutions including a shub in the unisex shower and paraplegic facilities. A spa and a sauna are options. Outside the BBQ and picnic area are inviting and there is an on-site store. Both takeaway meals and a hotel are next door. Perhaps the most flamboyant feature of this park is the display of Morris Minor cars and an aeroplane. Yes, pets are welcome. Your hosts Joelle Nicholson and Simon Vogel. Tent sites $16 for two. Power sites $17 for two. $30 for two.

28. Manapouri Glade Motor Park & Motels
Murrell Ave, PO Box 23 Manapouri (03) 249-6623

A canopy of trees shelters the entrance to this mini-park surrounded by beech trees. There are 12 power sites and 4 cabins, with forest tracks leading to the lake shore. The kitchen with its various appliances and the showers in the ablution block could only be described as quaint. The toilets are in a separate area. There is a laundry with washer and dryer. Check on the availability of sites, as it may be seasonally closed. Your host Ian Wentworth. All sites are $15 for two people. and .

29. Hollyford Valley Camp (Gunns Camp)
Hollyford Valley Road–via Te Anau

A page out of history. Set on the banks of a glacial stream at the bottom of the hill from the Homer Tunnel, this camp offers power sites. Nature's refrigerator is the small waterfall on the property. The Hollyford Track is close to this camp where there are plenty of tent sites and some nice cabins. "Jane," an ancient packhorse is still in residence here. You will also find a camp store with food available and a selection of greenstone and souvenirs for sale. There is a petrol pump too. There is no kitchen, and the ablutions are sparse, but clean. A tub is provided for the laundry. You may find a cabin available. Prepare to go back in time for the pioneer camping experience. Your host Murray Gunn. Tent sites are $4 per person.

 ### 30. Milford Road Conservation Campsites
S Hwy 94, Fiordland National Park–Department of Conservation
(03) 249-7921

People who want to take more time enjoying Fiordland National Park on their way to or from Milford Sound may choose to camp at one of 12 camping areas provided along the Milford Road from 17km north of Te Anau to Lake Gunn, 81km north of Te Anau. Many are located near walking tracks or excellent fishing rivers. Camping is permitted in these areas only. Fireplaces, picnic tables and toilets are provided. Water is available from rivers alongside the campsites. No pets here please. There are no bookings. Tent sites $4 per adult.

Cabins from	Dog friendly	
Tourist flat, and motels from		
On-site caravans from	Department of Conservation	

31. Milford Sound Lodge
Private Bag Te Anau–Milford Sound (03) 249-8071 (phone & fax)

The dramatic country of the Milford Sound has huge surrounding mountains and a fast-flowing river. The spectacular scenery and the road to Milford are worth experiencing. If you drive a mobile home please be cautious as bus traffic is frequent. The road is very steep in parts, with the Homer Tunnel rising 1 in 10 and barely enough room for two vehicles to pass. The Lodge is the main accommodation here with only 35 sites for camping, and there are only 15 with power. The ablutions are excellent. There is a gas kitchen with a large dining-recreation room and comfortable lounge with open fire. You will have to manage without TV or radio, but pool table, chess and music are a pleasant alternative. Restaurant meals from October to March are obtainable here. A self-sufficient holiday spot with its own shop too. This is sited in a National Park so pets are not permitted. The local wildlife include keas and voracious sandflies. Storage facilities for campers are provided at the Lodge. Inquire for prices. Your host Peter Teal. All tent sites are $8 per person or with power $9.

OTAGO

OTAGO DIRECTORY

Key to locations and maps in Otago district. Starts at Waitaki River and goes inland as far as Omarama. Returns towards the coast with a short diversion to Dansey Pass. Includes Oamaru and the mainly coastal areas. Through Hampden to turn inland at Palmerston. Along S Hwy 5 to explore Naseby, Ranfurly and back, with a deviation to Rock and Pillar. Resumes following the main route south via Palmerston to Dunedin and on to Milton. Goes inland as far as Cromwell. Returns towards the coast via Tapanui and Balclutha. Follows the eastern coastal settlements to finish at Curio Bay.

Waitaki	1.	Waitaki Mouth Motor Camp
Duntroon	2.	Duntroon Recreational Reserve
Kurow	3.	Kurow Holiday Park
Otematata	4.	Otematata Lodge & Camping Ground
Omarama	5.	Glenburn Holiday Park
Omarama	6.	Omarama Holiday Park
Oamaru	7.	Dansey Pass Holiday Camp
Oamaru	8.	Oamaru Gardens Holiday Park
Herbert Forest	9.	Herbert Forest Family Camping Ground
Hampden	10.	Hampden Motor Camp
Naseby	11.	Naseby Larchview Park
Ranfurly	12.	Ranfurly Motor Camp
Middlemarch	13.	Rock and Pillar Motor Camp
Palmerston	14.	Paradise Holiday Park

Palmerston	15.	Waiheamo Lodge Hotel & Caravan Park
Palmerston	16.	Moeraki Motor Camp
Waikouaiti	17.	Waikouaiti Camping Ground
Waikouaiti	18.	Waikouaiti Tourist Campervan Park
Dunedin	19.	Farmlands Camper-Caravan Park
Dunedin	20.	Portobello Village Tourist Park
Dunedin	21.	Leith Valley Touring Park
Dunedin	22.	Tahuna Park Seaside Camp
Dunedin	23.	Aaron Lodge Motel & Holiday Park
Mosgiel	24.	Mosgiel Caravan Park
Brighton	25.	Brighton Caravan Park
Taieri Mouth	26.	Taieri Mouth Motor Camp
Waihola	27.	Lake Waihola Holiday Camp
Milton	28.	Taylor Park Motor Camp
Lawrence	29.	Gold Park Motor Camp
Lawrence	30.	Beaumont Caravan Park
Millers Flat	31.	Millers Flat Motor Camp
Ettrick	32.	Ettrick Holiday Park
Roxburgh	33.	Roxburgh Family Motor Camp
Alexandra	34.	Alexandra Holiday Camp
Alexandra	35.	Pine Lodge Holiday Camp

OTAGO

Omakau	36.	Commercial Hotel & Caravan Park
Omakau	37.	Omakau Domain Camp
Clyde	38.	Clyde Holiday & Sporting Complex
Cromwell	39.	Cairnmuir Camp
Cromwell	40.	Cromwell Holiday Park
Tapanui	41.	Black Gully Camp
Tapanui	42.	Linsmoyle Park
Balclutha	43.	Balclutha Naish Point Camping Ground
Kaka Point	44.	Kaka Point Camping Ground
Pounawea	45.	Pounawea Motor Camp
Pounawea	46.	Keswick Park Family Camping Ground
Owaka	47.	Owaka Caravan Park
Tawanui	48.	Tawanui Camping Ground (DoC)
Papatowai	49.	Papatowai Motor Camp
Curio Bay	50.	Curio Bay Camping Ground & Store

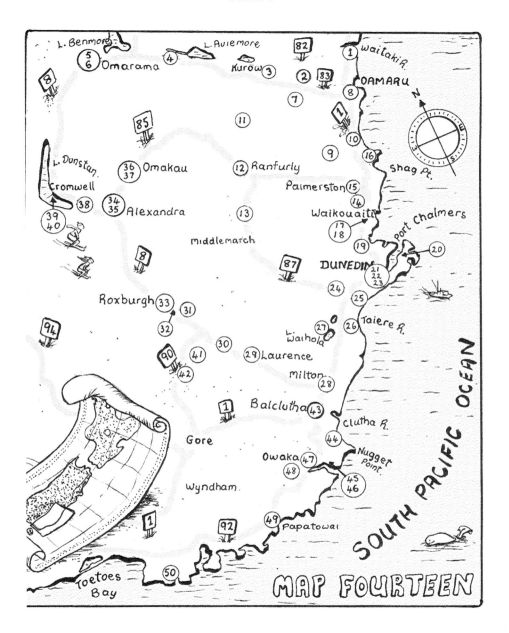

Chapter 14

OTAGO

Solid, conservative Otago encompasses three different and distinctive areas. It includes the populated coastal fringe, barren and challenging high country in the interior and the wildly beautiful Catlins coast.

On the coast, Dunedin is the principal city. Sprawling over a number of steep hills, many suburbs enjoy wonderful views of its extensive harbour. Dunedin has a tradition originating from the influence of its first Scottish settlers. The imposing architecture here has a timeless quality. Historic homesteads are open for inspection. A journey to the far end of the Otago Peninsula would not be complete without a visit to the albatross colony. A cruise is also available to enjoy close-up views of seals, cormorants and albatrosses in their natural environment.

Venture inland and you will find the feisty settlements that remain vestiges of the early goldrush boom. Hydro development has harnessed the mighty Clutha and New Zealand's largest (and most controversial) high dam is at Clyde, and well worth inspecting. There are a choice of lakes, some man-made, that offer a range of water-based activities, while orchards at Alexandra and Roxburgh produce quality apricots and other stone fruit.

Experience the vast emptiness of Central Otago, where occasional gorges slice through the landscape. For kilometres you may see nothing but the occasional rabbit. However there is interesting camping here, while good roads make the journey easy. The almost continental climate makes summer camping popular. Long days, high sunshine hours and mostly dry weather are to be expected.

Capture the spirit of this region. Its pre-European history includes the exploits of the moa hunters. The region was plundered of this now extinct bird and later of its greenstone and gold. Follow the Otago Heritage Trail through Clyde, Lawrence, St Bathans and Naseby. Take a gold pan and see if the rivers still yield their rewards to the patient.

The dramatic Catlins Coast has been the site of archaeological discoveries, including the fossilised forest at Curio Bay. This is a popular camping area in summer, but a quiet spot can usually be found in this otherwise sparsely populated location.

Otago should be on your itinerary if you enjoy scenic diversity. It is not noted for glitzy entertainment, but rather for voyages of discovery in a powerful countryside.

OTAGO

1. Waitaki Mouth Motor Camp
South Bank, Kaik Road Waitaki (03) 431-3880

Cast your worries aside. Located where the Waitaki River meets the sea is this anglers delight. You can try for salmon, trout or ocean fish. At the camp there are farm animals and pets are welcome. There is ample level ground for tenters and 48 power sites, plus cabin accommodation. There is a good kitchen here, but the ablutions are under-supplied for the capacity of the camp. A "no frills" laundry is provided. The camp has its own store with basic supplies. When you have eaten your fill of fish you can smoke, can or freeze your catch here. Warren and Allison Rintoul are your friendly hosts. Tent sites are $6 per person, or with power $8. ▦ $12.50 per person.

2. Duntroon Recreational Reserve
C/o Post Office Duntroon (03) 431-2732

In the region of the Waitaki River the settlement of Duntroon is an unlikely destination, but should you want to stop here take the track that runs parallel with the school and bridge to find this little camp. There is a football field adjacent to the tree-edged grounds with 4 power sites and some cabins. The kitchen has a stove and a TV room (minus the TV set) adjoining. The ablutions are in dubious condition. The laundry provides two basins which may not have hot water. In the grounds you will find a BBQ with a stack of wood. Crowding should not be a problem here. Call at the Duntroon Tavern opposite for keys. Camp sites are from $5.50 for two people. ▦ $6.50.

3. Kurow Holiday Park
76 Bledisloe Street, PO Box 27 Kurow (03) 436-0725 (fax 03 436-0812)

A combination resort complex and trout sanctuary. The choice of accommodation is varied with around 200 sites, 80 with power for campers. You can house your dog in the dog motels. The camping area is in two terraces; some sites have fences. On the upper level there is a large kitchen with dining space. There is a stove and a microwave and plenty of refrigeration. There are three blocks of ablutions and the ladies have a shub/ bath. The laundry has automatic equipment. The setting is landscaped and has some sheltering trees. There is a dump point here. Outdoor activities within the park include the use of free canoes and golf clubs for hire. Fishing, tramping, jet boating and golf, tennis and bowls are nearby. The Lodge has a lounge with open fire for all to use, and a room here is from $12 per person. Your hosts Ron and Alison Winsley. All camping is $8 per person, with other options from $17.

4. Otematata Lodge & Camping Ground
East Road, Otematata (03) 438-7826 (phone & fax)

There are a choice of lakes to discover in this central South Island location. Take the lovely lakeside drive west along the Waitaki River. This camp has 60 sites with power and 10 for tents. There is a large Lodge here, which tends to dominate the camp. The camp store/office has limited opening hours. You will find level sites with some shady trees and boats can be hired. A lot of outdoor activities are within reach here. The kitchen has hot-plate cooking and fridge. There is a very utilitarian look to the ablutions. The campers laundry has no dryer. Your hosts Joe and Robyn Collins. All sites $8 per person. Lodge beds $15.

5. Glenburn Holiday Park
S Hwy 83, PO Box 90 Omarama (03) 438-9624

Add extra luxury to your camping trip. For the mobile camper there are 19 power sites each with bathroom en suites, picnic tables, taps and waste disposal. Outside lighting and TV aerial connections are available. There are also cabins, motels and tent sites here. A children's playground is provided and there is a dump point for vans. Excellent kitchen and laundry facilities are available. The grounds are level and across the road from Lake Benmore, with a mountain backdrop. Your hosts Sue and Chris Aspinall close the camp in June and open again in mid-August. All sites are $8 per person. 🔲 $40 🔲 $70 .

6. Omarama Holiday Park
S Hwy 8 and 83 junction–PO Box 34 Omarama (03) 438-9875
(phone & fax)

This is an inviting park with all the ingredients for comfortable camping. The level, well groomed grounds have plenty of shady trees and a lazy stream meanders through the camp. There are 94 power sites, 100 tent sites and other accommodation units. There is a selection of shops, hotel, service station, meals etc in close proximity. In the camp a pleasant kitchen, with rangettes and microwave, has a recreation room adjoining. There is also fully automatic equipment in the adjacent laundry. The ablutions are first class, with pot-plant decor. In the grounds are two playgrounds for children and a coin-operated gas BBQ. The emphasis here is on family camping and groups are not encouraged. There are milk and vegetable deliveries here by arrangement. There is a dump point here. Your hosts Norman and Lynda Chamberlain. All camping is $17 for two people. 🔲 $30 for two. 🔲 $35. 🔲 $55.

7. Dansey Pass Holiday Camp
Livingston Road, 12C RD Oamaru (03) 431-2564

Just south of Duntroon turn off to Livingston Road. Stay on that road; the camp is signposted about 12 km along. The road is sealed all the way. The camp itself is snuggled into the surrounding hills along the banks of the Maerewhenua River. The grounds are well groomed and neatly edged with pine trees and there is a grass tennis court and a basketball net. Fly fishing is an attraction here, and you can also pan for gold or use the swimming hole in summer. The land is partially undulating and has 10 power sites, tent sites and cabins. The kitchen has a stove and deep freeze. The ablutions are refurbished to a moderately good standard. There are laundry facilities. Discover back-country camping, except when winter conditions make this camp inaccessible. Your hosts Carol and Neville Henderson. Tent sites $6 per person. Power sites $7 per person. ▥ $14.

8. Oamaru Gardens Holiday Park
Chelmer Street, Oamaru (03) 434-7666 (fax 03 434-7662)

A horseshoe of over 100 sites with a border of trees. Go across the little bridge and enjoy the lovely gardens with children's play area next door. This park has 60 power sites and some cabins. Two recently upgraded kitchens provide 3 full stoves plus hob cooking, fridge and plenty of table space. There are good ablutions with full paraplegic facilities. There is automatic laundry equipment. You can socialise in the recreation room. There is a dump station here. This camp is close to the town centre and tepid baths. Your friendly hosts Linda and Adrian. All camp sites are $18 for two. ▥ $28 for two.

9. Herbert Forest Family Camping Ground
Breakneck Road, Herbert Forest (03) 439-5644 or (03) 437-1820

Discover a little "Garden of Eden" where you can camp or picnic for a small fee. There are 25 sites but few have power. There is a combined kitchen-social room with basic appliances and dining space. It is cosy with a settee and heating. Toilet facilities are provided and there is a laundry with washing machine. Picnic tables and rubbish tins are in the grounds. The charming setting offers plenty of forest walks and perhaps meet the yellow-eyed penguins. Call at the Oamaru stone house prior to entering the grounds. Your hosts Mike and Jill Ramsay. All sites $7 per family.

10. Hampden Motor Camp
Carlisle Street, Hampden (03) 439-4825

Just north of Moeraki, this has plenty of tent sites and 25 power sites next to a riverside beach. The pleasant grounds have some nice trees. There are communal facilities for cooking, with a fridge. Toilet and showers and a laundry with automatic equipment. Your host Bill Lockerbie. Tent sites $10 for two. Extra $3 for power.

11. Naseby Larchview Camping & Caravan Park
Swimming Dam Road, PO Box 22 Naseby (03) 444-9904

This is an environmental treasure just 15km north from Ranfurly. It invites you to experience the invigoration of a woodland setting and fresh alpine air. Almost surrounded by extensive forest, it enjoys a dry climate and dramatic winter and summer temperatures. The camping sites are on many levels, greenery and larch trees giving great privacy. There are 48 power sites, innumerable tent sites and the other accommodation includes a self-contained house (sleep 7) $40 for two people. Although camp sites are not available in mid winter, you can stay at the house. For campers the amenities block is a central focal point. There is a great kitchen and living area with open fire. You can use the community freezer. The ablutions are satisfactory and clean. The laundry has automatic washer, but no dryer. There is a dump point here. At the park there is an adventure playground and a swimming dam. Enjoy a visit to the historic goldmining town of Naseby, where you will be able to replenish your supplies. Tent sites $11 for 2 people. Power $14.

12. Ranfurly Motor Camp
8 Reade Street, Ranfurly (03) 444-9144

The surrounding trees stand guard around this camp. Within the grounds the 42 power sites each have a tap and rubbish bin and are divided by flower beds, framed with logs. Plenty of tent space and some cabins are supplied. The kitchen has two stoves, fridges and freezers and meal space. There is a pergola-style BBQ for the outdoor cook. If the camp is not busy you will enjoy the showers with their plentiful hot-water supply. There is a good laundry with automatic equipment. A dump point is provided. Your hosts Sonia and Steven McGrath. Power sites for two people are $14. Tent sites are $9.50 ▭.

13. Rock and Pillar Motor Camp
Mold Street, Middlemarch (03) 464-3813

Somewhere to camp, perhaps, but "pot luck" access to any amenities. There are 14 sites with power and some cabins. There is a camp kitchen and ablutions. A dump point is provided. Even a tree house. All were unattended and locked when we called. ▭.

14. Paradise Holiday Park
S Hwy 1–Pleasant Valley, RD1 Palmerston (03) 465-1370 (phone & fax)

This park is just 3km south of Palmerston. The long established grounds are attractive, with a variety of terrain. These offer level sites and a peaceful glade of mature trees. There are 20 power sites and a multitude of sites for tents in a sheltered environment. There is a challenging adventure playground for children, plus an indoor playroom. The communal kitchen has a selection of appliances, with kettles. Pots and pans are available. The good hot showers in the ablutions will be appreciated. For the laundry free agitator washers are the only equipment. A variety of cabins and recreation activities are provided. This is a pet friendly place, which is also particularly suitable for large groups and backpackers. Your hosts Keith and Dena Henderson. All sites are $8 per person. 🔳 $10 per person.

15. Waiheamo Lodge Hotel & Caravan Park
Ronaldsay Street, Palmerston (03) 465-1700

In the heart of Palmerston lies this camping ground behind the hotel. There are only a handful of sites and you may not find any available. Ablutions and laundry are provided, but no kitchen. A site with power will cost $15 for two people.

16. Moeraki Motor Camp
Moeraki No.2 RD, Palmerston (03) 439-4759

This is a pretty camp only 3km off S Hwy 1 towards the coast. It overlooks a sheltered bay and has wonderful views, from the boat anchorage below to the distant horizon. From here you should take time to inspect the phenomenon of the Moeraki boulders and the nearby seal colony. A useful place to try fishing for salmon. There are 27 sites with power, also tent sites and self-contained units available. Good level camping on attractive grounds with some tree borders. The kitchen has a full stove and teamaker and there is a TV room. Modern ablutions are provided. The laundry is adequate. Your hosts Walter and Theresa Kiener. Tent sites are $7 per person or $15 for two with power.🔳 $20.

17. Waikouaiti Camping Ground
Waikouaiti Domain, Beach Street Waikouaiti (03) 465-7366

The beach adjacent to this camp has smooth white sand. The camp has 50 power sites on open flat ground. It has a large kitchen with minimal cooking, but plenty of freezer and refrigerator space and bristling with notices. The ablutions are sturdy, but old. The laundry boasts 4 machines of the manual variety. There are long-stay occupants as well as casual camping here. It has a friendly atmosphere. Your hosts Allison and Barry Smith. Tent sites $12 for two. Power sites $16 for two. 🚐 from $25.

NOTE. *The illustration on page 335 is of the incredible Moeraki boulders– well worth a visit.*

18. Waikouaiti Tourist Campervan Park
Pratt Street, Waikouaiti

A big name for a small facility. A total of 7 sites and one hut are the choice here. However there are 3 sites with power and en suite facilities. There is a small laundry, with hot plate and a few utensils. There is a shop next door and food available across the road. Your host W.B.Kerr. Tent sites $6 per person. Parking is $14 for two people with power and extras. Hut accommodation is $7.

19. Farmlands Camper-Caravan Park
Waitati Valley Road, Waitati Dunedin (03) 482-2730

Look for the signposts off S Hwy 1; this park is 15km north of Dunedin. On rambling rural grounds, it offers 24 power sites, but only 3 for tents. Amongst the farm animals and roaming peacocks is a donkey with a taste for freshly washed clothes! Children can enjoy the swings and flying fox. A log fire in a large comfortable lounge with dining area and window seat is attractive in the evenings. The kitchen and laundry are well equipped. The ablutions have paraplegic facilities. This is a peaceful farm setting, beside a stream. Canoes are available, and bush walks. There is a dump point here. A warm welcome awaits you from the Leslie family, who have supplies of fresh farm eggs and honey. All sites are $8.50 per person. ⬚ $28 for two.

20. Portobello Village Tourist Park
27 Hereweka Street, Portobello Dunedin (03) 478-0359

On the picturesque Otago Peninsula the location is 15km from Dunedin city. Not a large complex, but one which has that personal touch. There are 16 power points with sumps and taps. There is a newly developed tent area, nicely sheltered. The cosy kitchen has gas cooking, tables and chairs and TV. Enjoy a summer evening on the bricked and covered BBQ terrace where there is alternative cooking and seating for at least 20 people. Top-of-the-range ablutions include a good paraplegic suite and a babies bath with hand shower. The laundry has the latest automatic appliances. There is a dump point here. Your hosts Kevin and Sheryl Charles have established this camp over recent years. Tent sites $7.50 per person. Power sites $8.50 per person. ⬚ $12 per person.

21. Leith Valley Touring Park
103 Malvern Street, Dunedin (03) 467-9936

Sheltered by a barrier of trees this has neat level sites in a pastoral setting. There are 46 power sites available and a gentle stream around two sides. The kitchen is well equipped, with a combined dining and recreation area and a BBQ patio. Included in the main building is alternative indoor recreation with carpeted TV annexe and through the hallway is access to the toilets. Very good amenities include a paraplegic suite. Laundry facilities have automatic machines. There is a dump point here. You can leave your van tethered and use the bus service to the city. Your hosts Margaret and Brian McCammon. All camping $9 per person. Also 🚐 $30 for two.🏠 $50 double.

22. Tahuna Park Seaside Camp
41 Victoria Road, St Kilda Dunedin (03) 455-4690

A carefully tended camp with St Kilda Beach nearby. Quite extensive grounds that have 95 power sites, 40 tent sites and cabins en masse. There are two kitchens, one equipped with good commercial equipment. There is a separate TV lounge. The ablutions are good, very plentiful and the laundry has all automatic machines. A camp store is usually open, with takeaway meals available. There is a dump point here. This would be a good venue for groups. No animals here please. We appreciated the standard of housekeeping here, a credit to the hosts Eric and Diane Cochrane. Tent sites $8 per person. Power sites $16.50 for two.🏠 $28.

23. Aaron Lodge Motel & Holiday Park
162 Kaikorai Valley Road, Dunedin (03) 476-4725 (phone & fax)

This park is in close proximity to Dunedin city, although it is a hilly walk. There is quality camping here with a variety of options. For the camper there are 40 power sites and tent sites in secluded or group settings. The grounds have level, well groomed sites and there are gravel pads if you prefer. Plenty of taps are provided. A spa pool has been installed. A top feature here is the amenities block, well designed with covered walkways. There are two modern kitchens, each with TV and dining facilities. The ablutions are excellent and there are two automatic laundries. If you look for meticulous standards in an attractive environment you will enjoy it here. There is also a dump point. Your hosts Margaret and Lindsay McLeod. Tent sites $16 for two. Power sites $18 for two people. 🏠 $29. 🏠 $51. Look for further information on page 336.

24. Mosgiel Caravan Park
Gordon Road, Mosgiel (03) 489-3909 or (03) 489-4898

This local Memorial Park has pleasant grounds where privacy should not be a problem. There is a small capacity for campers with 12 sites that have power and paving as well as grass on each site. The kitchen is adequate for cooking and dining. The ablutions have individual LPG water heating for the showers. There is a laundry with automatic washer and dryer, plus a freezer. There is a swimming pool in the park, which is administered by the Dunedin City Council. If you need keys call at the Mobil Service Station in Factory Road. Diane Johnston takes care of this camp.

25. Brighton Caravan Park
1044 Brighton Road, Brighton (03) 481-1404

A seaside resort area on the south coast and an easy drive from Dunedin. The park presents a very practical and convenient layout for campers. The grounds are level with the 24 gravelled power sites edged with brick. All the facilities are clean and modern and well placed. The kitchen has stove and microwave and the additional trellised BBQ area is attractive. Excellent ablutions have paraplegic suites for both sexes. The laundry is equipped with automatic machines. There is a 7-day superette at the gate and the camp offers a choice of ocean beach swimming or a shallow estuary for the children. There is a camp boatshed and you can hire small boats. There is a dump point here. Your hosts are Eunice and Graham Lee. Almost no tent sites here. Power sites are $7.50 per person and there are ⌂ $27 for two.

 ### 26. Taieri Mouth Motor Camp
Moturata Road–via Waihola (03) 481-7818

From Waihola it is 18km towards the coast to Taieri Mouth camp. The last 10km are unsealed and hilly. This beachside camp is fairly unmemorable, with sand dunes and a local store for supplies. The secret could be in the fishing! There is a welcoming kitchen which combines good cooking equipment with a spot to relax; books on hand. The ablutions are of the primitive variety. There is a laundry. Dogs on a leash are allowed here. Your hosts Jim and Jan Clauson. Tent sites $6 per person. Power sites $14 for two.

27. Lake Waihola Holiday Camp
S Hwy 1, Waihola (03) 417-8908

On neat level grounds some 34km south of Dunedin, this park is almost at the edge of the calm waters of Lake Waihola. Bordered by trees, it has 76 power sites, on-site caravans, tent sites and some recently upgraded cabins. There are two amenities blocks. In one kitchen there is a TV alcove and dining space. The ablutions have a paraplegic toilet. The laundry is well equipped. You can hire fishing rods here; the lake offers a boat ramp and jetty. Good for swimming or water skiing. There is horse riding available too. Your hosts John and Lucy. Tent sites here are $6 per person, or with power $8. ⌂ $25 for two.

28. Taylor Park Motor Camp
Main Road, PO Box 123 Milton (03) 417-8109 (03) 417-8953

The environment for tenters is appealing on the Tokomairio Domain where this camp has private sites in nook and cranny situations. There are pleasantly random sites and an abundance of large old trees. The 30 power sites are on the perimeter of a playing field and a circular drive gives access. The camp features an 11-station Fitness Circuit and there are tennis courts and an indoor swimming pool complex alongside. A dump point is provided. The kitchen is adequate, and includes fridge. Basic ablutions include a wheelchair-access toilet. There is average laundry equipment. It is a well kept camp with a children's playground. This camp is administered by the Clutha District Council. Tent sites are $10 for two people, or with power $12.

29. Gold Park Motor Camp
Harrington Street, Lawrence (03) 485-9850

If you want a warm friendly atmosphere in a picturesque setting, this camp has both. If you want the most modern facilities and all the trimmings look elsewhere. This camp has 57 power sites and unlimited tent sites amongst gracious old trees, without crowding. A creek runs through the grounds and a flying fox and other adventures await the children. The amenities are yesterday's, but adequate. Milk and newspapers are available. The camp is 1km south from the main road, look for the signpost. Pets are welcome here. Family camping in a peaceful spot. Your hosts John and Sue Smith. All camp sites are $12 for two people. $10 per person.

30. Beaumont Caravan Park
S Hwy 8, Beaumont No.1.RD Lawrence (03) 485-9431 (phone & fax)

This facility is attached to an hotel and located inland from Lawrence and close to the Clutha River. The grounds are level and look poorly maintained but have 16 sites with power and a dump point. There are the usual camp amenities on site, but unavailable for us to view. Inquire from Bronwyn and Frank Murphy, who are in charge.

31. Millers Flat Motor Camp
Millers Flat (03) 446-6877 (phone & fax)

This Central Otago camp overlooks the Roxburgh Valley and has the Clutha River over the back fence. Well sited for salmon and trout fishing in the river or Lake Onslow, 75 power sites with around 20 tent sites and some cabins are available. There are three levels of sites, and a swimming pool and tennis courts. A border of trees defines the grounds. The kitchen has a full stove, plus hot plates and microwave cooking. There are plenty of fridges. Ample ablutions are available. The laundry has automatic and agitator washers, a dryer and an iron. There is an on-site shop. Your hosts Pat and Judy Dunick welcome families to this camp. We do not have a price for tent site. Power sites $15 for two. $10 per person.

32. Ettrick Park Camping Ground
S Hwy 8, Little James Street, Ettrick (03) 446-6610

Reclaimed as a holiday spot, this was once a village school. The playground equipment and the intact school library offer many attractions for the youngsters. The grounds are attractive with a well-tree'd border. There are ample tent sites and 23 that have power, most with taps and sumps. It is easy to find a shady spot. The kitchen has microwave and LPG hot plates and grill. There is also a fridge, freezer and kitchen tables. A communal dining and TV lounge is provided. The ablutions are well maintained and also have disabled facilities. There is an automatic washer and dryer in the laundry. Within the grounds are a tennis court and a swimming pool. Pets are permitted by prior arrangement. Musicians and chess players will receive a very warm welcome from Tony and Jenni Edwards. Spanish is spoken here. Tent sites $7 per person. Power sites $9 per person. Look for further information on page 336.

33. Roxburgh Family Motor Camp
11 Teviot Street, Roxburgh (03) 446-8093 (phone & fax)

Heartland Otago, noted for its apricots, also has this very pleasant mid-size camp on a recreation reserve with around 60 power sites, plus 10 for tents. Landscaped into three levels of sites, some with great views and trees. There is a swimming pool and BBQ. Both kitchens are good, with microwaves. There are freezing facilities and a smokehouse for all that salmon (in season). The ablutions have a bath/shub room for women. The showers are good too. There are wide-door toilets. Two laundries have automatic equipment. A large TV room is above the service block. There is a golf course below the camp. George Dickinson and Pam Williams are your hosts. Tent sites $7 per person. Power sites $8. ⬛ $10. ⬛

34. Alexandra Holiday Camp
Manuherikia Road, PO Box 7 Alexandra (03) 448-8297

Big on entertainment and scenery, this camp skirts the banks of the Manuherikia River. Landscaped into attractive sections surrounded by mature trees, there is nonetheless room for around 4000 campers. Over the busy Xmas holidays special programmes are arranged here. Even a shuttle bus is available for trips to local events, sightseeing or picnics. From the campsite you can fish or swim. Facilities range from functional ablution blocks, plus a paraplegic bathroom to a very well equipped laundry. There is a good kitchen/recreation room in an upstairs common area which is ideal for school or club groups. A couple of other kitchens provide serviceable communal equipment. A camp coolroom is available. The TV and dining area is an option, but lacking home comforts, though it is centrally heated in winter. For those who enjoy a social get-together there are many attractions here and the camp store is open in the summer holidays. No pets here please. A neighbouring market garden can supply fresh fruit and vegetables in season. Your hosts the Watson family. 📠 $20 for two. $16 for power sites and $14 for tent sites.

35. Pine Lodge Holiday Camp
Ngapara Street, PO Box 129 Alexandra (03) 448-8861

With fringes of pine trees, this camp offers a variety of accommodation plus 76 power sites and ample room for tents. Most sites have some large trees for shade and there are van sites enclosed by timber railings. Easy to reach, these sites are only one deep. A swimming pool is available in summer. Below the pool there is a children's play area. An outlook over this area can be gained from the roomy and functional kitchen. There is a games room and a TV room in rather stark surroundings. Included in the ablution block is a bathroom. There is a camp store open over Xmas holidays. Out of season you may bring your pets. Tent sites $7 per person. Power sites $16.50 for two. 📠 $26.50 for two.

36. Commercial Hotel & Caravan Park
PO Box 1, Omakau (03) 447-3715 (phone & fax)

A little gem in the "small camp" category. Stop over in comfort where individual en suite facilities are provided for motor homes. There are concrete stands for parking, plus water and drainage at each power site. There is some room for tents on beautifully groomed level lawns. A laundry with automatic machine is provided. Have a BBQ meal or eat at the hotel. Taking good care of you are Alison and Bruce Hebbard. Camp sites are $8 per person and there are 🚐 $18. Hotel beds are from $40 double.

37. Omakau Domain Camp
S Hwy 85 (or Alton Street), Omakau (03) 447-3814

A level camp near the foot of the Dunstan Mountains and 28km north of Alexandra. There are 40 sites with power here. With the appearance and upkeep typical of local sports clubs, the facilities are somewhat utilitarian. The multi-purpose kitchen, dining and recreation room has adequate cooking, fridges and plenty of tea makers. There are communal showers for the men, separate for the women. Well supplied with toilets (without visible designations) and there is a washing machine in the laundry. Close by is the hotel, general store and petrol station. Joan Kinney takes care of this camp. Tent sites $6 per person. Power sites plus $2.50.

38. Clyde Holiday & Sporting Complex
Whitby Street, PO Box 12 Clyde (03) 449-2713

New Zealand's largest hydro project, the mighty Clyde Dam, is close by. This camp offers the sports enthusiast golf, tennis, bowling, boating and swimming in season. There are 115 power sites and 53 for tents in three camping areas, with a central playing field. Two of these areas have shade from large mature trees. The kitchens are bright and spacious with stoves and plenty of dining space and TV. The ablutions lack a private dressing cubicle, but have an excellent paraplegic suite. Laundry equipment is fully automatic. A quiet camp, yet handy to the township. There is a dump point here. Your hosts Wilma and Bob Graham. Prices per person are $6 for tents, $7 with power and $28 for ⛺.

39. Cairnmuir Camp
Bannockburn Inlet, Cairnmuir Road, Cromwell (03) 445-0966

Take the road to Bannockburn where this camp occupies a sunny plateau above Lake Dunstan. Sheltered by well grown windbreaks, the grounds have 27 power sites, around 30 for tents and three cabins. The communal kitchen has stove and microwave and plenty of fridges, with a recreation room alongside. It is fairly basic. However there are excellent clean ablutions here and a well equipped laundry. Shopping is at Cromwell, 5km away. Your hosts Vina and Bruce Paterson. Tents site $7 per person, $2 extra for power. 🏠 $10 per person.

40. Cromwell Holiday Park
1 Alpha Street, Cromwell (03) 445-0164 (phone & fax)

"Sunhaven" was the former name for this camp. It has spacious level grounds with attractive large trees and offers 156 power sites plus almost as many for tents. Lake Dunstan is adjacent, as is a golf course. Children have a very nice playground provided. An appealing kitchen is well supplied with appliances and has dining in the centre. The TV room is a comfy and well used lounge, with a dining option. A superb new ablution block gives more facilities for campers. The laundry equipment is automatic. Cabins are available at random sites around the grounds. There is a dump point here. A camp store supplies basic requirements and there is a market garden stall across the road. Kay and John Searle and Richard and Catherine are your hosts. All camp sites are $16 for two people. 🏠 $22.

41. Black Gully Camp
Crookston, No 2 RD Tapanui (03) 204-2255

At Raes Junction head south on S Hwy 90 where there is a short journey off to the west, north of Tapanui. This camp is closed in mid-winter. Rugged terrain to negotiate, although the 14 power sites are level and there is tenting in the valley, which has a stream. You will need to be an independent cook (BBQs only). The ablutions are very challenging and you can use a motorised copper to tackle your laundry. The children's play area is a plateau on a hill top where there is accommodation and extensive views. This is wilderness camping and only for those with a sense of adventure. There is a refuge bunkhouse. Power sites and huts $6 per person.🔲.

42. Linsmoyle Park
81 Northumberland Street, Tapanui (03) 204-8501

A mini camp on S Hwy 90 which has a token number of sites, but the ones with power also have en suite facilities. It is in a quiet garden environment. A laundry is provided, but no kitchen. The entrance to this camp is off the lower road. Your hosts Marie and Alex Gow. Tent sites are $6 per person, or with power $8.50. There are 3 🚐 $10 plus camp charges.

43. Balclutha Naish Point Camping Ground
Charlotte Street, Balclutha (03) 418-0088

From an inviting entrance through seasonally flowering trees this camp came up to our expectations. The grounds are manicured with plenty of lovely trees and hedged stables for each power site. There are 12 with power and good concrete stands, also plenty of shady tenting spots and some cabins. The grounds are well lit at night and a coin phone is available. The kitchen is attractive, with full stove and opens to a carpeted dining and TV room. The ablutions are roomy with excellent appointments and a paraplegic toilet. There is a well equipped laundry. It is a short walk to shops and services. Your can bring pets here too. This is a fine example of a "small town" camp with all the comforts. Your new hosts Keith and Linda Cummings. Tent sites $7 per person. Power sites $8 per person. 🔲 $13 per person.

44. Kaka Point Camping Ground
RD1, C/o Kaka Point Store–Kaka Point (03) 412-8800

It is 22km to the southeast of Balclutha to this attractive beach settlement camp. Above a golden sand beach this is a nice, reasonably secluded spot with 25 power sites and plenty for tents. With a perimeter of trees, the grounds are spacious and level and there is a dump point here. All the amenities are modern and the ablutions include paraplegic facilities. Campers can use the tennis courts. There are bush walks and it is a downhill stroll to the beach. Your hosts Glennis and Norman Woods operate from the Kaka Point Store. Tent sites $10 for two. Power sites $14 for two.🔲 $20.

45. Pounawea Motor Camp
Pounawea–Catlins Coast (03) 415-8483

A mere dot on the map, Pounawea is on a coastal estuary on the outskirts of the Catlins. There are 36 power sites, tent sites and some cabins. Enjoy the natural surroundings, bush clad and with a conservation walking track. The other alternative is a little beach. You will find BBQ and picnic areas under the many trees. The central amenities block has excellent facilities. The kitchen has both microwave and other electric cooking and extends to a lounge with open fire. There is a dump point here. Tennis courts and a children's playground are close by. Your hosts Irene and Eric Miller. Tent sites $6 per person. Power sites $7 per person. 🚐 $15 per person.

46. Keswick Park Family Camping Ground
Pounawea–via Owaka (03) 415-8350

This camp specialises in lodge accommodation but has extensive tent sites and 16 with power. The land is level with some trees and good newish facilities. The recreation room is modern and well appointed. There are contemporary kitchen and ablution amenities. This camp caters mainly for travellers who enjoy a quiet, church-administered environment. Your host Jim Gear. Tent sites $4 per person. Power sites $5 per person.

47. Owaka Caravan Park
Ryley Street, Owaka (03) 415-8350

Adjacent to the Catlins Inn, south of Balclutha is a little camp behind the hotel. There are just a few power sites on a sloping grass ground with showers and toilets. Inquire from the hotel.

48. Tawanui Camping Ground
Tawanui–Department of Conservation (03) 477-0677

This camping ground is inland from Owaka and in the Catlins Forest Park, southeast Otago. The only facilities here are toilets and running water. For further information contact the Otago Conservancy, PO Box 5244 Dunedin.

49. Papatowai Motor Camp
Alexandra Street, Papatowai–No.2 RD Owaka (03) 415-8500

Sited in the dramatic and rugged Catlins, this environmental camp is fully serviced and located in Papatowai township, 64km south of Balclutha on S Hwy 92. There are 30 camp sites with power and at the camp entrance is a shop and petrol supplies. Base yourself here and take time to explore the Catlins at your leisure; a beach to yourself, walks through native forest to hidden waterfalls and a prolific wildlife which far outnumbers people. There is a sewer dump point here, and all the usual camp amenities. No animals here please. Your hosts Bronwyn and Deane Shute. Tent sites $5 per person. Power sites plus $2 .🚐 $25 for two. ▦ $20 for two.

50. Curio Bay Camping Ground & Store
Catlins Area via Waikawa (03) 246-8897 or (03) 246-8443

Tucked away on the far southeast coast of the South Island this pretty little bay has lovely views of the petrified forest. Tokanui is the nearest sizeable settlement. There are 23 sites with power and some on-site caravans. Each site is well sheltered by tall flax bushes, making them cosy and private. The camp store is not always open. Use of the showers and cookers costs 50 cents. The laundry has free use of a wringer-type washing machine. There is a small kitchen. Your hosts Lloyd and June Best. Tent sites $4 50. Power sites $7.50 per vehicle.

Note: Waitaki Reserves Lakeside Camping (for details see Chapter 11)
Private Bag 50058 Oamaru (03) 434-8060
(fax 03 434-8442)

A range of environmentalist camp sites are clustered on the edge of the hydro lakes. They are in magnificent positions, but they lack facilities, except for toilets. Most have boat ramps and effluent disposal. Inquire through the Waitaki Lakes Reserves. Camping is $6 per family or $115 for a season ticket. Write for details or phone as above.

These camps are open from 1 October to 6 May each year.

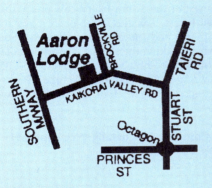

SOUTHLAND

SOUTHLAND DIRECTORY

Key to locations and map in Southland. Starts at Athol (south of Lake Wakatipu), and continues on S Hwy 6 to Lumsden. Turns west just before Winton going via Otautau and Clifden to lakeside camping within Fiordland National Park. Returns to Tuatapere and follows a mainly coastal route to Invercargill and Bluff. *Returns north on S Hwy 1 through Wyndham to Gore then veers northwest via Mandeville to Waikaia.

*Stewart Island, offshore from Bluff, has the last and southernmost camping.

Athol	1.	Glenquoich Caravan Park
Lumsden	2.	Lumsden Motor Camp
Mossburn	3.	Mossburn Country Park
Otautau	4.	Holt Park
Otautau	5.	Pourakino Conservation Campsite (DoC)
Clifden	6.	Clifden Historic Bridge Conservation Campsite
Lake Monowai	7.	Lake Monowai Conservation Campsite (DoC)
Lake Hauroko	8.	Lake Hauroko Conservation Campsite (DoC)
Tuatapere	9.	Mickalea Motor Camp
Tuatapere	10.	Tuatapere Motor Camp
Te Waewae Bay	11.	Orepuki Domain Camping Ground
Te Waewae Bay	12.	Monkey Island Camp
Colac Bay	13.	Colac Bay Pavilion

SOUTHLAND

Riverton	14.	Hillcrest Camp
Riverton	15.	Riverton Caravan Park & Holiday Home
Invercargill	16.	Lorneville Lodge & Campervan Park
Invercargill	17.	Invercargill Caravan Park
Invercargill	18.	Coachmans Caravan Park
Invercargill	19.	Beach Road Motor Camp & Tourist Flats
Bluff	20.	Argyle Park Motor Camp
Wyndham	21.	Wyndham Camping Ground
Gore	22.	Gore Motor Camp
Gore	23.	Dolamore Park
Mandeville	24.	Mandeville Motor Camp
Waikaia	25.	Piano Flat Conservation Campsite (DoC)
Stewart Island	26.	Stewart Island Camp

Chapter   15

SOUTHLAND

The forgotten land, at least as far as many tourists are concerned. This is a pity, for with very accessible destinations served by good roads and including some of New Zealand's most southern lakes, Southland holds a lot for visitors.

Leaving Manapouri, the scenic route via Tuatapere beckons. A lovely drive through level farm land where the road is quiet, the countryside picturesque, and the driving easy. This road brings you down to the coast, west of Invercargill. There are some interesting beach camp sites along this coast, with some benefiting from warm water currents. You will pass through Riverton, said to be the first landing spot used by the early settlers. This is an old and charming little seaside town, well worth a few days' stay.

Invercargill, New Zealand's southernmost city, is the centre of rich farming country, and has all the trappings of a busy urban centre. A number of alternative roads converge on Invercargill, from Lumsden in the northwest to Balclutha in the northeast.

A short trip further south reaches the largest protected wetlands in New Zealand at Awarua, while the southernmost tip at Bluff is home port for a large fishing fleet and boasts some of the world's largest oysters. You can depart by boat or by air to Stewart Island and visit New Zealand's smallest island 30km away. The small population there ensures that there are many unspoiled spots to discover. Bring your tent—yes, there is camping on Stewart Island.

A visit to Southland would be incomplete without calling in at Gore, New Zealand's Country Music Capital. So take along your old guitar and mosey on in to this friendly hospitable town. While you're there try and partake of some of the best brown trout in the world!

Before we say goodbye to Southland, remember this area has high summer temperatures and the longest summer days in the country, a very good reason to holiday here.

SOUTHLAND

SOUTHLAND

1. Glenquoich Caravan Park
Private Bag, Athol (03) 248-8863

Into the country via S Hwy 6 is this quiet little park on rolling grounds with shelter belts of young trees. There is the luxury of an en suite annexe at each power site, and there are also tent sites. A family-size lodge is also available. The campers will find free laundry facilities, but no kitchen, although there is a BBQ. There is a dump station and a car wash here. Other services (including supplies) are only about 1km away. As long as you have vaccination certificates you are welcome to bring your animals (but not in the lodge). Your host is Pam and sites are $15 for two people. You can also rent the whole lodge, or just a room.

2. Lumsden Motor Camp
S Hwy 6 Lumsden (03) 248-7076

Almost at the junction of the Te Anau Road and the Queenstown-Invercargill highway, this camp has immaculate grounds with a shelter belt of pines on two sides. There are also some lovely deciduous trees around the remainder of the camp, for summer shade. Each of the 30 power sites has a tap and rubbish tin supplied. There is plenty of room for tents. The BBQ garden is pleasant. Amenities buildings are adequate, featuring a homely kitchen with good new stove, teamakers, fridge and a large central table. Ablutions and laundry with wash and dry. Just down the road hotel meals are available and shopping and petrol in Lumsden. Bill Mitchell is the on-site caretaker. Tent sites are from $6 per person, or with power $13 for two. 🏠

3. Mossburn Country Park
Five Rivers Road, Mossburn–RD3 Lumsden (03) 248-6030

Truly a farming flavour to this park which is 3km north of Mossburn. A variety of sociable animals may come along to greet you. This is a peaceful spot with level camping, west of Lumsden. Shelter belts surround the camp and beyond are snowy mountains. There are 50 sites with power and taps, bisected by roads into small groups with BBQ areas. The kitchen has hot plate cooking only and opens to a patio. The ablutions are plentifully supplied with showers and toilets. The laundry has automatic equipment. There are good trout-fishing rivers nearby. Try the free-range eggs obtainable here. This is a very well appointed country camp with a dump point provided. Lex and Lyn Lawrence are your hosts. Tent sites are $8 per person, or with power $8.50. 🏠.

4. Holt Park
19 Hulme Street, Otautau (03) 225-8385 (03) 225-8674

Just a little park on gently sloping land that has trees around the perimeter. It will provide around 20 camp sites, although these may not have power. All the basic facilities are available, and there is automatic laundry equipment. Close to the Otautau township and 52km to Invercargill. Sheryl McNaught should be contacted for details. Tent sites are $7 per person or $8 with power.

5. Pourakino Conservation Campsite
Longwood Forest, Otautau–Department of Conservation (03) 214-4589

The distinctive low hills of the Longwood Range were once the focus for gold mining and timber milling activities. The Longwoods are today conserved for their scenic, historic, wildlife and recreation values. An informal camping area is sited near the Pourakino River where a walking track explores historic tramlines, a restored loco and milling relics. Fireplaces and toilets are provided. Water is collected from a nearby stream. This is a free camp which is closed during the winter.

6. Clifden Historic Bridge Conservation Campsite
Lillburn Valley Road, Clifden–C/o Southland District Council
(03) 218-7259 (fax 03 218-9460)

Limited space is available beside the historic Waira River Suspension Bridge, the longest remaining wooden suspension bridge in New Zealand. Basic toilet facilities suitable for picnickers are available on site. Excellent fishing can be found in the adjacent Waiau River. Limestone caves a short distance away are accessible to those equipped with a good torch and suitable clothing. Further information is available from The Southland District Council–15 Forth Street, Invercargill.

7. Lake Monowai Conservation Campsite
Borland Road, Monowai–Department of Conservation (03) 226-6607

Located beside peaceful Lake Monowai in Fiordland National Park, this campsite provides toilets, BBQ and picnic tables. There is good fishing and tramping here and a boat ramp is adjacent to the campsite. No pets here please. There are no bookings and fees are payable through the self-registration system on site. All sites are $4 per adult.

8. Lake Hauroko Conservation Campsite
Lillburn Valley Road, Clifden–Department of Conservation (03) 226-6607

Located within the Fiordland National Park, Lake Hauroko is the deepest lake in New Zealand. This camp is on a redevelopment programme and camping may be restricted. Several walking and tramping tracks start from the Lake Hauroko car park. A boat launching ramp is also located here. Toilets, BBQs, tap water and picnic tables are provided. No pets permitted here. There are no bookings and fees are payable through the self-registration system on site. All sites $4 per adult.

9. Mickalea Motor Camp
Peace Street, Tuatapere (03) 226-6474

A trim little camp on level grounds, sheltered on three sides. User-friendly facilities include a kitchen/dining with microwave. There is plenty of hot water in the ablutions. It is an easy walk to town which is reputed to be "The sausage centre of New Zealand". All sites here are $12 for two people.

10. Tuatapere Motor Camp
Half Mile Road, Tuatapere (03) 226-6474

The entrance through a glade of trees on the banks of the Waiau River belies the rather raw aspect of this camp. A fenced enclosure has 32 power sites provided, at varying distances from the amenities. Plenty of tenting space; share with the livestock. The facilities are unmemorable. Make inquiries from Alan Campbell at 33 Half Mile Road. The river offers trout fishing and swimming and it is 10km to the southern beaches. Vic Raymond is the caretaker here. Tent sites are $6 per family and power sites are $8 for two.🖼️.

11. Orepuki Domain Camping Ground
S Hwy 99, Te Waewae Bay

Also known as Hirshfield Domain, this is on the south coast road, west of Invercargill. There are neatly mown lawns with some power points. Macho camping with amenities to test the most experienced camper. Good luck!

12. Monkey Island Camp
Te Waewae Bay

This southernmost coast road leads to Invercargill and this camp is right on the beach, sheltered by some flax bushes. Pioneer camping with no power on and almost no facilities. The bay itself is attractive and you can share your swim with the visiting dolphins, usually from January to April. This is a safe swimming beach with a small island accessible at low tide.

SOUTHLAND

13. Colac Bay Pavilion
Colac Bay

The camping, with 4 power sites, is an offshoot with a tavern/catering complex as the focus. There is also a dairy. Facilities are minimal.

14. Hillcrest Camp
Pahia, 1 RD Riverton (03) 234-5129

Between Tuatapere and Riverton this is an interesting holiday option, with backpackers accommodation and 4 power sites, plus some tent sites on a working farm. From this elevated location you can take pony rides or visit old gold workings. There are basic supplies on-site including fresh milk and eggs. A loaf of hot bread is available each morning. Campers have use of the TV lounge in the Lodge. There is a kitchen/dining area with electric cooking and open fire. Just single shower and toilet for each sex. Laundry facilities are free. There is a car wash. Your friendly hosts are Trudy and Wayne Tecofoky. All sites are $8 per person.

15. Riverton Caravan Park & Holiday Home
Roy & Hamlet Streets, Riverton (03) 234-8526

Only a stone's throw from the beach, this camp has lovely views of Foveaux Strait. You can take the Bay Road turnoff to Towack Street for simple access to the camp. The camping sites surround the holiday house and cabins which are available to rent. There are 85 sites with power and some tent sites. The kitchen is large and bright with two stoves and extends to a convivial dining area with open fire and TV. The shower block has communal dressing area. The toilets are in a separate block, while the laundry is barely adequate. Some more attention to the upkeep would be an advantage. Riverton is an interesting historic area. This camp is pet friendly. Your hosts are Alan and Shirley Stenton. All camping is at $7 per person. 🗔.

16. Lorneville Lodge & Campervan Park
No.6 RD Invercargill (03) 235-8031 (phone & fax)

Check this out for somewhere different and appealing. On the northern outskirts of Invercargill, there are 20 power sites, tent sites, on-site caravans and cabins. Bed and breakfast is an option. This is all encompassed on a 7 ha farmlet. Delightful amenities with a log cabin kitchen/dining area that has comfort and all the "mod cons". Part of the recreation room (with mural depicting a tour of Southland) is a working shearing shed. Here you can enjoy watching sheep shearing from the comfort of your chair. There are two indoor range/coal BBQs in there own special area. The ablutions are kept spotless and supplied with bathmats and hand towels. The laundry is good too. This is a popular destination with a welcome from your thoughtful hosts Pauline and Bill Schuck. All camping is $8.50 per person. Please inquire for other options, including meals. 🔲 and ⌂.

17. Invercargill Caravan Park
A & P Showgrounds, 20 Victoria Ave, Invercargill (03) 218-8787

Handy to the city (turn at McDonald's corner), the Showgrounds on which this camp resides are neat and level. There are over 100 sites, some occupied long term. 40 sites with power are available for casual campers. Basic shopping is provided on site. The canteen style kitchen and dining have fridge and microwave. There is a well used TV room, plus a recreation room. The ablutions appear to be plentiful and efficient. The laundry has automatic washers and dryers. It has an urban atmosphere and will provide vehicle storage. There is a dump point here. Your hosts are Bill and Rosemary Sadlier. Two persons can camp here for $14, or $16 with power. ⌂ and 🔲 $26 for two.

18. Coachmans Caravan Park
705 Tay Street, Invercargill (03) 217-6046 (fax 03 217-6045)

This could be a convenient stopover, with a good selection of shops opposite. It is not right in Invercargill City, and is on level grounds with some dividing hedges. Central in the grounds is a 2 storey amenities block with accommodation units at either end. The facilities look clean, but utilitarian. The complex contains a licensed restaurant and bar. There is a dump point here. Possibly guest accommodation is a priority. We understand new management may be in residence now.

19. Beach Road Motor Camp & Tourist Flats
Oreti Beach, No.9 RD Invercargill (03) 213-0400

This camp is 1km from the beach and well planted, with a maze of pine trees near the back and appealing pockets for camping. There are 100 tent sites, plus 25 with power and a number of cabins. The kitchen has adequate cooking and a fridge. The indoor recreation room contains TV, piano and pool table and is obviously not "smoke-free". The ablutions include a bath, and are refurbished with new fittings. The laundry has free washing machines, and metered dryers plus ironing equipment. Upkeep here is a bit patchy. There is a coin phone provided and a general store next door. Your host is Don Black. Tent sites are $12 for two people, or with power $16. 🔲 $13 per person. 🔲 $27.

20. Argyle Park Motor Camp
Gregory Street, Bluff (03) 212-8722

It might be small, but it won't be crowded. This camp has rather open and bumpy grounds with plenty of tent space plus 7 power sites (4 have hard stands). The camp is divided into two sections by a hedge with amenities at one end, which include a small kitchen, providing 2 stoves and fridge, with meal space. There are basic ablutions and a laundry. Your host is Veronica Rouse. Camping is $5 each, or with power $6. 🔲 $8 per person.

21. Wyndham Camping Ground
Cardigan Road, Wyndham (03) 206-4547

Although this is in pine-tree country, this camp is on a very open paddock with only the occasional tree for shade. It is a quiet rural situation with 12 power sites and plenty of room for tents. There is a homely kitchen, pleasant, with mini-dining area. The showers are modern and roomy. The toilets (possibly a public facility) are separate, with a fresh coat of paint. These are adjacent to two hard tennis courts and a bowling green. There is also a golf course nearby. Managing this camp is A.R.Townley, 40 Alma Street, Wyndham. Tent sites are $7 for two persons and power sites for two are $9.

22. Gore Motor Camp
35 Broughton Street, Gore (03) 208-4919

This camp stretches between S Hwy 1 and Broughton Street, where guests will enter the grounds. This is a pretty setting with 50 power sites, nice sheltered tent sites and some cabins clustered to one side. Sites are level, some with gravel stands and these tend to monopolise the area around the main amenities block. There are two kitchens equipped with microwave and TV. Double ablution blocks too and automatic equipment in the laundry. There is a dump station here. This area is noted for its brown trout fishing at the nearby Mataura River. The camp has good upkeep and is handy to local services. Your hosts Annette and Graham Avery. Power sites are $9 per person, or $8 for tents. 🔲.

23. Dolamore Park
North of Gore–Gore District Council

Lush with trees this discovery is 8km from the main road and 2km north of the township.The park is immaculately kept and will gratify the most ardent environmentalist. 4 sites have power, and all sites have good shelter and shade. Don't expect to find upmarket facilities here. However there are clean showers and toilets, also washing-up sinks and boiling water available in the kitchen. The grounds have picnic tables, BBQs and some play equipment for children.

No animals are permitted here. An arboretum with a conifer collection, plus bush walks, are a delight. A classroom display of flora and fauna is worth inspecting. Local school children make use of this facility. This best kept secret requests donations if possible. There are no camp charges. The helpful caretaker advises that no bookings are taken. First come first served.

24. Mandeville Motor Camp
S Hwy 94, Mandeville (03) 208-9662

Look for Mandeville Tearooms (with bar licence) and Store. This busy watering hole is open daily. Services include camping or bed and breakfast. The location is 20km west of Gore. There are 16 power sites or you can tent anywhere you choose. The grounds are level and have a tap and sump at each power point. A former hotel on the site has been called into service to supply some rooms for guests and the amenities for campers. The aspect is homely, with all the usual facilities, but a little lacking in "spit and polish". Good for a country stopover, where you can get a meal if required. There are paraplegic facilities provided for both guests and campers. Your friendly host David Soper. Tent sites are $6 per person, or with power $7.

25. Piano Flat Conservation Campsite
Waikaia Forest, Waikaia–Department of Conservation (03) 204-8441

Grassy river terraces surrounded by beech forest make Piano Flat an ideal picnic and camping site. Walking tracks and tramping tracks leave from the campsite. Fishing, hunting, horse riding and mountain biking are popular activities. The area enjoys good weather in summer. Toilets, BBQs, picnic tables and tap water are provided. There are no bookings and fees are payable through the self-registration system on site. All sites are $4 per adult.

26. Stewart Island
PO Box 117, Halfmoon Bay, Stewart Island (03) 219-1218 (fax 03 219-1555)

The most southerly of New Zealand's islands, with a permanent population of about 450, this peaceful settlement is rich in bush and birdlife. You will find it quiet, even here, in the centre of town where a local pub and takeaway food outlet will sustain you. It is also handy to the wharf and airline depot. Camping is on lawn sites serviced by basic amenities but you will need your own cooker. Of the 4 showers available two have meters ($2). Flush toilets and a washing machine are provided. Luggage storage is offered here. Tents and mats can be hired. Visitors come to walk the tracks and to hunt and dive. You can cross Foveaux Strait by catamaran or passenger plane. Your hosts Lesley and Alan Gray. Tent sites are from $5 per night.

Please help us–so that we can help you

DISCOUNT ENTITLEMENT

Your personal comments are greatly valued by us; take the time to send this page back to us, and next year's edition will be mailed directly to you at the discounted price of $17.50 including postage.

Name---

Address--

Phone number...

The New Zealand Camping Guide was helpful because—

Signed--------------------------------You may quote me Yes/No

INDEX

Blue Lake Holiday Park 151

Blue Skies 256

Boat Harbour (DoC) 248

Boomerang Motor Park 78

Boundary Creek Reserve (DoC) 305

Bowentown Holiday Park 115

Bridge Motor Caravan Park 198

Brighton Caravan Park 328

Brinkworths Motor Camp 112

Broken Hills (DoC) 92

Brook Valley Motor Camp 231

Brooklands Motor Camp 256

Buffalo Beach Resort 87

Bushlands Farm Camp 193

Bushy Park Homestead 195

Buxton Camping Ground 250

C.J. Talbot Motor Camp 277

Cairnmuir Camp 332

Cambridge Domain Motor Camp 109

Camp Elsdon 211

Capitol Seaside Resort 210

Carlyle Beach Camp 194

Carnival Park Motor Camp 216

Castlecliff Motor Camp 196

Castlecourt Caravan Park 46

Castlepoint Motor Camp 216

Cedar Wood Resort 150

Charleston Motor Camp 290

Chartridge Park 234

Cheviot Caravan Park 250

Cheviot Trust Caravan Park 249

Clarks Beach Holiday Park 73

Clifden Historic Campsite 342

Clifton Beach Motor Camp 178

Clive Motor Camp 175

Closeburn Alpine Park 309

Club Habitat 158

Clyde Holiday Complex 332

Coachmans Caravan Park 345

Colac Bay Pavilion 344

Collingwood Motor Camp 225

Commercial Caravan Park 331

Cooks Beach Motor Camp 89

Coppermine Caravan Camp 181

Coromandel Farm Parks (DoC) 82

Coromandel Motels and Park 80

Coronation Park Motor Camp 264

Cosy Corner Motor Camp 120

Cosy Cottage Park 145

Cow Shed Bay (DoC) 234

Cromwell Holiday Park 332

Crossroads Holiday Park 228

Culverden Domain 252

Curio Bay Campground 335

Dansey Pass Holiday Camp 323

Danniverke Motor Camp 181

De Bretts Thermal Resort 156

Deer Valley (DoC) 293

Delhaven Caravan Park 253

Dickeys Flat 113

Dickson Holiday Park 78

Discovery Motel, Park 160

Dolamore Park 346

Domain Motor Camp (Te Kuiti)142

Donneraille Park 169

Duddings Picnic Park 197

Duncannon Caravan Park 239

Duntroon Recreational Reserve 321

Duvauchelles Camp ing 260

Dyers Motel & Auto Park 30

Eivens Lodge & Motor Camp 159

Eketahuna Motor Camp 215

Elizabeth Gardens Holiday Park 119

Epworth Centre 111

Eskdale Holiday Park 172

Ettrick Holiday Park 330

Falls Motor Caravan Park 23

Farmlands Caravan Park 326

Fearons Bush Motor Camp 228

Ferguson Farms 296

Fernwood Holiday Park 228

Finlay Park 111

Fiordland Holiday Park 311

Fisherman's Lodge Holiday 151

Fishermans Lodge 288

Fitzroy Beach Motor Camp 189

Flaxmill Bay Hideaway Camp 88

Forest View Motor Camp 106

Fox Glacier Motor Park 298

Foxton Beach Motor Camp 207

Frankton Motor Camp 308

Franz Josef Holiday Park 298

French Pass (DoC) 232

Gateway Campervan Park 189

Gateways Caravan Park 279

Geraldine Motor Camp 274

Gillespies Beach (DoC) 299

Glenbrook Motor Camp 143

Glenburn Holiday Park 322

Glendhu Bay Motor Camp 307

Glenmark Motor Camp 276

Glenorchy Holiday Park 310

Glenquoich Caravan Park 341

Glentaki Holiday Camp 279

Glentanner Park 281

Glentunnel Holiday Park 262

Glinks Gully 52

Glow-Worm Motor Home Park 298

Goat Island Camping 46

Gold Park Motor Camp 329

Golden Bay Caravan Park 226

Golden Bay Holiday Park 226

Golden Grove Motor Park 119

Golden Springs Holiday Park 153

Goldsborough Camping (DoC) 295

Goose Bay Motor Camp (DoC) 248

Gore Bay Camping Ground 250

Gore Motor Camp 346

Great Lake Holiday Park 154

Green Acres Caravan Park 71

Greengrove Holiday Park 147

Greenmeadows Holiday Park 200

Grenfelt Caravan Park 239

Greta Valley Caravan Park 252

Greymouth Seaside Park 294

Greytown Motor Camp 214

Grove Bridge Holiday Park 238

Haast Highway Accommodation 300

Haast Motor Camp 300

Hahei Holiday Resort 89

Haldon Arm Motor Camp 279

Hamilton East Tourist Court 108

Hampden Motor Camp 323

Hanmer River Holiday Park 251

Hans Bay (DoC) 295

Harataonga (DoC) 83

Harbour Lights Caravan Park 42

Harbourside Holiday Park 88

Harcourt Holiday Park 212

Harihari Caravan Park 297

Mawley Park Motor Camp 214

Mayfair Camping Ground 130

Mayfair Caravan Park 118

McDonalds Creek (DoC) 298

McKee Memorial Reserve 229

Meadow Park Holiday Park 258

Meadowcourt Caravan Park 71

Medlands (DoC) 84

Mercury Bay Motor Camp 88

Merge Lodge Caravan Park 149

Methven Caravan Park 263

Mickalea Motor Camp 343

Mickeys Place Campground 83

Milford Road (DoC) 313

Milford Sound Lodge 314

Millers Flat Motor Camp 329

Miranda (Hot Springs) Park 77

Moeraki Motor Camp 325

Moke Lake Reserve (DoC) 310

Mokihinui Domain 288

Momorangi Bay (DoC) 235

Monkey Island Camp 343

Morere Camping Ground 171

Morrinsville Camping Ground 107

Mosgiel Caravan Park 327

Mossburn Country Park 341

Motueka Vineyard Tourist Unit 228

Motuihe Island (DoC) 69

Motuoapa Motor Camp 157

Motuora Island Camping Ground 48

Motutara Farm Camp 29

Motutere Bay Caravan Park 157

Mountain View Holiday Park 251

Mowhanau Motor Camp 195

Mt Maunganui Motor Camp 119

Mt Nimrod (DoC) 278

Mt Somers Domain 273

Mt Somers Holiday Park 273

Mt Thomas (DoC) 254

Municipal Motor Camp 109

Murphy's Motor Camp 123

Nape Nape (DoC) 250

Narrows Park Christian Camp 109

Naseby Larchview Park 324

Nelson Cabins & Caravan Park 231

Nelson Creek (DoC) 293

Ngaherenga (DoC) 143

Ngunguru Bay Holiday Park 39

North Shore Caravan Park 64

North South Airport Park 258

Nosloc Gardens 117

NZ Holiday Parks 72

Okains Bay Motor Camp 261

Oakiawa Domain Camp 191

Oakura Beach Camp 191

Oakura Motels & Caravan Park 28

Oamaru Bay Tourist Flats 81

Oamaru Gardens Holiday Park 323

Oasis Motels & Caravan Park 159

Ocean Pines Motor Park 120

Ohakune Motor Camp 161

Ohakuri Dam 144

Ohau Channel Lodge 147

Ohawe Beach Camp 192

Ohiwa Family Holiday Park 125

Ohope Beach Holiday Park 124

Okarito Camping Ground (DoC) 297

Okiwi Holiday Park & Lodge 232

Okopako 31

Okoroire Hot Springs 111

Omakau Domain Camp 331

Omana Regional Park 72

Omapere Tourist Hotel & Motel 32

Omarama Holiday Park 322

Omihi Reserve (DoC) 248

Omokoroa Tourist Park 116

Onaero Domain Camp 188

Onamalutu (DoC 234

Opal Hot Springs Park 112

Opape Motor Camp 127

Opononi Beach Motor Park 31

Opotiki Holiday Park 126

Opoutere Park Beach Resort 92

Opunake Beach Resort Camp 191

Orari Gorge (DoC) 274

Orepuki Domain 343

Orere Point Holiday Park 75

Orewa Beach Holiday Park 49

Orongo Bay Holiday Park 25

Orua Bay Motor Camp 74

Otahuhu Caravan Park 71

Otaika Motel & Caravan Park 42

Otaio Gorge (DoC) 278

Otaki Beach Motor Camp 209

Otaki Forks (DoC) 210

Otama Beach Remote Area 86

Otamure Campsite (DoC) 29

Otautu Bay Motor Camp 82

Otematata Camping Ground 322

Otorohanga Caravan Park 141

Owaka Caravan Park 334

Owhango Holiday Park 159

Paeroa Camping Ground 113

Pagoda Lodge Holiday Park 22

Pahi Motor Camp 51

Paia Point (DoC) 249

Pakawau Beach Motor Camp 225

Pakiri Beach Motor Camp 45

Paku Lodge & Caravan Park 90

Palm Beach 70

Palmerston North Holiday Park 200

Palms Caravan Park 117

Panorama Resort 24

Papa Aroha Holiday Park 81

Papamoa Beach Holiday Park 120

Paparoa Motor Camp 51

Papatowai Motor Camp 334

Paradise Holiday Park 324

Paradise Point Motor Camp 43

Parklands Farm 141

Parklands Marina Village 237

Parklands Motor Home Park 158

Pauanui Airtel & Auto Park 91

Peel Forest Camp (DoC) 273

Peketa Camping Ground (DoC) 248

Pelorous Bridge (DoC) 232

Penrith Park 306

Piano Flat (DoC) 347

Picton Campervan Park 236

Pigeon Bay Motor Camp (DoC) 261

Piha Domain Motor Camp 66

Pikowai Domain 122

Pine Grove Motels 299

Pine Lea Motor Camp 91

Pine Lodge Holiday Camp 331

Pine Tree Lodge Motor Camp 30

Pineacres Holiday Park 255

Pinedale Motor Camp 233

Pinefield Holiday Park 93

Pinewoods Motor Park 50

Pioneer Park (DoC) 275

Piropiro Flats (DoC) 143

Playford Park Motor Camp 208

Pleasant Flat (DoC) 300

Pleasant Point Motor Camp 277

Plummers Point Caravan Park 117

Pohara Beach Camp 226

Porangahau Beach Camp 180

Port Waikato Motor Camp 105

Portobello Village Tourist Park 326

Pounawea Motor Camp 334

Pourakino (DoC) 342

Pourere Beach 179

Prebbleton Holiday Park 259

Presbyterian Camp 192

Princes Tourist Court 189

Pukehina Motor Camp 122

Pukenui Holiday Camp 16

Puketi Forest Camping (DoC) 21

Punakaiki Motor Camp (DoC) 290

Purau Motor Camp 262

Puriri Park Holiday Complex 49

Putangirua Reserve (DoC) 217

Queen Charlotte Holiday Park 235

Queens Park Camping Ground 198

Queenstown Creeksyde Park 308

Queenstown Motor Park 309

Quinneys Bush 229

Raceview Motel & Holiday Park 175

Raetihi Motor Camp 161

Raglan Wagon Cabins 106

Rainbow Resort 146

Rakaia Gorge 263

Rakaia River Holiday Park 262

Ranfurly Motor Camp 324

Rangemoore Farmlands 110

Rangiora Holiday Park 255

Rapahoe Motor Camp 291

Rarawa Beach Campsite (DoC) 16

Rawene Motor Camp 31

Redwood Motel & Holiday Park 150

Reeds Farm 154

Reefton Domain Camp 292

Remuera Camping 68

Rendezvous on the Coast Park 128

Riccarton Motor Camp 259

Richmond Motel & Holiday Park 230

Rimutaka Forest Park (DoC) 212

Riverhideaway Motor Camp 159

Riverlands Outback Retreat 173

Riversdale Beach Motor Camp 216

Riverside Caravan Park 45

Riverside Motor Camp 172

Riverton Caravan Park 344

Riverview Motor Camp 290

Riviera Motor Camp 187

Rock & Pillar Motor Camp 324

Rocky Valley Camp 116

Ross Motor Camp 296

Rotherham Hotel 251

Rotoma Holiday Park 148

Rotorua Thermal Holiday Park 144

Roxburgh Family Motor Camp 330

Ruakaka Reserve Motor Camp 43

Ruataniwha Motor Camp 280

Ruby Bay Backpackers Lodge 229

Russell Holiday Park 25

Russley Park Motor Camp 259

Sailors Cutting 280

Sandspit Motor Camp 47

Sandspit Motor Camp 73

Sanson Caravan Park 199

Sapphire Springs Holiday Park 116

Seadown Holiday Village 276

Seal Colony Tourist Park 289

Searidge Holiday Park 248

Seaview Motor Camp 187

Seddon Motor Camp 239

Seddonville Motor Camp 288

Selwyn Holiday Park 276

Selwyn Park Camping Ground 109

Selwyn Park Motor Camp 52

Settlers Motor Camp 92

Shakespear Regional Park 50

Shanghai Camp (DoC) 296

Sheepworld Caravan Park 47

Shelly Beach Motor Camp 80

Shelly Beach Reserve 35

Showground Motor Camp 257

Showgrounds Park Camp 169

Silver Birch Thermal Park 118

Ski Haus 160

Skipper-Mt Aurum (DoC) 310

Slab Hut Creek (DoC) 292

Smiths Holiday Camp 25

Solitaire Guest House 32

South Auckland Caravan Park 75

South Beach Motor Park 294

South New Brighton Camp 257

Spencer Park Holiday Camp 256

Spring Creek Holiday Park 238

St Andrews Recreation Reserve 278

Stewart Island Camp 347

Stillwater Motor Camp 63

Stratford Top 10 Holiday Park 192

Sullivans Motor Camp 178

Surf n'Sand Holiday Park 124

Tahuna Beach Holiday Park 231

Tahuna Park Seaside Camp 327

Taieri Mouth Motor Camp 328

Taipa Caravan Park 19

Tairua Holiday Park 90

Takapuna Beach Motor Camp 63

Takou Bay Camp 21

Tangimoana Motor Camp 199

Tapapakanga Regional Park 75

Tapotupotu Bay (DoC) 15

Tapu Creek Farm 79

Tapu Motor Camp 79

Taradale Holiday Park 174

Tarawera Caravan Park 173

Tatum Park 209

Taupo All Seasons Holiday Park 155

Taupo Bay Motor Camp 19

Taupo Motor Camp 154

Tauranga Bay Motor Camp 20

Tauranga-Taupo Fishing Lodge 157

Tawanui Camping Ground 334

Tawharanui Regional Park 47

Taylor Park Motor Camp 328

Te Anau Motor Park 312

Te Anau Mountain View Park 312

Te Aroha Holiday Motor Park 113

Te Aroroha Holiday Park 129

Te Kaha Holiday Park 127

Te Mahia Bay Holiday Resort 235

Te Pua Reserve 16

Te Puia Springs Park 129

Te Puke Holiday Park 121

Te Rata Bay (DoC) 152

Te Tapahoro Bay (DoC) 152

Te Wera Camp 193

Temple Forest (DoC) 280

Temuka Holiday Park 275

The Barn 227

The Cottages Inn the Woods 24

The Esplanade Holiday Park 247

The Farmyard Holiday Park 274

The Forks Bunkhouse 297

The Glade Holiday Resort 91

The Orange Centre 22

The Park 17

The Park (Paihia) 24

The Pines Motor Camp 252

The Staging Post 249

The Tree House 30

Thornton Beach Motor Camp 123

Tikokino Hotel & Caravan Park 179

Tinopai Camp 52

Tinwald Caravan Park 264

Tirohanga Beach Motor Camp 126

Titoki Point Garden 199

Tokerau Beach Motor Camp 18

Tokomaru Bay Beach 129

Tolaga Bay Motor Camp 130

Totara Reserve 200

Totaranui (DoC) 227

Travellers Hostel (Ruawai) 52

Treasure Island Trailer Park 41

Tropicana Holiday Park 40

Trounson Kauri Park Campsite 54

Tuatapere Motor Camp 343

Tui Glen Motor Camp 65

Turakina Beach Camp 197

Turangi Holiday Park 158

Tutira Recreational Reserve 172

Twin Pines Tourist Park 23

Two Macs Seaside Camp 179

Urenui Domain Motor Camp 188

Uretiti Campsite (DoC) 43

Urupukapuka Island (DoC) 26

Victoria Park Motor Camp 278

Vinegar Hill Reserve 198

Wagener Tourist Park 16

Waharau Regional Park 76

Wai-iti Beach Camp 187

Waiapu Hotel & Caravan Park 129

Waiau Motor Camp 250

Waihau Bay Holiday Park 129

Waihau Bay Lodge 128

Waiheamo Lodge Caravan Park 325

Waiheke Backpackers 69

Waihi Beach Holiday Park 114

Waihi Gorge Camping Area (DoC) 274

Waihi Motor Camp 114

Waihi Waterlily Gardens 114

Waikanae Beach Holiday Park 169

Waikaremoana Motor Camp (DoC) 170

Waikari Reserve Camping 252

Waikawa Bay Holiday Park 237

Waikawa Stream (DoC) 209

Waikite Valley Thermal Pool Camp 153

Waikouiti Camping Ground 325

Waikouiti Tourist Campervan Park 326

Waikuku Beach Camp 254

Waimana Valley 8 Acre (DoC) 125

Waimarama Holiday Park 179

Waimea Town & Country Club 230

Waingaro Hot Springs 108

Wainui Bay 20

Waiohine Gorge (DoC) 214
Waioumu Bay Holiday Park 78
Waiouru Welcome Inn 161
Waipapa Camp Ground 247
Waipapakauri Hotel 17
Waipatiki Beach Motor Camp 172
Waipawa Motor Camp 180
Waipoua Forest Campsite (DoC) 54
Waipu Cove Reserve Motor Camp 44
Waipukurau Holiday Park 181
Wairakei Thermal Valley 154
Wairoa Domain 194
Waitaki Mouth Motor Camp 321
Waitangi Motor Camp 24
Waiterere Beach Motor Camp 208
Waiteti Trout Stream Holiday Park 147
Waitiki Landing 15
Waitomo Caves Motor Camp 142
Wakavale Farmstay 233
Wanaka Motor Park 306
Wanaka Pleasant Lodge 306
Waterfront Camp (Muriwai) 66
Water's Edge Motor Lodge 87
West Bay Camping Ground (DoC) 240
Western Caravan Park 65
Westport Chalet Holiday Park 289
Westshore Holiday Park 174
Whakanewa Regional Park 70
Whakapapa Holiday Park (DoC) 160
Whakatane Caravan & Motor Park 124
Whananaki Motor Camp 29
Whananaki School Camp 29
Whangamata Motor Camp 93
Whangamomona Village 193

Whangaparapara (DoC) 83
Whangapoua Campground 84–5
Whangarei Falls Caravan Park 39
Whangaroa Harbour Motor Camp 20
Whangaruru Campsite (DoC) 27
Whangaruru Harbour Motor Camp 28
Whangateau Camp Ground 46
Whatamonga Bay (DoC) 235
Whataroa Hotel Camper Park 297
Whatawhiwhi Holiday Park 18
Whatipu Lodge 66
White Horse Hill (DoC) 281
Whites Bay (DoC) 236
Whitianga Holiday Park 86
William Jones Motor Camp 40
Winchester Domain Motor Camp 275
Windsor Lodge Caravan Park 156
Woodend Beach Motor Camp 254
Woodville Caravan Stop 181
Wyndham Camping Ground 346